A NOTION AT RISK

A NOTION AT RISK

PRESERVING PUBLIC EDUCATION AS AN ENGINE FOR SOCIAL MOBILITY

Richard D. Kahlenberg, Editor

A CENTURY FOUNDATION BOOK

2000 ◆ THE CENTURY FOUNDATION PRESS ◆ NEW YORK

The Century Foundation, formerly the Twentieth Century Fund, spon-
sors and supervises timely analyses of economic policy, foreign affairs,
and domestic political issues. Not-for-profit and nonpartisan, it was
founded in 1919 and endowed by Edward A. Filene.

LIBRARY OF CONGRESS CATALOGING-IN-PUBLICATION DATA
A notion at risk: preserving public education as an engine for social mobility
/ Richard D. Kahlenberg, editor.
    p. cm.
  Includes bibliographical references and index.
  ISBN 0-87078-455-2 (alk. paper)
  1. Educational equalization—United States. 2. Education—Social aspects—
United States. 3. Public schools—United States. 4. Educational change—
United States. I. Kahlenberg, Richard D.
  LC213.2 .N68 2000
  379.2'6'0973—dc21

                                                              00-010644

Manufactured in the United States of America.

FOREWORD

Capitalism and democracy owe a large measure of their dynamism and success to the fact that, while they do not prevent substantial inequality, they do offer extensive opportunity for upward mobility. The United States, where the rags-to-riches story remains a national fable, provides what is probably the best historical manifestation of this phenomenon. Even today, Americans enjoy a potential for upward mobility that is unusual by international standards, but the advantages available to the rich and wellborn also are numerous and noticeable.

In the public sector, for example, the log-cabin-to-the-presidency version of reality is scarcely the norm. Indeed, as this is written, the presidential contest is between the son of a president and the son of a senator. And, generally, there is a strong correlation between income and election to high public office. Although there are complaints about this state of affairs, Americans seem remarkably complacent about the prominent place of money and position in their politics. In private life, however, Americans still hold tightly to the notion that there should be ample opportunity for movement well up the economic ladder for all citizens. Any evidence that this part of the American Dream is at risk or in decline is likely to be disquieting to citizens.

One of the twentieth-century keys—perhaps the central one—to achieving upward mobility in the United States was the public education system. Thus, data suggesting that American education, in some cases, is having the effect of reinforcing existing inequalities is real cause for alarm. One of several pieces of evidence pointing to this disturbing conclusion is a recent study that found that the reading gap between the average student in high-poverty and low-poverty schools—measured in terms of relative standing on a percentile scale—starts at twenty-seven points in first grade and grows to forty-three points by eighth grade. Such studies call into question the whole notion of an educational dynamic of opportunity and highlight the necessity to reform our weakest public (and, for that matter, private) schools.

Findings such as these already have given rise to intense concern and debates between conservatives and liberals, with each group, not surprisingly, offering quite different solutions. Conservatives put forward ideas such as private school vouchers that are based on an underlying belief in less government and more markets. Progressives advocate a response based on an underlying philosophy that government action is essential for overcoming social problems, arguing for more resources and more reform within the public school system. In the heat of argument, both sides sometimes seem to lose touch with a significant reality: there is good evidence that the nation's public schools are performing as well as or better than ever (and even that most parents are happy with their children's schools). Still, many of our schools in high-poverty areas are performing miserably, so miserably that few readers of this volume would send their own children willingly to such schools. Those are the kinds of schools that are not providing the first steps so necessary to upward mobility.

Although much of the analysis has wider applications, this volume focuses on the needs and shortcomings of urban public schools, especially those in poor neighborhoods. The authors offer numerous wise observations about our schools today and a strong set of recommendations about how to make them better. While they scarcely speak with one voice, taken together the volume gives a practical and thoughtful view of some of the best ideas about school reform currently under discussion. Richard Kahlenberg, a senior fellow at The Century Foundation, organized and edited the volume. His introduction provides a useful overview of the topic, as well as a road map to the essays that follow, which explore teaching, school financing, summer school, discipline, charter schools, standards, and public opinion—all examined through the lens of inequality.

Over the years, The Century Foundation has supported a number of projects on American education, including Warren Bennis's *The Leaning Ivory Tower* (1973); *Making the Grade*, a 1983 Task Force Report on Federal Elementary and Secondary Education Policy; and *Facing the*

Challenge, a 1992 Task Force Report on School Governance. We recently have reinvigorated our education efforts with the publication of *Hard Lessons: Public Schools and Privatization*, by Carol Ascher, Norm Fruchter, and Robert Berne (1996); Richard Rothstein's *The Way We Were? The Myths and Realities of America's Student Achievement* (1998); and Gordon MacInnes's white paper, "Kids Who Pick the Wrong Parents and Other Victims of Voucher Schemes" (1999).

In the coming months, we will be releasing a full-length book by Richard Kahlenberg, *All Together Now: Creating Middle-Class Schools through Public School Choice* (Brookings Institution Press), and two volumes edited by Gary Orfield, one examining Title I reform, the other exploring the effects of high-stakes testing in public education. Other Foundation projects under way include a working group on inequality in K–12 education, a Task Force on Low-Income Students in Higher Education, and two book-length projects, one by Richard Rothstein and James Guthrie on school financing, the other by Joan Lombardi on child care policy and educational opportunities.

RICHARD C. LEONE, *President*
The Century Foundation
July 2000

CONTENTS

1.

INTRODUCTION:
MAKING K–12 PUBLIC EDUCATION
AN ENGINE FOR SOCIAL MOBILITY

RICHARD D. KAHLENBERG

Since the 1983 publication of *A Nation at Risk*, most of the focus on education reform has centered around raising overall levels of achievement, while the core concern over equity that animated *Brown v. Board of Education* and the 1965 Elementary and Secondary Education Act has been given short shrift. Democratic and Republican administrations alike have framed their education efforts primarily in terms of raising achievement generally rather than closing the gaps between disadvantaged and advantaged students. The public policy debate, as noted journalist Peter Schrag observes, "has largely been an argument between center and right: charters and tougher standards as alternatives to vouchers and the free market."[1]

Ironically, it is conservative proponents of private school vouchers who are most vocal in articulating the goal of equity, emphasizing the unfairness of assigning poor children to failing schools. The Century Foundation has supported research advancing two arguments against such voucher proposals. Gordon MacInnes's 1999 paper, "Kids Who Pick the Wrong Parents and Other Victims of Voucher Schemes," details why the poor will in fact be hurt by private school vouchers. And Richard Rothstein's 1998 report, *The Way We Were? The Myths and Realities of America's Student Achievement*, demonstrates that the public schools are in fact serving students far better than privatization advocates acknowledge.

But so long as the average low-income twelfth grader reads at the same level as the average middle-class eighth-grader,[2] it is incumbent upon opponents of vouchers to propose specific ways to better realize the promise of public schools as promoters of equal opportunity. Indeed, the conservative emphasis on equity in the voucher debate presents an important opportunity to reinvigorate this component of the education discussion. Equity goes hand in glove with public education. Although the United States may have less progressive public policies than other Western industrialized countries on issues such as housing, welfare, and health care, our schools have historically been more egalitarian. Indeed, part of the reason Americans tolerate inequality of result is the belief that the public schools will provide a rough equality of opportunity. The conservative attack on public education has gained traction in some measure because many Americans believe that public schools are not in fact providing the educational opportunity that has always been their central justification. Restoring equal opportunity is therefore a key to the entire defense of public education as an enterprise.

So, too, is equal opportunity necessary to promoting the goal of large overall achievement gains. On the merits, we do not have a systemic crisis in public education; we have a dire need to improve achievement in high-poverty schools, where performance levels drag down the overall level of achievement. Improving equal opportunity is not the enemy of quality; it is a prerequisite.

This volume seeks to systematically identify the leading sources of inequality and propose concrete public policy remedies. The chapters explore inequality in the home and various facets of inequality in schooling: finances, curriculum, teachers, peer groups, and discipline. The authors examine the strengths and weaknesses of various responses— summer schooling, federal aid to education, standards, teacher enhancement, charter schools, and zero-tolerance policies.

The book begins where inequality of opportunity begins, in the home. In chapter 2, Doris Entwisle, Karl Alexander, and Linda Steffel

Olson of Johns Hopkins University describe the large gaps in achievement that develop between poor and middle-class children on average before they enter school and then outline the important role that summers off from school can play in perpetuating and magnifying that gap. While middle-class children continue to learn during the summer, the academic learning of low-income children virtually ceases.

Expanding summer schooling would seem to provide an obvious remedy to this inequity, and the movement against social promotion has raised the salience of such programs. But the authors note that most summer school programs to date have proved highly disappointing. After reviewing the research, they conclude that summer schooling might be more effective in raising achievement if two important steps are taken. First, efforts should be focused earlier, in the lower elementary grades when cognitive growth is most rapid. And second, summer programs should provide poor children with the types of enriching experiences that middle-class children receive during the summer, as opposed to the traditional approach of reviewing curriculum taught during the year.

In chapter 3, Richard Rothstein of the Economic Policy Institute and the *New York Times* takes on one of the core inequities in public education: unequal financial resources. Despite reform efforts, in the aggregate poor schools still have fewer financial resources to spend than wealthier schools, particularly after the greater needs of poor students are factored in. While controversy continues to rage over the effectiveness of spending in raising achievement, research suggests that effectively targeted expenditures can produce better educational results.

Rothstein outlines five types of spending inequality: unequal spending among states (Type I), among districts within states (Type II), among schools within districts (Type III), among tracks within schools (Type IV), and within individual classrooms (Type V). While almost all public policy efforts have focused on Type II inequality, Rothstein's key insight is that in fact Type I inequality contributes more to the problem and should receive far greater attention than it currently does. Federal funding under Title I of the Elementary and Secondary Education Act has done little to equalize spending among states, he notes, because federal dollars are tied to individual state spending levels. Rothstein estimates the "capacity" of each state to provide education spending using a formula based on personal income per student, and estimates that in order to raise all states with below average capacity to the national average in spending would require $21 billion in new federal funding (as of 1996). Rothstein also provides guidance on addressing other forms of school spending inequality, and he urges that more resources be provided to improve the social capital of disadvantaged families outside of schools through programs that improve nutrition and housing.

In chapter 4, Adam Gamoran of the University of Wisconsin takes on the issue of unequal expectations and curricula, both between rich and poor schools and within schools, and examines whether raising standards across the board will remedy this inequity. Gamoran finds that in poor schools, curricula and expectations are often substantially watered down, and that significant differences exist between tracks within schools. Raising standards can arguably promote greater equity and greater quality at the same time, but Gamoran cautions that in order to have positive effects, standards must be implemented carefully. Within schools, Gamoran concludes that extreme forms of tracking should be eliminated, but that some form of ability grouping is appropriate so long as all students face high standards. More generally, in order for standards to work, he says, they must be consistent (not fragmented and shifting); coherent (with assessments aligned with curricula and professional development); and address issues of capacity (providing adequate resources to disadvantaged children).

In chapter 5, Linda Darling-Hammond and Laura Post of Stanford University outline the differences in teacher and principal quality between poor and better-off schools and examine strategies for enhancing teaching and leadership in poor schools. They note that in the aggregate, the least-qualified teachers tend to end up in high-poverty schools, where the best teachers are most desperately needed. Teachers often consider it a "promotion" to move from a high-poverty to a middle-class school, where there are fewer discipline problems, better school supplies, more active parents, and greater degrees of professional autonomy.

The stakes are high. Recent research finds that the difference in teacher quality may represent the single most important school resource differential between black and white children. New research also finds that teacher quality can explain much more of the variance in student achievement than previously thought. Likewise, principals are thought to be very important to a school's success, and high-poverty schools often can find it difficult to attract the strongest leaders.

What can be done to ensure that more of the most-qualified teachers and principals end up in high-poverty schools? The authors note that currently districts with mostly poor and minority populations must pay more than middle-class districts just to attract equally qualified teachers, and that the limited research on so-called combat pay to lure teachers to high-poverty schools suggests such incentives are often insufficient. Instead, they call for a comprehensive program, including streamlined teacher selection procedures in high-poverty districts, new mentoring and induction programs for beginning teachers, professional development that better ensures success, and better salaries and working conditions. While some have suggested that teacher tenure rules contribute to inequality (because it is very hard to fire bad teachers, they are simply transferred out of middle-class schools to high-poverty school dumping grounds), Darling-Hammond and Post argue that reforming teacher tenure provisions would hurt rather than help students in disadvantaged schools. Tenure is one of the few remaining plums to keep good teachers in the profession, they note, and removing tenure guarantees might be particularly unfortunate in highly politicized urban districts.

In chapter 6, Amy Stuart Wells and her coauthors Jennifer Jellison Holme, Alejandra Lopez, and Camille Wilson Cooper of the University of California at Los Angeles take on the critical issue of school integration, which relates to two important sources of inequality: access to motivated peers and access to parents who are active in the school. In schools with high concentrations of poverty, the lower aspirations and higher mobility rates of peers can have the effect of reducing achievement; moreover, students in such schools are cut off from important employment networks. Wells and her colleagues address the important question: does the charter school movement mean more or less integration?

In theory, the student bodies of charter schools, because they are derived through a process of parental choice rather than residential assignment, might be more economically and racially integrated than the student bodies found in neighborhood public schools. But Wells and her colleagues find the opposite is true. While the aggregated national data put forth by the U.S. Department of Education and charter school advocates suggest that charter schools are serving populations similar to, or even more diverse than, the general public school population by race and income, a closer analysis finds that charter schools often exacerbate economic and racial segregation. National data that lump together different states, districts, and schools mask the way in which subsets of charter schools may be predominantly white and affluent or predominantly poor and minority. In a fascinating new discovery, the authors find that as a general rule, in states with diverse public school populations, charter schools seem to provide an outlet for white and middle-class students seeking to avoid diversity. By contrast, in states with more affluent and segregated schools, charter schools tend to provide an outlet for poor and minority students dissatisfied with segregated public schools. Meanwhile, those charter schools that serve mostly "at-risk" children, the authors find, often have the fewest resources and least-challenging curriculum.

What can be done to better capitalize on the charter school movement to promote integration rather than foster further segregation? Wells and her colleagues reviewed laws in thirty-six states and the District of Columbia and found that provisions affecting integration were generally weak or not enforced. They therefore argue that incentives should be put in place to encourage integration. Where today many charter schools use word-of-mouth recruitment and rely heavily on parental contracts as a screening device, charters might promote integration if information were disseminated to all parents, informal selection devices were discouraged, student transportation paid for by the state, and schools given incentives to seek diverse student bodies.

In chapter 7, Paul Barton of the Educational Testing Service examines the issue of school disorder, which is a key source of inequality between rich and poor schools, though it is not commonly thought of in those terms. Barton then evaluates the effectiveness of a number of strategies used to promote greater discipline in schools. He confirms that one of the major impediments to learning is lack of school discipline, and that discipline issues are a much larger problem in poor schools than in middle-class schools. Moreover, he notes, the lack of order has negative spinoffs, helping to fuel the flight of good teachers and good students from disadvantaged schools. Barton's analysis finds that while the nation is transfixed by horrible incidents of school violence, in fact such phenomena are rare (and declining) and the far more pressing issue is rising levels of school disorder. He reviews a number of approaches that are being taken by local jurisdictions—including zero tolerance, character education, and alternative schools—and concludes that since many of these programs are relatively new, more research is needed to know which are the most effective. He also calls for more research about whether different strategies are needed in high-poverty schools, where the issue of disorder is particularly daunting.

Chapter 8 concludes the discussion with an analysis of public opinion data touching on the various reforms discussed in the volume. Ruy Teixeira of The Century Foundation examines public support for the initiatives discussed: summer schooling, school financing, standards, teacher quality, integration through charter schools, and school discipline. He also reviews polling data on private school vouchers and the overall level of confidence in public education.

Teixeira finds that Americans are at once deeply committed to the institution of public education and fairly pessimistic about the current state of public schools—suggesting the time is ripe for public school reform. He also finds basic support for themes advanced by a number of individual authors in this volume, though not necessarily all of the specifics.

On the issue of summer schooling, Teixeira finds strong support for policies that eliminate social promotion and general support for summer schooling, though he found no evidence regarding the alternative "enrichment" program advocated by Entwisle and her colleagues. On the issue of school financing, Teixeira finds "overwhelming" support for an overall increase in spending and says that programs to equalize spending may also find support, at least where they do not involve taking away from wealthier districts and where there are assurances the money will be well spent. On the issue of standards, Teixeira finds strong support for holding all students to high standards (even if that means some loss of local control). And on the issue of teacher quality, the public supports more teacher testing, but also higher teacher salaries—and, apparently, even wage premiums for teachers in high-xpoverty schools.

Teixeira notes that many people are not familiar with charter schools but says that there is strong support for public school choice and for the concept (if not the working reality) of charter schools. Likewise, there is strong support for the idea of school integration, though about 75 percent of whites oppose forced busing to achieve it. Interestingly, when the two ideas are combined—integration through public school choice—support rises to 61 percent of whites and 65 percent of blacks. Better school discipline is a high priority for the public, and there is strong support, across racial lines, for zero-tolerance policies against disruption.

The essays in this volume make clear that so long as poor children attend different schools than their more advantaged peers, they will face a baseline inequality of opportunity on several levels. Two major responses are possible. In the short term, a number of the important initiatives outlined in this volume can begin to chip away at inequality in financing, curriculum, teaching, and discipline. In the longer term, the underlying premise of voucher proponents—that mandatory assignment of children to local schools is harmful—raises a bigger question: should we harness the trend toward public school choice to reduce the number of high-poverty schools altogether, striking at the root of unequal curricula and expectations, unequal peer influences and parental support, unequal teacher and principal quality, unequal learning environments, and unequal financial resources, in one fell swoop?[3]

Either approach to the tough issues of inequality will run into some resistance. But it is important to recall that federal aid to education was first introduced exactly one hundred years before passage of the Elementary and Secondary Education Act in 1965. That long-fought effort, which today represents a secure and important part of America's program to improve education for poor kids, eventually prevailed. The belief that public education should be an engine for social mobility is thoroughly American. The essays in this volume lay out the blueprint for the next crucial steps in realizing that aspiration.

2.

SUMMER LEARNING AND HOME ENVIRONMENT

DORIS R. ENTWISLE, KARL L. ALEXANDER,
AND LINDA STEFFEL OLSON

In seeking to explain why poor children do worse academically than children from middle-class and wealthy families, analysts have focused on two major topics: differences in schools and differences in home environments. Because the government has more control over schooling than over the home environment, public policy has emphasized the former. However, as we have argued in previous work, this single-minded emphasis on schools is misplaced since differences in elementary schools do not create the achievement gap between rich and poor children: virtually the entire gap reflects differences in home environments.[1] In fact, children from poor and middle-class families make comparable gains during the school year, but while the middle-class children make gains when they are out of school during the summer, poor and disadvantaged children make few gains, or even move backwards academically. These findings are consistent with a growing body of research showing substantial differences between the home environments of poor and middle-class families.

9

So far, one seemingly obvious method of reducing the achieve-ment gap—summer school—has turned out to be highly ineffective. If summers are the time when differences are established, why does sum-mer school do so little to close the gap? This chapter examines the link between family socioeconomic status and school outcomes, reviewing studies of summer school programs and addressing the reasons why sum-mer school is less effective at improving the attainment level of poor children than had been hoped. We then propose a new strategy while considering the broader issues involved in school reform.

POOR CHILDREN AND SCHOOLING

The United States today is faced with the fact that too many of its children continue to suffer the adverse effects of inadequate home envi-ronments. These effects include a slower rate of cognitive development and lower levels of school achievement.[2] Identifying exactly how a family's socioeconomic status affects children's development, while far from easy, is the first step in determining how these negative outcomes might be offset or eliminated.

Family Economic Status and School Outcomes

There is no doubt that family economic status is strongly correlated with children's schooling, whether in terms of how well they do or how long they stay in school. Children from impoverished backgrounds leave school sooner than their better-off classmates,[3] with those living in poverty for at least one year 6 percent less likely to graduate from high school than those not raised in poverty.[4] Overall, national dropout rates hover around 10 percent,[5] but youth whose families are in the lowest income quintile have a dropout rate of close to 25 percent, while the rate for children from families in the highest income quintile is only 2 percent.[6] Put somewhat differently, by age twenty-four, people who lived in affluent households as adolescents completed more than two additional years of schooling on average than those who lived in low-income households.[7]

In urban school systems with large numbers of disadvantaged stu-dents the situation is by far the worst. Their dropout rates approach 40 or 50 percent.[8] It hardly needs to be said that lack of a high school degree leads to more unemployment and lower earnings later in life, especially for members of minority groups.[9]

In addition to leaving school prematurely, children from impoverished backgrounds do not do as well on standardized tests of achievement as their better-off classmates. Research on primary-school-age children is limited, but family background probably matters more for their test scores than it does for older children's,[10] and the strong relationship between family economic background and children's test scores begins early.[11] Children from advantaged homes arrive at first grade with their verbal and math skills at a higher level than children from disadvantaged homes,[12] and the achievement scores of children five to seven years old are especially diagnostic. Susan Mayer compared children in the richest quintile with those in the poorest quintile from one national sample. She reports that by age six, low-income children score considerably lower than affluent children on vocabulary knowledge, a difference that amounts to about nine months of cognitive growth for an average child.[13]

Even within disadvantaged groups, samples from specific locations reveal differences in achievement patterns by family income. For example, in a representative sample of children beginning first grade in Baltimore in 1982,[14] two-thirds of whom were below the poverty line, average scores on standardized tests of reading comprehension and math reasoning were significantly below national norms.[15] In addition, the difference between the poorest and the not-so-poor was striking, even within this generally disadvantaged group. Baltimore students qualifying for the federal meal subsidy program[16] had reading and math scores when they began first grade considerably below the scores of Baltimore students who did not qualify.[17]

Low achievement scores when children start first grade mean that those from economically disadvantaged families are at greater risk of failing a grade right from the start. Nationally, there are no comprehensive data on retention,[18] but among the sons of parents who dropped out of high school and are living in poverty, retention rates by age fifteen reach 50 percent. These compare with rates of less than 20 percent for sons in an "average household" (a husband-wife family with income above the poverty level, in which the wife has a high school degree and either does not work outside the family or works part-time).[19] Similarly, the 1988 National Education Longitudinal Survey of eighth-graders shows that, compared to the richest 25 percent, about four times as many children in the poorest 25 percent of the population repeated a grade at some point.[20]

The Baltimore Study enlarges upon this picture, showing how retention cumulates over children's school careers.[21] In one Baltimore school where more than 90 percent of the students lived below the poverty line when they started first grade, less than half had reached fifth grade five years later; the majority had either been retained or placed in special education classes. By contrast, of those who started first grade in schools where the majority of students lived above the poverty line, more than three-quarters were in fifth grade five years later.

The consequences of retention for students' overall academic careers are not as clear as they might be because most summaries lump together middle-class and poorer students, and retention can have benefits for some poorer students.[22] Still, failing a grade is an important predictor of dropping out of high school,[23] even when other risk factors like minority status and poverty background are taken into account.[24] Nationally, about 40 percent of those who have failed a grade drop out, compared to only 10 percent of those who were never held back.[25] Young people drop out of school for many reasons, but the specific connections between dropping out and retention early in children's school careers are becoming clearer and clearer.[26]

Explaining the Linkage

Many hypotheses could explain the correlation between parents' economic status and children's school performance, the most common being that better-off families have more resources to buy things that help children learn. Books, games, and computers top the list, but family trips to museums, zoos, science centers, historical sites, and sporting events; summer camp attendance and tutoring; as well as the purchase of bicycles, musical instruments, and hobby equipment also count as things that better-off families are able to provide.[27] In line with this hypothesis, the Baltimore Study children on meal subsidy in 1990 were less likely than those not on subsidy to have a daily newspaper, magazines, encyclopedias, or an atlas in the home, and less than half as likely to have a computer.[28] In summers when they were in the first few grades, the low-income children were also less likely to go to state or city parks, zoos, science centers, fairs, or carnivals; to take trips and vacations; to borrow books from the library; to play sports; or to take music or dance lessons. In particular, the number of books children read and their use of the public library over the summer both correlate significantly with socioeconomic status.[29]

Higher economic status implies much more than having a computer or taking trips, however. As Mayer points out, the relationship between parental income and children's schooling is more complicated and less important for children's progress in school than many social scientists have thought. She emphasizes a second hypothesis: those parental characteristics that employers value, such as skills, diligence, honesty, good health, and reliability, are important resources that improve children's life chances. Children of parents with these attributes do well even when their parents do not have much income.[30]

The flavor of the day-to-day interactions and psychic investments that parents make in their children may actually be the critical issue, rather than the specific items parents can purchase. Better-off parents are likely to have more rewarding and intellectually complex jobs, and the quality of the home environment when parents have these higher-level jobs is better than that of homes where parents have lower-level jobs.[31] Compared to poorer parents, not only do better-off parents have more reading materials in the home, visit more places, and do more things with their children, but they also tend to have the kinds of interpersonal skills that foster children's development. They avoid negative feedback (saying "no" all the time). They use more complex language, whether in terms of sentence structure or vocabulary. And they emphasize relationships among concepts; for example, in reading a story about cats and dogs, they tend to add comments such as that both are "animals." They also emphasize self-direction: they expect children to monitor their own behavior.[32]

In line with these ideas about parents' psychological resources, before the Baltimore children started first grade, the poorer parents on average expected somewhat lower marks in both reading and math on their children's first report cards and aspired to lower-status jobs for them in adulthood than did the better-off parents. The poorer parents also rated their children less favorably on the personal qualities that help children do well in school; for example, they rated them lower on classroom cooperation, but higher in aggression.[33]

Baltimore parents' expectations for children's marks turned out to be an amazingly good barometer of many other parental attitudes and behaviors. Parents with higher expectations tended to have warmer feelings about their children than did parents with lower expectations. In the second year, for example, when the Baltimore parents rated their children on whether they were "enthusiastic and liked to do things," were "high-strung or fidgety," or were "happy and well-liked," the parents who held high expectations for their children's school performance rated them quite positively. Parents with low expectations rated their children considerably lower on such personal qualities. Parents with high expectations thus saw their children as having appealing personalities, while parents with low expectations saw their children as less appealing. Children who are happy and popular tend to do better in school, perhaps because they are easier to get along with, but no doubt a warm and positive relationship between parent and child helps support children's achievement growth as well.

Baltimore parents' expectations were not just a state of mind; expectations matched the actions parents took.[34] Compared to parents who expected a low mark, for example, parents who expected an "excellent" mark in reading more often read aloud to the child and were twice as likely to see that their children borrowed books from the library in the summer, to take summer trips, and to have seen the child's school records during the past year. Having seen the child's records indicates parental concern in a number of ways. It usually means the parent has conferred with the teacher, visited the school, and has some understanding of the standards the school holds. It also means that a parent has some idea of a child's strengths and weaknesses.

Parents and Schooling

Do these parent opinions and activities matter? For every indicator of school achievement, whether dropout, retention, or test scores, the Baltimore research shows parents' expectations to be among the strongest predictors, and stronger by far than children's own expectations.[35] In addition, parents' initial expectations when children started school—before any report cards were issued—predicted children's academic self-images and feelings of competence and had large *negative* correlations with academic or other problems children developed in first grade. Parents' expectations also forecast whether or not children were held back or placed in special education classes.

Baltimore parents' expectations and family economic status were the two major predictors of children's gains on standardized tests over the first two years of school.[36] In fact, parents' expectations and their economic standing are of roughly the same importance and contribute *separately* to forecasting the gains children make on tests. Not only do better-off parents have more reading materials in the home and take more trips, but they also have more of the psychological capital that fosters children's development, such as high expectations.

The family's willingness to make large investments in children relative to the resources available probably deserves more attention than particular family activities do.[37] For example, a high-income family may purchase all kinds of educational books and toys but have little day-to-day contact with a child, while a low-income family may not be able to buy books but can take the child to the library and read books aloud. Parents of all economic levels, even those in the most limited circumstances, can supply psychological supports that help children do well in elementary school, and these supports have strong positive effects that are virtually independent of financial supports.[38]

Parents' expectations relate directly to the level of schooling children are likely to achieve. Baltimore parents' expectations for their children's marks at the beginning of first grade correlated with whether parents expected the children to go to college. Whether or not children can go to college depends on the programs they take in high school and before, and Baltimore parents who had high expectations in first grade had children who were twice as likely to take algebra and a foreign language in eighth grade, even when family economic status and the child's actual first-grade performance are also taken into account. Unless they take these subjects in middle school, high school students cannot be admitted to the college preparatory curriculum.

Seasonal Learning

Many studies besides the Baltimore Study indicate that when schools are closed for summer vacation the achievement scores of children from disadvantaged families either stay the same or slip back a little.[39] That is, poor children do not continue to grow in terms of reading and math skills over the summer when schools are closed, while scores of children from economically advantaged families continue to increase over summer periods. The summer gains of better-off children are smaller than the gains they make during the winter when schools are open but are still substantial. Seasonal patterns in learning are obviously an important clue for understanding how parents' resources affect schooling, but they are generally overlooked.

To see how important these seasonal patterns are for understanding children's achievement, we calculated how much the Baltimore children's scores on standardized tests increased in the summer when schools were closed, separately from how much scores improved in the winter. (The children are a random sample of almost eight hundred students who began first grade in the Baltimore city public schools in 1982.) The achievement levels of children from families of both high and low socioeconomic status moved up substantially during the winter of first grade.[40] Between the fall and spring of that first year, children from families of low socioeconomic status in the Baltimore sample gained fifty-seven points in reading and forty-nine points in math, and their counterparts from families of high socioeconomic status gained almost exactly the same number of points (sixty-one points in reading and forty-five points in math).[41] In the summer, however, while children from families of high socioeconomic status gained fifteen points in reading and nine points in math, the children from families of low socioeconomic status lost ground. For example, in the summer after first grade, they lost four points in reading and five points in math. Differences in summer growth rates thus accounted for an increasing gap between rich and poor, as poorer children's growth was confined to the school year.

The results are similar for the total of all five summers in elementary school. Over this period, the low-income students gained less than one point altogether in reading and lost eight points in math. By contrast, over these same five summers the high-income children gained a total of forty-seven points in reading and twenty-five points in math.[42] Over all five winters however, when children were in school, both the low- and high-income groups gained virtually the same amount (in reading, 193 points for low-income versus 191 points for high-income, and 186 points for both in math). The increasing gap in test scores between children from families of high and low socioeconomic status over the elementary-school period thus accrued entirely from the differential gains they made when school was closed: that is, during the summer months.[43]

An important consideration when thinking about the achievement gap in children's cognitive growth rates is that rates decelerated as children progressed up through elementary school; that is, yearly gains of all children became smaller and smaller. Still, the seasonal patterns continued through the entire five-year period.

The seasonal data from Baltimore are not a statistical fluke; they agree with seasonal data for children in Atlanta,[44] New Haven,[45] and several other localities.[46] All show that summer gains depend strongly on family socioeconomic status.

Faucet Theory

We think a "faucet theory" makes sense of these seasonal patterns. When school was in session, the resource faucet was turned on for all children, and all gained equally; when school was not in session, the school resource faucet was turned off. In summers, poor families could not make up for the resources the school had been providing and so their children's achievement plateaued. Middle-class families could make up for the school's resources to a considerable extent and so their children's growth continued, though at a slower pace than during the school year.

Standardized tests administered once a year, the testing schedule followed in most schools, cannot distinguish between children's progress in winter and summer. When gains are calculated from one spring to the next, the seasonal differences in growth rates are ignored. Therefore, yearly scores convey the distinct but wrong impression that middle-class children learn more over the entire year than poorer children. With seasonal differences hidden inside the yearly test score gains, it looks as though home and neighborhood resources help year round. The seasonal scores, however, show that home and neighborhood resources matter mainly—or only—in summer.

Families, of course, live in neighborhoods. For this reason resources in high-income neighborhoods, as well as in the families that inhabit them, could help supply the resources children need to learn in the summer. We therefore examined the relationship between Baltimore children's achievement gains in the summer and several measures of neighborhood quality.[47] Over the first three years of school, with effects of family poverty and parent education removed, children's gains over the summer were related to the percentage of families in their neighborhoods who were above the poverty line.[48] After family resources were taken into account, the summer gains Baltimore children made on standardized tests of reading and math were significantly higher in neighborhoods where the poverty rate was lower, but there was no correspondence between gains children made on standardized tests over winter periods and measures of the quality of their neighborhoods. In fact, children who lived in the poorer neighborhoods gained a little more over the winters than did their counterparts in better neighborhoods.[49] Baltimore schools in winter thus tended to make up for the lack of both neighborhood resources and family resources. When the school's faucet was open in winter, neither family nor neighborhood resources were important.

Parents with more income typically select better neighborhoods. In fact, the elementary school's reputation is often a primary factor in their selection of a neighborhood. Poor neighborhoods accentuate the disadvantages of family poverty and are qualitatively different from middle-class neighborhoods.[50]

Since poorer children have lower scores when they first begin school, and gains are usually proportional to starting scores, the amount of progress they do make when school is open is quite extraordinary. If we could get poorer children up to speed before they start school, perhaps schools could do even more to help poorer children close the gap.

For formulating policy to deal with the gap in school performance between rich and poor, it is crucial to understand that a family's socioeconomic status boosts children's achievement scores by helping them learn more in summers when school is closed, not by helping them do better when school is in session. Some families can turn on a "resource faucet" in the summer, others cannot.

Explaining Summer Gains

What happens in the summer in middle-class families and neighborhoods that does not happen in poorer ones? First of all, middle-class parents see themselves as partners in the learning game, while blue-collar or poorer parents see education as the school's job.[51] Because middle-class parents take an active role they know more about their children's school programs than poorer parents do. They understand how schools work, what determines success, how to get along in a complex bureaucracy, and how present actions relate to future interests. Middle-class parents themselves have been successful in school (for example, they are more highly educated) and in the workplace (for example, they have higher income and job status), so they are in a position to encourage activities at home that will lead to success in school. Indeed, parent involvement in school and home-school partnerships help parents acquire precisely the skills and understanding that could support children's learning in the summer.[52]

For many of the poor, schools are intimidating—the school's rules and conventions are foreign and the middle-class professionalism of school personnel threatening. Poor parents tend to defer to school personnel, they advise their children to "follow the rules,"[53] and they rely on "professional authority" to decide what needs to be done for their children rather than deciding themselves. Middle-class parents act more independently, often as advocates on their children's behalf.[54]

Poor parents' goals for their children are not too low, however. Typically they are high,[55] but effective follow-through is lacking. That is, poor parents are not as likely to adjust their expectations in terms of feedback from the school.[56] Continuing to hold "too high expectations" does not serve the interests of minority and low-income parents or their children—in earlier Baltimore research we found that when parents' expectations were too high, as is typically the case, children began to ignore them.[57]

Another possible reason for the poverty–summer deficit link is that low family income is associated with high levels of stress in the home,[58] and children spend more time at home in the summer than during the school year. Direct evidence is thin, but maternal stress interferes with both the quality of maternal care and maternal sensitivity to children's needs.[59] Poor children experience double jeopardy because, first, they are exposed more frequently to family stress and other negative life conditions at home, and second, they experience more serious consequences from these risks than do children from higher-income families, particularly if poverty is long-term.[60]

In sum, we know that higher family income allows expenditures for books, games, computers, and other resources that could promote learning in the summer, but parents' financial capital also correlates with their human capital, their social capital, and especially their psychological capital. In the Baltimore Study, parents' psychological capital, as measured by parents' expectations for children's school performance *before* they started school, was of about the same importance in predicting cognitive growth as family socioeconomic status. For policy purposes, it is good to know that parents' psychological capital is an independent predictor of school performance that adds on to the predictive power of income.[61] The two predictors overlap, but an important piece of each is distinct from the other.

Marks figure prominently in the dynamics of children's daily learning, and the link between low marks and low family income may be the most telling in terms of explaining why poor children have summer deficits. It gives us some insight into how schools might undercut poor parents' views of their children.

Researchers use standardized test scores rather than teachers' marks to gauge children's progress in school because marking standards vary so much from one school to another and from one teacher to another. Most families and children, however, pay much more attention to marks than to test scores. In fact, many do not even understand test scores, but even the youngest children and the poorest parents know a low mark when they see one. Further, children come home every day with marks on papers and homework, and they receive report cards several times a year whereas standardized test scores only appear once a year. Marks are a crucial aspect supporting the link between poverty and learning deficits because parents judge how well children are doing in school mainly by the marks they see. Parents who see low marks react by believing that their children are not learning very much, but are often at a loss as to what they should do. Children themselves are disappointed and also confused by low marks.

In the Baltimore Study the levels of children's marks followed the socioeconomic status of their neighborhoods. In schools where 30 percent or fewer children were in poverty, the first reading mark of over one-third of the children was an A or a B, while in schools with more than 30 percent of children in poverty only 5 percent of children received an A or a B. It strains credulity, but in one school where 88 percent of children received meal subsidies, all Baltimore Study students failed reading in the first quarter of first grade.

The disconnect between the level of children's marks and their growth as measured by test score gains is striking. Recall that over the first-grade school year, gains on standardized tests in reading were on average the same in schools serving families of low socioeconomic status as those serving families of high socioeconomic status. Children in schools where most children were from poor families were nevertheless perceived and treated differently than children in other schools, even though all were doing equally well as judged by the gains they made on standardized tests. In the winter, when school was open, children in schools of all economic levels gained equal amounts on tests of achievement in reading and math on average, so the differences by socioeconomic status in marks and expectations are not triggered by differences in the rate of children's cognitive growth. Instead, children were not being marked in terms of how much they gained during the school year but in terms of where they started.[62] Tragically, the message sent home on report cards was thus that many of these children were already academic failures. This negative picture helps to shape poor parents' reactions to their children, thus further eroding parents' valuable psychic capital, which is an essential undergirding to children's long-term academic prospects.

Marks also affect how teachers think about their students. At the end of first grade, when asked to predict how their students would perform in second grade, teachers' predictions shadowed the marking patterns of the school. In the top ten schools in terms of socioeconomic status, teachers expected their pupils to get more As and Bs in reading than Cs or below, while teachers in the bottom ten schools expected almost all their students to get Cs or below. Teachers' ratings of children's classroom behavior also corresponded to marks. In a school with only 11 percent of children on meal subsidy, teachers rated their pupils significantly higher in general interest and classroom participation than did teachers in a school where 90 percent of children were on subsidy. In fact, the correlation between the meal subsidy level of the school and teachers' average ratings of their students' class participation is almost perfect.[63] In schools with high percentages of children on subsidy, some children were rated so low on class participation that they were at the bottom of the scale.[64] In the more affluent schools, no student was rated at the bottom of the scale on these qualities.

The overall picture is one of poor children receiving poor marks, expected by teachers to get poor marks, and perceived as deficient in classroom behaviors known to foster learning. The great inequity is, of course, that during the school year the poor children learn at a rate equivalent to that of the better-off children in the same school system.

Parents and the community as a whole react to the evaluations they receive even though the level of these evaluations reflects children's social addresses rather than children's progress in reading or math on standardized tests.

We believe that schools account for little of the variation in young children's achievement because when they are open they furnish sufficient resources for poorer children to learn just as much as other children. This lack of variation in learning does *not* mean that schools are unimportant. Rather, they are so effective that nothing else matters when they are open. They enable poor children to overcome resource deficits in their families and neighborhoods and progress at a rate equal to or faster than that of better-off children.

The School's Role

According to the research discussed so far, school systems and society in general are misinformed about the origins of social differences in children's school performance. The strong impression most people have is that home resources help all year long, but this impression is mistaken. Instead, family resources make a difference mainly when school is closed. One implication is that schools are doing a far better job than they have been credited with. Another is that middle-class parents' aspirations, attitudes, activities, and psychic investments in their children are a major reason for the differences among social classes in children's cognitive growth when schools are not open.

To sum up, when Baltimore children started school their prereading and premath skills reflected their uneven family situations, but despite this, children of all socioeconomic levels progressed at the same rate over first grade. In June of first grade, however, the unevenness in test scores present at the start was still there. Poor children started from a lower point than better-off children did, so when school let out for the summer they ended up at a lower point even though both groups made equal gains during the year. In addition, in the summer the poor children's growth virtually stopped, while that of better-off children continued to rise. These seasonal patterns of learning related to children's family backgrounds are hidden completely when tests are given only once a year.

SUMMER SCHOOL AS A SOLUTION

The preceding section emphasizes that economically disadvantaged children fall behind their better-off classmates in the summer.[65] Immediately one thinks that attending summer school could, or should, bring poorer children up to speed. Unfortunately, this seemingly obvious course of action so far does not work. Before explaining why this is so, a word of warning.

A large number of research studies focus on "summer learning loss," the relatively slower rate of achievement of *all* students in the summer as compared to the school year.[66] That is, when students attend summer school, they usually make some progress but do not grow as fast as they do in the winter. This slower rate of summer learning for all students is not our focus. Our focus rather is on research studies showing that among children who attend summer school, middle-class children grow faster than disadvantaged children. Attending summer school increases the gap between the two groups.[67] The following evidence supports this statement.

Negligible Gains for Poor Children

On average, the summer school gain for students of all socioeconomic levels is quite small, roughly one month on average or a few test points (out of three or four hundred) on standardized tests like those used in the Baltimore Study.[68] This small gain is for rich and poor combined, however. Thus, the first question is whether disadvantaged students attending summer school make any gains. The literature suggests they do not.

In a comprehensive tally of findings from ninety-three studies of summer school learning by Harris Cooper and his colleagues, only a handful examined whether poor children learned more than rich children; that is, whether summer school reduced the gap between rich and poor. The consensus of these few studies is that summer programs increased rather than reduced the gap.[69]

Other research, not included in that tally, is more conclusive on this issue. For example, Barbara Heyns solidly concluded that poorer children do not benefit from summer school in her reanalysis of the Sustaining Effects Study, the only national study of the relative size of summer gains made by rich and poor students. This research involved

120,000 students in three hundred elementary schools who were followed for three successive years.[70] It examined specifically how poor or minority children in the first two grades fared in summer programs compared to better-off children. In both reading and math, poor and minority children derived less benefit, and as a consequence the racial and socioeconomic inequality among students' scores was heightened.[71] Heyns's conclusion is consistent with that of Cooper and his colleagues—wealthier students profit more than poorer students from summer school—but draws specifically on research directed at this particular issue. In addition, Heyns's own, large, Atlanta study of fifth-, sixth-, and seventh-graders shows the same pattern. During the summer, among students enrolled in summer school, socioeconomic and racial inequality across test scores increased dramatically.[72]

The distinction between summer school in general, and summer school as a means to close the gap in cognitive skills between rich and poor students, is critical to understand. Summer schools with good programs and facilities on average can improve students' performances, but the few careful evaluations that have focused on attending summer school for the purpose of closing the gap between social groups (racial, economic, or both) find just the opposite. Summer school increases the gap.

Why Summer School Does Not Close the Gap

The failure of summer school to narrow the learning gap is disappointing but not really surprising. Many other programs, undertaken in the past with high hopes of reducing differences between children from families of low and high socioeconomic status, also have had disappointing results. For one illustration, a major aim of *Sesame Street* was to reduce the knowledge gap between minority (or poor) preschool children and their majority (or better-off) counterparts. *Sesame Street* clearly benefited preschoolers on average, but backfired in terms of decreasing the learning gap because the gap between rich and poor grew larger rather than smaller.[73] This is not the place to discuss all the reasons for such a disappointing outcome, but like summer school, the counterintuitive outcome of *Sesame Street* is an example of a "Matthew effect"—roughly translated as "unto those who are well-off shall even more be given." Providing add-on services across the board benefits rich students more than poor, bright more than not-so-bright, majority more than minority, and so on. Why? For one thing, the richer parents of higher-scoring children find out about special programs and see that their children attend them more often than do poorer parents. In Atlanta, where summer school was voluntary, the children whose parents enrolled them in summer school had higher achievement levels during the school year than those who did not attend.[74] Similarly, today the children least likely to attend preschool programs are children from low-income and single-parent families and those whose parents have the least education.[75] For summer school and other programs to close the learning gap, they have to be designed especially for poor children and provided only for them, as has been done with some compensatory education preschool programs.

Proposing a Strategy

In order to figure out how to boost the summer achievement of poorer children, that is, to determine the content of a summer program, we need to know the kinds of learning experiences these children lack. Then the question is when to offer such programs. An important consideration for timing of programs is that children's cognitive growth slows down precipitously as they progress upward through the grades.[76] Reading achievement of Baltimore Study children improved twice as fast in grade one as grade three, for example, and the gap in summer gains between better-off and poorer children decreased over time.

Considering (1) the relatively small gap in children's test scores associated with family income at the point when they start first grade, (2) the seasonal profiles of achievement growth, with better-off children gaining more in the summer, and (3) the marked deceleration in the rates of cognitive growth over the early school years, we suggest the following course of action: provide poor children with high-quality preschools, and then follow up with summer school just for poor children in the summers before and after first grade.

Preschool Programs

A good place to start reform would be with the gap in academic performance that separates rich and poor children at the beginning of first grade by providing programs to help bring poorer children up to speed before they start. We already know this can be done: scientifically impeccable data show that good preschools can improve the early school success of disadvantaged children by enabling them to do better in first grade than disadvantaged children who do not attend preschools.[77]

Good preschool programs can reduce retention among disadvantaged first-graders. The retention rate in first grade is higher than it is in any subsequent grade,[78] and holding poor children back in first grade jeopardizes their futures. By age twenty-three, Baltimore students were three times more likely to have dropped out of school if they had been retained in first grade, with family economic status, minority status, and even actual school performance allowed for.[79]

The lack of preschools for disadvantaged youngsters is presently an insidious way that school tracking by family income takes hold early. A few extra test points conferred by attending a good preschool could be enough to protect economically disadvantaged youngsters against early retention and low placements in first-grade reading groups.[80] However, it is important to note that all of the large-scale studies that show preschools can help poorer children to negotiate the first-grade transition exclusively enrolled low-income children.[81] Keeping in mind the Matthew effect, we believe only preschool programs directed exclusively at poor children will help close the gap.[82]

More disadvantaged children also need to attend kindergarten, a kind of "preschooling." Because kindergarten is not compulsory, a surprisingly large number of children do not attend or only attend part-time. Again, as the Matthew effect predicts, those who do not attend are poorer children. In Baltimore City, which is one of the poorest school districts in Maryland, 10 percent of first-graders in our study had not attended kindergarten,[83] compared to about 1 percent nationwide.[84]

In addition, the Baltimore Study children who came from the poorest families were more often enrolled in half-day than full-day sessions. (Of children who attended half days, 77 percent were on meal subsidy, compared to 32 percent of those who attended full days.) The benefits of full-day as compared to half-day kindergartens for the Baltimore children were striking. Allowing for family background and many other variables, first-graders who attended full-day kindergarten were absent fewer days in first grade, were less often retained, and earned higher marks and test scores than the half-day attendees.[85] So in addition to preschools (age four and younger), full-day kindergarten (age five) for poorer children could help close the achievement gap.

Summer School Programs

The next logical step after improving preschooling is to develop summer school programs for poor children. Preschools can reduce the achievement gap when children start first grade, but then we need to keep the faucet open and provide the extra resources for poor children when school is closed that middle-class parents provide for their children.

We believe that summer programs for disadvantaged six- and seven-year-olds who had earlier attended high-quality preschools would help to keep the gap small. The basis of this recommendation is an ongoing study of a school-year program for disadvantaged children in Chicago that shows that intense exposure to supplemental learning resources in the first two grades helps poor children maintain the academic edge they get from attending a good preschool.[86] The Chicago program is far different in content and timing from the summer strategy we are proposing, but nevertheless demonstrates that extra programs following preschool can help disadvantaged children do better over first grade, and that these benefits then continue. Likewise, summer programs for disadvantaged children just before and just after first grade, we believe, would help maintain the gains conferred by preschooling and perhaps induce summer gains like those made by middle-class children.

What should these summer programs consist of? Summer activities related to reading top the list. Low-income children involved in Atlanta's summer schools tended to read more on their own than did students not attending.[87] Likewise, in Baltimore, first- and second-graders who went to the library more often and took out more books in the summer did better than other children. Both math and reading growth benefited from library activities.[88]

Better-off children also do things in the summer that are different from what they do during the school year: they attend day camps, take swimming lessons, go on trips, visit local parks and zoos, and play organized sports, to name a few. Summer programs for disadvantaged children should feature such activities to provide different experiences from what they have during the school year. Activities that include a substantial amount of physical activity for both boys and girls should also be included, especially games like soccer, field hockey, and softball that take very little equipment but have complicated rule systems and require children to take multiple roles.[89] Adult leaders need to be cast in the role of coach rather than teacher.[90]

Program content is not the only concern, however. Higher-income parents have psychological capital of a kind that summer school coaches could emulate: using positive rather than negative reinforcement, teaching productive problem solving strategies, encouraging children to be self-directed, having high expectations, and seeing that the means are there for children to meet high expectations. Perhaps most important, coaches need to encourage children to enjoy themselves.[91]

The logistics of summer programs need planning, especially in terms of teachers who can establish strong attachments to students and parents.[92] The programs need to be located near pupils' homes so children can get to them easily and so parents can become involved. Changing the summer environment of children in low-income families may require community intervention.[93]

No single approach is likely to close the academic gap between low- and high-income children, but summer programs bracketing first grade especially, for disadvantaged children alone, could help. High-quality preschools and kindergartens can definitely improve the school performance of low-income children as they go through the first three grades.[94] The summer programs should not be scheduled as "make-up" or billed as being for children who have "failed." The success of these programs, we believe, hinges on their nonschool flavor and on providing them only for disadvantaged children.

At age six, when children's cognitive development is proceeding at probably twice the rate it does two or three years later,[95] the trajectory of children's long-term educational careers is being established. For this reason, it is imperative to concentrate on the pre- and primary schooling of disadvantaged youth.

CONCLUSION

The key for achieving more equity in school outcomes is to bring poorer children up to speed before they start school, and then keep them there by providing the extra resources they need, especially over the first-grade transition. Less advantaged children *can* be brought up to speed by attending preschools.[96] In the first few grades children take their biggest cognitive strides, especially in reading,[97] and to keep pace in the summer children from disadvantaged families need more resources than their families can furnish. Providing poor children with additional resources just before they get to first grade and then in summers very early in their school careers could give them the chance to correct their academic deficits early, and keep more of them "on track."

We propose:

1. Getting more children into Headstart or other good preschool programs designed exclusively for disadvantaged children.

2. Then getting these children into full-day public kindergartens.

3. Before and after first grade for disadvantaged children only, following up with summer programs modeled along the lines of the summer activities that middle-class families provide.

The Larger Picture

A fascination with inequality is part of the human condition. Why is inequality perpetuated?[98] How can we get those at the very bottom of the ladder to move up? Social theorists and policymakers alike have looked to public schools to provide solutions. The imagery is strong that a set of occupational slots is waiting for students as they graduate from school, and that those who win out in school and attend the longest will win out in the labor market as well.

To us the idea of sorting children toward the end of their schooling seems upside down because elementary schools already reflect the social stratification between neighborhoods. Families sort themselves by income into neighborhoods; then neighborhood schools tend to eliminate any real contest between students from different income levels. The engine that drives the system is located mainly in the individual family because of the unequal distribution of resources across families (and neighborhoods). This inequity so far has not been solved by tinkering with schools as they presently exist, and, judging from the available research, we believe inequity would likely be exacerbated by noncompulsory summer schools open to all children.

The good news is that despite poverty and family disruption, young children's ability to learn during the school year seems little impaired by scarce family resources. In seeking to address the achievement gap between rich and poor, we should begin by recognizing the efficacy of elementary schools in leveling the playing field. Most press coverage of American education today emphasizes the system's failures, especially its failures with respect to the most disadvantaged students. These negative perceptions often undercut popular support for elementary schools and public education in general. Missed in these perceptions is the extent to which schools make up for deficits in poor children's backgrounds. The tragedy of current American educational practice is that schools are organized and children perceived as though the more advantaged groups are better able to benefit from the schooling process. Lower-status children are assumed to be "slower" learners, less capable of absorbing the curriculum, and these lower expectations feed into poor parents' own perceptions about their children's academic futures. This is especially unfortunate in the early grades when students' achievement trajectories are being set and their cognitive growth is most rapid.

The recognition of the power of schools to make a difference in the lives of poor students needs to be coupled with efforts to involve parents and communities in the schooling process so that all parents, not just middle-class parents, are active collaborators in the education of their children. Preschool and summer programs, properly organized, can help to potentiate economically disadvantaged parents and their neighborhoods as active supporters of children's academic endeavors. These parents need to know, for example, that such simple activities as reading aloud to their children can have big payoffs in supporting children's academic careers. Neighborhoods need playgrounds and coaches to encourage organized sports and craft activities in the summer. Workshops and other outreach efforts could help disadvantaged adults develop some of the psychological and social capital that is so important in undergirding their children's learning.

3.

EQUALIZING EDUCATION RESOURCES ON BEHALF OF DISADVANTAGED CHILDREN

RICHARD ROTHSTEIN

The achievement gap between students from socially and economically disadvantaged families and others has narrowed since the mid-1960s, but it remains substantial. For the better part of a generation, reform energies have emphasized a litigation strategy to reduce differences in average per pupil spending between districts within a state. These efforts have partly succeeded in closing the differential between high- and low-spending districts, consistent with the gains in achievement made by disadvantaged children. Yet, "no one has been able to show that the narrowed spending differentials achieved by successful school finance equity cases in the 1970s and 1980s directly led to a narrowing of educational achievement differentials."[1]

While narrowing intra-state inequalities may be helpful, these are not the only, and perhaps not even the most important, sources of blame for the achievement gap, despite the priority given to them in reform strategies. Differences in real resources consumed by schools within districts also may make substantial contributions to differences in student performance. Further, a systemic approach that focuses on the social and economic background issues that figure in student achievement may recommend governmental action outside the educational sphere that may be as productive in terms of equipping students to learn as school spending itself.

Strictly within the realm of schooling, the most important policy initiative should be a new focus on differences in per pupil spending *between* states, which are a greater cause of disadvantaged students falling behind their counterparts than any other school resource inequality. The least well-off students in high-spending states receive considerably more school spending than the most privileged students in low-spending states. Existing federal aid to education programs, notably Title I, do little to ameliorate this inequality and, because Title I distributions are adjusted to existing per pupil spending levels in states, may actually exacerbate it in some cases.

A new system for redistributing federal education aid is the only solution to these problems. Federal support to education should be adjusted not only for regional cost differences between states but also for the intensity of child poverty and for states' ability to pay. States with relatively low levels of personal income per student and relatively high levels of child poverty cannot be expected to mount an effort to increase revenues dedicated to the schooling of disadvantaged children that is comparable to what wealthier states can sustain. Litigation aimed only at the distribution of school resources within a state cannot solve this problem. Stepped-up federal aid is the one sure way to overcome inequalities rooted in disparities between states and regions in regard to overall levels of prosperity and concentrations of disadvantaged families.

ENHANCING RESOURCES TO
NARROW THE ACHIEVEMENT GAP

The gap in mean academic outcomes between students from disadvantaged backgrounds and others is substantial. (I use the terms "advantaged" and "disadvantaged" children to encompass differences in children's economic circumstances as well as their racial minority status. Children can be disadvantaged because of family economic circumstances, racial minority status, or both.) In 1998, 58 percent of poor and near-poor fourth graders had reading scores that the National Assessment Governing Board considers below the "basic" level of proficiency for children that age. Only 27 percent of nonpoor children had below "basic" proficiency.[2]

By some measures, the gap between advantaged and disadvantaged children has narrowed in the past quarter century, with the former maintaining or slightly improving their achievement levels while the latter posted more rapid gains. In 1996, black seventeen-year-olds had an average reading-scale score on the National Assessment of Educational Progress (NAEP) that was at about the twenty-seventh percentile of white scores. But this is a much smaller gap than in 1971, when black seventeen-year-olds had an average reading score at about the ninth percentile of white scores.[3] Only a portion of the gains made by black students during that period can be attributed to circumstances relating to improved social and economic background, so it is likely that more effective schooling is at least partially responsible.[4] Students of all races and ethnicities in 1996 whose parents had not graduated from high school had an average reading-scale score that was 29 points below that of students whose parents had attended college. In 1971, the gap had been 32 points. Trends have been similar in mathematics.[5]

There is no scholarly consensus either about what caused the gap to narrow or about the reasons why it has not narrowed further, but some oft-repeated explanations seem reasonable. Some portion of the narrowing of the achievement gap may not have resulted from greater school resources but rather from the improved use of existing ones. For example, teacher expectations regarding the academic proficiency of disadvantaged children may have increased during the past quarter century. Resource enhancements may also have played a role. In particular, class sizes and pupil-teacher ratios have declined; smaller classes and more individualized instruction may have had more of an impact on the achievement of disadvantaged than other children. But even if the resources money can buy do make a difference, it is unlikely that disadvantaged children's academic outcomes would improve significantly, relative to those of their peers, if all children had access to equal school funding. Narrowing the gap more may require further enhancements in the instruction of disadvantaged children. Further reductions in class size for these children, as well as expanded summer school and the addition of prekindergarten programs, are widely believed to be measures likely to narrow the achievement divide further. Disadvantaged children are often concentrated in larger schools in overcrowded, inner-city communities. Breaking up such large institutions into smaller ones characterized by less anonymity is another expensive reform likely to generate significant results. Another major expenditure that could be helpful is salary inducements to attract more qualified teachers to inner-city placements. However, even if school resources for disadvantaged children are made greater, it is impractical to expect that this alone can eliminate the performance gap entirely. Bringing underachieving students from circumstances of deprivation fully into the mainstream of accomplishment would require addressing the large differentials in background social and economic advantages themselves.

In an important 1995 report (based on 1989–90 figures) from the National Center for Education Statistics, Thomas Parrish, Christine Matsumoto, and William Fowler examined expenditure data from all school districts nationwide to determine variations in resource use.[6] They found that districts with the greatest poverty spent considerably less than those with the least poverty. Specifically, high-poverty districts spent, on average, only 79 percent of the level of the most affluent districts. Spending in high-poverty districts was virtually identical to that in moderately affluent districts and was actually about 9 percent higher than spending in moderate-poverty districts.[7] Parrish, Matsumoto, and Fowler found lesser disparities when disadvantage was defined more narrowly, as not poverty alone but also living with a single mother who had not graduated from high school: districts with a large proportion of students at risk by this definition spent 5 percent less than districts where few students were deemed at risk but 7 percent more than districts with a moderate number of at-risk students.[8]

In a multivariate analysis, Parrish, Matsumoto, and Fowler found smaller disparities in spending between districts when they controlled for socioeconomic background and student need. However, their findings reflect suppositions that require further consideration. (While scholars of school finance as well as litigants now frequently conduct "need-adjusted" analyses of school spending, it often seems that more effort is devoted to making the calculations than to examining the underlying assumptions.) For example, Parrish and colleagues assume that children living in poverty or having limited English proficiency require 20 percent more resources than other children; students who are both poor and come from non-English-speaking households are deemed to require 40 percent more. There is no research basis for such assumptions, however.

The report's authors attribute this estimate to Henry Levin, but Levin actually guesses that the weighting for disadvantaged students should be 1.5, not 1.2 (that is, disadvantaged students require 50 percent more resources than regular students, not 20 percent).[9] The 1.2 figure was apparently derived from Levin's calculation of actual Chapter 1 (federal aid for districts with disadvantaged students, now referred to as Title I) spending patterns, which Levin did not presume adequate.

Indeed, the 1.2 estimate does not even accurately describe the additional funding currently applied to the education of disadvantaged children, because approximately two-thirds of the states have their own compensatory education programs that supplement Title I funds and about half the states provide extra resources for limited-English-proficient students as well.[10] In states that do provide such additional funds, most allocate them according to formulas that weight recipients at between 1.2 and 1.3 of the norm.[11] When added to Title I funds, these generate a pupil weight in excess of 1.5 for the disadvantaged. While some policymakers consider this level of extra aid sufficient, others do not. William Clune, for example, cites a figure closer to 2.0, while Andrew Reschovsky and Jennifer Imazeki estimate that 2.1 would work.[12]

However, the approach of estimating a fixed weight for the additional costs of educating students in poverty is probably flawed regardless of the number chosen. Because of the powerful influence of peer expectations and role models, the concentration of school poverty probably has a more important impact on the cost of educating poor children than an individual's poverty status itself. Thus, the weight given ought to be smaller in schools where there are few poor children and greater in schools where there are many.[13] Nonetheless, the flawed 1.2 estimate has now become the conventional definition of the extra resources required for disadvantaged children and is used frequently in authoritative analyses of school spending.[14]

The implication of any statistical weighting system for student need is that if financing in the specified increments is applied, equal outcomes can be achieved. There is no evidence, though, that school resources, even with the most effective deployment, can on their own fully compensate for the social and economic disadvantages that hinder academic achievement. There is a conspicuous need for research on school finance to specify how much of the achievement gap any resource weighting system is capable of closing.

Parrish, Matsumoto, and Fowler also control for differences in purchasing power in various districts utilizing median household income adjusted for cost-of-living disparities and for the value of owner-occupied housing, not adjusted on a regional cost basis. There are reasonable technical arguments for such an approach, but the matter has not been settled definitively.

It is unfortunate that the multivariate regressions were not reported using alternate assumptions, to see how results might have differed. In particular, it would be useful to know how the adjusted distribution of funds would be affected by a disadvantaged pupil weight that was closer to 1.5 than to 1.2.

The NCES authors conclude that high-poverty districts spent 93 percent as much as affluent districts, and that spending in high-poverty, moderate-poverty, and moderately affluent districts was almost identical in cost-adjusted (for differences in purchasing power) and need-adjusted (for differences in poverty) dollars.[15] They also found that districts with high proportions of minority students spent more in cost- and need-adjusted terms. Different definitions of cost and need controls would, of course, cause these estimates to change.

Because the American education system is not a unitary one, an examination of inequality of funding that merges all districts into a single statistical analysis can provide only partial policy guidance. Because school finance is primarily a state and local matter, this chapter focuses on spending inequalities between and within states.

FIVE TYPES OF SCHOOL RESOURCE INEQUALITY

The pages that follow refer to five types of resource inequalities, corresponding to five institutional levels at which disadvantaged children could be shortchanged.

Type I: Disadvantaged children may live disproportionately in states that spend less money on education than do other states.

Type II: Within any state, disadvantaged children may attend schools in districts that spend less on education.

Type III: Within any district, disadvantaged children may attend schools that command fewer real resources than others.

Type IV: Within any school, disadvantaged children may be placed in classrooms that have fewer real resources at their disposal.

Type V: Within any classroom, disadvantaged children may be offered less adequate assistance than others.

Type IV and Type V resource inequalities result primarily from tracking systems within schools and classrooms; from the assignment of teachers of uneven qualities to the different tracks, or from different class sizes for faster and slower tracks, or from variable facility access (for example, to computers or laboratories), or even from teacher attitudes or approaches toward certain kinds of students. Types IV and V inequality are not addressed in this chapter, for reasons of space and the fact that these types of inequality are more difficult to quantify. Economists recognize that a less capable teacher represents a lesser "real" resource than a better teacher, but if both are paid on the same salary schedule, available school finance data will not be able to measure this (Type IV) inequality. Similarly, if teachers have lower expectations of disadvantaged children than their ability warrants and therefore devote less time and energy to them, there is no fiscal measure of this (Type V) inequality. While these forms of resource inequality will not be discussed further here, they can have a significant impact on student outcomes.[16] This chapter is primarily concerned with resource inequalities of Types I to III, differences in spending between states, between districts within states, and between schools within districts.

TYPE I INEQUALITY: DIFFERENCES IN SCHOOL SPENDING BETWEEN STATES

Table 3.1 (pages 38–41) presents data related to Type I resource inequalities for the school year 1996–97. Column 1 shows total dollars raised by state and local governments for education, divided by total public elementary and secondary school enrollment. This column does not include revenues received by states or school districts from the federal government, and it only includes what is generated from tax sources—it does not include funds raised by school districts from student tuitions or fees (for summer school, transportation, textbook sales, school lunch sales, student activities, etc.).[17] Column 2 displays the total state and local spending for each state as a percentage of average per pupil spending nationwide. Considerable disparities exist in state and local nominal (unadjusted) spending for education. New Jersey, New York, and Connecticut are the

TABLE 3.1. PUBLIC EDUCATION SPENDING BY STATE, 1996–97

	(1)	(2)	(3)	(4)	(5)	(6)	(7)	(8)	(9)
	1996–97 NOMINAL STATE AND LOCAL PER PUPIL SPENDING		1996–97 STATE AND LOCAL PER PUPIL SPENDING ADJUSTED FOR REGIONAL COST DIFFERENCES		1996 % OF CHILDREN, AGES 5–17, IN POVERTY		PERSONAL INCOME PER ENROLLED STUDENT		
	($)	As % of U.S. AVG.	($)	As % of U.S. AVG.	(%)	As % of U.S. AVG.	($)	ADJUSTED FOR REGIONAL COST DIFFERENCES ($)	ADJUSTED FOR REGIONAL COST DIFFERENCES AS % OF U.S. AVG.
United States	6,081	100	6,081	100	19	100	140,553	140,553	100
Alabama	4,525	74	4,943	81	21	110	113,784	124,926	89
Alaska	8,031	132	7,356	121	10	52	113,247	103,035	73
Arizona	4,868	80	4,973	82	30	157	116,848	118,599	84
Arkansas	4,516	74	5,055	83	20	103	103,020	115,894	82
California	5,500	90	4,592	76	24	124	140,400	116,456	83
Colorado	5,487	90	5,632	93	11	59	145,128	147,962	105
Connecticut	8,714	143	7,172	118	24	124	210,393	172,986	123
Delaware	7,232	119	6,692	110	12	66	178,410	165,923	118
Dist. of Col.	8,054	132	7,255	119	38	202	234,755	212,497	151
Florida	5,490	90	5,563	91	20	105	153,333	156,163	111

State									
Georgia	5,503	90	5,806	95	20	104	124,711	132,222	94
Hawaii	5,829	96	4,635	76	16	83	158,718	125,376	89
Idaho	4,674	77	4,993	82	16	86	95,485	101,334	72
Illinois	6,094	100	6,063	100	17	87	159,632	159,295	113
Indiana	7,231	119	7,742	127	8	42	131,755	141,498	101
Iowa	5,645	93	6,114	101	12	62	124,784	135,571	96
Kansas	5,982	98	6,441	106	11	57	125,865	135,947	97
Kentucky	5,151	85	5,571	92	27	143	115,247	125,268	89
Louisiana	4,495	74	4,927	81	28	147	107,273	118,167	84
Maine	6,619	109	6,309	104	14	74	121,418	115,621	82
Maryland	6,766	111	6,059	100	15	79	168,667	151,796	108
Massachusetts	7,266	119	6,100	100	13	69	192,738	161,663	115
Michigan	7,293	120	7,641	126	16	83	138,668	145,727	104
Minnesota	6,624	109	6,865	113	13	69	138,447	143,950	102
Mississippi	3,704	61	4,129	68	26	138	93,558	104,813	75
Missouri	5,579	92	5,933	98	11	60	134,733	143,722	102
Montana	5,206	86	5,542	91	25	132	100,506	106,301	76
Nebraska	5,927	97	6,564	108	12	63	128,960	143,255	102
Nevada	5,574	92	5,434	89	8	44	146,783	142,136	101
New Hampshire	6,079	100	5,378	88	7	36	154,472	136,521	97

cont. on next page

TABLE 3.1. PUBLIC EDUCATION SPENDING BY STATE, 1996–97 (CONT.)

	(1)	(2)	(3)	(4)	(5)	(6)	(7)	(8)	(9)
	1996–97 NOMINAL STATE AND LOCAL PER PUPIL SPENDING	As % of U.S. AVG.	1996–97 STATE AND LOCAL PER PUPIL SPENDING ADJUSTED FOR REGIONAL COST DIFFERENCES	As % of U.S. AVG.	1996 % OF CHILDREN, AGES 5–17, IN POVERTY	As % of U.S. AVG.	PERSONAL INCOME PER ENROLLED STUDENT	ADJUSTED FOR REGIONAL COST DIFFERENCES	ADJUSTED FOR REGIONAL COST DIFFERENCES AS % OF U.S. AVG.
	($)		($)		(%)		($)	($)	
New Jersey	9,667	159	8,166	134	14	74	204,755	172,816	123
New Mexico	4,687	77	4,945	81	32	170	95,679	100,285	71
New York	8,748	144	7,506	123	25	132	185,144	158,731	113
North Carolina	4,841	80	5,170	85	18	93	133,194	142,973	102
North Dakota	4,429	73	4,800	79	10	54	108,081	117,513	84
Ohio	6,134	101	6,351	104	17	88	139,616	145,014	103
Oklahoma	4,537	75	5,039	83	24	128	102,707	114,653	82
Oregon	5,813	96	6,001	99	18	97	136,015	139,495	99
Pennsylvania	7,418	122	7,004	115	16	84	163,630	154,347	110
Rhode Island	7,359	121	6,804	112	12	66	159,043	146,914	105
South Carolina	5,196	85	5,588	92	21	112	112,456	121,548	86

South Dakota	4,548	75	5,058	83	12	61	105,183	117,325	83
Tennessee	4,151	68	4,529	74	21	109	127,829	140,163	100
Texas	5,246	86	5,625	92	23	119	111,074	119,678	85
Utah	4,159	68	4,322	71	9	46	80,646	83,246	59
Vermont	7,141	117	6,998	115	16	86	122,286	119,722	85
Virginia	6,034	99	5,607	92	18	95	151,767	141,725	101
Washington	6,206	102	6,095	100	16	82	141,345	137,897	98
West Virginia	6,183	102	6,857	113	22	119	108,455	120,894	86
Wisconsin	7,133	117	7,482	123	10	55	135,273	142,323	101
Wyoming	6,072	100	6,413	105	9	49	104,313	109,448	78

Note: State and local spending does not include funds raised from tuition payments, lunch sales, bus passes, textbook sales, or other nontax sources.

Sources:

Column 1: U.S. Department of Education, Office of Educational Research and Improvement, *Statistics in Brief: Revenues and Expenditures for Public Elementary and Secondary Education, School Year 1996-97*, NCES 1999-301, National Center for Education Statistics, 1999, Table 1; Spreadsheet provided to author by National Center for Education Statistics, July 12, 1999, LOCREV97.wk1; U.S. Department of Education, Office of Educational Research and Improvement, *Digest of Education Statistics 1998*, NCES 1999-036, National Center for Education Statistics, 1999, Table 40.

Column 2: Calculated from column 1.

Column 3: See text.

Column 4: Calculated from column 3.

Column 5: U.S. Department of Education, *Digest of Education Statistics 1998*, Table 20.

Column 6: Calculated from column 5.

Column 7: U.S. Department of Commerce, Bureau of Economic Analysis, "Regional Accounts Data, State Personal Income," 1999, http://www.bea.doc.gov/bea/regional/spi/pi.htm.

Column 8: See text.

Column 9: Calculated from column 8.

highest-spending states. The District of Columbia, Alaska, Pennsylvania, and Rhode Island also spend considerably more per pupil than the national average. At the other extreme, Mississippi, Tennessee, Utah, North Dakota, Louisiana, Arkansas, Alabama, Oklahoma, and South Dakota spend only about half as much per pupil as the three highest-spending states. Other low-spending states include Idaho, New Mexico, North Carolina, and Arizona.

Adjusting Interstate Disparities for Differences in Regional Costs

These data, however, are misleading, because there are substantial differences in the costs of education between states. School districts in states with low prices for goods and services (most importantly the services of teachers) can operate with budgets considerably below what it would take for districts to purchase resources of comparable quality in high-cost states. Column 3 adjusts for these differences, displaying a cost-adjusted per pupil spending figure for each state. It takes the nominal per pupil spending figure of column 1 for each state and expresses that outlay as though the education dollars in that state had average nationwide purchasing power.[18]

Disparities in state education spending are narrower after this adjustment is made but still substantial. New Jersey spends at a rate more than a third above the national per pupil average, and Indiana and Michigan spend more than 25 percent above the average. Other high-spending states include New York, Wisconsin, Alaska, the District of Columbia, Connecticut, Pennsylvania, and Vermont. At the other extreme, Mississippi, Utah, and Tennessee spend much less than the national average. The next-lowest-spending states are California, Hawaii, North Dakota, Louisiana, Alabama, New Mexico, Arizona, Idaho, Oklahoma, Arkansas, and South Dakota.

Interstate Disparities in the Context of Differences in Need—Child Poverty

Column 5 displays the percentage of children in each state, aged five to seventeen, whose families had income below the poverty line in 1996.

Column 6 shows the ratio of this percentage to the national child poverty average of 19 percent. Here again there is great disparity. The District of Columbia had a child poverty rate more than twice that of the nation as a whole, and seven other states (New Mexico, Arizona, Louisiana, Kentucky, Mississippi, New York, and Montana) had relatively high child poverty rates. At the other extreme, five states (New Hampshire, Indiana, Nevada, Utah, and Wyoming) had child poverty rates that were less than half the U.S. average, and another six states (Alaska, North Dakota, Wisconsin, Kansas, Colorado, and Missouri) also had rates considerably below the national average.

Differing Capacities of States to Pay for Education

The last three columns of Table 3.1 present data on the capacity of states to provide public education for their children. Column 7 shows the total personal income of the residents of each state divided by the number of enrolled public school students in 1996–97.[19] This gives a figure of state personal income per student (PIPS). Column 8 adjusts these data for cost of living differences between states.[20] As column 9 shows (in terms of percentage of the national average), the capacity of states to provide for the education of their children also varies greatly. Citizens of the District of Columbia have the means to provide for public education with the greatest ease; total PIPS is 51 percent greater than the national average.[21] Connecticut and New Jersey have PIPS that is more than 20 percent greater than the national average; Delaware and Massachusetts have PIPS that is more than 15 percent greater than the national average. At the other extreme, citizens of Utah must make the greatest sacrifice to provide for public education—PIPS is only 59 percent of the national average. Six other states (New Mexico, Idaho, Alaska, Mississippi, Montana, and Wyoming) have PIPS that is less than 80 percent of the national average.[22]

States with High Poverty and
Low Capacity Spend Less in Real Terms

Nominally, Type I inequality exists simply to the extent that unadjusted per pupil spending differs from state to state. Real Type I inequality is based not only on school spending after regional cost adjustment but also on educational need and the capacity of a state's citizens to bear this burden. If a truly equitable school spending regime would dedicate more resources to disadvantaged than to other children, then states with greater need (that is, those with more disadvantaged children) should also be those states that spend more of their own resources, on average, per pupil. And from a standpoint of concern with Type I equality, ideally states with greater need and higher per pupil spending of state and local resources should also be those states where fiscal capacity is greater. On the other hand, a system with great Type I inequality would exist if in places where poverty was high, state and local per pupil spending and fiscal capacity were both low.

Simple statistical analyses confirm Type I inequality. There is a positive, statistically significant relationship between cost-adjusted average per pupil spending by state (1996–97) and cost-adjusted PIPS. An additional $1,000 in PIPS corresponds to approximately $25 in increased per pupil spending.[23] And there is a negative, statistically significant relationship between spending and poverty. A 1 percent increase in a state's child poverty rate corresponds to a $35 decline in spending.[24] These relationships, taken together, indicate the presence of Type I inequality—states with greater need and lower capacity spend less. Both coefficients are quite small, but they point in the opposite direction from what we should expect of a system that worked to minimize Type I inequality.

Table 3.2 compares the rankings of states on three measures. Column 1 displays states in order of cost-adjusted per pupil spending (1 to 51, with 1 being the state with the highest spending, calculated from columns 3 or 4 of Table 3.1).[25] Column 2 displays state ranks in the intensity of child poverty (calculated from columns 5 or 6 of Table 3.1). Column 3 displays how states fare in regard to fiscal capacity (calculated from columns 8 or 9 of Table 3.1).

Column 4 calculates the disparity between a state's rank in cost-adjusted per pupil spending and its rank in the intensity of child poverty. (Column 4 equals the difference between column 2 and column 1.) A very high positive number in column 4 indicates that, in comparison to other states, a state has high per pupil expenditure while having less need for spending because it has relatively few children in poverty.[26] The state with the greatest disparity in this respect is Indiana: it ranks second in per pupil spending but fiftieth in child poverty. Other states

TABLE 3.2. RANKINGS OF PUBLIC EDUCATION SPENDING BY STATE, 1996–97

	(1) 1996–97 STATE AND LOCAL PER PUPIL SPENDING, ADJUSTED FOR REGIONAL COST DIFFERENCES (RANK)	(2) 1996 PERCENTAGE OF CHILDREN, AGES 5–17, IN POVERTY (RANK)	(3) 1996 PERSONAL INCOME PER ENROLLED STUDENT, ADJUSTED FOR REGIONAL COST DIFFERENCES (RANK)	(4) DISPARITY IN RANK (SPENDING VS. NEED)	(5) PIPS RANK COMPARED TO SPENDING/NEED DISPARITY
Alabama	44	15	32	–29	–61
Alaska	6	46	48	40	–8
Arizona	42	3	37	–39	–76
Arkansas	39	19	42	–20	–62
California	48	10	41	–38	–79
Colorado	28	42	11	14	3
Connecticut	8	11	2	3	1
Delaware	14	36	4	22	18
Dist. of Col.	7	1	1	–6	–7
Florida	33	17	8	–16	–24
Georgia	27	18	29	–9	–38

cont. on next page

TABLE 3.2. RANKINGS OF PUBLIC EDUCATION SPENDING BY STATE, 1996–97 (CONT.)

	(1) 1996–97 STATE AND LOCAL PER PUPIL SPENDING, ADJUSTED FOR REGIONAL COST DIFFERENCES (RANK)	(2) 1996 PERCENTAGE OF CHILDREN, AGES 5–17, IN POVERTY (RANK)	(3) 1996 PERSONAL INCOME PER ENROLLED STUDENT, ADJUSTED FOR REGIONAL COST DIFFERENCES (RANK)	(4) DISPARITY IN RANK (SPENDING VS. NEED)	(5) PIPS RANK COMPARED TO SPENDING/NEED DISPARITY
Hawaii	47	28	30	-19	-49
Idaho	41	25	49	-16	-65
Illinois	23	24	6	1	-5
Indiana	2	50	22	48	26
Iowa	20	39	28	19	-9
Kansas	16	43	27	27	0
Kentucky	32	5	31	-27	-58
Louisiana	45	4	38	-41	-79
Maine	19	32	43	13	-30
Maryland	24	31	10	7	-3
Massachusetts	21	34	5	13	8
Michigan	3	29	13	26	13

Minnesota	11	35	15	24	9
Mississippi	51	6	47	-45	-92
Missouri	26	41	16	15	-1
Montana	34	8	46	-26	-72
Nebraska	15	38	17	23	6
Nevada	35	49	20	14	-6
New Hampshire	36	51	26	15	-11
New Jersey	1	33	3	32	29
New Mexico	43	2	50	-41	-91
New York	4	7	7	3	-4
North Carolina	37	22	18	-15	-33
North Dakota	46	45	39	-1	-40
Ohio	18	23	14	5	-9
Oklahoma	40	9	44	-31	-75
Oregon	25	20	24	-5	-29
Pennsylvania	9	27	9	18	9
Rhode Island	13	37	12	24	12
South Carolina	31	14	33	-17	-50
South Dakota	38	40	40	2	-38

cont. on next page

TABLE 3.2. RANKINGS OF PUBLIC EDUCATION SPENDING BY STATE, 1996–97 (CONT.)

	(1) 1996–97 STATE AND LOCAL PER PUPIL SPENDING, ADJUSTED FOR REGIONAL COST DIFFERENCES (RANK)	(2) 1996 PERCENTAGE OF CHILDREN, AGES 5–17, IN POVERTY (RANK)	(3) 1996 PERSONAL INCOME PER ENROLLED STUDENT, ADJUSTED FOR REGIONAL COST DIFFERENCES (RANK)	(4) DISPARITY IN RANK (SPENDING VS. NEED)	(5) PIPS RANK COMPARED TO SPENDING/NEED DISPARITY
Tennessee	49	16	23	-33	-56
Texas	29	12	36	-17	-53
Utah	50	48	51	-2	-53
Vermont	10	26	35	16	-19
Virginia	30	21	21	-9	-30
Washington	22	30	25	8	-17
West Virginia	12	13	34	1	-33
Wisconsin	5	44	19	39	20
Wyoming	17	47	45	30	-15

Sources: Column 1 calculated from Table 3.1, column 3; column 2 calculated from Table 3.1, column 5; column 3 calculated from Table 3.1, column 8; column 4 calculated from columns 2 and 3; column 5 calculated from columns 3 and 4.

with great positive disparities include Alaska, Wisconsin, New Jersey, Wyoming, Kansas, Michigan, Minnesota, Rhode Island, Nebraska, and Delaware.

A very low negative number in column 4 indicates that, in comparison to others, a state spends relatively little per pupil in spite of having greater need for such spending because of its relatively large number of children in poverty. The state with the greatest disparity in this respect is Mississippi: it ranks at the very bottom in adjusted per pupil spending but close to the top (sixth) in child poverty. Other states with great negative disparities include New Mexico, Louisiana, Arizona, California, Tennessee, Oklahoma, Alabama, Kentucky, and Montana.

Policies to correct Type I inequality could either encourage greater state expenditure in low-spending states with severe need or arrange a redistribution of spending from the federal government. (The term "redistribution" used here encompasses policies that supplement spending in needy states without necessarily requiring an offsetting reduction in federal contributions to states with lesser need.) The first option would make sense in cases where states have reasonably sufficient fiscal capacity (PIPS) but choose not to utilize it for education. Redistribution would make sense in cases where low-spending states also have limited fiscal capacity with which to address their own considerable needs.

Column 5 of Table 3.2 compares a state's ranking in PIPS to the disparity in its cost-adjusted spending and child poverty rankings (the difference between columns 3 and 4). A very low negative number in column 5 suggests that while a state may spend little given its need, it has relatively little ability to address this shortfall without outside help. States falling most clearly into this category include Mississippi, New Mexico, Louisiana, California, Arizona, Oklahoma, Montana, Idaho, Arkansas, Alabama, and Kentucky. States with less negative or positive numbers are those that have greater ability than the first group to correct, without federal aid, spending shortfalls in relation to how widespread are their conditions of child poverty. Some states that have great spending versus need disparities yet may have capacity to increase the flow of revenues to education to solve this problem on their own are North Carolina, Virginia, Florida, the District of Columbia, and Oregon.

These calculations are only suggestive, not definitive. Differences between rank numbers on any of these measures do not necessarily reflect equal intervals. Determining whether a state is spending sufficiently to address its own needs, or whether its mean personal income is adequate to increase such spending as much as necessary, depends on a calculation of the cost of an adequate education for disadvantaged children. Because there is no consensus regarding this amount, it is not possible to gauge, in anything but a suggestive manner, whether federal aid is required to correct Type I inequality in school spending and, if so, how much. However, based on these rankings, it appears that there is a positive relationship between inadequate spending and low state income. Table 3.2a illustrates this relationship more vividly. It is identical to Table 3.2 but is sorted by column 4, "Disparity in Rank." States appearing at the top of Table 3.2a are those with low rankings in per pupil spending combined with relatively high percentages of poor children. As can be seen by examining column 3, these states tend to be those with low levels of personal income per student. Of the ten states with the greatest spending versus need disparity, only one (Tennessee) is above the median in PIPS.

The Limitations of Existing Federal Education Aid

Federal aid to education does very little to redress these inequalities because federal funds represent only about 7 percent of school expenditures.[27] The largest federal education category is the child nutrition (free and reduced-price lunch) program of the Department of Agriculture. Next is Title I, grants to schools serving disadvantaged students. Other federal aid (for example, bilingual and immigrant education, "school improvement," and "Goals 2000" funds) could also be used by states to enhance teaching, materials, or facilities at schools serving students in poverty. However, federal spending does not seem to have reduced Type I resource inequalities. It may even exacerbate them. Title I funding is distributed to states based on the number of children in poverty, which should tend to reduce Type I inequality. But allocations are adjusted based on each state's average per pupil spending.[28] This adjustment could actually aggravate the problem because states that spend less typically are also those with less fiscal capacity.

Table 3.3 (pages 55–56), column 1, shows total per pupil spending by state, including state, local, and federal funds, adjusted for regional cost differences. Column 2 shows each state's rank on this measure, with the highest-spending state (New Jersey) ranked 1 and the lowest-spending state (Utah) ranked 51. Column 3 (identical to column 1 in

TABLE 3.2A. RANKINGS: PUBLIC EDUCATION SPENDING BY STATE, 1996–97, SORTED BY DISPARITY IN RANK (SPENDING VS. NEED)

	(1) 1996–97 STATE AND LOCAL PER PUPIL SPENDING, ADJUSTED FOR REGIONAL COST DIFFERENCES (RANK)	(2) 1996 PERCENTAGE OF CHILDREN, AGES 5–17, IN POVERTY (RANK)	(3) 1996 PERSONAL INCOME PER ENROLLED STUDENT, ADJUSTED FOR REGIONAL COST DIFFERENCES (RANK)	(4) DISPARITY IN RANK (SPENDING VS. NEED)	(5) PIPS RANK COMPARED TO SPENDING/NEED DISPARITY
Mississippi	51	6	47	–45	–92
Louisiana	45	4	38	–41	–79
New Mexico	43	2	50	–41	–91
Arizona	42	3	37	–39	–76
California	48	10	41	–38	–79
Tennessee	49	16	23	–33	–56
Oklahoma	40	9	44	–31	–75
Alabama	44	15	32	–29	–61
Kentucky	32	5	31	–27	–58
Montana	34	8	46	–26	–72

cont. on next page

TABLE 3.2A. RANKINGS: PUBLIC EDUCATION SPENDING BY STATE, 1996–97, SORTED BY DISPARITY IN RANK (SPENDING VS. NEED) (CONT.)

	(1) 1996–97 STATE AND LOCAL PER PUPIL SPENDING, ADJUSTED FOR REGIONAL COST DIFFERENCES (RANK)	(2) 1996 PERCENTAGE OF CHILDREN, AGES 5–17, IN POVERTY (RANK)	(3) 1996 PERSONAL INCOME PER ENROLLED STUDENT, ADJUSTED FOR REGIONAL COST DIFFERENCES (RANK)	(4) DISPARITY IN RANK (SPENDING VS. NEED)	(5) PIPS RANK COMPARED TO SPENDING/NEED DISPARITY
Arkansas	39	19	42	−20	−62
Hawaii	47	28	30	−19	−49
South Carolina	31	14	33	−17	−50
Texas	29	12	36	−17	−53
Florida	33	17	8	−16	−24
Idaho	41	25	49	−16	−65
North Carolina	37	22	18	−15	−33
Georgia	27	18	29	−9	−38
Virginia	30	21	21	−9	−30
Dist. of Col.	7	1	1	−6	−7
Oregon	25	20	24	−5	−29

Utah	50	48	51	-2	-53
North Dakota	46	45	39	-1	-40
Illinois	23	24	6	1	-5
West Virginia	12	13	34	1	-33
South Dakota	38	40	40	2	-38
Connecticut	8	11	2	3	1
New York	4	7	7	3	-4
Ohio	18	23	14	5	-9
Maryland	24	31	10	7	-3
Washington	22	30	25	8	-17
Maine	19	32	43	13	-30
Massachusetts	21	34	5	13	8
Colorado	28	42	11	14	3
Nevada	35	49	20	14	-6
Missouri	26	41	16	15	-1
New Hampshire	36	51	26	15	-11
Vermont	10	26	35	16	-19
Pennsylvania	9	27	9	18	9
Iowa	20	39	28	19	-9

cont. on next page

TABLE 3.2A. RANKINGS: PUBLIC EDUCATION SPENDING BY STATE, 1996–97, SORTED BY DISPARITY IN RANK (SPENDING VS. NEED) (CONT.)

	(1) 1996–97 STATE AND LOCAL PER PUPIL SPENDING, ADJUSTED FOR REGIONAL COST DIFFERENCES (RANK)	(2) 1996 PERCENTAGE OF CHILDREN, AGES 5–17, IN POVERTY (RANK)	(3) 1996 PERSONAL INCOME PER ENROLLED STUDENT, ADJUSTED FOR REGIONAL COST DIFFERENCES (RANK)	(4) DISPARITY IN RANK (SPENDING VS. NEED)	(5) PIPS RANK COMPARED TO SPENDING/NEED DISPARITY
Delaware	14	36	4	22	18
Nebraska	15	38	17	23	6
Minnesota	11	35	15	24	9
Rhode Island	13	37	12	24	12
Michigan	3	29	13	26	13
Kansas	16	43	27	27	0
Wyoming	17	47	45	30	–15
New Jersey	1	33	3	32	29
Wisconsin	5	44	19	39	20
Alaska	6	46	48	40	–8
Indiana	2	50	22	48	26

Source: Table 3.2.

TABLE 3.3. RANKINGS: PUBLIC EDUCATION SPENDING BY STATE, 1996–97, WITH AND WITHOUT FEDERAL FUNDS INCLUDED

	(1)	(2)	(3)	(4)
			STATE AND LOCAL PER PUPIL SPENDING[a]	DIFFERENCE IN RANK, WITH AND WITHOUT FEDERAL SPENDING
	TOTAL PER PUPIL SPENDING[a]			
	($)	(RANK)	(RANK)	
Alabama	5,495	45	44	−1
Alaska	8,373	2	6	4
Arizona	5,496	44	42	−2
Arkansas	5,511	42	39	−3
California	5,006	48	48	0
Colorado	5,954	33	28	−5
Connecticut	7,438	9	8	−1
Delaware	7,252	12	14	2
Dist. of Col.	8,113	4	7	3
Florida	6,025	32	33	1
Georgia	6,241	27	27	0
Hawaii	5,050	47	47	0
Idaho	5,358	46	41	−5
Illinois	6,480	21	23	2
Indiana	8,089	5	2	−3
Iowa	6,461	22	20	−2
Kansas	6,834	17	16	−1
Kentucky	6,151	28	32	4
Louisiana	5,597	38	45	7
Maine	6,671	19	19	0
Maryland	6,401	25	24	−1
Massachusetts	6,413	24	21	−3
Michigan	8,190	3	3	0
Minnesota	7,189	14	11	−3
Mississippi	4,826	50	51	1
Missouri	6,323	26	26	0
Montana	6,144	29	34	5

cont. on next page

TABLE 3.3. RANKINGS: PUBLIC EDUCATION SPENDING BY STATE, 1996–97, WITH AND WITHOUT FEDERAL FUNDS INCLUDED (CONT.)

	(1)	(2)	(3)	(4)
	TOTAL PER PUPIL SPENDING[a]		STATE AND LOCAL PER PUPIL SPENDING[a]	DIFFERENCE IN RANK, WITH AND WITHOUT FEDERAL SPENDING
	($)	(RANK)	(RANK)	
Nebraska	7,006	15	15	0
Nevada	5,679	36	35	−1
New Hampshire	5,576	40	36	−4
New Jersey	8,470	1	1	0
New Mexico	5,681	35	43	8
New York	7,943	6	4	−2
North Carolina	5,586	39	37	−2
North Dakota	5,497	43	46	3
Ohio	6,782	18	18	0
Oklahoma	5,519	41	40	−1
Oregon	6,416	23	25	2
Pennsylvania	7,416	10	9	−1
Rhode Island	7,194	13	13	0
South Carolina	6,127	30	31	1
South Dakota	5,622	37	38	1
Tennessee	4,983	49	49	0
Texas	6,106	31	29	−2
Utah	4,620	51	50	−1
Vermont	7,345	11	10	−1
Virginia	5,910	34	30	−4
Washington	6,487	20	22	2
West Virginia	7,486	8	12	4
Wisconsin	7,826	7	5	−2
Wyoming	6,873	16	17	1

[a] Adjusted for regional cost differences

Note: Nontax revenues not included.

Sources: Column 1 same as Table 3.1, column 1 (see text for adjustment methodology); column 2 calculated from column 1; column 3, Table 3.2, column 1; column 4 calculated from columns 2 and 3.

Table 3.2) shows these rankings without federal funds included. Column 4 shows how the addition of federal funds affects a state's rank in regard to per pupil spending. It is apparent that there is very little change. Federal aid is currently too insignificant to have much of an impact in this regard. Except for New Mexico and Louisiana, those with the greatest need for subsidy (Mississippi, New Mexico, Louisiana, California, Arizona, Oklahoma, Montana, Idaho, Arkansas, Alabama, and Kentucky) show virtually no change in rank.[29]

Federal aid for the education of disadvantaged children could be considered to have zero impact on nominal Type I inequality if each state received the same proportion of total federal education dollars as its proportion of the total number of children in poverty. Federal aid could be said to offset inequality if states with less ability to pay (PIPS) for education received a greater share of federal dollars than their share of children in poverty, and could be said to exacerbate inequality if the opposite were true.

Table 3.4 (pages 58–61), parts A and B, shows that federal aid does not reduce Type I inequality, but rather may exacerbate it in many cases. Part A includes the twenty-two states whose PIPS is greater than the national average. Column 1 shows the percentage of total cost-adjusted Title I funds received by each state; column 2 shows the percentage of all cost-adjusted federal elementary and secondary education funds received by each state;[30] column 3 shows the percentage of the nation's population of poor children residing in each state. If federal funds neither diminished nor exacerbated Type I inequality, one would expect columns 2 and 3 to be identical; column 1 should also be similar to column 3. Instead, with the exception of six states (Connecticut, New York, Virginia, Massachusetts, New Jersey, Maryland), states with greater than average PIPS also get a greater than proportional share of federal funds. Indiana is the most extreme case—with only 0.8 percent of the nation's poor children, it receives 1.7 percent of the nation's Title I funds, 211 percent of its proportional share. Rhode Island, with only 0.2 percent of the nation's poor children, receives 0.3 percent of Title I funds, or 50 percent more than its proportional share.

Part B of Table 3.4 features the twenty-nine states whose PIPS is less than the national average. If federal funds had the effect of compensating for this disadvantage, one would expect these states to receive a greater ration of federal funds than their share of the nation's poor children. This is true for twenty of these states. But for the remaining

TABLE 3.4. SHARE OF FEDERAL EDUCATION SPENDING BY STATE, 1996–97, COMPARED TO STATES' SHARES OF THE NATIONAL POPULATION IN POVERTY AND ABILITY TO PAY FOR EDUCATION

	(1) 1998 TITLE I ALLOCATIONS BY STATE,° AS % OF TOTAL TITLE I ALLO-CATIONS	(2) 1996–97 TOTAL FEDERAL SPENDING BY STATE,° AS % OF TOTAL SPENDING	(3) 1996 CHILDREN, 5–17, IN POVERTY AS % OF TOTAL CHILDREN IN POVERTY	(4) RATIO, % OF TOTAL FEDERAL SPENDING TO % OF CHILDREN IN POVERTY (%)	(5) RATIO, % OF TITLE I SPENDING TO % OF CHILDREN IN POVERTY (%)	(6) PERSONAL INCOME PER ENROLLED STUDENT AS % OF U.S. AVG.
PART A. STATES WITH GREATER ABILITY TO PAY FOR EDUCATION:						
Indiana	1.7	1.7	0.8	206.8	211.2	101
Rhode Island	0.3	0.3	0.2	156.6	171.4	105
Wisconsin	1.9	1.5	1.1	138.0	170.7	101
Michigan	4.9	4.6	3.0	155.0	163.1	104
Missouri	1.9	1.8	1.3	140.0	152.3	102
Delaware	0.2	0.3	0.2	174.7	136.5	118
Pennsylvania	4.4	3.7	3.6	101.8	121.9	110
Nevada	0.3	0.3	0.3	136.6	121.2	101
Nebraska	0.5	0.6	0.4	151.1	117.0	102
Massachusetts	1.7	1.5	1.5	96.7	115.7	115
Ohio	4.4	4.0	3.8	103.8	115.3	103

Illinois	4.6	4.1	4.0	101.7	113.9	113
Colorado	1.0	1.1	0.9	117.1	110.6	105
New Jersey	1.9	1.8	1.9	96.7	102.5	123
Florida	4.9	5.2	4.8	108.5	101.7	111
Minnesota	1.3	1.4	1.4	100.9	94.3	102
North Carolina	2.1	2.5	2.3	108.8	92.1	102
New York	8.3	6.2	9.1	68.2	91.4	113
Maryland	1.3	1.4	1.4	98.0	89.0	108
Dist. of Col.	0.3	0.3	0.3	104.5	87.1	151
Virginia	1.5	1.7	1.9	87.2	76.9	101
Connecticut	0.8	0.7	1.7	42.1	48.3	123
PART B. STATES WITH LESSER ABILITY TO PAY FOR EDUCATION:					
Wyoming	0.2	0.2	0.1	240.3	257.5	78
North Dakota	0.3	0.4	0.1	308.5	202.6	84
West Virginia	1.2	1.0	0.6	163.7	199.7	86
South Dakota	0.3	0.4	0.2	242.3	184.1	83
New Hampshire	0.2	0.2	0.1	143.9	162.6	97
Maine	0.4	0.4	0.3	142.0	144.4	82
Kansas	0.8	0.9	0.6	156.8	144.0	97

cont. on next page

TABLE 3.4. SHARE OF FEDERAL EDUCATION SPENDING BY STATE, 1996–97, COMPARED TO STATES' SHARES OF THE NATIONAL POPULATION IN POVERTY AND ABILITY TO PAY FOR EDUCATION (CONT.)

	(1) 1998 TITLE I ALLOCATIONS BY STATE,ᵃ AS % OF TOTAL TITLE I ALLOCATIONS	(2) 1996–97 TOTAL FEDERAL SPENDING BY STATE,ᵃ AS % OF TOTAL SPENDING	(3) 1996 CHILDREN, 5–17, IN POVERTY AS % OF TOTAL CHILDREN IN POVERTY	(4) RATIO, % OF TOTAL FEDERAL SPENDING TO % OF CHILDREN IN POVERTY (%)	(5) RATIO, % OF TITLE I SPENDING TO % OF CHILDREN IN POVERTY (%)	(6) PERSONAL INCOME PER ENROLLED STUDENT AS % OF U.S. AVG.
Alaska	0.2	0.7	0.2	368.9	125.8	73
Louisiana	3.0	2.7	2.5	108.7	122.6	84
Vermont	0.2	0.2	0.2	92.8	122.5	85
Utah	0.5	0.7	0.4	174.5	118.8	59
Mississippi	2.0	1.8	1.7	103.5	117.2	75
Alabama	2.0	2.1	1.8	116.6	111.3	89
Arkansas	1.2	1.0	1.1	95.2	110.5	82
Texas	9.7	9.2	8.9	103.1	108.4	85
Iowa	0.8	0.9	0.7	117.9	108.2	96
Georgia	2.9	2.9	2.9	101.3	101.3	94
Kentucky	2.0	1.9	2.1	89.8	93.4	89
Washington	1.5	1.9	1.6	114.8	90.9	98

South Carolina	1.5	1.8	1.6	109.8	90.3	86
Oregon	1.0	1.1	1.2	94.5	84.8	99
Tennessee	2.0	2.1	2.4	85.3	83.3	100
Montana	0.4	0.5	0.5	102.2	79.5	76
Idaho	0.3	0.4	0.4	105.9	78.8	72
Oklahoma	1.4	1.5	1.8	82.7	76.6	82
Hawaii	0.2	0.4	0.3	115.4	67.5	89
New Mexico	0.9	1.2	1.4	85.3	65.3	71
California	9.8	11.6	15.4	75.7	63.4	83
Arizona	1.6	2.1	3.0	67.8	53.6	84

a Adjusted for regional cost differences.

Sources:

Column 1: Calculated from U.S. Department of Education, "FY 1998 Title I Allocations to States for School Year 1998–99," 1999; http://www.ed.gov/offices/OUS/us98.htm; for adjustment methodology, see text.

Column 2: Calculated from U.S. Department of Education, Office of Educational Research and Improvement, *Statistics in Brief, Revenues and Expenditures for Public Elementary and Secondary Education, School Year 1996–97*, NCES 1999-301, National Center for Education Statistics, 1999, Table 1. For cost adjustment methodology, see text.

Column 3: Calculated from U.S. Department of Education, Office of Educational Research and Improvement, *Digest of Education Statistics 1998*, NCES 1999-301, National Center for Education Statistics, 1999, Table 20.

Column 4: Calculated from columns 2 and 3.

Column 5: Calculated from columns 1 and 3.

Column 6: Table 3.1, column 8.

nine, federal funds have the effect of worsening inequality. Five of these states are in the West or Southwest, three are in the Southeast, and one (Vermont) is in the Northeast.

In 1996–97, the coefficient of variation (a statistical measure of inequality) of cost-adjusted per pupil state and local spending by state was about 16 percent. With federal funds added, the coefficient of variation was reduced only to about 15 percent. The results are barely different if each state's per pupil spending is readjusted, utilizing the assumption that it costs 50 percent more to educate disadvantaged students. In that case, the coefficient of variation is 17.5 percent without federal funds and about 16 percent after federal funds have been added.[31]

The conclusion that federal aid makes a minimal contribution toward ameliorating inequality differs from that of the Parrish, Matsumoto, and Fowler analysis of school districts nationwide (without regard to the state in which they are located). They find that school districts confronting high poverty receive more than four times as much federal funding as affluent districts, two and one-half times as much as moderately affluent districts, and 68 percent more than moderate-poverty districts.[32] However, even in the high-poverty cases, federal aid represents only 10 percent of total spending, so the equalizing effect is weak.

Estimating the Cost of Reducing Type I Inequality

Because federal funds are so small a share of elementary and secondary education budgets, new policies to reduce Type I inequality must augment as well as redirect federal spending. A state's ability to pay for education (as measured, for example, by PIPS) should become an explicit criterion for the distribution of federal education funds to states. How much federal spending should be enhanced depends on judgments, first, about what states should be expected to allot to education at a given PIPS level and, second, about what constitutes an adequate level of spending per child, and particularly per poor or near-poor child.

Because the financing of public education has always been primarily a state and local, not a federal, matter, very little policy attention has been devoted to Type I inequality. Yet this might be the most serious financing problem in American education. As noted, per pupil expenditures in the lowest-spending states, on average, amount to only about half of per pupil expenditures in the highest-spending states. Kentucky, the state at the seventy-fifth percentile of states' school spending distribution (state and local funds), spends only 72 percent of what Wisconsin, the state at the twenty-fifth percentile, does. The highest-spending districts in Kentucky allocate less than the lowest spending districts in Wisconsin.[33] And the poorest children in high-spending states receive an education richer in resources than the wealthiest children in low-spending states. Thus, even if all intrastate school spending were equalized, inequalities—interstate (Type I) inequalities are as significant, if not more so, as intrastate (Type II) inequalities—would remain. A national program to subsidize all states whose mean state and local per pupil spending is below average, bringing these states' spending up to the national mean, would have cost $23 billion in 1996. If subsidies were restricted only to those states that spent below the national average and whose PIPS was also below the national average, the total cost would have been $21 billion. If subsidies were restricted only to those states that spent below the national average and whose PIPS was less than 85 percent of the national average, the total cost would have been $11 billion. In 1996–97, federal elementary and secondary spending was about $20 billion, so a program to correct Type I inequalities could easily double federal education spending.[34]

While there has been considerable policy focus on Type II school spending inequality, Type I inequality has barely changed in over a generation. As mentioned, in 1996–97, the coefficient of variation of cost-adjusted per pupil state and local spending by state was 16 percent. In 1969–70 it had been 19 percent. For per pupil state and local spending at the seventy-fifth percentile, the ratio was 74 percent of spending by the state at the twenty-fifth percentile in 1969–70, barely distinguishable from the 72 percent figure just cited for Kentucky versus Wisconsin in 1996–97.[35] An analysis of 1992 school district expenditures nationwide found that about 65 percent of the variance was interstate, and only 35 percent was attributable to differences within state. These percentages were about the same as twenty years earlier.[36]

TYPE II INEQUALITY:
DIFFERENCES IN SPENDING BY DISTRICTS WITHIN STATES

In the American fiscal system, the federal government has mostly relied for revenue on personal income taxes; state governments have mainly depended on sales taxes, and local governments, primarily on property taxes. These distinctions are a matter of tradition and convenience and are not absolute: the federal government gets revenue from sales (excise) taxes and other sources; some states lean heavily on business license or mineral severance fees, while others increasingly rely on income and property taxes; and certain localities top off property tax revenue with local sales and income taxes.

Throughout American history, public education has been controlled mostly at the local level and as a result has relied primarily on property taxes for revenue. But state governments have increasingly supplemented local financing for schools. In 1930, states provided only 17 percent of school funds, while localities provided 83 percent. The state share increased to about 40 percent in 1950 and then continued to grow, surpassing the local share in 1979.[37] By 1996–97, state and local shares were about equal (48 and 45 percent, respectively), with the federal government making up the rest.[38] The federal government has not traditionally provided general ("block grant") support to schools but has restricted its financing to "categorical" grants—that is, funds provided for schools to carry out specific, federally designed programs, with the most important of these being nutrition and compensatory education for poor children.

Reliance on local property taxes for a substantial part of school funding has generated Type II inequalities for several reasons: Localities differ in property wealth, so the same tax "effort" (tax rate per dollar of assessed value) by citizens might yield vastly different revenue streams in property-rich and property-poor communities. Moreover, citizens in different localities might differ in the importance they place on education, leading to variations in rates of property taxation. Inequalities could result simply from communities with unusually valuable property being able to fund schools at a high level while making very little effort at revenue raising to do so. Inequalities also result from inter-community differences in the ratio of children to adults; a district with a large number of children might generate less per pupil revenue with the same property wealth and tax effort as others.

Many states have, for decades, taken responsibility for "equalizing" property tax revenue by ensuring, with subsidies, that equal "effort" generates a minimally required revenue stream. In general, this approach has rested on the stipulation of a "foundation level" of per pupil funding, guaranteed by the state—if a community taxes its own property at a state-standardized rate, and if this does not generate sufficient funds to reach the "foundation level," the state makes up the difference. The rationale for such adjustment is that the democratic choice of local citizens to provide their children with better or worse schools should be respected, but the result should not be determined by the accidental wealth of the community.

The foundation formula, however, has proved inadequate to equalize resources between districts because the level of guaranteed support has not kept pace with Americans' more demanding definition of a minimally adequate level of resources for education. States with foundation systems have seen their finance systems grow increasingly unequal as the per pupil revenue in high-property-wealth communities rises over time relative to the state's guarantee of the minimum.

This potential for inequality is not inherent in the tradition of having local communities depend on property rather than sales or income taxes. A similar potential for inequality would exist if schools depended primarily on local sales or income taxes. Communities with a higher concentration of retail businesses, or with high average incomes, would still be able to support schools at a high level more readily than would communities without high sales revenues or with a lower-income population.

It is generally the case that children who are poor and members of disadvantaged minority groups suffer from this local autonomy of school finance, but this is not always the case. Poor children may live in communities with high tax bases, either because these have valuable industrial property or because the local jurisdiction is large enough to include both very wealthy and very poor residents. Our largest cities have great property wealth coexisting with schools that enroll relatively poor populations. The extremes in school financing inequality occur, rather, in poor rural or homogeneous satellite urban communities on the one hand and very wealthy suburbs on the other. Recall that, when all school districts nationally are compared, districts with large percentages of poor children spend about as much per pupil as moderately affluent districts (that have few poor children), and they actually spend more per pupil than moderately poor districts.

Litigation to Reduce Interdistrict Spending Disparities

For the past quarter century, efforts to reduce school finance inequality have concentrated on Type II inequalities. This pattern was stimulated by the U.S. Supreme Court's 1954 *Brown* v. *Board of Education* desegregation decision that applied the Fourteenth Amendment's equal protection clause to education. Although the Court did not define education as a constitutionally significant "fundamental right," it did say that "education is perhaps the most important function of state and local governments."[39] This being the case, it was hardly a giant leap for the advocates of school finance reform to assume that the equal protection clause not only required racial minorities to have access to education equivalent to that enjoyed by the majority but that those living in communities with little property wealth should have access to education that was comparable in quality to that enjoyed by those living in communities with great property wealth. The blossoming of litigation as a reform tool inevitably directed reformers' attention to Type II, not Type I, inequalities because the Fourteenth Amendment restricts the extent to which a state can discriminate against its own citizens; it does not require that citizens of different states be treated equally. An almost exclusive focus on litigation (or to some extent, on state legislative action to preempt litigation) in the wake of the *Brown* decision thus excluded from policy concern the most important source of financing inequality. While no constitutional provision precludes congressional action to equalize spending between states, or political action to provoke Congress to take up the issue, those concerned with inadequate school spending for disadvantaged children, committed to a strategy of litigation to redress these grievances, reserved their energies for that area where they stood on the firmest legal ground, inequities among districts within a state.

The movement to make litigation a central plank in school finance reform was initiated with a 1971 California Supreme Court decision (*Serrano* v. *Priest*) finding that education was a "fundamental right" and that the state's property-tax-based education finance framework violated the U.S. Constitution's equal protection clause because it left students in districts of differing property wealth with educational systems having greatly varying funding levels. In California as in other states, disparities could be substantial even between neighboring communities. The *Serrano* court noted that per pupil spending in Beverly Hills was twice that in Baldwin Park, although both were in the same county. But in 1973, the U.S. Supreme Court negated the California court's constitutional interpretation, ruling (in *San Antonio Independent School District* v. *Rodriguez*) that education was *not* a fundamental right and that states were therefore free to balance the values of local control and equality of educational resources.[40] With education declared not to be a fundamental right, property wealth that varied from community to community was not to be regarded as a "suspect classification," and thus inequality in school spending was not unconstitutional. Although the case was decided by only a 5–4 margin, there have been no indications that the Court is prepared to reconsider the *San Antonio* decision.[41]

Following *San Antonio*, advocates of school finance equalization reoriented their tactics to focus on language in state constitutions that might be more sympathetic to equity among school districts. Only a month after the Supreme Court's ruling, the New Jersey Supreme Court found (in *Robinson v. Cahill*) that, while education was not a fundamental U.S. constitutional right, wide disparities in average spending by school districts, owing to differences in community property wealth, violated New Jersey's own constitutional requirement that the state maintain a "thorough and efficient" system of education. The state legislature was ordered to design a new system. Similar litigation in other states soon followed. By 1976, the California Supreme Court reaffirmed its *Serrano* decision, concluding that if the state's property-tax-based education finance system did not violate the U.S. Constitution, it violated the California Constitution's own equal protection clause.

Since *San Antonio*, state court judicial decisions have invalidated the school finance systems of nineteen states while upholding the arrangements in twelve states (or, at least, rejecting challenges to them on procedural grounds). In some of the latter cases, however, methods of financing were upheld only after legislative reform to avoid adverse judicial action.[42] In twelve additional states, cases are still being litigated or are on appeal. In only six states has there been no significant school finance equalization litigation.[43] Table 3.5 (pages 68–70) displays states by litigation status.

The divergent outcomes of these cases are partly attributable to differences in status given to education in state constitutions, but mostly they result from varying state court interpretations of similar language. For example, while the New Jersey Supreme Court ruled that its state constitutional requirement of a "thorough and efficient" school system necessitated equality of resources, the Oregon Supreme Court in 1976 found that its consitutional requirement of a "uniform and general" school system did not.[44] Yet, "uniform" did imply equality according to the Wyoming Supreme Court in 1980.[45]

TABLE 3.5. CHANGES IN STATE SPENDING, GROUPED BY SCHOOL FINANCE LITIGATION STATUS

	(1) YEAR OF DECISION	(2) REAL PER PUPIL SPENDING GROWTH, STATE AND LOCAL FUNDS, 1969–70 TO 1996–97[a] (%)
United States, nationwide		34
United States average[b]		50
1. STATE COURT INVALIDATED SCHOOL FINANCE SYSTEM		
California	1971	−5
New Jersey	1973	71
Connecticut	1977	83
West Virginia	1979	100
Wyoming	1980	31
Arkansas	1983	93
Kentucky	1989	86
Montana	1989	10
Texas	1989	65
Alabama	1993	90
Massachusetts	1993	37
Missouri	1993	45
Tennessee	1993	55
Arizona	1994	13
New Hampshire	1997	36
North Carolina	1997	73
Ohio	1997	68
Vermont	1997	43
Washington	1998	23
Group average[b]		54
Average of states with 1970s decisions		62
Average of states with 1980s decisions		57
Average of states with 1990s decisions		48

	(1)	(2)
		REAL PER PUPIL SPENDING GROWTH, STATE AND LOCAL FUNDS,
	YEAR OF DECISION	1969–70 TO 1996–97[a] (%)

2. STATE COURT REFUSED TO INVALIDATE SCHOOL FINANCE SYSTEM (INCLUDES CASES WHERE COURT LEGISLATIVE REFORM PRECEDED COURT DECISION)

Idaho	1975	38
Georgia	1981	85
Michigan	1984	76
Oklahoma	1987	65
Kansas	1992	55
Nebraska	1993	93
North Dakota	1994	33
Virginia	1994	60
Maine	1995	66
Rhode Island	1995	54
Florida	1996	37
Alaska	1997	61
Group average[b]		60

3. LITIGATION PENDING (INCLUDES CASES WHERE SCHOOL FINANCE SYSTEM WAS NOT INVALIDATED BUT DECISION IS ON APPEAL OR A NEW CASE HAS BEEN FILED)

Colorado	1982	34
Maryland	1983	28
Pennsylvania	1987	55
South Carolina	1988	68
Wisconsin	1989	59
Minnesota	1993	46
New York	1995	21
Illinois	1996	17
Oregon	1997	13
Louisiana	no decision	45
New Mexico	no decision	38
South Dakota	no decision	56
Group average		40

cont. on next page

TABLE 3.5. CHANGES IN STATE SPENDING, GROUPED BY SCHOOL FINANCE LITIGATION STATUS (CONT.)

	(1) YEAR OF DECISION	(2) REAL PER PUPIL SPENDING GROWTH, STATE AND LOCAL FUNDS, 1969–70 TO 1996–97[a] (%)
4. NO LITIGATION, OR DORMANT CASE		
Delaware	—	21
Iowa	—	33
Mississippi	—	64
Nevada	—	15
Utah	—	9
Indiana	—	117
Group average[b]		43
5. UNITARY SYSTEMS		
Hawaii	—	3
Dist. of Col.	—	88
Group average[b]		46

[a] Adjusted for regional cost differences.
[b] Simple average of state growth rates.

Sources:
  Column 1: Paul Minorini, "School Finance Litigation: Box Score (4/15/98)," chart distributed at panel on educational adequacy at the annual meeting of the American Education Research Association, San Diego, April 1998.
  Column 2: Table 3.1; 1969–70 data provided to the author by the National Center for Education Statistics from its Common Core of Data. For inflation and regional cost adjustments, see text.

Increased, and More Equal, Spending within States

Even if Type II inequality has diminished in the wake of litigation and legislative remedies, this does not necessarily imply increased school spending overall. The early suits did not require states to raise their school spending, and parity can be accomplished by capping or reducing expenditures in rich districts while increasing them in poor ones. If taxpayers in property-rich school districts resent reforms that increase the share of their taxes that benefit children in less wealthy districts, these taxpayers could conceivably vote to reduce their own spending, leading to an equalized system but with fewer total resources. In New Jersey and Texas, legislators initially attempted to enact "Robin Hood" laws to take property tax revenues from wealthy school districts and give them to poor districts, but these met with strong political resistance. After such a scheme was enacted by the legislature in Texas, it was reversed in a 1993 statewide referendum by the overwhelming margin of 63 percent to 27 percent. Kansas, on the other hand, disguised a redistribution plan by having state government assume control of the local property tax system, collect all property taxes directly, and make per pupil grants to districts. At the present time, Vermont is involved in a dispute in which, following a court-mandated plan to redistribute property tax revenues, property-rich districts ("gold towns") have been reducing their tax rates so that no excess will be generated and instead have established private foundations through which citizens voluntarily donate substantial funds to their local schools.[46] In general, however, state legislatures have avoided conspicuous redistribution and have reacted to equalization pressures by "leveling up," adding money to the local property tax receipts of poor districts from state revenues while keeping rich districts whole, or by placing some limits on the right of rich districts to increase spending further while poorer districts were catching up. California, where litigation to promote equity first appeared, was, until recently, a conspicuous exception to this trend. *Serrano* was followed there by a taxpayers' revolt, and real school spending actually declined over the next two decades.[47] Recently, however, average school spending in California as well has begun to increase.

Michigan's experience illustrates the complexities of education finance reform. Twice, in 1973 and 1984, the state's supreme court upheld a school finance system that was among the nation's most dependent on property taxes (these provided two-thirds of all school funds). Voters in 1989 rejected a proposal for the state to take over the financing of schools by raising sales taxes.[48] By 1993, property-rich districts were spending nearly $11,000 per pupil, while poor, rural districts spent barely $3,000.[49] Then, a small, rural, low-property-wealth district at the northern tip of the state voted to close its public schools rather than further raise its tax rate, which was already higher than that of better-endowed districts. Embarrassed, Republican governor John Engler, supported by both Democratic and Republican legislative leaders, agreed to replace much of the local property tax system with state revenues, to be raised by a tripling of the cigarette tax and an increase in the state sales tax rate from 4 to 6 percent.[50] The tax hike was submitted to a referendum, with the threat that if the proposal were defeated, the legislature would instead raise the state income tax.[51] The referendum passed with 69 percent of the vote, and Michigan suddenly had one of the most state-dependent school finance systems in the nation, with nearly 80 percent of funds coming directly from Lansing.[52]

Michigan's new system immediately raised per pupil spending in the poorest districts by one-third. To reduce inequality further, it also prohibited the richest districts from raising their local property taxes more than 1.5 percent a year; yet voters in the rich districts also supported the new proposal by substantial margins.[53] Overall, Michigan's average per pupil spending continued to increase (about 3 percent a year, after inflation) in the 1990s.

The range of real average per pupil spending increases seems to have been similar in states whose courts have equalized spending, in those where courts have declined to do so (sometimes because legislatures acted before court decisions), in those where litigation is pending, and in those where no litigation has been filed. Column 2 of Table 3.5 lists states, grouped according to their litigation status, by their real growth in per pupil spending from 1969–70 (prior to the first *Serrano* decision) to 1996–97.[54] From this column, it seems that, while school spending growth varied considerably across states, the range of variation is similar within each litigation category. These calculations are only suggestive because they compare spending growth for the full 1970 to 1997 period for all states, although states varied greatly in the time frame for which a litigation decision might be presumed to be influential. Nonetheless, even when states are grouped more narrowly, similar patterns prevail. States with equalization court decisions in the 1970s had real spending growth of 62 percent from 1969–70 to 1996–97 (although California's atypical history influences this number); states with decisions in the 1980s had real spending growth of 57 percent over the entire period; and states with decisions in the 1990s had real spending growth of 48 percent. On an annual basis, these are small differences over a twenty-seven-year period. Clearly, litigation was not the only force driving growth in school spending during these decades. Overall, states with successful litigation had spending growth of 54 percent, compared to 60 percent in states where courts declined to invalidate funding systems. Again, this is a very small difference—between a 1.6 percent average annual increase in the first case and 1.8 percent in the second.

In a more sophisticated econometric analysis, Sheila Murray, William Evans, and Robert Schwab estimate that if a state court finds a school finance system unconstitutional, subsequent reform causes a 23 percent increase in school spending over what would have occurred absent such a court finding.[55] This may understate the impact of litigation because the analysis cannot account for spending increases enacted by legislatures to preempt a court-ordered solution.

While spending has increased across the board, litigation seems to have been effective in decreasing Type II inequalities within the context of broad, overall spending growth. G. Alan Hickrod calculated that the coefficient of variation of district spending in states with successful equalization litigation declined by 22 percent; in states with moderately successful litigation, by 8 percent; in states with unsuccessful litigation, the coefficient of variation increased by 2 percent; in states with unsuccessful litigation but with further litigation filed, it increased by 23 percent; in states with no court decision yet, it increased by 6 percent; and in states with no litigation filed, it decreased by 6 percent.[56] Murray, Evans, and Schwab found that court decisions themselves were responsible for a reduction in interdistrict inequality of from 19 to 34 percent. This happened because court-ordered reforms increased education outlays in the lower-spending and median districts while leaving spending in the higher-spending districts unchanged.[57]

There is, however, less evidence that the successes in remedying Type II inequality have consistently benefited the disadvantaged students who most need additional help. This is because an assumption that low-income families are clustered in low-spending districts may not be entirely accurate. Indeed, lack of evidence for a strong inverse correlation between student poverty and district property wealth was an important reason given by the Supreme Court in *San Antonio* for declining to get involved in disputes about equity in interdistrict finances. While a strong negative relationship between poverty and property may have been commonplace when most poverty was rural, the poorest children now are concentrated in urban areas, some of which (New York City, Los Angeles, Chicago) are quite prosperous and have substantial commercial and residential property. And, as described in the discussion of Type I inequalities, the District of Columbia has some of the nation's poorest children, along with some of its most affluent taxpayers.

While districts with concentrations of poor children may not raise as much money per pupil as low-density, very wealthy, suburban communities, they may raise more than the typical district that is more uniformly middle class.[58]

The Shift from "Equity" to "Adequacy" in Litigation

Recently, therefore, the focus of state equity litigation has changed. The seeds of change were planted in the very first judicial decision, *Robinson v. Cahill* in New Jersey, where the court used not only spending data but an outcome standard by which to measure whether the state's school system was "thorough and efficient": the schools, the *Robinson* court decreed, must provide adequate education so that all students have equal opportunities to play roles as citizens and to compete in the labor market. Other courts increasingly have taken a similar approach. What matters is not merely whether funding is equalized between districts but rather whether funding is sufficient to provide the resources needed to deliver a quality education as implied by state constitutions. Courts in Kentucky, Massachusetts, Ohio, West Virginia, Wyoming, and elsewhere now insist that an equal amount of too little is not enough. Their decisions demand, instead, that the state guarantee to each district an "adequate" level of resources. Further, the court decisions recognize that what is adequate for ordinary children may not be so for disadvantaged children. In consequence, several courts have now explicitly interpreted their state constitutions as requiring not equality, but resources matched to the unequal needs of students in the state.

While applying unequal resources to unequal needs may be good social and educational policy, the resolution of such questions in state courts has required a degree of judicial activism for which courts are poorly suited. It is one thing to litigate whether school districts have equal funding. Judges can easily compare the revenues produced by comparable tax "effort" and can mandate states to compensate for resulting inequalities. But how are judges to decide how much it costs to deliver an "adequate" education and how costs vary according to student needs? These are questions to which educators and social scientists have only the most tentative answers. Requiring judges to go beyond what even experts can determine has spawned a huge industry of competing expert witnesses, traveling from state to state, from one "adequacy" hearing to another. Litigants (both plaintiffs and defendants, usually state attorneys general) have thus become important funders of education policy research.

Courts cannot figure out what an adequate level of resources might be without first determining what results these resources should aim to produce.[59] Consider one of the early attempts by a state court to define adequate outcomes, that of the West Virginia Supreme Court in 1979, requiring the legislature to fund schools to develop "in every child" these capacities:

- literacy;

- ability to add, subtract, multiply, and divide;

- knowledge of government to the extent that the child will be equipped as a citizen to make informed choices among persons and issues that affect governance;

- self-knowledge and knowledge of his or her total environment to allow the child to intelligently choose life work—to know his or her options;

- work training and advanced academic training as the child may intelligently choose;

- recreational pursuits;

- interests in all creative arts, such as music, theater, literature, and the visual arts; and

- social ethics, both behavioral and abstract, to facilitate compatibility with others in this society.

Other courts have required funding adequate to develop similar competencies. Few of these developments can be measured by standardized reading and math tests that states increasingly utilize for purposes of accountability. Whether, for example, the same resources that produce mathematical competency also train for adequate performance in, or appreciation of, the fine and performing arts is a question that as yet has been barely addressed by education finance theory. Nor have theorists assessed whether disadvantaged children need the same resources in all of these domains, or whether the degree of necessary augmentation differs from one domain to another.

How, then, can a state, whether because of court mandate or political desire, determine how much money each district requires to provide not only an equal education but an adequate one? In attempting to comply with court decisions, the Ohio state board of education set an impossibly high bar for adequacy: it assumed that a "thorough and efficient" (the state's constitutional language) education meant that schools should not merely narrow the gap between the achievement of disadvantaged and other children. Rather, the board implied, schools should produce the same outcomes for all children, regardless of the differences in social and economic background that children bring to schooling: a practical test, the board stated in 1990, would be to ask parents whether they would "be willing to have [their] children educated in any of the 612 school districts in Ohio." If not, then "the system would appear to be suspect."[60]

The state then hired experts John Augenblick and John Myers to identify school districts that generated adequate outcomes and then calculate how much these districts spent.[61] Ohio assumed that if these districts could generate adequate student achievement with the funds available to them, then any district could generate similar results with identical funding. However, the Augenblick approach has been rejected by the Ohio Supreme Court on appeal, and the state is now struggling with new methods to satisfy the judiciary's demand for "adequacy."

Augenblick and Myers's pioneering Ohio work still left important questions unanswered:

- It utilized academic test scores to identify districts with adequate outcomes, yet such test scores may not suffice to form judgments of what constitutes an adequate education. But no other objective measures of adequacy currently exist.

- Districts with large numbers of at-risk students fail to generate outcomes given the same funding levels—similar to districts with mainly middle-class students. But should adequacy be defined differently for poorer districts, or should Ohio assume that they can achieve satisfactory performance if only given more money? This question remains unanswered.

◆   The obligation to generate adequate achievement requires only
    that districts have the funds necessary to generate it. But some
    districts are more efficient than others. By assuming that what ade-
    quately performing districts spend is the same as what they must
    necessarily spend, this method incorporates inefficient spending
    patterns into the definition of adequacy.

Illinois governor James Edgar's Commission on Education Funding
used a similar "empirical" method in 1996 to estimate the cost of an
adequate education and retained Fordham University professor Bruce
Cooper, acting on behalf of the Coopers & Lybrand accounting firm, to
calculate it. He tried to solve some of the problems raised in Ohio.
Cooper grouped schools by prevalence of poverty and in each group
identified schools where scores on the Illinois Goals Assessment
Program were in the top quartile of that group. This implicitly adopts a
different definition of adequacy for various socioeconomic groups. Of
these high-performance schools, those for which per pupil expenditures were below average were presumed to be efficient and, therefore,
to have adequate funding. The commission's report, however, was never
adopted by the state legislature.[62]

Augenblick, Myers, and Amy Anderson report that a similar
empirical approach has now been adopted by Mississippi, which has
identified thirty successful schools based on test scores and concluded
that the costs of operating these schools is "reasonable."[63] What is spent
on education in these thirty schools is being defined as the cost of adequacy, with adjustments made for districts with varying costs of living,
student poverty rates, and so forth. As of this writing, however, the
Mississippi method has not been described in the published education
finance literature.

Two states, Wyoming and Maine, have taken a different approach,
modeling prototypically adequate schools and then pricing the resources
that go into realizing these prototypes. In 1995 the Wyoming Supreme
Court ordered the legislature to design a new school finance system
that delivered the "best" education to each student in the state, a system in which all per pupil spending differences had to be justified in
terms either of differences in districts' special needs (for example, percentages of at-risk students) or in cost (for example, higher living costs
might make it more expensive for some districts to attract qualified
teachers). A team led by James Guthrie surveyed national research

along with the informed opinions of nationally and state-recognized expert educators to estimate the resources required to deliver an adequate education.[64]

Although school prototypes designed by the Guthrie team were adopted by the legislature, another round of appeals is now under way. One group of plaintiffs claims that the level of teacher salaries funded by the legislature is inadequate in today's market to attract college graduates of sufficiently high quality to deliver an adequate education. Another group of plaintiffs allege that the additional resources in the legislature's model are insufficient for areas of the state where the cost of living is higher than elsewhere.

In Maine, prototypes were commissioned by the legislature (but have not yet been fully implemented or adopted) in 1995, the year that the Maine Supreme Court dismissed a challenge to the state's school finance system. David Silvernail and others relied on examination of resource patterns in Maine schools that performed particularly well on state tests, as well as on national research literature and the opinions of experts about necessary levels of resources, to guide the construction of prototypes.[65]

It is noteworthy that this method, delving into national research and expert opinion to model prototypical resources, has been adopted by two states where the number of disadvantaged children is relatively small. Nowhere have prototypical models been litigated with the primary purpose of prescribing how much additional money districts must expend to provide adequate educations to disadvantaged children.

The prototypical-model method also has disadvantages, namely, that professional opinion seems more subjective than empirical analysis. One expert may decide that well-funded athletic programs are necessary to build character, while another concludes that athletics are an option, not part of the state's obligation to fund a minimally adequate education. There are no test scores on character whereby such disputes can be resolved. Policymakers, educators, and voters must enter these debates, comparing their own best judgments to those of the "experts." The success of a model depends on the integrity and credibility of those who design it, and on the thoroughness with which they distill and synthesize available research about effective means of delivering adequate achievement.

It is certain, however, that courts will continue to adjudicate the "adequate" resource level for different categories of students, and judges will continue to make decisions about educational theory that go far beyond what is known by educators and researchers themselves. These decisions may, however, reflect a consensus of educators' opinions in one regard: bringing underprivileged children up to the level of the mainstream is likely to require spending more per pupil on them.

The latest New Jersey decision again breaks new ground. In 1990, the New Jersey Supreme Court issued a decision that almost fully dispatched the notion that nominal "equalization" could be a constitutional goal. *Abbott v. Burke* decreed that not only must poor urban school districts receive funds comparable to those of wealthy suburban districts; they must be granted additional funds because of their special needs. Initially, the court ordered that "special-needs" districts be awarded an increment of 5 percent of the foundation guarantee.[66] But the court soon was persuaded that this was insufficient to guarantee adequacy. The final court order in *Abbott* requires the state to finance full-day preschool for three- and four-year-olds in the special-needs districts as well as make substantial expenditures for repair and renovation of their school buildings.[67]

Type III Inequality:
Differences in Spending in Schools within Districts

Even if inequality of Types I and II were corrected—states and districts had at their respective levels equalized financial support, adjusted for differences in student need—resources might still be distributed unequally if schools within districts were unequally endowed or if some schools were failing to meet the particular needs of their students. Inequality between schools locally (Type III) could exist because, for example, population growth within a district is unequal, leaving children in rapidly growing poor communities in more overcrowded schools and larger classes. If the disadvantaged population is isolated—as in many cities—in inner-core areas that have been abandoned by the middle class, facilities attended by poor children may not only be more crowded but deteriorating and in need of replacement.

The most serious cause of Type III inequality, however, is the maldistribution of teachers within urban districts. In most, union contracts permit senior teachers to transfer to fill openings in the schools they choose, before new teachers are hired. The result is that, in diverse metropolitan districts, predominantly suburban-style, middle-class, and white schools generally have a more experienced teaching force than do inner-city, poor, and minority schools. The problem is aggravated by the time consumed by seniority moves: each opening that occurs in a middle-class school and is filled by a transferring senior teacher then triggers an opening in another city school that the teacher leaves. By the time seniority moves are complete, it may be very close to the beginning of the school year, forcing inner-city schools suddenly to scramble to fill unexpected vacancies with unqualified personnel. More difficult (because their students come to school less prepared to learn) inner-city schools already have fewer experienced teachers; seniority rules exacerbate the situation.

Senior teachers are not always better than junior ones, nor do teachers gain in quality in direct proportion to their experience. It is typically the case that teachers gain in effectiveness during their first seven to ten years on the job, at which point their effectiveness levels off but does not decline.[68] In other words, even if they were paid the same, an inexperienced teacher is not comparable in human resource value to an experienced one. The fact that teacher salary schedules reward teachers for years of experience confirms this inequality but does not cause it. The problem cannot be solved by leveling teacher pay, increasing that of junior teachers and reducing that of senior ones. Students in schools with a high proportion of teachers with less than seven years' experience are likely to receive educations inferior to those of students in schools with a low proportion of such teachers.

Simply demanding that teacher unions in urban districts abandon their seniority rights will not itself solve this problem. It is unreasonable to insist that teachers who have accumulated experience should have no opportunity to move to teaching positions where discipline is easier, children come to school more ready to learn, and schools (and teachers) get public credit for their students' easier-to-achieve successes. Not all experienced teachers will want to make such moves, but a district cannot prevent those who wish to transfer from doing so. If it attempts to eliminate seniority considerations from teacher assignments, it will ensure that more of its experienced teachers simply abandon the profession, or apply for openings in nearby suburban districts.

Even with some restriction on seniority transfer rights, however, the solution to this problem is ultimately economic: districts must pay teachers in hard-to-staff schools enough of an increment to compensate for the more difficult working conditions. Teacher unions, as well as tax-conscious school boards, will resist this solution, primarily because unions are naturally dominated by more experienced teachers who work in less challenging locations and will not support bargaining platforms that distribute new monies disproportionately to recently hired, inner-city staff. Yet the problem is negotiable: in some big cities, teacher unions have agreed to inner-city pay increments, though the amounts have been token, insufficient to bring parity to teacher experience levels in schools attended by poor and middle-class children. Unless a lot of new money becomes available to urban districts, union resistance to this important reform is moot.

New York City, however, recently offered 15 percent bonuses to experienced teachers who volunteer for its forty lowest-scoring schools.[69] This is probably close to $10,000 per year per teacher in additional compensation. If this incentive turns out to be sufficient to attract more seasoned teachers back to schools with large numbers of disadvantaged children, massive amounts of money will be required to replicate it on a nationwide scale. In 1996, there were about 8.6 million poor children in America's schools. If we assume that half of them were in hard-to-staff schools and that attracting experienced teachers to these schools will cost, on average, about $7,000 each in additional compensation (somewhat lower than what New York put forward because costs are higher there than elsewhere), then this reform alone would require nearly $2 billion in additional funds for elementary and secondary education across the country.

Hobson v. *Hansen:* Mandating Intradistrict Equality

There has been only one judicial decision regarding Type III inequality, in a federal desegregation case decided in 1968.[70] The plaintiff in *Hobson v. Hansen* charged the District of Columbia school system with a variety of practices that perpetuated a pre-Brown-era segregated system, not all of which are relevant for our purposes.[71] (Some important issues litigated in the case involve Type IV and Type V inequalities, school and classroom tracking.) But the court also found Type III inequalities characteristic of segregated school districts in Washington, D.C. It discovered that predominantly black schools were more overcrowded, had fewer experienced teachers, fewer instructors with advanced degrees, and more temporary positions. An overcrowded school realizes apparent administrative economies of scale, spending less per pupil, for example, on a principal's salary than an ordinary school of similar size. Salary costs for less experienced, less credentialed or less degreed teachers are lower. In large schools, teacher assignment can be more efficient as well, leading further to lower per pupil costs—for instance, a music teacher can instruct more pupils in a single school than when traveling between smaller schools.

The court's initial order required Washington, D.C., schools to adopt a "color-conscious" teacher assignment policy to facilitate faculty integration: voluntary transfers of highly paid white teachers from predominantly white to predominantly black schools were encouraged, and new teachers were subsequently assigned to schools in ways to achieve a target of having no school deviate by more than 10 percent from the racial composition of teachers citywide. However, there were too few volunteers and too few new teachers to make much of a difference. Three years after the court's decision, per pupil teacher expenditures were still 40 percent higher in some predominantly white schools than in some predominantly black ones, and total per pupil expenditures at some schools were nearly three times as great as at other schools. Plaintiffs returned to court, seeking an order requiring per pupil expenditures at any school to vary by not more than 5 percent from the districtwide average. The court instead adopted an order with the plus-or-minus 5 percent requirement applying only to teachers' salaries, not all expenditures. The court's reasoning was that other expenditure variations (for example, stemming from more dilapidated buildings in poorer areas) were more beyond district officials' control than teacher assignment policies.

This remedy, too, was ineffective. The District of Columbia complied primarily by redistributing "resource" teachers (music, art, enrichment) between schools, not by reshuffling teacher experience in regular classrooms. To the limited extent that regular classroom teachers' assignments changed, it is not clear that this truly represented a real resource equalization because the relationship between teacher experience and quality is hardly perfect. Since most researchers believe that the learning curve flattens out after about seven to ten years' experience, teachers with twenty years' experience may not generally be better at their job than those with ten, though the former may receive 25 percent greater compensation. In the District of Columbia case, a court

would have to believe that the twenty-year teacher provides 25 percent more effective instruction than the ten-year teacher if distributing
teachers among schools so as to equalize salaries were to be deemed a
valid strategy. Education research has yet to identify the precise relationship between teacher experience and quality. Thus, in districts
resembling those of many big cities, where more experienced teachers
cluster in schools serving the relatively well-off, it is not clear how to
fashion a legal remedy for an acknowledged injustice.

The Los Angeles Consent Decree: Equalizing School Resources within a District

Perhaps because of this difficulty, there have been no further court decisions regarding Type III inequality. But in 1986 a Los Angeles lawsuit
made allegations similar to those underlying the *Hobson* case, and in
1992 the Los Angeles Unified School District negotiated a settlement.
The consent decree in *Rodriguez* v. *LAUSD* required the district, within five years, to bring the per pupil spending of 90 percent of its elementary schools to within $100 of the districtwide average.[72]

While the consent decree allowed for more nuance than a judicial
order, still the mechanical formulas of the decree were imperfect
approximations of greater equality. The decree relied on the fact that
senior, higher-paid teachers tended to transfer to more middle-class and
white schools, while inexperienced teachers were typically hired to fill
vacancies in inner-city, poor, and heavily minority schools. Prior to the
decree, per pupil spending varied by as much as $400 per pupil between
schools, largely because of the differences in teacher experience and
salaries but also because of economies of scale reflected in the lower
administrative costs associated with bigger, overcrowded, inner-city
schools—the school district's highest-spending elementary school
enrolled 185 students, while the lowest-spending enrolled 1,467.

But while these patterns were unmistakable, they were not universal. Some inner-city schools had a full complement of senior teachers, and some suburban schools had mostly junior teachers. Under the
consent decree, the former were also required to reduce spending,
whereas the latter could increase it.

The Los Angeles teachers' union was a party to the settlement,
and it insisted on a provision prohibiting mandatory transfers of

teachers to fulfill the consent decree's goals. While high-spending schools complied by hiring only junior teachers when they had vacancies, other techniques were employed as well. These were possible because the Los Angeles consent decree attempted to equalize a variety of school resources and gave schools some discretion about how to spend their budgets. Thus, it went farther than *Hobson*, in which only teacher salary costs had been put on an even footing. In Los Angeles, schools with concentrations of inexperienced teachers were given additional funds to spend on other necessities. Compliance was achieved by such means as hiring mentor teachers, counselors, or nurses; reducing class sizes in schools with low payrolls; or requiring principals of high-spending small schools to supervise more than a single facility. The five-year period for phasing in compliance made the adjustments more palatable than they otherwise might have been.

Resources Required by Schools Serving Disadvantaged Children

It is impossible to say whether, in general, Type III inequalities have more significance in major urban areas than Type I or II inequalities because of the difficulty of establishing a precise method of assessing the relationship of teacher quality to experience. Suffice it to say that, while a broad, Type II judicial remedy, directing more resources to districts with large proportions of disadvantaged children, might be effective, a more targeted policy would steer funds not only to those districts but to particular schools within them.

There is a growing consensus of educational researchers and policymakers that such a targeted resource policy should include:

♦ differentiated pay scales, so that schools with large numbers of disadvantaged children can utilize pay increments to attract highly skilled teachers to schools where their talents and experience are most needed;[73]

♦ smaller class sizes for disadvantaged children;[74]

♦ prekindergarten programs that begin at age four or earlier for disadvantaged children;

- ◆ summer school: credible research has concluded that the biggest gaps between the academic skills of disadvantaged children and others develop in the summer, when advantaged children repair to intellectually stimulating environments while disadvantaged children lose some of the skills gained in the previous year;[75]

- ◆ mentor teachers to assist inexperienced teachers in inner-city schools;[76] and

- ◆ downsizing of large, urban schools to prevent student anonymity and create communities for learning.[77]

The Importance of Concentrated Disadvantage

Formulas that allocate additional resources to schools with disadvantaged children in direct proportion to the numbers of such children are inadequate. It is the concentration of disadvantage itself that requires the strongest remediation. An expectation of the social and academic benefits a disadvantaged child would derive from being schooled alongside advantaged peers was a fundamental sociological support of the *Brown v. Board of Education* decision to desegregate schools. This insight was confirmed in James S. Coleman's pathbreaking 1966 report, *Equality of Educational Opportunity*: the achievement and socioeconomic status of a disadvantaged student's peers is a better predictor of that student's achievement than his or her own socioeconomic status.[78] Because we have failed, since *Brown*, to integrate schools either racially or by social class, concentrated disadvantage reinforces itself in urban schools. Schools with intensive poverty require not simply additional resources but disproportionately more than others.

INEQUALITIES IN SOCIAL CAPITAL

Secretary of Education Richard Riley noted recently that today everybody demands more from schools: "You know, people didn't expect much from Title I fifteen years ago. Now they expect [disadvantaged students] to do the same thing as every other kid. The bar has been lifted."[79] But this expectation may be inappropriate.

Even if all (Types I through V) school resource inequalities could be eliminated, it is unlikely that achievement differences between disadvantaged and more privileged children would vanish. For decades, education researchers have been able to associate only about 25 percent of the variation in student achievement with the influences of schools. The other 75 percent results from differences in the educational habits and attitudes (social capital) that children get from their families, their communities, and their peers.

Of course, the statistical analyses upon which these conclusions rest are limited by the real-world nature of the data they describe. It is possible that school influences are relatively weak only within the parameters of resource allocation currently found in American schools. Perhaps if disadvantaged children had vastly improved access to quality education, good schools could remedy more than 25 percent of the gap. But while this is conceivable, there is yet no solid evidence to support such an inference. Indeed, those schools that seem to produce relatively better results for disadvantaged children are characterized not merely by better resources but also by organizational cultures that meld existing assets and personnel into focused teams emphasizing high expectations with incentives and accountability for results. But there is no certainty that even in such high-performing schools the achievement gap can be entirely eliminated.

Improving Achievement through Expenditures to Improve Social Capital

It may be, however, that the greatest opportunities for lifting the academic achievement of disadvantaged children lie not in school spending but in spending to improve these children's social capital. What is needed is a systemic approach in which, with the goal of academic achievement in mind, the opportunity costs of dollars spent in schools and other institutions are compared.

For example, children with abnormally low weights for their age, a result of nutritional deficiencies, perform more poorly on academic tests than well-nourished children. In experimental studies, children given vitamin and mineral supplements "showed test score gains that significantly exceeded the controls."[80] These supplements are relatively inexpensive. Dollars spent to combat nutritional deficiencies in poor communities might, in addition to their direct benefits, be more effective levers for raising achievement than class size reduction or similar school interventions.

One study found that children from families who received housing subsidies (as through the federal Section 8 housing program)[81] were less likely to have abnormally low weights for their ages than were children from families who were on waiting lists for such subsidies. Families with housing assistance spend more of their incomes on food than eligible families without them, thereby averting low-weight crises and the consequent depressing effects on academic achievement.[82]

Keeping Students from Transferring Repeatedly between Schools through Investments in Housing

Housing subsidies may also improve outcomes by making accessible lower-cost apartments with more adequate space for children to study and do homework. Or subsidies may help achievement by stabilizing families' living arrangements, permitting their children to remain in the same schools. Repeated student transfers may be an important cause of low achievement in poor communities: "Moving generally keeps children of lower SES [socioeconomic status] from attaining their normally expected achievement and grade level."[83] About one-sixth of all third-graders nationwide have attended three or more schools since first grade. These frequent movers are disproportionately low income and minority: 30 percent of children from families with incomes below $10,000 have attended at least three different schools by the third grade, while only 10 percent of children from families with incomes above $25,000 have done so.[84] An analysis of Chicago mobility found that in a *typical* elementary school, half the students are not enrolled in the same school after three years; over a two-year period, 5 percent of Chicago students attended four or more different elementary schools; three-fourths of these students on the move were African American.[85] In the Los Angeles Unified School District, the average annual elementary school transiency rate (students who enter or leave school during a single year) was 43 percent in 1989–90, and at one site it was 96 percent.[86] This mobility may contribute more to poor academic performance than the teacher seniority differences dealt with in the *Rodriguez* v. *LAUSD* consent decree.

Too-mobile students suffer from discontinuity of instruction, lose familiar peer relationships that provide security for learning, and cannot readily take advantage of remedial programs for which diagnoses emerge only over time or programs for which eligibility must be established, such as Title I reading services.[87] Not only are test scores depressed and dropout rates elevated for these students themselves, but achievement of all students in schools characterized by this sort of instability suffers because teachers must devote instructional time to reviews for newcomers and to the organizational tasks of incorporating them into classrooms. Schools with high rates of students moving around frequently reconstitute classroom lists to avoid placing all newcomers in a single class. In one typical inner-city school, a research team observed class rearrangements affecting stable as well as mobile students four times in a single academic year.[88] Even without such reorganization, teaching strategies falter in schools confronted with high student mobility: instructors are more likely to teach discrete units rather than integrating instruction across subjects and are more likely to spend time reviewing old material than introducing new concepts.[89] The American public's stress on greater accountability is also frustrated in schools facing these conditions: students who remain in one place may make achievement gains that are disguised by including in school averages the test scores of recent arrivals for whose lack of progress the new school is not fully responsible.

Student mobility can have several causes, including dislocations resulting from parental job loss or transfers, school choice programs, or family breakup or reorganization. But in poor communities, an important cause is inadequate housing. A serious housing shortage challenges low-income urban residents, and many families with children intermittently double up with friends or relatives, or move when they cannot keep up with rent payments. In extreme cases, families move in and out of shelters or other nonstandard housing.

Of 1.7 million renter families with children in 1995 who were "working poor" (that is, whose income from work equaled at least half-time, year-round work at the minimum wage), 80 percent spent more than 30 percent of their incomes for rent and utilities, and 42 percent spent more than 50 percent of their incomes for rent and utilities. One-third of these families with children either lived in overcrowded housing or were doubled up with other families.[90]

A long history of research showing the deleterious effects of excessive student mobility on achievement drives policymakers to consider how schools can accommodate special needs—by improving the speed with which student records follow school transfers, by providing busing so students can avoid changing schools when families move, or by offering remedial tutoring for students who are subject to repeated moves.[91] Some educators believe that residential stability can be encouraged by urging parents to consider the impact on their children's lives before deciding to move, and some school policymakers have attempted such an approach.[92] Educational research, however, rarely considers whether steering resources directly toward keeping families settled, by means, for example, of housing subsidies, might be a cost-effective approach to improving test scores, quite aside from producing other beneficial results. If dollars are available either to reduce school finance inequalities or to improve students' social capital by guaranteeing more stable housing to their families, which expenditure would generate the greater academic achievement gains?

Publicly funded housing subsidies are necessary to reduce student mobility. New York City families in homeless shelters who received housing subsidies within the next five years were twenty-one times more likely to be stable (in the same apartment for at least twelve months) than families who did not receive subsidies.[93] Nationwide, only one-quarter of working poor families with children received public housing assistance in 1995: 569,000 working poor families received no housing assistance and paid more than 50 percent of their incomes for rent and utilities; another 463,000 paid between 30 and 50 percent of their incomes.[94] The Department of Housing and Urban Development estimated in 1997 that the average cost of housing subsidies is $5,499 per year per unit.[95] Thus, an immediate expansion of the Section 8 program to cover all working families with children who at present spend more than 50 percent of their incomes for rent would cost only $3.1 billion annually. Covering all working families with children spending more than 30 percent of their incomes for rent would cost $5.7 billion annually.

An annual housing expenditure of $5.7 billion is equivalent to a per pupil spending increase of about $121, spread across all elementary and secondary pupils. No research has yet been undertaken to determine relative gains in student achievement from the expenditure of $5.7 billion on Section 8 housing vouchers—as opposed to school interventions like class size reduction or recruitment of more qualified teachers—but the possibilities are sufficiently intriguing that such research should be a high priority.

CONCLUSION

Although the academic achievement differential between disadvantaged children and others has narrowed, it stubbornly persists. Part of the remaining gap could be attributable to lesser resources received by disadvantaged children, and part could be attributable to less efficient use of resources directed at disadvantaged children. Children may be disadvantaged when they receive fewer material, social, and cultural resources in their families, their communities, their schools, or in all of these. Improving the level and quality of resources in schools serving such children should be one important tool for improving their achievement.

Schools can be inadequate for disadvantaged children because the states in which they reside provide fewer resources generally to schools than do other states. This interstate inequality (termed here Type I inequality) is the source of the greatest disparities in school funding, although it receives relatively little attention from policymakers.

Disadvantaged children can also be shortchanged because they live in districts that provide fewer resources to schools than do others in their state (Type II inequality). Type II, interdistrict inequality attracts the greatest public attention. Disadvantaged children also can lose out because they attend schools that are less adequately endowed than other schools in their district (Type III inequality), because they are tracked into classrooms that are allocated fewer resources than others in their schools (Type IV inequality), or because their classrooms are organized to deliver instruction and support unequally (Type V inequality). This chapter has explored Types I, II, and III inequality, as well as the relative importance of resources given directly to schools as opposed to measures taken outside the educational arena to enhance students' social capital.

For the past thirty years, public policy has addressed issues of equity for disadvantaged children primarily by leveling expenditures by districts within a state. Districts serving large proportions of poor children may have fewer resources than others, yet these same districts require more because of the greater educational challenges they face. Advocates for disadvantaged children have pursued strategies to equalize school spending between districts within states, relying on both legislation and litigation. These strategies have been reasonably successful in many states; intrastate spending inequality has been reduced more in states with successful litigation, although per pupil spending (benefiting the disadvantaged as well as children generally) has grown in all states, regardless of whether litigation was successfully pursued. As these cases have evolved, attention has shifted from attempts to equalize resources, regardless of their adequacy, to questions of how to define a minimally adequate level of spending for disadvantaged students, with their greater than typical needs.

Little policy effort has been directed toward the remediation of Type III (intradistrict) inequalities. To do so would require, primarily, attracting higher-quality teachers to poorer areas and reducing class sizes, particularly for the youngest children, to a greater extent than is done in more affluent parts of the district. This will prove politically difficult, although a recent consent decree in Los Angeles, requiring the district to increase per pupil spending in some schools, may be a preview of future trends. Attracting more qualified teachers to inner-city communities could cost about $2 billion annually on a nationwide basis.

More important, public policy has failed to focus on Type I (interstate) inequalities, which are generally greater in magnitude than the widely acknowledged Type II (intrastate) disparities. Even if all resources were distributed equally to districts within states, most of the inequity overall would remain. This is because, at present, the most disadvantaged students in states with the highest average spending receive substantially more public funding than the most advantaged students in states with the lowest average spending.

States that spend too little cannot necessarily correct this problem easily because many of them also have a low capacity to raise revenue for education. (A state's capacity to fund education is defined here as its total personal income per enrolled student.) A serious effort to provide equal, or at least adequate, school resources to the nation's disadvantaged children must help the low-spending states, and in particular those states that have higher than typical rates of poverty and less capacity to boost spending for education.

Thus, the most important initiatives to improve school conditions for disadvantaged students require federal funds. Existing programs, particularly Title I, have done little to equalize educational opportunity because federal funds represent only a small (about 7 percent) share of total school expenditure and because the distribution formula for Title I funds includes an adjustment for current state spending levels. States that spend less per disadvantaged pupil because of lower fiscal capacity also receive fewer Title I funds per disadvantaged pupil owing to their low spending levels. A national program to subsidize all states whose state and local per pupil spending is currently below the national average, and whose fiscal capacity is also below average, bringing these states up to par, would have cost about $21 billion in 1996.

While public attention is drawn to whether disadvantaged children have adequate school funding, enhancing their school resources may not necessarily be the only or even the most efficient strategy for improving their academic performance and narrowing the achievement gap. Devoting efforts to enhancing the social capital of disadvantaged families and communities may have effects on academic achievement that compare favorably with supplementing school finances. For example, significant achievement gains for inner-city children might be brought about by reducing the frequency with which they change schools, a task that requires improving the housing stock available to their families. Expansion of the Section 8 housing voucher program to cover all working families with children that presently allocate more than 30 percent of their incomes to rent would require $5.7 billion annually. The cost-effectiveness of such expenditures as a way of narrowing the educational achievement gap, relative to outlays to reduce school resource inequalities, has not been examined by policymakers. It should be a priority.

4.

HIGH STANDARDS: A STRATEGY FOR EQUALIZING OPPORTUNITIES TO LEARN?

ADAM GAMORAN

Will high standards for student achievement help solve the problems of unequal learning opportunities that afflict American schools? If standard-setting raises the bar for the quality of students' experiences in schools, and not just their performances on tests, then it holds some promise for reducing inequality as well as enhancing levels of learning. If standards mean nothing more than standardized tests on a wider scale, they may serve to highlight inequalities that already exist, but they will do little to ameliorate the problem.

Proposals for raising standards have come from many actors and take many forms. In the 1999 State of the Union Address, President Clinton announced that "with [federal] support, nearly every state has set higher academic standards for public schools, and a voluntary national test is being developed to measure the progress of our students." High state standards generally refer to attaining a certain level on a statewide examination. Most of these tests are designed to examine students on a specified curriculum. High standards are also a prominent feature of local reforms in many districts and schools.

The challenge confronting standards initiatives is not just that achievement is too low and too unequal, but that learning opportunities that produce achievement are unequal. Students who attend different schools, as well as students enrolled in different tracks and classrooms within schools, encounter varied curricular content, activities, and expectations, leading to differences in how much they learn. Often the differences in classroom experiences are tied to social background; that is, unequal opportunities for learning lead to wider gaps in achievement among students from different backgrounds. A strategy designed to reduce inequality as well as to raise standards for achievement must respond to the inequalities in students' experiences in schools. This chapter will (1) show how extensive differences in opportunities for learning are and document their impact on unequal achievement, (2) discuss the prospects for high standards as an approach to reducing inequality, and (3) offer recommendations for using standards effectively.

UNEQUAL OPPORTUNITIES FOR LEARNING

Among the many differences that pervade our decentralized and diverse system of American education, perhaps the most profound are the differences in academic content and classroom experiences that confront students in the same grade level but different schools, classes, and instructional groups. These differences exist at both the elementary and the secondary levels, and they occur both from school to school and within a single school.

Unequal Opportunities in Elementary Schools

Teachers in elementary schools with large numbers of low-income students face extraordinary challenges. Inadequate health and nutrition, high rates of student mobility, language barriers, and a lack of resources and stability in the home environment all pose special difficulties that teachers must overcome.[1] On one level, teachers may be considered remarkably successful in the face of these challenges. Some researchers have found that during the school year, elementary students from disadvantaged backgrounds learn about as much, on average, as their more advantaged peers. Similarly, African-American elementary school students tend to keep pace with whites during the school year. According to this research, it is during the summer, when school is not in session, that the gap between advantaged and disadvantaged students widens, year after year.[2]

On another level, elementary schools have not been successful enough. Even though elementary schools do not create these achievement gaps, they do not prevent them from occurring nor do they stop them from widening during the summer, and the inequalities are carried through as students move on toward middle and high school. Rather than finding ways to close the gap during the school year, educators in elementary schools often respond to these inequalities by altering their expectations for student achievement.

INEQUALITIES BETWEEN ELEMENTARY SCHOOLS. Michael Knapp provides a vignette from a fifth-grade classroom that illustrates how teachers commonly respond to low-income, low-achieving youth:

> It is time for mathematics. Mr. Gates asks the children to switch from the dictionary skills worksheet they have been working on to the mathematics homework. The students, a mixed group of Anglo and Hispanic children from a nearby housing project, fumble for their homework sheets. Some never find them; a few—primarily a handful of boys (mostly Hispanic) sitting in seats around the edge of the room—pay little attention to what is going on, but the teacher appears not to notice (for the moment, the nonparticipants are quiet). The next 15 minutes are devoted to a review of homework, which involved long division. Mr. Gates proceeds in rapid-fire fashion, asking for the correct answer and providing it if some member of the class fails to give it. . . . The class shifts to a 15-minute presentation by Mr. Gates on the finer points of long division. . . . Many students fidget during the explanation; the nonparticipating students are beginning to be louder and more noticeable. ("This class just doesn't seem to get it," he explains at the end of the class; his game plan appears to be to repeat the explanation "till they understand it.") The class ends with a period of seatwork—more practice with long division problems. The class works at this task, but the contingent of nonparticipating boys does little. Once again, Mr.

Gates pays little attention to them (he explains later that he
has tried hard to involve them and they "just don't respond;
they don't care about learning, so I don't spend much time
with them").[3]

Three key points are evident in this vignette. First, instruction
consists of filling out worksheets, listening to the teacher's explanations, and reciting answers. There is little conversation between teacher
and students; rather, students provide short answers to narrow questions. Second, students who listen but who do not understand simply
hear the same explanation over and over. Third, students who do not
listen receive little attention from the teacher. Mr. Gates has learned to
lower his expectations, and we can see that a vicious cycle is in place as
the teacher's low expectations and the low level of learning among
some children perpetuate one another.

Low expectations for poor children are also reflected in grading
standards. One study found that the same test score that earned a C in
low-poverty schools rated an A in high-poverty schools.[4] Even with this
"grade inflation," teachers in high-poverty schools expect their students
to receive low marks. A study of Baltimore schoolchildren reported that
the higher the proportion of poor children in a school, the lower teachers' expectations for students' future performance.[5] For example, when
first grade teachers were asked to predict students' marks in second grade,
those in schools with less than 50 percent of students on free or reduced-
price lunch predicted their students would receive more As and Bs than
Cs, whereas teachers in schools with higher proportions of children in
poverty predicted mostly Cs for their students.[6] The authors of the
Baltimore study do not claim that low expectations *caused* under-
achievement; rather, low expectations *reflect* low levels of learning.

In research on seven elementary schools in the Chicago area,
Robert Dreeben and Adam Gamoran noted wide disparities in the challenges that students encountered during first-grade reading instruction.[7] In schools attended by African-American students and students
from low-income families teachers tended to cover less curricular material. Where less material was covered, student reading achievement
was lower. Even if they are not the cause of achievement inequality,
such differences in curriculum and expectations between high- and
low-poverty schools are barriers to eliminating it because they prevent
inequality from being addressed.

INEQUALITIES WITHIN ELEMENTARY SCHOOLS. Differences within schools in student achievement are even more salient than differences among schools: about 80 percent of all the differences in achievement among students can be found within a typical school, while only about 20 percent of the differences among students reside in comparisons of one school to another.[8] Consequently, it is essential to examine differences in opportunities for learning that lie within schools. The main reason that students in the same elementary school do not always encounter the same instruction is that schools divide students into separate classes, and sometimes into instructional groups within classes, according to teachers' perceptions of students' capacities for learning. Almost all American elementary schools use some sort of "ability grouping" or "tracking" system to divide students in this way.[9] Although grouping and tracking are supposed to enhance achievement for all students, in practice they often fail to meet that goal. Instead, assignment to different classes and groups typically leads to achievement gaps that widen as the school year goes by.[10]

Why do achievement gaps tend to expand? Several researchers have demonstrated that the pace and complexity of classroom instruction favor students assigned to high-level classes and groups and work against those placed in lower levels. For example, Brian Rowan and Andrew Miracle observed that teachers in higher-level reading classes covered more stories with their students than those in lower-ranked classes.[11] Similarly, Rebecca Barr and Robert Dreeben showed that high-level reading groups covered more material at a faster pace, compared to lower-level groups in the same classroom.[12] Gamoran obtained the same results in a follow-up study.[13] These differences in instructional pace and coverage resulted in significant learning differences among students over the course of the school year.

Studies of ability-group assignment in elementary schools show that placement is determined by test scores at the beginning of the school year, and neither race nor socioeconomic background has an independent effect on assignment after initial test scores are taken into account.[14] Ability groups are nonetheless *stratified* by socioeconomic status because test scores and social class are related to one another at the beginning of the school year, and, as mentioned earlier, that association becomes more powerful year after year due to differential learning during the summer. Background differences in the composition of ability groups are compounded by differences among schools, which also tend to be segregated by social class and, in many contexts, by race and ethnicity. Thus, schools and classrooms become increasingly segregated by social background each year, and opportunities for learning are differentiated accordingly.

In an important review of research on ability grouping, Robert Slavin concluded that, whereas broad tracking is harmful, some types of grouping may help rather than hinder student achievement.[15] Elementary schools that reorganized students across grade levels for reading and schools that used within-class grouping for mathematics seemed to foster higher levels of achievement overall, even for those with initially low test scores, than schools that did not use such grouping. Slavin attributed the positive results to the way the groups were organized: they were limited to a specific subject, the assignment of students was based on criteria relevant to that subject, and the content of instruction was tailored to meet the needs of the students assigned to each group. Despite these findings, many elementary schools continue to use broader and more rigid forms of grouping (such as dividing students into high, middle, and low classes for the entire day) that make it difficult to match instruction with students' needs in particular subjects, and instructional modifications that do occur often underestimate the capacity of low-achieving students to keep pace with their peers.[16]

Unequal Opportunities in Secondary Schools

Even though elementary schools promote the same rate of learning for students of all backgrounds during the school year, achievement inequality grows over time. Because of stratification in the wider society, and because schools reflect that stratification in the way they are organized, students from different racial, ethnic, and economic backgrounds end up in very different positions from one another as they make the transition from elementary to middle schools and middle to high schools. Building on the way students are sorted among and within elementary schools, middle and high schools also offer separate programs that tend to segregate students along the lines of social background. Thus, stratification in elementary schools feeds into stratification at the secondary level and serves as a further basis for unequal access to high expectations and a meaningful academic curriculum.

INEQUALITIES AMONG SECONDARY SCHOOLS. At the secondary school level, an even smaller proportion of student achievement differences are found from one school to the next—closer to 10 percent of the variation than to the 20 percent found at the elementary level.[17] This means that most of the inequality in achievement may be found inside each school. Still, schools with different populations of students face distinct challenges and offer varying opportunities to students, and it is important to explore these differences.

Substantial inequalities exist among secondary school students from different family backgrounds. For example, African-American and Hispanic students are more than twice as likely as non-Hispanic white students to score below the basic level on mathematics and reading achievement tests in eighth grade, and they are also more than twice as likely to drop out of high school by the tenth grade.[18] Among those from the same socioeconomic background, dropout rates are similar among the racial and ethnic groups but inequalities in achievement remain. Moreover, socioeconomic disadvantages make dropping out more likely. After taking race and ethnic differences into account, students whose parents are poorly educated and in low-status jobs were about seven times more likely to drop out by tenth grade, compared to those whose parents are educated professionals.[19] Educators who teach in schools with high concentrations of poor and minority students face substantial challenges to keep students in school and to bring about enough academic success to make postsecondary education a possibility.

Instead of reducing these inequalities, the way secondary schools are typically configured usually makes them worse. In a statistical analysis of a national sample of high schools, David Monk and Emile Haller discovered that the higher the average social class of the student body, the more academic credits were offered in the school curriculum.[20] In another national study, Jeannie Oakes found a similar pattern for mathematics and science opportunities. She reported, "Students attending the junior high and middle schools with the largest concentrations of *low-income students* had access to considerably less-extensive programs in both science . . . and mathematics . . . than those attending more affluent schools."[21] Moreover, schools serving wealthy populations are more likely to offer algebra to eighth graders than schools serving children in poverty. Although algebra is only one course, its presence or absence is especially significant because it provides access to higher-level mathematics.[22]

Oakes also reported differential access to courses at the high school level. For example, schools with large concentrations of affluent students have the most extensive science programs. Moreover, calculus, the most advanced mathematics course at the high school level, was far more likely to be available in schools with affluent students than in schools with economically disadvantaged students. Similarly, 80 percent of schools serving predominantly white students offered calculus, whereas only half the schools in which all or almost all students came from minority backgrounds did so.

Corresponding to the differences in course availability, schools with more affluent students also tend to have more fully qualified teachers. The larger the concentration of poor students, the greater the shortage of qualified teachers in middle and high school mathematics and science courses.[23] Schools serving disadvantaged children are more likely than others to staff their courses with teachers who lack a major or minor in the subject that they are teaching.[24]

High schools reflect their student bodies in more subtle ways as well. Mary Metz led a team of researchers that conducted in-depth visits to eight high schools located in different types of communities.[25] At one level, teachers followed a "common script" in all the schools. Schools and classrooms had a common look and on the surface were characterized by common activities, and administrators, teachers, and students played the same roles regardless of the community context. At a deeper level, however, the adherence to a common script obscured more fundamental differences among schools. In middle-class communities conventional approaches were largely successful, but in schools located in poor neighborhoods they were not. Instead, as Metz explains,

> Even where there was incontrovertible evidence that students were not learning well, both students and teachers were frustrated or alienated, and there was an evident lack of connection between students and standard strategies and curricula, teachers did not respond by suggesting alternative strategies that would significantly change the common script. . . . Teachers did make informal, *de facto* changes in the script, however. Much of the difference between the schools in daily curriculum-in-use, in the sense of time, and in relationships resulted from adjustments that students and teachers created together through informal processes.[26]

Metz goes on to describe modifications such as diluting the curriculum without changing its formal outline, reducing homework assignments, or reducing the amount of class time devoted to academic work as coping strategies in schools serving working-class and low-income populations. These changes were put into place without adjusting the outward appearance of the school or class session.

Does it matter whether high schools serving poor children offer rigorous academic courses? It seems obvious that students can only enroll in such courses if they are offered, so the lack of access to high-level courses would appear to be a barrier for low-income students. Yet the research on high schools shows that simply offering such courses has no impact on student achievement. For example, Gamoran's analysis of a national survey of schools and students revealed that offering advanced placement (AP) courses had no effect on achievement in mathematics, science, vocabulary, reading, writing, or civics.[27] Moreover, about half the schools offered special programs for gifted and talented students and half did not, yet achievement growth was the same in either case. Even more surprisingly, the number of advanced courses in mathematics offered in a school had no impact on mathematics achievement, and the number of advanced science courses offered did not influence science achievement. How can that be? Achievement was closely related to the number and type of courses in which students actually *enrolled*, especially in mathematics and science, but it was unrelated to course *availability*. Schools that did not offer advanced courses must have contained very few, if any, students who would have enrolled in the courses, had they been available.

Should we conclude, therefore, that offering advanced courses is irrelevant to raising standards and reducing inequality? Not at all. Instead, we should recognize that offering courses is only one part of a two-part problem. The second part is enrolling students. Because of profound divisions within schools, many students typically lack access to advanced courses even when they are offered in the school. Students who attend schools where such courses are absent would have been "tracked" away from advanced courses if the courses were present, making it appear as if offering courses makes no difference. In fact, offering courses could make a difference, if it were combined with a policy that enrolled disadvantaged students in advanced courses.

INEQUALITY WITHIN SECONDARY SCHOOLS. To realize the benefits of reducing inequalities among schools in course offerings, it is first

necessary to understand inequalities *within* schools in course enrollment. Many research studies show that ability grouping and tracking in
secondary schools tend to widen the gaps in achievement that students
bring with them when they enter school each year.[28] Students enrolled
in high-level classes achieve more than otherwise similar students in
mixed-ability classes, and students enrolled in low-level classes fall
behind their peers.[29] These findings come mainly from middle schools,
where it is possible to compare ability-grouped and mixed-ability classes that are formed with similar students in different schools.

In high schools, it is difficult to compare grouped and ungrouped
classes because almost all high schools use some form of grouping.[30]
Still, one can see the pattern of increasing inequality in high schools in
the widening achievement gap among students enrolled in different
"tracks" (college preparatory, general, and vocational) and different
classes (such as honors, regular, and remedial). Two students whose test
scores are initially similar but who are placed in different types of classes complete the school year with different levels of achievement. These
differences are often very large. For example, one study demonstrated
that the achievement gaps among track levels are as large as the differences between students who are in school and those who have dropped
out by the end of high school.[31]

Small-scale studies of ability grouping have been less consistent
than those with national samples: some find positive effects, some negative, and some no differences related to grouping.[32] Rather than interpreting these findings as evidence that ability grouping is inconsequential,
however, these studies reveal that the effects of grouping may depend on
how it is implemented.[33] For example, Gamoran showed that high
schools with more rigid tracking systems, preventing students from
moving up or down over time, tend to produce more inequality than
schools with more flexible tracking systems.[34]

Why do ability groups and curriculum tracks magnify achievement
differences among students? It is not merely that students in different
classes have varied achievement levels at the start—even after taking
those differences into account, achievement becomes more unequal
over time. The major reason is that students in different classes and
tracks encounter different curricula and have different classroom experiences. Students enrolled in college preparatory programs, for example,
take more academic courses, and in particular more advanced academic courses, compared with students enrolled in general and vocational

programs.[35] These course work differences contribute to achievement inequality. In sequentially organized subjects such as mathematics, students who are judged to have low skills at the beginning of high school are consigned to low-level courses such as general math, where they repeat the skills of arithmetic over and over. Meanwhile, students whose achievement is higher when they enter high school progress through the sequence of algebra, geometry, and more advanced courses.[36] In subjects such as English, the level of the class affects curricular content. Students in honors or advanced classes are more likely to read classic literature, whereas students in basic or remedial classes read less, and what they do read is more likely to be young-adult fiction.[37] Students in high-level classes also write more extensively, while demands for writing are less in low-level classes.[38]

Observers have further noted that students in low-level classes respond to instruction less vigorously—they are more likely to misbehave during class and more likely to neglect their homework—compared to students in higher-ranked classes.[39] The research does not say whether low-track students' lack of response brings on the slow-paced instruction, or boredom in the face of fragmented and repetitive teaching leads to students' unresponsiveness; most researchers conclude that both processes are occurring.[40] In the view of Gamoran and his colleagues, classroom instruction is not what teachers do to students, but what teachers and students do together.[41] In this sense, a weak curriculum and unresponsive students go hand in hand and may constitute a vicious cycle.

In a case study of a suburban high school, James Rosenbaum noted that high-track teachers spent more time preparing and were more enthusiastic in class, compared to teachers in low-track classes.[42] In a later case study, Reba Page observed that even when the curriculum appeared similar in high- and low-track classes, teachers tended to reduce instruction to smaller bits of information in the low-track classes to meet what they perceived as their students' needs for narrowly focused tasks.[43] Page viewed low-track classes as "caricatures" of regular classes, in that the formal elements of classroom knowledge were fragmented and trivialized in their transmission to low-track students. Her observations from a high school social studies class illustrate her findings:

Mr. Ellison [the teacher] "joshes" lower-track students to establish a less authoritarian, easygoing relationship with them. His paper-wad tosses and stretched puns demonstrate that Additional Needs [a euphemism for low-track] students should not judge him strictly as a teacher, because those are not teacherly behaviors, but should consider him a "good fellow." Nevertheless, like his attempts to be friendly, such a strategy to establish goodwill and control often goes awry. Although it may allay openly hostile and anti-educational confrontations, it creates an atmosphere of irony in which genuine educational encounters rarely happen.[44]

In some schools, teachers compete with one another for the opportunity to teach the honors classes, and those with less experience or weaker reputations may be consigned to the lower tracks.[45] Low-track teachers are also less likely to be fully qualified for their assignments.[46] Oakes noted that differences between tracks in teacher qualifications are especially sharp in schools serving low-income urban communities. For example, whereas teachers in low-track math and science classes of suburban schools were almost as likely to be certified in their subject matter (82 percent) as their counterparts in high-track classes (84 percent), only 39 percent of low-track math and science teachers in urban schools were certified in their subject compared with 73 percent of those in high tracks.[47] These findings suggest that differences within and between schools may compound one another to heighten the inequities for low-achieving, disadvantaged youth.

As in elementary schools, test scores and other measures of academic competence are still the primary criteria for ability group assignments in high schools; but unlike elementary schools, social background plays a direct role in the placement process at the secondary level.[48] For this reason, grouping and tracking not only magnify the differences between high and low achievers, but they expand inequality of achievement among students of different social class backgrounds. In addition, even though race and ethnicity do not affect assignment directly, because race and ethnicity are related to prior achievement and social class, grouping and tracking also contribute to growing racial and ethnic inequality in student achievement over the high school years. Moreover, all else being equal, students assigned to the college track are less likely to drop out than their nonacademic peers, so the underrepresentation of low-income and minority students in the college track contributes indirectly to inequality in high school graduation rates.

Critics of tracking tend to focus on its impact on inequality: because tracking widens achievement gaps, they argue, it should be eliminated. The critics often neglect the findings that, in many cases, high-achieving students are better-off in high-ability classes than they would be if tracking were eliminated. Meanwhile, supporters of tracking focus on the benefits for high achievers, but ignore tracking's persistent effects on magnifying inequality. If tracking is eliminated, the program that replaces it must find a way to challenge high achievers so that they do not lose ground; to the extent that tracking continues, it will continue to promote inequity unless low-track classes are eliminated or dramatically improved.[49]

In a few instances, tracking has been implemented in ways that appear less damaging to low achievers. In the United States, Catholic high schools exhibit less inequality of achievement between college preparatory and general tracks compared to public high schools, apparently because course requirements for non-college-bound students are more rigorous in Catholic schools.[50] This is also the main reason that Catholic schools exhibit less inequality between students of different socioeconomic backgrounds, compared to public high schools.[51] In a study of ability grouping in twenty-five middle and high schools, Gamoran found two examples of low-track classes in which students kept up with their peers in other classes, instead of falling behind, and both classes were located in Catholic schools. Gamoran attributed the success of these low-track classes to three common elements: (1) high teacher expectations, manifested in a refusal to relinquish a serious academic curriculum; (2) extra efforts on teachers' parts to encourage oral discourse in the classroom, instead of relying on seatwork to maintain order; and (3) no system of assigning weak or inexperienced teachers to low-track classes. In another study, Gamoran found further evidence that high expectations in lower-level classes promoted achievement in a restructured public school.[52] These examples are rare, especially in public schools, but they could become more common if high expectations were effectively implemented in lower-level classes.

Andrew Porter and his colleagues examined new initiatives in high school mathematics designed to improve the quality of mathematics instruction for low-achieving, disadvantaged youth.[53] In four urban school districts, educators had created new classes that replaced general math with "transition" courses that were supposed to provide a bridge to college-preparatory mathematics. Evaluation of the transition courses found that they were more successful than general math at promoting achievement and leading students to a curriculum that prepared them for college. Moreover, despite the more rigorous requirements, students were no less likely to accumulate the credits they needed to graduate. Despite these successes, statistical analyses indicated that students of equivalent grades and/or test scores as they entered high school would have been better-off bypassing the transition courses and going straight into the college-preparatory classes; that is, students were much better-off in the transition courses than in general math, but not as well-off as those who enrolled in college-preparatory mathematics when they first entered high school.

In countries that have national examinations at the end of secondary school, different class levels within academic programs may help low-achieving students succeed on the tests. In Israel, for example, academically oriented students may enroll in academic courses at a variety of levels. Comparative research shows that while sorting students into levels tends to magnify inequality in American schools, in Israel it tends to reduce inequality, apparently because students in all levels have access to a meaningful curriculum and the examination provides a realistic incentive for students in all levels.[54] If American high schools had such incentives for teachers and students, dividing students into levels might be helpful rather than harmful. At present, however, expectations for low-level classes are minimal, as reflected in diluted curricula and limited academic demands.[55]

A combination of curriculum and achievement standards probably accounts for the more successful use of different levels in academic courses in Israel as compared with the United States. Within core academic subjects, Israeli students at all levels follow a prescribed curriculum. In addition, students at all levels take a national examination that is required for access to higher education and is valued in the job market. Both the curriculum and the examination are more demanding at higher levels within a subject, but they are meaningful for students' future destinations at all levels. By contrast, low-level academic courses in the United States tend to have diluted course content, and they are weakly connected to students' future opportunities.[56]

Successful use of tracking, though apparently not impossible, is exceedingly rare in the United States. At a minimum, the most rigid forms of tracking should be eliminated. These include tracking into separate classes for the entire day in elementary school and tracking into fixed programs that determine all of a student's courses in high school. The evidence is further clear that dead-end courses such as general math should be eliminated. To the extent that low-level classes are maintained, it is essential that they occur in a context of high expectations for academic progress.

HIGH STANDARDS AS A RESPONSE TO UNEQUAL CURRICULA

If curriculum inequality magnifies achievement inequality, can we reduce inequality by promoting the same high standards for all students? Although this sounds promising in principle, many important challenges make implementation difficult. Three approaches to implementing high standards—detracking, whole-school reform, and state and district standards for curriculum and assessment—reveal the challenges and potential benefits of standards-based reform.

Detracking

How may detracking reforms use high standards to improve teaching and learning? Advocates argue that by eliminating tracking, educators can provide the same high-quality instruction with the same beneficial results as currently occur in high-track classes. Ideally, then, detracking reforms would raise standards for all students, providing access to high-quality curricula and instruction to students of all backgrounds.

In reality, however, detracking has been difficult to implement. Jeannie Oakes, the nation's most articulate critic of tracking, has identified three main barriers to its elimination: (1) normative barriers, which result from the pervasive belief that children vary by nature and thus should be divided within schools; (2) political barriers, which reflect the strong interests that persons such as teachers of high-track classes or parents of high-track students have in maintaining a stratified system of classes; and (3) technical barriers, which embody the challenge of providing instruction to a more academically heterogeneous group of students than teachers usually encounter.[57]

Oakes and her colleague, Amy Stuart Wells, carried out an important study of detracking in ten diverse secondary schools located in different regions of the United States.[58] Despite strong detracking goals, none of the schools eliminated tracking entirely. Most eliminated their remedial tracks, but all maintained honors classes in at least some subjects. Educators committed to detracking encountered substantial resistance, sometimes from other teachers or administrators within their own schools and sometimes from parents or administrators outside their schools. In exploring the reasons for this opposition, the researchers focused on normative and political problems encountered by detracking reformers. "[The reformers] ran headlong into deeply held beliefs and ideologies about intelligence, racial differences, social stratification, and privilege. Conventional conceptions of intelligence, ability, and giftedness combined with the local community culture and politics around race and social class to fuel enormous resistance."[59] These findings are consistent with other research that identifies parent resistance as an impediment to detracking, and also research suggesting that mathematics and foreign language teachers may resist detracking more strongly than teachers of other subjects due to their beliefs in a sequential, hierarchically organized subject matter.[60]

This line of research pays scant attention to the third barrier identified by Oakes: the technical problem of instructing students of widely varying academic competencies, all in the same classroom. When teachers resist detracking, Oakes and her team ascribe the opposition to teachers' normative beliefs about students and subject matter. A new study by Tom Loveless indicates that many teachers find it hard to teach mixed-ability classes, especially if they have been accustomed to instructing students in a narrower range of academic performance. As one teacher explained, "I think they [teachers in an experimental heterogeneous class] have found some real problems to some degree. They're trying to teach to the middle. The lower students are struggling to keep up; and then, of course, the higher students are bored and unchallenged."[61]

Are these difficulties inherent in the nature of teaching, or do they merely reflect the entrenched beliefs of educators, without a basis in the practical demands of instruction? It is especially important to answer this question because many of the normative and political challenges of detracking have their roots in the technical difficulties. If these difficulties could be resolved—that is, if teachers were better prepared to provide high-quality instruction to mixed-ability classes, and if such instruction could be successfully demonstrated to observers—normative and political resistance to detracking would diminish.

The limited research that currently exists shows the difficulty but also the possibility of providing high-quality teaching in heterogeneous classes. Detracking is less controversial at the elementary school than at the secondary school level. Mixed-ability classes, typically with regrouping for reading and math, have long existed at the elementary school level. Also, the student body is less heterogeneous at the elementary than at the secondary level. Moreover, teachers have more flexibility at the elementary school level in how they arrange their time and how they cover curriculum. If they need to spend extra time with individual students, or to spend extra time on reading and math at the expense of social studies, they usually have the autonomy to do so.

The challenge of detracking is far greater at the secondary school level, when the gaps between students are wider and the demands of subject matter are more rigorous. Gamoran and Matthew Weinstein examined how a set of highly restructured schools responded to the problems of tracking.[62] Among the eight high schools in their sample, three did not divide students into tracks or class levels. In two of these three, expectations for students were low and academic rigor was weak. For example, in one large urban high school serving a minority population,

> teachers geared pedagogy and curriculum content for the lower-achieving students in the mixed-ability classes. Almost none of the observed classes exhibited more than a minimal amount of thoughtfulness and depth. . . . Two [math] teachers acknowledged that they had lowered their standards for heterogeneous classes, and one said he had given up trying to cover all the intended material. This resulted in students being promoted without being prepared for the next math course.[63]

In the third case of mixed-ability classes, however, the researchers found the highest level of instructional quality in their study, as well as the highest level of achievement. In this urban school serving a diverse population, teachers were committed to providing rigorous instruction to students who varied widely in their academic performances. In mathematics, the teachers had rejected the idea that the sequential organization of subject matter means students cannot tackle complex problems if they have not mastered the basics. Instead, students were expected to obtain extra tutoring in the basics while the class addressed more complex issues.

As one teacher explained, "I've told the kids, 'If you need to work on your basic math skills, I don't slow down for you. You're supposed to be putting in extra time. We have somebody here on Saturdays. You can stay after school. . . . On Saturday the library is open. There are two teachers and a resource teacher there to tutor.'"[64]

Several important features of this school led to its success with mixed-ability classes. First, a visionary leader had selected a staff with a strong, collective commitment to teaching without tracking. Second, students who attended the school were highly motivated. There were no academic selection criteria and the school was racially and economically diverse, but students either came from a feeder school with a similar philosophy or went through an interview as part of the admissions process. Third, the school had outside resources that enabled it to hold class sizes to twenty students and to create a tutoring program for students in danger of falling behind.

If secondary school mathematics is among the subjects most resistant to detracking, then evidence that detracking can succeed in that context is especially important. A curriculum called the Interactive Mathematics Program (IMP), which was designed for instruction of students with widely varying competencies, is an example of a program that seems to promote high achievement. Researchers have shown that students in the IMP program obtain test scores that are as high as those of students in the traditional algebra and geometry sequence.[65] Moreover, a study of high-achieving students in one school indicated that the top-performing students did just as well in the IMP program as in the traditional sequence.[66] These results, though based on very small samples, are promising enough to suggest that a solution to the technical problem of detracking is possible, even in secondary school mathematics.

Other evidence that detracking is warranted comes from analyses of what happens to low-achieving students when they enroll in college-preparatory mathematics. That is the goal of the Equity 2000 Project, a program of the College Board, which is working with urban districts across the nation to enroll all students in algebra and geometry. Findings from Equity 2000 districts indicate that far more students pass algebra now than before Equity 2000 was implemented. For example, in Milwaukee, one of the Equity 2000 pilot sites, the proportion of students enrolled in ninth-grade algebra (or a more advanced course) rose from 31 percent to 99 percent between 1991 and 1997. At the same time, rates of students passing algebra rose from 25 percent to 55 percent.[67] These findings are substantiated by Gamoran and Eileen Hannigan's analysis of national survey data which showed that all students benefit from taking algebra in their freshman or sophomore years, regardless of their mathematical competencies when they entered high school.[68] These findings raise questions about one of the key claims of tracking proponents: that low-achieving students cannot keep up with college-preparatory material. On the one hand, it is clear that expectations have been too low: many more students can successfully complete college preparatory mathematics than have previously been enrolled. On the other hand, substantial numbers of disadvantaged students still fail their math courses, so simply placing all students into advanced courses may not suffice.

Overall, it seems clear that eliminating dead-end classes such as general math is an effective strategy for raising standards. The evidence is less conclusive on what system should replace the low tracks. Teachers are skeptical about effectively instructing classes of widely varying achievement levels, particularly in subject areas such as mathematics that they perceive as sequentially organized. When disadvantaged students are enrolled in college preparatory classes many more succeed than might have previously been expected, but many students still fail. Successful detracking has been documented in case studies, but it seems to require extraordinary commitment and resources (such as small classes, extra tutoring, and innovative curricula). The alternative approach of reorganizing instruction for low-achieving students so that it raises standards even while students are taught in a separate group has also yielded partial success, so it may also be an appropriate solution.

Whole-School Reform

A limitation of many detracking reforms is that they change one aspect of the school while leaving the rest of the structure and beliefs in place. By contrast, whole-school reform initiatives aim to transform schools entirely. High standards are an important component of many whole-school reforms. Are they an effective way of reducing the inequality that results from varied opportunities?

Surprisingly, little research evidence exists to answer this question. Recently, the American Institutes for Research (AIR) released a report, commissioned by five professional educators' groups, entitled *An Educators' Guide to Schoolwide Reform*.[69] The report examined twenty-four prominent models of schoolwide reform. Although the models have been adopted by thousands of schools across the United States, most have not been systematically tested. According to the AIR report, strong evidence of benefits to student achievement exists for only three of the twenty-four models: Direct Instruction, an approach used in elementary schools that focuses on teaching clearly defined knowledge and skills using specific instructional routines; Success for All, another elementary school program that emphasizes early reading and uses one-on-one tutoring to make sure all students learn to read; and High Schools that Work, a secondary school program that emphasizes rigorous course work for students who do not intend to enroll in college. Most of the models that lack evidence of benefits to achievement have not been proven ineffective, but rather their impact has not been carefully assessed.

Several common features of the three programs cited for positive effects are worth noting. First, all three make prominent use of performance standards. In Direct Instruction, teachers assess student achievement levels frequently and target their instruction toward student progress in a specified curriculum. The key element of Success for All is its insistence on all students learning to read, a demanding minimum standard in the low-income, urban schools in which it is used. Schools that adopt High Schools that Work eliminate "basic" courses such as general math, enroll all students in college preparatory courses, and attempt to integrate academic and vocational studies.

Second, all three use some form of grouping by achievement level, with modifications that may help prevent the typical harm that grouping does to low achievers. Both Direct Instruction and Success for All use within-class and cross-grade grouping on a subject-specific basis, approaches that appeared to be beneficial in Slavin's review of elementary school grouping.[70] Both models assess and regroup students frequently so that instruction can be closely matched to students' skills, and the extra tutoring provided in Success for All supplements regular instruction rather than replacing it. High Schools that Work offers a program for students who are not bound for college, but eliminates low-track courses and integrates academic and vocational studies. These approaches may be seen as alternatives to detracking that, instead of providing weak, trivialized instruction to low achievers, use high standards to work toward all students' success.

A third similarity among the three programs is that they are high-ly scripted, prescribing particular courses of study. This is especially true for the two elementary school programs, Direct Instruction and Success for All. This quality has opened the programs to charges that they are too narrow, focusing on basic skills at the expense of higher-order think-ing. No data exist to refute this criticism, as the evidence of success for Direct Instruction and Success for All come from standardized tests of basic skills. Another concern is that while the programs have been judged successful in raising levels of achievement, their impact on inequality among students within the same schools has not been exam-ined. However, because these programs have yielded benefits in schools with high proportions of disadvantaged students, it is likely that they tend to reduce inequality as well as raise overall levels of achievement on the tests by which they are judged.

An important reason for weak research findings from many of the schoolwide reform models is that they have been implemented incon-sistently. Even though most of the models insist that teachers vote to adopt their programs, implementation is not easy. A series of RAND studies has examined implementation in the New American Schools, a set of schoolwide reform designs originally sponsored by business lead-ers.[71] The RAND scholars have found that although implementation improves over time, even after three years most schools have yet to implement fully the programs they have adopted. Teacher support is an important element of more extensive implementation. Other factors include clarity of communication by the team that designed the reform and the level of economic resources available for implementation. These reforms are not cost-free—they range from several thousand to several hundred thousand dollars in the first year. High Schools that Work, for example, anticipates first-year costs of $48,000, while the costs for Direct Instruction and Success for All are estimated at $244,000 and $270,000, respectively, per school in the first year.[72] Funds to support the reform may come from the district, from outside sources, or both.

It is not only the amount of funds but the way they are used that matters for implementation. The RAND research indicates that funds for professional development and teacher planning are especially impor-tant.[73] In addition, implementation occurs more fully when educators have flexibility and authority in determining how funds are allocated within their schools; when schools have chosen a design, rather than having one mandated; when there is stable leadership in the district, school, and design team; and when there is consistency between the design for reform and the criteria by which educators are held accountable for success.

In conclusion, limited evidence suggests that schoolwide reforms that emphasize high standards can succeed in improving opportunities and outcomes for disadvantaged students. Most schoolwide reforms lack sufficient evidence for determining their value, but it seems clear that continued experimentation is warranted. Interestingly, the three programs that have strong evidence of success may be seen as alternatives to detracking.

State and District Standards

A limitation of the schoolwide reform approach is that it relies on changing one school at a time. Implementation is difficult even when consensus exists about the need for reform and about reform strategies; where such consensus is lacking, schoolwide reform seems beyond reach. Mandates for high standards from state and district authorities are an approach to bringing about reform regardless of the preferences of individual educators and schools. While some educators view mandates as infringing on their professional discretion, others find standards a stimulating challenge.

PERSPECTIVES ON STANDARDS. Advocates maintain that high standards can improve learning and reduce inequality in two ways. First, standards provide a clear vision of what constitutes important content, excellent teaching, and meaningful learning. By providing this vision, standards let everyone in the educational system know what to aim for. Second, standards offer a means of holding educators—and their students—accountable for teaching and learning. When teachers and students are held accountable, they presumably have more incentive to perform at their best. Standards may also reduce inequality, if those who benefit most from high standards are students who would otherwise have been subjected to lower-quality content, instruction, and learning.

Critics of standards generally raise three major complaints. Some writers offer a philosophical objection to the idea of creating a common framework for education. Elliot Eisner, for example, argues that excellent

teaching and learning cannot be mechanized or routinized, so it is fruit-
less to strive for uniformity in teaching and learning.[74] According to
this view, curricular diversity adds richness to American culture, so we
should not try to define a common standard for what all students should
know and do. Eisner recalls John Dewey's distinction between *criteria*
and *standards*: we should develop criteria for judging what is excellent,
but we should not enact standards that dictate what everyone should do.
A variant of this argument focuses on the long tradition of local control
over education, noting that if states determine standards for teaching and
learning, the autonomy of local districts is diminished.[75]

A second objection views standards as an attack on teachers' professionalism. According to this view, teachers need the autonomy to
exercise their professional discretion in selecting content and determining instructional methods.[76] Such choices largely result from teachers' professional knowledge and from the particular needs of the students
in the class. From this perspective, state guidelines may serve as helpful
resources, but they should not dictate content, process, or levels of
learning because they cannot take into account students' diverse needs
and capabilities.

A third critique of standards deems it unfair to hold students
accountable for showing mastery of material they have not been
taught.[77] If some schools or classrooms provide inadequate opportunities
for learning, then their students are at a disadvantage when it comes to
testing, through no fault of their own. In response to this concern, some
writers have advocated "opportunity-to-learn" standards, or standards
for the content and delivery of instruction, as a precursor to standards
for student performance.[78] However, proposals for opportunity-to-learn
standards have intensified the opposition to standards as a threat to
local control over education.[79] In addition, Andrew Porter has explained
that focusing on opportunity-to-learn standards draws attention away
from outcomes in favor of inputs, a strategy that has failed to ensure
equal educational opportunity and has not led to equal achievement for
students from different backgrounds.[80]

Despite these concerns, virtually all states and many school districts throughout the United States are establishing standards for student performance. Two features of standard-setting activities seem to
respond to some of the criticisms. First, most educational authorities
recognize the need to align standards for student performance with
standards for instructional content. Second, states and districts devote

resources for professional development to help teachers prepare for helping their students to reach the standards.[81]

IMPACT OF STANDARDS. An early version of standards reform occurred in the 1980s and early 1990s when most states, responding to charges of educational "mediocrity," increased requirements for high school graduation. This change led high school students to take more academic courses. Although some observers found the quality of academic courses undiminished, others noted a tendency to add courses at lower levels.[82] Moreover, higher graduation requirements do not necessarily raise test scores. Although students take more academic courses when graduation requirements are higher, the courses provide weaker contributions to achievement, so there is no net gain. Evaluating these findings, Thomas Hoffer surmised that the courses are more "watered down" when graduation requirements are higher.[83]

Instead of regulating the "inputs" to student achievement (such as academic courses), the current wave of standards reform emphasizes "outcomes": that is, student achievement itself as the performance standard. Although most of today's standards reform efforts are too recent for evaluation of their impact, results from some of the earliest cases are promising. Since the early 1990s, Diane Massell and her colleagues at the Consortium for Policy Research in Education have monitored state and district efforts to engage in standards-based reform.[84] Case study reports are available that describe progress throughout the 1990s for five states: California, Florida, Kentucky, Minnesota, and Texas. These states differ in the timing of reforms, so we can compare them to get a sense of the impact of standards. Table 4.1 contrasts three "early reformers" (Kentucky, Minnesota, and Texas) with two "late reformers" (California and Florida). Kentucky, for example, established rigorous, coordinated standards for instructional content and student performance in 1990. In contrast, California set standards in fits and starts: a testing system created in the early 1990s was abandoned by 1994; only in late 1997 was a new statewide testing program adopted; and the tests were given for the first time in 1998.

If standards make a difference for student performance, greater gains during the 1990s would be expected in states that had implemented consistent standards early on than in states that established standards later. Using average state scores on the National Assessment of Educational Progress for comparison, Table 4.1 shows that the early

TABLE 4.1. NAEP ACHIEVEMENT GAINS IN STATES THAT IMPLEMENTED STANDARDS AT DIFFERENT TIMES

EARLY STATE REFORMS

STATE	YEAR OF STANDARDS IMPLEMENTATION[a]	READING GAINS[b] 1992–98 GRADE 4	MATHEMATICS GAINS[c] 1992–96 GRADE 4	1990–96 GRADE 8
Kentucky	1990	+5	+5	+9
Minnesota	1980s	+1	+4	+9
Texas	1984	+4	+11	+12
Average state gains for early reformers		+3.3	+6.67	+10

LATE STATE REFORMS

STATE	YEAR OF STANDARDS IMPLEMENTATION[a]	READING GAINS[b] 1992–98 GRADE 4	MATHEMATICS GAINS[c] 1992–96 GRADE 4	1990–96 GRADE 8
California	1998	0	+1	+6
Florida	1996	−1	+2	+8
Average state gains for late reformers		−0.5	+1.5	+7
NATIONAL AVERAGE GAINS		0	+4	+8

[a] From Diane Massell, Michael Kirst, and Margaret Hoppe, *Persistence and Change: Standards-based Reform in Nine States* (Philadelphia: Consortium for Policy Research in Education, 1997); Diane Massell, *State Strategies for Building Capacity in Education: Progress and Continuing Challenges* (Philadelphia: Consortium for Policy Research in Education, 1998).
[b] From Patricia L. Donahue et al., *NAEP 1998 Reading Report Card for Nations and the States*, document no. NCES 1999-500 (Washington, D.C.: U.S. Department of Education, 1999).
[c] From Clyde M. Reese et al., *NAEP 1996 Mathematics Report Card for the Nation and the States*, document no. NCES 97488 (Washington, D.C.: U.S. Department of Education, 1997).

reformers made substantially greater gains in reading and mathematics than the late reformers. Moreover, the gains in the early-reforming states outstripped the national averages, whereas the gains in the late-reforming states lagged behind.

Minnesota is a somewhat contradictory case in that it implemented statewide testing as far back as the 1980s, but the tests were not aligned with content standards. Only in 1998 did Minnesota implement a new

set of statewide tests aligned with standards for content. It is interesting
to note that Minnesota's gains were the least among the three early
reformers, possibly a reflection of the lack of alignment between the
curriculum and the early tests.

Although these findings are suggestive, they are hardly conclusive. A host of other state-level conditions, including changes in population, resources, and other policies, may account for the test score
gains in Kentucky, Minnesota, and Texas, and these need to be ruled
out before one can safely conclude that state standards are responsible
for the gains. Moreover, one cannot tell what the implications of these
gains are for equity. Which students are making gains in these states, all
students or only some? The gains in test score levels would reflect a
reduction in inequality only if weaker students are gaining faster than
stronger students.

A recent analysis by RAND researchers David Grissmer and Ann
Flanagan lends confidence to the interpretation of state NAEP trends
as a reflection of standards.[85] Grissmer and Flanagan noted that Texas
and North Carolina have exhibited the most extraordinary gains on
recent NAEP assessments. (Gains in North Carolina were +5, +11, and
+17 on the tests listed in Table 4.1 for fourth-grade reading and math, and
eighth-grade math, respectively.) Could these gains be due to high standards in these states? First, the authors ruled out competing explanations:
neither student populations, nor funding for education, nor teacher qualifications changed in ways that might account for the test-score gains.
Hence, the explanation of standards is plausible. Grissmer and Flanagan
argued that eight common elements in the two states' educational reform
programs may account for their apparent success. These are:

- clear objectives for what students should know at each grade level,
  coordinated with textbooks, curricula, and professional development for teachers;

- statewide assessments aligned with the learning objectives;

- results of testing available widely through a computerized system;

- accountability for educators focuses on gains as well as on absolute
  scores, allowing educators of low-achieving students to succeed if
  their students improve;

◆   application of standards to all students, regardless of family back-
    ground;

◆   flexibility for educators, so they can find their own paths to reach-
    ing the objectives;

◆   reallocation of resources to schools with more disadvantaged stu-
    dents; and

◆   stable and consistent participation of business and political leaders
    in educational reform.

Despite the overall achievement gains in these states, the impact
of standards on equity is still in doubt. In Texas, African-American
and Hispanic students made larger gains in test scores than non-
Hispanic whites during the 1990s. In North Carolina, however, there
was no decline in racial or ethnic inequality.

International comparisons support the claim that testing high
school students on a rigorous academic curriculum promotes higher
achievement. John Bishop suggested that such tests, which are used in
many nations including most of Europe and Asia, create incentives
for learning that are otherwise absent.[86] Examining two international
tests, and taking into account population differences, Bishop showed
that scores are higher in countries that require curriculum-based examinations than in countries without such tests. He found the same pattern in a comparison of Canadian provinces that do and do not require
curriculum-based tests. Finally, Bishop argued that there is one state in
the United States—New York—that has a long-standing policy of testing students on a specified high school curriculum, namely the Regents
examinations. On both the NAEP and SAT scores, Bishop showed that
New York students outperform students in other states, a result that
Bishop attributed to the incentives created by the Regents examinations. Once again, however, these analyses focus on overall levels of
achievement and do not reveal whether testing promotes greater equality of outcomes among students from different backgrounds.

One international study suggests that higher standards can support
more equitable outcomes. In Scotland, students take a national examination at around age sixteen. Formerly, only the more academically

oriented students were permitted to take the examination, which is the gateway to more advanced academic study. During the 1980s, the examination was revamped and opened to all students. Not only did average scores on the examination rise, but the gap between economically advantaged and disadvantaged students diminished as a result of this change. However, even though the test score gap declined, advantaged students still scored higher, and inequality in access to higher education did not change, at least in the short run.[87]

IMPLEMENTATION OF STANDARDS REFORMS. Research on the impact of standards to date leaves open two major questions. The first is the impact on equity; no further evidence is yet available to address this question. The second question has to do with implementation: what conditions have led some states and districts to implement standards more successfully than others? Several case studies of states and districts shed light on this question. The case studies cover the past decade or so, with some beginning in the early 1990s (for example, Kentucky), and others that are more recent, developing standards that have not yet taken effect (for example, New York City). Drawing on the case studies, one may identify three crucial elements in the implementation of standards that seem to be associated with success: consistency, coherence, and capacity.

♦   CONSISTENCY. One of the most striking features of the reforms in Texas and North Carolina is their consistency over a long period of time.[88] Their current testing systems date from the mid-1990s, but they have strong roots in earlier systems that go back to the previous decade. Moreover, these states have witnessed a stability of business and political leadership that undergirds the educational reform. Despite changes in the political landscape, educational reforms proceeded, supported by coalitions of lawmakers from both parties. Grissmer and Flanagan concluded that:

> Perhaps the most important aspect of the reform initiatives in both states is the establishment of a substantial "infrastructure" for supporting a process of continual improvement in education. This infrastructure includes . . . a mix of public, non-profit, and private sector participation and organizations. . . . [It] generates a continuing

series of educational improvement plans—each building on previous agendas. It includes continuing analysis and evaluation of the results of previous reform as an important element. . . . [P]erhaps the most important part of this infrastructure is the relationships built upon the shared experience of working together over many years to improve education that has developed among taxpayers, educators, policymakers and business leaders.[89]

Kentucky is another state that has followed a stable, long-term agenda toward standards-based reform. Test results from Kentucky, both on the NAEP and on internal, statewide assessments, show a consistent rise over time.[90] Other states experienced substantial turmoil as they worked through standards reforms, mandating tests and eliminating them later, sometimes even before the tests had been implemented.[91]

Within districts and schools, a consistent and unified approach to standards also contributes to success. A study in the state of Washington of elementary schools whose students took a new fourth-grade test concluded that:

Effective changes in teaching methods and materials are focused and school-wide, not random and fragmented. In the two years since statewide testing began, most schools have made changes in what and how they teach. However, schools whose scores increased made changes that affected the whole school and unified the efforts of all teachers; schools whose scores did not increase added on new programs or materials that affected some teachers and not others and did not lead to a more unified school-wide approach.

Similarly, a case study of seven urban districts responding to standards reform found that "the district challenge is to maintain that focus [on a specific change] over time, even as leaders and state agendas change."[92] Stable leadership within schools is another aspect of consistency. In a study of elementary schools in Kentucky, responses to standards-based reform were undermined in schools that changed principals frequently.[93]

♦   COHERENCE. Reforms in Kentucky, North Carolina, and Texas, among other states, were developed carefully to ensure that state assessments were aligned with the curriculum. Ideally, curriculum standards are designed first, followed by assessments that test mastery of the curriculum. This pattern was followed in each of these states and may account for their success in implementation. Alignment between curriculum and assessments is an essential element of standards-based reform.

Another key aspect of implementing coherent standards is the creation of incentives for both educators and students. When only educators are accountable, they find it difficult to motivate students to perform well. When only students are accountable, educators may lack sufficient incentives to ensure that learning opportunities are adequate.

Some states have made their tests voluntary for students. This practice may result in turmoil, as in the case of Michigan, where students quickly learned that they could be penalized for failing the tests but not for skipping the tests altogether. Many high-achieving students simply avoided the tests, since they had little to gain from them and thus apparently could only lose.[94] Consequently, while voluntary tests may respond to criticisms about local autonomy, they are unlikely to be implemented successfully.

♦   CAPACITY. A clear vision and strong incentives for success are not enough to raise achievement, and certainly not enough to reduce achievement inequality, if teachers and students lack the resources to respond to their mandates. Perhaps the most important element of building capacity for standards-based reform is professional development for teachers that provides both content knowledge and pedagogical strategies consistent with the standards. Professional development can help build acceptance of standards, as well as enhance teachers' abilities for successful implementation. In the mid-1990s, most states did not mandate professional development geared toward standards reform; Kentucky was one of the few states that did.[95] Studies of district and school responses to standards indicate that professional development for teachers was effective when it was used strategically. As one principal explained, "Our staff decides the best use of staff development funds. We decided that if teachers were going to get paid for training, they'd have to come back and teach others what they learned. So we didn't go out and get any canned presentations. What we did was take a group of teachers and look at other schools, programs that worked. We also invested in training people to be specialists. When we needed a reading specialist, we spent money on training one."[96]

These case studies stress the value of involving entire school faculties in professional development over a sustained period of time. Professional development that builds capacity for meeting high standards does not rely primarily on traditional workshops but creates opportunities for intensive, collaborative work among teachers.[97] Both the Washington State study and an evaluation of standards-based reform in Chicago indicate that implementation is more successful when teachers and principals can decide for their own schools how resources are spent and which models of reform are adopted.[98]

Another aspect of building capacity is the allocation of extra resources for disadvantaged students. Grissmer and Flanagan note that this policy may have helped educators in Texas and North Carolina succeed with low-achieving students. Jane David and Patrick Shields echoed this conclusion in their study of urban districts: "[L]ow-performing students need extra time, help, and structure. Without these reports, standards-driven reform risks becoming 'another way to fail students,' as one teacher expressed her fear. This extra time must consist of a well-designed program taught by well-trained teachers, not the usual remedial and repetitive work. And it must start early, not wait until children are several years behind."[99]

The lack of focused attention on equity issues is a key failing in most standards-based reforms to date. Although rhetoric about equity is plentiful, most states and districts have not taken decisive action toward equity goals, and little evidence is available to assess changes in achievement outcomes among students of varied racial, ethnic, and socioeconomic backgrounds. Few educational authorities have ensured that all students will have opportunities to learn the tested material. The Chicago school district has attempted to respond to this challenge by creating special programs to help students to pass a subsequent attempt when they have failed the tests that are required for promotion. These programs remain controversial, and evidence is not yet available for a rigorous evaluation.[100]

Lacking assurance of equal opportunities for learning, the use of a common test with serious consequences for all students is problematic. For example, as of the year 2003, all students in New York will be required to pass the Regents examinations in order to graduate from high school. In light of the difficulty of the tests and many students' lack of preparation, it seems certain that a large proportion of students will fail the tests and will be unable to graduate, particularly in disadvantaged areas such as New York City. Anticipating this type of situation, the authors of *High Stakes*, a National Academy of Sciences report on the development of voluntary national tests, concluded that it is inappropriate to use tests as the sole criterion for high-stakes decisions such as high school graduation and promotion from one grade to the next. In addition to potential inequalities in preparation for tests, no test is perfectly reliable, so multiple criteria should be used in making high-stakes decisions. Therefore, the writers concluded that, "Scores from large-scale assessments should never be the only sources of information used to make a promotion or retention decision. No single source of information—whether test scores, grades, or teacher judgments—should stand alone in making promotion decisions. Test scores should always be used in combination with other sources of information about student achievement."[101]

In the case of high school graduation, it seems likely that the negative consequences for students who fail to graduate will outweigh the positive consequences that testing can have on student motivation. An alternative approach to linking test performance to graduation would be to allow students to graduate on the basis of performance in courses and to use test performance at high school exit as an indicator of "qualifications," or mastery of specific curricular material. The tests would still have serious consequences if they were used as criteria for entry into higher education and for selection in the job market, but they would not serve as barriers to high school graduation, a consequence that is likely to reduce opportunities for the most disadvantaged students, compared to opportunities that are currently available.

RECOMMENDATIONS AND CONCLUSIONS

Research on high standards as a strategy to combat unequal opportunities yields six recommendations:

1. **Extreme forms of tracking and ability grouping should be eliminated.** Elementary schools should refrain from rigidly grouping students for all subjects on the basis of a single criterion. At the secondary level, dead-end courses such as general math should be dropped because viable alternatives are available.

2. **In a context of high standards, some forms of differentiation (that is, divisions among students) can help reduce achievement inequality.** These include limited within-class and cross-grade, subject-specific grouping at the elementary level and integration of academic and vocational curricula with an emphasis on careers at the secondary level. Whole-school reform models such as Direct Instruction, Success for All, and High Schools that Work confirm the value of these limited forms of differentiation. In each case, clear standards of curriculum and performance ensure high-quality learning opportunities for low-achieving students.

3. **Where tracking is completely eliminated, care must be taken to ensure that standards for high-achieving students are not lowered.** In some cases to date, detracking has resulted in watered-down instruction for all students. Avoiding this pattern requires a strong vision of success, a curriculum that is appropriate for students with diverse abilities, and professional development to help teachers learn how to instruct students who vary widely in their performance levels.

4. **Where some degree of tracking is maintained, it is essential to implement high standards for low-achieving students.** Most uses of tracking result in poor instruction for low achievers. Avoiding this pattern requires high expectations, innovative academic curricula, and strong efforts by educators to ensure that low-achieving students receive the attention they need to keep pace or catch up to their higher-performing peers.

5. **Consistency, coherence, and capacity are key elements of state and district standards-based reforms.** Educational authorities must work toward a clear vision of standards, rather than the fragmented and shifting approaches that prevail in many cases. Assessments must be aligned with curricula and professional development to ensure that a coherent focus is maintained. Opportunities for teachers' professional development that emphasize long-term, collaborative growth are important for developing teachers' capacities for change. In addition, shifting resources toward schools with high proportions of low-achieving students may enhance capacities for providing equal learning opportunities.

6. **High stakes—that is, serious consequences—must be used judiciously to provide incentives for the performances of educators and students.** Both educators and students must be motivated to perform. However, implementing high stakes when success is out of reach is counterproductive. Using test scores as the sole criterion for high school graduation will probably increase the proportion of students who fail to graduate. Consequently, it may be more productive to use examinations at the time of high school graduation to indicate mastery. These examinations could still have high stakes attached to them, if they are used as selection criteria for college entry and in the labor market.

Standards-based reform in the United States is faced with a fundamental dilemma. If we are serious about raising expectations for what students should know and be able to do we must have examinations to hold students and educators accountable for performance. Yet raising the stakes in this way will highlight the vast inequalities within and among schools that already exist in American education. In the long run, the only way out of this dilemma is to improve opportunities for disadvantaged youth by using less tracking, by enhancing instruction, and by providing extra resources that are needed to prepare low-achieving students for high-stakes tests. In the short run, standards must be applied carefully to ensure that existing inequalities are not exacerbated.

5.

Inequality in Teaching and Schooling: Supporting High-Quality Teaching and Leadership in Low-Income Schools

Linda Darling-Hammond and Laura Post

Few Americans realize that the U.S. educational system is one of the most unequal in the industrialized world, and students routinely receive dramatically different learning opportunities based on their social status. In contrast to most European and Asian nations that fund schools centrally and equally, the wealthiest 10 percent of school districts in the United States spend nearly ten times more than the poorest 10 percent, and spending ratios of three to one are common within states. Poor and minority students are concentrated in the less well funded schools, most of them located in central cities and funded at levels substantially below those of neighboring suburban districts.[1] In addition, policies associated with school funding, resource allocations, and tracking leave minority students with fewer and lower-quality books, curriculum materials, laboratories, and computers; significantly larger class sizes; less qualified and experienced teachers; and less access to high-quality curriculum.

The fact that the least-qualified teachers typically end up teaching the least-advantaged students is particularly problematic. Recent studies have found that the difference in teacher quality may represent the single most important school resource differential between minority and white children and that it explains at least as much of the variance in student achievement as socioeconomic status. In fact, as we describe below, disparate educational outcomes for poor and minority children are much more a function of their unequal access to key educational resources, including skilled teachers and quality curriculum, than they are a function of race or class.

Just as capable teachers are important to students' success, excellent principals are critical to a school's success and to its ability to attract, retain, and mobilize able teachers. Along with other resources, high-poverty schools often also have difficulty attracting the strongest leaders. But this is not a necessary outcome of our educational system. What can be done to ensure that low-income schools are organized to attract and retain more highly qualified teachers and principals and to develop schools organized to support successful teaching and learning? Many states and districts have enacted policies that have sharply reduced or even eliminated the disparities in access to high-quality teachers, teaching, and schooling for low-income and minority students in urban and poor rural areas. Their strategies are as important to understand as the widespread problems. This chapter details both the sources of typical inequalities and the possibilities offered by solutions that have been found successful in the real world.

WHAT MATTERS MOST: HOW TEACHERS AND PRINCIPALS AFFECT TEACHING AND LEARNING

Despite conventional wisdom that school inputs make little difference in student learning, a growing body of research suggests that schools do make a difference, and a substantial portion of that difference is attributable to teachers. Recent studies of teacher effects at the classroom level using longitudinal databases in Tennessee and Dallas, Texas, have found that differences in teacher effectiveness are an extremely strong determinant of differences in student learning, far outweighing the effects of differences in class size and heterogeneity.[2] Students who are assigned to several in-effective teachers in a row have significantly lower achievement and small-er gains in mathematics and reading—yielding differences of as much as fifty percentile points over three years—than those who are assigned to several highly effective teachers in sequence.[3] These studies also find trou-bling indicators for educational equity, noting evidence of strong bias in assignment of students to teachers of different effectiveness levels, includ-ing indications that African-American students are nearly twice as likely to be assigned to the most ineffective teachers and about half as likely to be assigned to the most effective teachers (see Figure 5.1).

How Teachers Matter

A growing body of research indicates that teacher expertise is one of the most important factors in determining student achievement, followed

FIGURE 5.1. CUMULATIVE EFFECTS OF TEACHER EFFECTIVENESS: STUDENT TEST SCORE PERCENTILES (5TH-GRADE MATH), BY EFFECTIVENESS LEVEL OF TEACHERS OVER A THREE-YEAR PERIOD, FOR TWO METROPOLITAN SCHOOL SYSTEMS

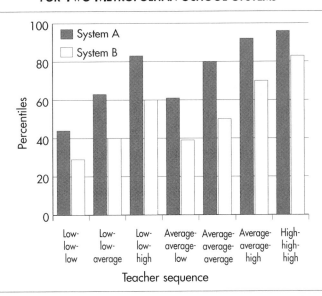

Source: W. L. Sanders and J. C. Rivers, *Cumulative and Residual Effects of Teachers on Future Student Academic Achievement* (Knoxville: University of Tennessee, 1996).

by the smaller but generally positive influences of small schools and small class sizes. That is, teachers who know a lot about teaching and learning and who work in environments that allow them to know students well are the critical elements of successful learning. In an analysis of nine hundred Texas school districts, Ronald Ferguson found that teachers' expertise—as measured by scores on a licensing examination, master's degrees, and experience—accounted for about 40 percent of the measured variance in students' reading and mathematics achievement at grades 1 through 11, more than any other single factor. He also found that every additional dollar spent on more highly qualified teachers netted greater increases in student achievement than did less instructionally focused uses of school resources.[4] The effects were so strong and the variations in teacher expertise so great that, after controlling for socioeconomic status, the large disparities in achievement between black and white students were almost entirely accounted for by differences in the qualifications of their teachers (see Figure 5.2).

Ferguson and Helen Ladd repeated this analysis with a less extensive data set in Alabama that included much rougher proxies for teacher knowledge (master's degrees and ACT scores instead of teacher licensing examination scores) and still found sizable influences of teacher

Figure 5.2. Influence of Teacher Qualifications on Student Achievement: Proportion of Explained Variance in Math Test Score Gains (from Grades 3 to 5) Due to:

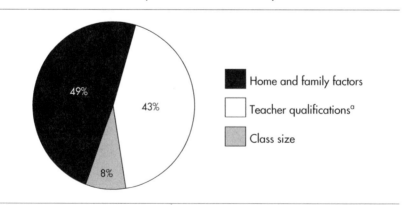

[a] Licensing examination scores, education, and experience.

Source: Developed from data presented in Ronald F. Ferguson, "Paying for Public Education: New Evidence of How and Why Money Matters," Harvard Journal on Legislation 28 (Summer 1991): 465–98.

qualifications and smaller class sizes on student achievement gains in mathematics and reading.[5] These influences held up when the data were analyzed at both the district and school levels. In an analysis illustrating the contributions of these variables to the predicted differences in average student achievement between districts scoring in the top and bottom quartiles in mathematics, they found that 31 percent of the predicted difference was explained by teacher qualifications and class sizes, while 29.5 percent was explained by poverty, race, and parent education.

In North Carolina, Robert Strauss and Elizabeth Sawyer found a similarly strong influence on average school district test performance of teachers' average scores on the National Teacher Examinations that measure subject matter and teaching knowledge.[6] After taking account of community wealth and other resources, teacher qualifications had a strikingly large effect on students' success on the state competency examinations: a 1 percent increase in teacher quality (as measured by NTE scores) was associated with a 3 to 5 percent decline in the percentage of students failing the exam. The authors' conclusion is similar to Ferguson's:

> Of the inputs which are potentially policy-controllable (teacher quality, teacher numbers via the pupil-teacher ratio and capital stock) our analysis indicates quite clearly that improving the quality of teachers in the classroom will do more for students who are most educationally at risk, those prone to fail, than reducing the class size or improving the capital stock by any reasonable margin which would be available to policy makers.[7]

These findings are reinforced by those of a recent review of sixty production function studies, which found that teacher education, ability, and experience, along with small schools and lower teacher-pupil ratios, are associated with significant increases in student achievement.[8] In this study's estimate of the achievement gains associated with expenditure increments, spending on teacher education substantially outpaced other variables as the most productive investment for schools (see Figure 5.3, page 132). Many other studies came to similar conclusions. For example, a study of high- and low-achieving schools with similar student populations in New York City found that differences in teacher qualifications accounted for more than 90 percent of the variations in student

**FIGURE 5.3. EFFECTS OF EDUCATIONAL INVESTMENTS:
SIZE OF INCREASE IN STUDENT ACHIEVEMENT FOR EVERY $500 SPENT ON:**

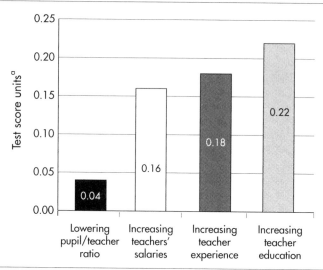

[a] Achievement gains were calculated as standard deviation units on a range of achievement tests in the sixty studies reviewed.
Source: Rob Greewald, Larry V. Hedges, and Richard D. Laine, "The Effect of School Resources on Student Achievement," *Review of Educational Research* 66, no. 3 (1996): 361–96.

achievement in reading and mathematics at all grade levels tested.[9] Research using national data and studies in Georgia, Michigan, and Virginia have found that students achieve at higher levels and are less likely to drop out when they are taught by teachers with certification in their teaching field, by those with master's degrees, and by teachers enrolled in graduate studies.[10]

The National Assessment of Educational Progress has documented that the qualifications and training of students' teachers are also among the correlates of reading achievement: students of teachers who are fully certified, who have master's degrees, and who have had professional coursework in literature-based instruction do better on reading assessment than students whose teachers have not had such learning opportunities. Furthermore, teachers who have had more professional coursework are more likely to use an approach that integrates the teaching of reading with literature and writing, which is associated with stronger achievement. For example, teachers with more staff development hours in reading are much more likely to use a wide variety of books, newspapers, and materials from other subject areas and to engage students in regular writing, all of which are associated with higher reading achievement. They are also less likely to use reading kits, basal readers, and workbooks, which are associated with lower levels of reading achievement.[11]

Reviews of research over the past thirty years have concluded that both subject matter knowledge and knowledge of teaching are important to teacher effectiveness, and that fully prepared and certified teachers are better rated and more successful with students than teachers without this preparation.[12] As Carolyn Evertson and colleagues conclude in their research review: "[T]he available research suggests that among students who become teachers, those enrolled in formal preservice preparation programs are more likely to be effective than those who do not have such training. Moreover, almost all well planned and executed efforts within teacher preparation programs to teach students specific knowledge or skills seem to succeed, at least in the short run."[13]

Studies of underprepared teachers consistently find that they are less effective with students and that they have difficulty with curriculum development, classroom management, student motivation, and teaching strategies. With little knowledge about how children grow, learn, and develop, or about what to do to support their learning, these teachers are less likely to understand student learning styles and differences, to anticipate students' knowledge and potential difficulties, and to plan and redirect instruction to meet students' needs. They are also less likely to see it as their job to do so, often blaming the students if their teaching is not successful.[14] Thus, policies that resolve shortages by allowing the hiring of unprepared teachers serve only to exacerbate the inequalities low-income and minority children experience.

Expert teachers are a prerequisite for the successful implementation of challenging curriculum. Teachers who are well-prepared are better able to use teaching strategies that respond to students' needs and learning styles and that encourage higher-order learning.[15] Since the novel tasks required for problem-solving are more difficult to manage than the routine tasks associated with rote learning, lack of knowledge about how to manage an active, inquiry-oriented classroom can lead teachers to turn to passive tactics that "dumb down" the curriculum, busying students with workbooks and end-of-chapter fill-in-the-blank tests rather than complex tasks like lab work, research projects, and experiments that require more skill to orchestrate.[16]

How Principals Matter

The recruitment and retention of well-prepared teachers and the support of high-quality teaching is the major function of a principal who functions as an instructional leader. In his research on effective schools, Ron Edmonds found that strong instructional leadership on the part of the principal was a crucial element in school effectiveness.[17] Reviewing research by others as well as his own work,[18] Edmonds cited as first among six indispensable characteristics of effective schools the "strong administrative leadership without which the disparate elements of good schooling can neither be brought together nor kept together."[19]

The nature of this leadership matters for the quality of teaching and for the retention of high-quality teachers. Virtually all of the most recent research on school leadership connects teacher commitment with a collaborative and value-based style of leadership—one aimed at enhancing professional commitment, using symbolic and transformational values as touchstones. Collaborative leadership styles focus on developing a clarity of mission; cultural cohesion through shared norms, values, and beliefs; and reward systems that reinforce those cultural values.[20] Not surprisingly, administrative leadership styles and teacher participation are strongly related to one another. Mark Smylie found that the principal-teacher relationship was the most powerful predictor of teachers' willingness to participate in personnel, curriculum, staff development, and administrative decisionmaking.[21] Michael Fullan and Thomas Sergiovanni have both found that principals who support norms of collegiality and encourage teacher development and self-management raise individual and group commitment to teaching.[22] In these studies, teachers who participate in creating the culture of the school and the values that drive that culture tend to be more committed to teaching and to the school organization.

School leadership and culture are two conditions that encompass most other workplace conditions. School culture refers to the dominant ethos of the organization, its values and visions, and the everyday experiences of members of the school community. Studies often find that indicators of school culture are powerful predictors of teachers' work, career, and organizational commitment.[23] Teachers' perceptions of their principals are almost always found to be directly related to their perceptions of the school culture.[24]

These perceptions directly influence the supply and turnover of teachers. Eileen Sclan found that the ways in which schools structure decisionmaking and collegial relations significantly influence beginning teachers' commitment to the profession. Beginning teachers appear to evaluate school leadership by how effectively it creates a school culture that is collaborative and supportive. The more beginning teachers feel that they can actively participate in making important decisions in their schools, the more positive their view of school leadership; the more collaborative and supportive the school leadership, the more involved teachers appear to be and the more likely they are to want to stay at the school. Whether and how schools provide opportunities for involvement in decisionmaking, for collaborative work with other teachers, and for engagement in curriculum building and other professional tasks strongly determines whether they plan to remain in the profession.[25]

While there is no evidence about the relative competence of principals in low-income schools versus schools generally, there is evidence that, all else being equal, principals' leadership has a great deal to do with which schools are hard to staff. Study after study has noted that good schools in low-income communities have strong principals who serve as instructional leaders. While resources and working conditions certainly matter, research suggests that teachers who have options choose to enter and remain in schools where they feel well supported by the local administrator, irrespective of student wealth or poverty, and that schools with poor leadership typically have difficulty attracting and retaining teachers.[26] In national surveys of teachers about their decisions to remain in teaching, administrative supports matter far more than the characteristics of the student body or even variables like student behavior and parent involvement.[27]

Clearly, teachers and principals matter. The question for those concerned about equity then becomes, How can schools serving poor and minority students enhance their ability to get and keep well-prepared teachers and capable leaders?

THE PROBLEMS OF STAFFING LOW-INCOME SCHOOLS

Using the most conservative estimates, the nation will need to hire at least two million teachers over the next ten years. Although this level of demand is daunting, the country has for many years graduated more new teachers than it hires. Usually only about 65 to 70 percent of newly prepared teachers take full-time teaching jobs in the year after they graduate.[28] Although there are many new teachers who cannot find jobs, there are also many job openings for which schools have difficulty finding teachers. In almost every field, schools with the largest numbers of low-income and minority students are much more likely than other schools to report that they have difficulty filling vacancies.[29] These schools are also more likely to fill vacancies with unqualified teachers, substitutes, or teachers from other fields, or to expand class sizes or cancel course offerings when they cannot find teachers.

National Center for Educational Statistics' data confirm that difficulty filling teaching positions varies by field and school location. Overall, 15 percent of all schools reported in 1991 that they had vacancies that they could not easily fill with a qualified teacher. Nearly one-fourth of central-city schools (23.4 percent) found that they had difficulty filling vacancies with qualified persons. Schools with minority enrollments of more than 20 percent, whether in central cities, urban fringe, or rural areas, had the most difficulty filling vacancies.[30] Minority and low-income students in urban settings are most likely to find themselves in classrooms staffed by inadequately prepared, inexperienced, and ill-qualified teachers because funding inequities, distribution of local power, and labor market conditions conspire to produce shortages of which they bear the brunt. Shortages of qualified teachers also translate into larger class sizes, lack of access to higher-level courses, and poorer teaching.[31]

These "shortages," though, are largely a problem of distribution rather than of absolute numbers. Wealthy districts that pay high salaries and offer pleasant working conditions rarely experience shortages. Districts that serve low-income students tend to pay teachers less and offer larger class sizes and pupil loads, fewer materials, and less desirable teaching conditions, including less professional autonomy. They also often have cumbersome and inefficient hiring systems that make the selection process particularly slow and grueling for candidates. For obvious reasons, they have more difficulty recruiting teachers. In 1993–94, for example, schools serving larger numbers of minority and low-income students were four times as likely as whiter and wealthier schools to hire unqualified teachers (see Figure 5.4). As we show later, there are exceptions to these practices that illustrate how state and local policies can reverse the usual trends and provide qualified teachers for all students.

Currently, teaching in most parts of the country is faced with the perennial problem it has experienced for centuries: disparities in salaries

FIGURE 5.4. QUALIFICATIONS OF NEWLY HIRED TEACHERS, BY SCHOOL TYPE,[a] 1994

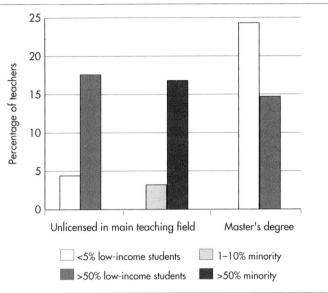

☐ <5% low-income students   ▨ 1–10% minority

▨ >50% low-income students   ■ >50% minority

[a] Newly hired teachers excluding transfers.

Source: Robin R. Henke et al., Schools and Staffing in the United States: A Statistical Profile, 1993–94 (Washington, D.C.: National Center for Educational Statistics, U.S. Department of Education, 1996).

and working conditions, along with a panoply of backward-looking personnel policies, have recreated teacher shortages in central cities and poor rural areas. And, for a variety of reasons, the response of many governments continues to be to lower or eliminate standards for entry rather than to create incentives that will attract and retain an adequate supply of well-prepared teachers. As a consequence, this era is developing an even more sharply bimodal teaching force than ever before. While some children are gaining access to teachers who are more qualified and well-prepared than in years past, a growing number of poor and minority children are being taught by teachers who are sorely unprepared for the task they face. This poses the risk that we may see heightened inequality in opportunities to learn and in outcomes of schooling—with all of the social dangers that implies—at the very time we most need to prepare all students more effectively for the greater challenges they face. If the emerging reforms of schooling are to succeed, and if students are to have a fair shot at meeting the high standards states and districts are increasingly insisting they meet, teaching as an occupation must be able to recruit and retain able and well-prepared individuals for all classrooms, not just the most affluent.

Problems in Hiring Qualified Teachers

The number of newly hired teachers entering the field without adequate training has been increasing in recent years. In 1991, 25 percent of new entrants to public school teaching had not completed the requirements for a state license in their main assignment field. This proportion increased to 27 percent in 1994, including nearly 11 percent who had no license at all in their main field.[32] The least-qualified teachers were most likely to be found in high-poverty and predominantly minority schools and in lower-track classes. In fact, in schools with the highest minority enrollments students had less than a 50 percent chance of getting a science or mathematics teacher who held a license and a degree in the field he or she taught.[33]

On virtually every measure, teachers' qualifications vary by the status of the children they serve. Students in high-poverty schools are not only the least likely to have teachers who are fully qualified, they are also least likely to have teachers with higher levels of education— a master's, specialist, or doctoral degree.[34] Whereas only 8 percent of public school teachers in low-poverty schools taught without at least a minor in their main academic assignment field, fully one-third of teachers in high-poverty schools taught without at least a minor in their main field, and nearly 70 percent taught without at least a minor in their secondary teaching field.[35] This is problematic given the studies that show lower levels of achievement for students whose teachers are not prepared and certified in the subject area they teach.

While hiring statistics show more teachers entering with marginal qualifications, about 17 percent of beginning teachers and about 25 percent of all newly hired teachers entered the profession with a master's degree in 1993–94, a substantial increase over a decade earlier.[36] Most of these were prepared in five- or fifth-year programs that add a year of training beyond the bachelor's degree to allow the completion of a major in the field to be taught as well as intensive education coursework and extended student teaching (usually thirty weeks rather than the typical twelve to fifteen weeks). This represents a substantial increase in preparation beyond the traditional four-year education degree for a subset of entering teachers. Graduates of the new five-year program models that resulted from the 1980s reform efforts of the Holmes Group of education deans from research universities have been found to enter and stay in teaching at higher rates and to be more effective than graduates of traditional four-year programs.[37] However, while some of these programs successfully prepare teachers for urban schools (for example, the programs at Trinity University in San Antonio, Texas, University of Cincinnati in Ohio, University of Texas at El Paso, and University of Washington in Seattle), on average the better-prepared recruits are generally less likely to be hired in high-poverty schools (see Figure 5.4). These statistics illustrate the dual standard increasingly characterizing entry to teaching, one that provides teachers of very different qualifications to different students and that exacerbates educational inequalities between the rich and the poor.[38]

This state of affairs is not true everywhere, however. Inequality is most pronounced in the states and districts that have invested the least in preparing and hiring high-quality teachers. In states like Connecticut, Iowa, Minnesota, Montana, and Wisconsin, nearly all teachers hold both full certification and a major in the field they teach, and few if any are hired on emergency credentials.[39] Not surprisingly, students in these states rank at the top of the distribution in mathematics and reading achievement on the National Assessment of Educational Progress. One might speculate that this distribution is largely a function of states' student populations; however, research on the determinants of these outcomes has found that states' levels of student performance are much more strongly predicted by the proportion of well-qualified teachers (those holding full certification plus a major in the field they teach) in the state than by student poverty, language status, or other background variables.[40] As described later, these states have adopted specific policies that have allowed them to provide well-qualified teachers to all students. By contrast, states like Alaska, California, and Louisiana, which rank much lower on overall achievement, have many fewer teachers who are well qualified (that is, who hold certification plus a major in their field) and large numbers of teachers teaching out of field or on emergency credentials.[41] These differently prepared teachers are allocated along class and racial lines.

In addition to the fact that states have widely varying require-ments for licensing, school districts do not always insist on hiring well-qualified teachers. Nationwide, only two-thirds of districts require their new hires to hold at least a college minor in the field to be taught, along with full certification and preparation from a state-approved insti-tution. In some low-scoring states, like Georgia, fewer than half of all districts insist upon these hiring requirements, and these districts serve more advantaged students.[42] In other states, like Iowa, Minnesota, Kentucky, and Wisconsin, almost all of them do. On the other hand, some districts, such as School District 2 in New York City and the dis-trict of New Haven, California, have created comprehensive systems of recruitment, preparation, and induction to ensure that they get and keep the best-qualified teachers, even in difficult labor markets. We describe how they have done this in a later section of this chapter.

RESOURCE DIFFERENTIALS. An ongoing problem in recruiting well-prepared teachers to poor school districts is the continued inequality in funding that plagues American schools. Teacher salaries vary widely across districts and states. For example, average salaries in 1997–98 ranged from $27,839 in South Dakota to $51,727 in Connecticut.[43] Even within a single labor market, there is often a marked difference in teachers' salaries based on the wealth and spending choices of various districts. Typically, teachers in affluent suburban districts earn more than those in central cities or more rural communities within the same area. In 1994, for example, the best-paid teachers in low-poverty schools earned at least 35 percent more than those in high-poverty schools (see Figure 5.5).

Teachers' salaries are not high relative to those of college graduates in other occupations. Of all college graduates, those with education majors generally receive the lowest average starting salaries.[44] This sit-uation is partly a function of how school systems allocate their funds. For example, in the United States only 52 percent of education dollars are spent on instruction and only 43 percent of education staff are class-room teachers. Only 36 percent of education dollars are spent on teach-ers' salaries. In other industrialized nations, about three-fourths of education resources are spent directly on instruction and classroom teachers represent from 60 to 80 percent of all staff. More than half the budget in these countries is spent on a greater number of better-paid and better-prepared teachers.[45]

Figure 5.5. Top Public School Teacher Salaries, by Poverty Status of Students, 1993–94

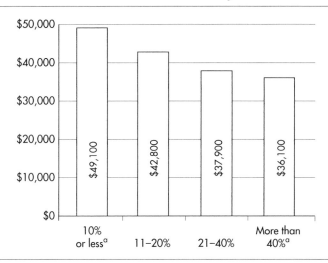

ᵃ Students receiving free/reduced-price lunch.

Source: "America's Teachers: Profile of a Profession, 1993–94," National Center for Education Statistics, U.S. Department of Education, Washington, D.C., 1993.

TRACKING. The practice of tracking is another well-documented phenomenon that contributes to unequal access to educational opportunities for low-income and minority students. A number of studies have found that students placed in lower tracks ultimately achieve less than students of similar aptitude who are placed in academic programs or untracked classes.[46] Tracking persists in the face of growing evidence that it tends not to benefit high achievers and puts low achievers at a serious disadvantage.[47] This is in part because good teaching is a scarce resource that tends to get allocated to the students whose parents or advocates have the most political clout. In addition, teachers who are adequately prepared to use the wide variety of strategies needed to succeed with diverse learners are relatively few. Evidence suggests that teachers themselves are tracked, with those judged to be the most competent and experienced assigned to the top tracks.[48] Within a school the more expert experienced teachers, who are in great demand, are rewarded with opportunities to teach the most enriched curricula to the most advantaged students. Meanwhile, underprepared and inexperienced teachers are often assigned to the students whom others do not care to teach, which leaves them practicing on the students who would bene-fit most from highly skilled teachers.

Although part of the reason for curriculum differentiation is the strongly held belief that only some students can profit from a chal-lenging curriculum, another reason for the restricted access to the more rigorous courses is the scarcity of teachers who can teach in the fashion such a curriculum demands. This was the case at one very diverse school that tried to "detrack" its mathematics curriculum. The school had offered a rote-oriented curriculum to most students and a conceptually oriented program to selected students. Despite a short-lived effort to offer the more advanced program to all students, after a few years the school returned to a tracked system, in which most white students received a substantially more challenging curriculum than most stu-dents of color. The principal explained that most of the teachers found the more conceptual curriculum too difficult to teach; they lacked the mathematics and teaching skills needed to use it well. And so tracking for the students was revived primarily as a means for dealing with unequal capacities of teachers.[49]

In classrooms where teachers are poorly trained, students tend to receive a steady diet of worksheets and rote learning guided by superfi-cial texts. In large part as a function of the limited skills of their teach-ers, students in poor schools and those placed in the lowest tracks too often sit at their desks for long periods of the day, matching the picture in column A to the word in column B, filling in the blanks, copying off the board. They work at a low cognitive level on boring tasks that are not connected to the skills they need to learn. Rarely are they given the opportunity to talk about what they know, to read real books, or to construct and solve problems in mathematics or science.[50] When their teachers do not know other ways to teach, the curriculum students are taught—and what they consequently learn—is quite different from what students learn in schools where good teaching is widespread.

CONDITIONS OF TEACHING. Teaching conditions are also distributed differently across different types of schools and of students. The lower fiscal capacity of inner-city schools that deters qualified teachers is fur-ther compounded by the nonprofessional working conditions many such schools offer, ranging from lower levels of teacher participation in decisionmaking to more dysfunctional administration. Teachers in more advantaged communities have much easier working conditions, including smaller class sizes and pupil loads, and much more control over decisionmaking in their schools.[51] In addition, reforms in teachers' workplace conditions are more evident in schools outside central cities. The uneven pace and distribution of reform across the public school system may contribute to both the causes and the effects of what is becoming a bimodal distribution of teachers.

Between 1988 and 1994, teacher attrition rates climbed from 5.6 percent to 6.6 percent of all teachers.[52] This was partly due to growing retirements and partly due to the continuing high rates of attrition for beginning teachers, more than 30 percent of whom leave within the first five years of teaching.[53] Of those who left, about 27 percent retired, 37 percent left for family or personal reasons, and 26 percent were dissatisfied with teaching or sought another career.[54] Not surprisingly, attrition rates were higher in high-poverty than low-poverty schools, and those who left high-poverty schools were more than twice as likely to leave because of dissatisfaction with teaching as those in low-poverty schools.[55]

Teachers' plans to remain in the profession are highly sensitive to their perceptions of their working conditions. About 33 percent of public school teachers and 49 percent of private school teachers plan to remain in teaching as long as they are able, but these plans are highly dependent on how they feel about administrative support, teacher influence in decisionmaking, faculty cooperation, and resource provision. These professional factors matter even more to teachers in their decisions about where to teach than characteristics of students or communities (see Figure 5.6, page 144).[56]

Control over salient elements of the work environment is also an important factor in teacher retention. Those who left teaching for other employment in 1994 were more satisfied in their new jobs with their influence over policy, professional prestige, resources available, support from administrators, and manageability of work than were current teachers.[57] Many talented teachers leave teaching because their workplaces do not sustain teachers' adaptability, individuality, and the autonomy that they need to teach.[58] Research over the past twenty years shows that most teachers want more opportunities to be involved in decisionmaking, especially in areas of school policy that affect teaching, and this is related to their satisfaction, stress, and loyalty.[59] Yet in 1993–94, fewer than 40 percent of all teachers (and an even smaller proportion of public school teachers) felt they had much influence in determining

FIGURE 5.6. PERCENTAGE OF TEACHERS WHO PLAN TO REMAIN IN TEACHING AS LONG AS THEY ARE ABLE, BY PERCEPTIONS OF THEIR WORK ENVIRONMENTS, 1993–94

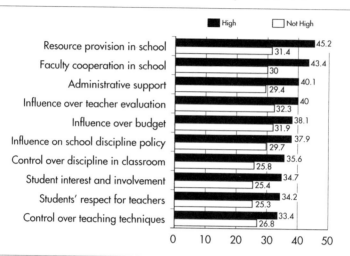

Source: "America's Teachers: Profile of a Profession, 1993–94," National Center for Education Statistics, U.S. Department of Education, Washington, D.C., 1993.

school policies such as curriculum, content of in-service training, or discipline policy.[60] Nearly half of all teachers in 1990 (up from one-quarter in 1987) said they were not satisfied with the control they had over their professional lives.[61] And one out of four first-year teachers in 1990–91 reported that they had to follow rules that conflicted with their best professional judgment—a situation highly correlated with lower levels of commitment and planned retention in teaching.[62]

Teachers in central city schools and those schools with higher minority enrollments are least likely to report having influence over school policies in any category and most likely to believe that they have too little power at the school level.[63] Teachers in high-poverty schools are much less likely than others to say that they have influence over decisions concerning curriculum, texts, materials, or teaching policies. They are also much less likely to be satisfied with their salaries or to feel they have the necessary materials available to them to do their job.[64] This compounds the other disincentives for teaching in these schools—disincentives that include lower salaries and larger class sizes—which feed, in turn, into the disparities in teacher qualifications and teaching quality that students in different schools experience.[65]

In cities that have mandated the use of "teacher-proof curricula" in the form of highly detailed, prescribed lesson plans, curriculum packages, scripted lessons, pacing schedules, and the like, the disincentives for attracting and retaining thoughtful teachers have been noted in a number of studies.[66] While untrained teachers sometimes welcome scripted lessons, better-prepared teachers complain that they cannot meet the nonstandardized needs of their students if they are constrained by highly prescribed curricula that are based on unvarying assumptions about when, how, and how quickly individual students will learn particular material. In recent years, such curriculum controls have been reinstated in Chicago, Washington, D.C., and Philadelphia (after similar programs were abandoned in the 1980s). Anecdotal evidence suggests that these efforts have encouraged some talented teachers to leave these districts. Similar disincentives for responsive teaching can occur if schools use scripted teaching programs, such as the most prescriptive versions of Open Court's reading program, as mandates rather than as tools that can be adapted to support instruction for different students.

Finally, there is very different access to the kinds of mentoring supports that new teachers need, especially in challenging environments. Traditionally, the newest teachers are assigned to the neediest schools and students and are left, without mentoring, to sink or swim. Many leave after a short time, and others learn to cope rather than to teach effectively.[67] The good news is that some states are creating induction programs to provide mentoring and support for beginning teachers. Among teachers with less than five years of experience, 55 percent report that they experienced some kind of formal induction program during their first year of teaching.[68] By contrast, only 16 to 17 percent of teachers with more than ten years of experience had had such help when they entered the profession.[69]

Like all other education policies, however, access to high-quality induction programs varies widely across the country. More than three-quarters of beginners report having experienced induction supports in states that put such programs in place several years ago—Connecticut, Florida, Indiana, Kentucky, Missouri, North Carolina, Oklahoma, and Pennsylvania. However, in states like Rhode Island and Massachusetts that have relied on local initiatives, fewer than 15 percent of beginning teachers have received any kind of systematic mentoring. Inner-city schools with stretched resources and disproportionate numbers of in-experienced teachers (and commensurately fewer expert veterans) are least likely to offer adequate mentoring supports.

Meanwhile, professional development investments are often paltry, and most districts' offerings, limited to "hit and run" workshops, do not help teachers learn the sophisticated teaching strategies they need to address very challenging learning goals with very diverse populations of students. And teachers have little time to learn from one another. In U.S. schools, most teachers have only three to five hours a week in which to prepare their lessons, usually in isolation from their colleagues. They rarely have opportunities to plan or collaborate with other teach-ers, to observe and study teaching, or to talk together about how to improve curriculum and meet the needs of students.

In combination, these findings intersect with a growing body of research on teacher efficacy, retention, and commitment that suggests that retaining and supporting effective teachers will require restructur-ing schools to provide teachers with greater administrative supports, more decisionmaking input and control over their work, more useful feedback and opportunities for collegial work, and provision of mater-ial resources and supports.[70]

District Management Also Matters

While there are labor force issues and resource inequities that often put urban school systems at a disadvantage, the ways in which districts choose to organize their efforts and use their resources also matter greatly. Districts' hiring practices strongly affect the quantity and quality of teach-ers in the labor pool and the distribution of teachers to different types of school systems. Studies have found that some districts hire unqualified teachers for reasons other than shortages, including out-and-out patron-age; a desire to save money on salaries by hiring low-cost, less qualified recruits; and beliefs that more-qualified teachers are more likely to leave and less likely to take orders.[71] A RAND Corporation study, for example, found that many districts emphasize teachers' ability to "fit in" and their willingness to comply with local edicts rather than their professional expertise.[72] When these and other new teachers leave in frustration because they are underprepared for teaching and undersupported by the current induction practices, the hiring scramble begins all over again.

Furthermore, many school districts fail to hire the most qualified and highly ranked teachers in their applicant pool because they have inadequate management information systems and antiquated hiring procedures that discourage or lose good applicants in a sea of paperwork.[73] These problems are particularly likely to occur in large, urban districts. Reports of vacancies and information on candidates are not always accessible to district decisionmakers. Hiring procedures are often cumbersome and bureaucratic, sometimes including fifty or more discrete steps that take many months to complete. Candidates repeatedly have their files lost, fail to receive responses to repeated requests for information, cannot secure interviews, and cannot get timely notice of job availability. Late budget notification from state or city governments and union contracts requiring placement of all internal teacher transfers prior to hiring of new candidates can put off hiring decisions until August or September, by which time candidates have decided to take other jobs. As a result of these inefficiencies, large, urban districts often lose good candidates to other districts and to nonteaching jobs.[74]

Other state and school district practices also can undermine high-quality teacher recruitment and development. For example:

- Many states will not accept licenses from other states without requiring new fees, tests, and often redundant course requirements. The lack of reciprocity makes it hard to get teachers from states with surpluses to those with shortages. Many districts will not hire veterans with more than seven to ten years of experience.

- Most impose a cap on salaries they offer experienced candidates; as a consequence, highly educated and experienced teachers often find themselves passed over in favor of inexperienced and even uncertified teachers. Some are forced to take a cut in pay if they move to a new locality and want to continue to teach. Many end up leaving the profession.

- Few districts provide reimbursement for travel and moving expenses.

- Many districts place beginning teachers in the most difficult schools with the highest rates of teacher turnover, the greatest numbers of inexperienced staff, and the least capacity to support teacher growth and development. Without induction supports, many teachers leave.

Just as policies can create shortages, they also can eliminate them. Case studies of urban districts that are successful in hiring the teachers they most want and need have found that they have developed pro-active outreach systems for recruiting from local colleges and from other regional and national sources, streamlined personnel systems using sophisticated information technology to make information about vacancies available to candidates and information about candidates readily available to decisionmakers, and developed systems for predicting teacher demand and making offers early in the spring, as well as strategies for ensuring that those who receive offers are made to feel welcome, wanted, and well-inducted into the school district.[75]

WHAT ARE THE ALTERNATIVES?

While there are many challenges in recruiting teachers to urban and rural schools, education policy can make a difference. For example, in the post-Sputnik years, highly focused teacher recruitment programs created new pathways for attracting and preparing teaching talent (for example, the National Defense Education Act of the 1950s and the Education Professions Development Act of the 1960s). During the early 1970s, the federal Career Opportunities Program provided a total of $129 million to support fifteen thousand teacher aides on pathways into teaching and the Urban Teachers Corps. Federal support also created Masters of Arts in Teaching programs and supported pathways for college graduates into teacher preparation and teaching. National Science Foundation initiatives in the 1960s and 1970s targeted the preparation and recruitment of mathematics and science teachers. In part because of these programs, shortages of teachers that began to appear in the 1960s were eliminated by the 1970s. In more recent years, many states and districts have overcome teacher shortages even in central cities. Proactive policy can make a difference in the availability of qualified teachers to all schools.

Subsidies for High-Quality Training

An important point to consider when solving problems related to the supply of qualified teachers is that better-prepared teachers enter and stay in teaching at much higher rates than those who are less prepared.

For example, studies suggest that teachers from five-year programs have entry and retention rates significantly higher than those from four-year undergraduate programs, who in turn have retention rates significantly higher than those from short-term alternative or emergency certification programs. These differences are so substantial that it is actually less expensive to prepare a teacher in a high-quality program—once the costs of preparation, recruitment, induction, and replacement due to turnover are taken into account—than to train a teacher through a quick route that will leave her underprepared and vulnerable to dropping out of the profession (see Figure 5.7).

Lowering the financial and opportunity costs of acquiring teacher preparation is one means to improve recruitment, particularly for minority students. Although the funding for federal recruitment programs was discontinued in the early 1980s, some states created their own recruitment incentives when demand for teachers began to grow again in the late 1980s. One such initiative is the North Carolina Teaching Fellows program. The Fellows program, funded by the state legislature at $8 million a year, provides $20,000 service scholarships to four hundred highly able high school seniors a year who enroll in intensive

FIGURE 5.7. AVERAGE RETENTION RATES FOR DIFFERENT PATHWAYS INTO TEACHING

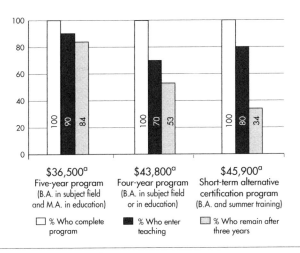

$36,500[a]
Five-year program
(B.A. in subject field
and M.A. in education)

$43,800[a]
Four-year program
(B.A. in subject field
or in education)

$45,900[a]
Short-term alternative
certification program
(B.A. and summer training)

☐ % Who complete
program

■ % Who enter
teaching

▨ % Who remain after
three years

[a] Estimated cost per third-year teacher per program.

Source: Linda Darling-Hammond, *Solving the Dilemmas of Teacher Supply, Demand, and Quality* (New York: National Commission on Teaching and America's Future, 2000).

teacher education programs throughout the state. These programs include special coursework and summer programs in addition to the usual preparation teaching entrants would receive. The fellows do not have to pay back their scholarships if they teach for at least four years in North Carolina schools. The program has recruited more than four thousand fellows to teaching—a disproportionate number of them males and minorities and many in high-need fields like math and science and in urban school districts.

A recent study of the program found that 75 percent of all fellows had completed their four-year obligation and were still teaching in the public schools.[76] In another recent evaluation, principals reported that the fellows' first-year classroom performance far exceeded that of other new teachers in every area assessed. The fellows, who had had more extensive preparation than most other new teachers in areas relating to student diversity and assessment, felt that their teacher education programs had prepared them well for the multiple and demanding roles they play as teachers. They stressed both the importance of this preparation and a desire for additional learning opportunities.[77]

Some urban districts have pursued their own recruitment initiatives for teacher preparation. In recent years, New York City—once a hiring source for thousands of unlicensed teachers annually—has worked to ensure qualified teachers for all of its students by streamlining hiring procedures and aggressively recruiting well-prepared teachers through partnerships with local universities. In 1997, New York filled two-thirds of its fifty-five hundred vacancies with fully qualified teachers, whereas in 1992 it had filled only one-third of a smaller number of positions with qualified teachers. During these years the number of uncertified teachers in the city was decreased by more than half.

Key to this success are a series of efforts that bring the city's recruiters directly to students in local preparation programs each spring; offer interviews and tests on college campuses; recruit teachers in high-need areas like bilingual and special education by offering them scholarships and forgivable loans to complete their training; work with universities and local districts to bring well-trained prospective teachers into hard-to-staff schools as student teachers, interns, and visitors; make offers to well-qualified candidates much earlier in the year; and streamline the exchange of information and the processing of applications. More efforts are under way to create automated systems for projecting vacancies and processing information, to decentralize interviews to principals and committees of teachers in local schools, and to strengthen partnerships with local colleges.

Salaries

Clearly, recruitment into teaching is also a function of the competitiveness of wages and other job benefits. In fact, based on his research in Texas, Ron Ferguson argues that districts with greater numbers of low-income and minority students need to pay a higher salary to attract the same quality of teachers as districts with students from more affluent families.[78] In recent years, a few districts have experimented with bonuses or added salary increments to attract recruits for fields with shortages or for hard-to-staff schools; however, only about 10 percent of all school districts are trying any of these strategies (see Figure 5.8, page 152).

There is little evidence about the effectiveness of most of these targeted efforts. In his research on what are sometimes called "combat pay" programs, James Bruno found that incentives such as paying bonuses to teachers in hard-to-staff schools are not sufficient to retain them or enhance their teaching. Rather, combat pay programs "tend to be superficial approaches to a problem that demands careful study to determine why teachers are leaving certain schools in the first place."[79] Bruno identifies several problems that have resulted from this strategy: draining teachers from similar schools that do not qualify for combat pay; district difficulties in maintaining the financial obligation over time (particularly once any special funding for the program has expired); and the lack of support and supervision after teachers are hired to ensure that the goals of the program—teacher retention and instructional improvement—are being met. He concluded that if teacher support and classroom performance are not addressed as well, combat pay or similar programs based on financial compensation will not be successful in improving students' education.

A more systematic approach seeks to address teacher salaries and supports through reallocation of state resources. One major cause of teacher shortages in cities and poor rural districts is that few states have equalized school funding or teachers' salaries so that districts can compete equally in the market for well-prepared teachers. Having experienced severe shortages of qualified teachers in its cities for more than two decades, Connecticut sought to rectify this situation in 1986. With

FIGURE 5.8. PERCENTAGE OF PUBLIC SCHOOL DISTRICTS THAT OFFERED VARIOUS FINANCIAL INCENTIVES TO RECRUIT AND RETAIN TEACHERS IN LESS DESIRABLE LOCATIONS OR IN FIELDS OF SHORTAGE, 1987–88 AND 1993–94

Less Desirable Locations

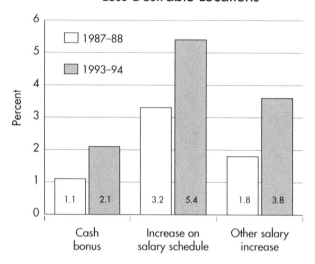

Fields of Shortage

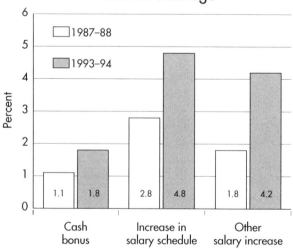

Source: "America's Teachers: Profile of a Profession, 1993–94," National Center for Education Statistics, U.S. Department of Education, Washington, D.C., 1993.

a major investment through its Educational Enhancement Act, Connecticut spent over $300 million in 1986 to boost minimum beginning teacher salaries for qualified teachers in an equalizing fashion that allocated more funds to needy districts than to wealthy ones. This made it possible for low-wealth districts to compete in the market for qualified teachers and for all districts to offer market-competitive wages. This initiative eliminated teacher shortages in the state, even in the cities, and created surpluses of teachers within three years. At the same time, the state raised licensing and teacher education standards, instituted performance-based examinations for licensing and a state-funded mentoring program for beginning teachers, required teachers to earn a master's degree in education for a continuing license, invested in training for mentors, and supported new professional development strategies in universities and school districts. Since then, Connecticut has posted significant gains in state rankings, becoming one of the top-scoring states in the nation in mathematics and reading despite an increase in the proportion of students with special needs during the 1990s.[80] Equalization of salaries and improvements in teacher education and induction have led to similar reductions in teacher shortages and improvements of teacher qualifications in states such as Kentucky and North Carolina as well.[81]

Streamlined Selection and Proactive Recruitment

As noted above, many large districts have hiring procedures that are so cumbersome and dysfunctional that they chase the best-prepared candidates away instead of aggressively recruiting them. Large districts like New York City, Chicago, and Los Angeles with underfunded, non-automated personnel offices may have thousands of qualified candidates annually who are not hired because their files are lost, their calls are not returned, or they become discouraged after waiting months to get an interview. New York City's efforts to address these problems made a major dent in the city's teacher shortage during the late 1990s.

Another glimpse of the possible can be seen in the New Haven Unified School District, located midway between Oakland and San Jose, California, which serves approximately fourteen thousand students from Union City and south Hayward. Three-quarters of these students are minorities, and most of them are from low-income and working-class families. Twenty years ago, the district was the most impoverished district in a low-income county, and it had a reputation to match. Families who could manage to do so sent their children elsewhere to school. Today, the New Haven Unified School District, while still a low-income district, has a well-deserved reputation for excellent schools—despite its lower per pupil expenditures than many surrounding districts. Every one of its ten schools has been designated a California Distinguished School. All have student achievement levels well above California norms for similar schools. The district has had to close its doors to out-of-district transfers because schools are bulging at the seams. Still, families try every trick in the book to establish a New Haven district address because they know their children will be well taught.

When school districts across California scrambled in recent years to hire qualified teachers, often failing to do so, New Haven had in place an aggressive recruitment system and a high-quality training program with local universities that allowed it to continue its long-term habit of hiring well-prepared and committed teachers from diverse backgrounds to staff its schools.[82] One factor in this success is that New Haven spends the lion's share of its budget on teachers' salaries. But the efficient recruitment system is also instrumental in maintaining a high-quality teaching staff. For example, while nearby Oakland spends substantially more money per pupil, New Haven's beginning teacher salaries are nearly one-third higher. And as Oakland hires large numbers of unqualified teachers as its dysfunctional personnel operations keep many qualified teachers from entering the system,[83] New Haven's personnel office uses technology and a wide range of teacher supports to recruit from a national pool of exceptional teachers. Its website posts all vacancies and draws inquiries from around the country. Each inquiry receives an immediate e-mail response. With the use of electronic information transfer (for example, the personnel office can send vacancy information directly to candidates and applicant files to the desktop of any administrator electronically), the district can provide information to potential applicants that urban districts might never think would be available to them. Viable applicants are interviewed within days in person or via video-conference (through a local Kinko's), and if they are well qualified with strong references, they may be offered a job that same day. Despite the horror stories one often hears about the difficulty of out-of-state teachers earning a California teaching credential, New Haven's credential analyst in the personnel office has yet to lose a teacher recruited from out of state in the state's credentialing maze.

Mentoring and Induction for Beginning Teachers

Another significant strategy for recruiting teachers to the New Haven Unified School District is its long-term investment in teacher education. The district was one of the first in the state to implement a Beginning Teacher Support and Assessment Program that provides support for teachers in their first two years in the classroom. All beginning teachers receive support from trained mentors who are given a lighter teaching load to free-up enough released time for this responsibility. Many beginning teachers report that they chose to teach in New Haven because of the availability of this strong support for their initial years in the profession. In addition, with the California State University at Hayward, the district designed an innovative teacher education program that combines college coursework and an intensive internship conducted under the close supervision of school-based educators. Because interns function as student teachers who work in the classrooms of master teachers rather than as independent teachers of record, the program simultaneously educates teachers while protecting students from untrained novices and providing quality education. The fruits of these efforts show in New Haven's steadily rising student achievement as well as its success in finding and keeping good teachers.

New Haven's investment in mentoring beginning teachers has been replicated elsewhere, with similar results. The number of teachers who participated in formal induction programs almost doubled during the decade from 1981 to 1991 and more than tripled since the early 1970s.[84] By 1991, 48 percent of all teachers with fewer than three years' experience and 54 percent of public school teachers had participated in some kind of induction program during their first year. Depending on how the programs are designed and the kinds of supports they provide, these induction initiatives may make a substantial difference in teacher recruitment and retention.

The importance of mentors to new teachers is now well documented in research on induction and learning to teach.[85] When teacher educators were surveyed about critical issues in teacher education in 1989, the issue ranked highest was the need for mentoring beginning teachers during their first year of practice.[86] Teachers of all experience levels agree on the importance of supervised induction. When asked what would have been most helpful in their first years of teaching, 47 percent of respondents in a Metropolitan Life survey of teachers said a skilled, experienced teacher assigned to provide advice and assistance and 39 percent said more practical training, such as a year's internship before having their own classroom.[87] In addition to providing vital guidance and learning for new teachers, teacher mentoring reduces the attrition of beginning teachers from the profession.[88]

The likelihood that mentor programs will have these salutary effects depends on how they are designed. Across the country, mentor programs vary in the amount of resources they provide for participating teachers. Some are unfunded and voluntary, and mentors and participants consult on their own time. Others provide compensation for the mentor in the form of additional pay and release time. In some districts, mentors are released from classroom responsibilities full- or part-time for one or two years. In other districts, mentors and beginning teachers are provided a limited amount of release time, so they can visit and observe in each others' classrooms.

Previous research on state-level teacher induction programs shows major differences in the strategies adopted during the 1980s. While places like California and Connecticut funded mentor programs, many other first-wave induction programs focused on evaluation rather than mentoring, requiring new teachers to pass an observational evaluation before they received a continuing license. Most such programs did not fund mentoring, and the mandated evaluation strategies typically rated new teachers on how well they demonstrated a predetermined list of behaviors rather than on whether they developed effective practices appropriate to their contexts and content areas. Since then, more states and districts have sought to create programs that support new teachers in the guided development of good practice through mentoring and self-assessment that promote higher levels of effectiveness.[89]

Successful programs allow mentors to be flexible in addressing the individual needs of each new teacher. Gayle Wilkinson surveyed first-year teachers about their needs for assistance in planning lessons and for help with classroom procedures, teaching methods, making difficult decisions, and making decisions about discipline.[90] She found that new teachers had very diverse responses regarding the amount of assistance they desired in these categories. Instead of a prescriptive induction program,

Wilkinson recommends programs that are designed to "accommodate beginning teachers who are developmentally at different stages, who have different needs and require various types of assistance."[91] This recommendation is supported by Terry Wildman and colleagues who studied 150 mentor-beginner pairs and concluded that the diversity of contexts for mentoring requires flexibility in mentors' roles, which should not be overly prescribed. They conclude that "[m]entoring, like good teaching, should be defined by those who carry it out."[92]

There is no one formula for mentoring, but successful models have some common features. Connecticut's statewide induction program, Beginning Educator Support and Training (BEST), which began in 1986, is designed with a three-tiered training model for mentors to accommodate their different degrees of prior mentoring experience. The BEST program also includes an assessment component, which ultimately determines licensure for new teachers. From the beginning, BEST has involved classroom teachers in the planning and development of the program. Teachers serve both as mentors and evaluators, but different people serve each function. The fact that mentors are responsible for helping teachers develop classroom competencies that will ultimately be observed and assessed creates an incentive for the recruitment and selection committee to choose strong mentors.[93] Mentoring in the BEST program provides many different kinds of assistance to new teachers. Mentors confer with beginners, demonstrate lessons, model strategies, and observe and are observed by the beginners. University-based seminars designed to help each new cohort of beginning teachers understand the state standards and assessments—and the teaching they call for—are also now a part of the beginning teacher program. An emphasis is placed on reflection in the seminars as well as in the mentoring program; a recent study found that "the thinking of both the beginning teacher and the mentor is enhanced as they 'puzzle about' and discover reasons for classroom decisions together."[94]

The BEST program serves a vital role for the mentors as well as the beginners: "New opportunities for professional growth, specifically in developing analytical, reflective, and communication skills, have been cited by nearly all mentors as having had a major impact on their perception of themselves and as having improved their teaching."[95] Extremely low attrition of beginning teachers in Connecticut contributes to continuing surpluses; and the state has eliminated the revolving door that had once required the state to replace large numbers of teachers each year.

Connecticut's practice of establishing cohort groups comprised of new teachers is supported by research suggesting that novice teachers benefit from working with other novices to solve problems collabora-tively as well as to develop a sense of solidarity with others in similar cir-cumstances.[96] Providing opportunities for beginning teachers to observe skilled veterans as well as to be observed by them is another important component of new teacher induction. It combats the isolation that has traditionally kept teachers from growing professionally while fostering norms of collegiality and continual learning.[97] Leslie Huling-Austin reports that when mentors discuss their practices with novices, it is important for them to make their thought process explicit.[98] She and others also recommend that new teachers should be paired with men-tors of the same grade level or subject if possible. This enables new teachers to pursue specific questions about content.[99]

One local program that includes these features is the Los Angeles Unified School District's partnership with California State University, Dominguez Hills, a program that focuses on the retention of new teach-ers in two low-income regions of the school district that suffered from high annual teacher attrition rates (in many years, attrition rates were in excess of 50 percent).[100] In this program, lead teachers were selected based on experience, excellence in teaching, and leadership, as well as their abilities to be nurturing and nonjudgmental.[101] These lead teach-ers were trained in observation and coaching, so they were able to pro-vide feedback and support confidentially. They did not have an evaluative role. Each lead teacher was matched with two to four teach-ers in their first or second year of teaching based on common grade level and subject area as well as classroom proximity. The teams met every week to plan together and solve problems collaboratively. Teacher teams, including the lead teacher, enrolled together in specially designed university classes; lead teachers were thus able to help the new teachers implement the strategies they learned there.

This program included a provision for stipends to be paid to all participants for work during noncontract hours. The costs of the uni-versity courses were also covered. The program costs were justified by research that has shown that "the most cost effective projects provided high-intensity assistance by experienced teachers who were paid for their time."[102] After three years of this program, over 95 percent of the beginning teachers who participated were still teaching (89 percent remained in their original districts) and only 1 percent had left teaching.[103] In addition, the quality of teaching among new teachers was positively affected. An evaluation of the project found that "project beginning teachers used more effective instructional planning practices, provided more learning opportunities for students, and had higher student engagement rates than non-project participants."[104]

Several other urban districts have created models of beginning-teacher induction and career-long learning that have been replicated with significant success in other urban settings. Peer review and assistance programs initiated by the American Federation of Teachers (AFT) and the National Education Association (NEA) locals in Toledo, Cincinnati, and Columbus, Ohio; Rochester, New York; and Seattle, Washington, are successful in helping beginners learn to teach. They also have helped veterans who are having difficulty either to improve their teaching or to leave the classroom without union grievances or delays. Each program was established through collective bargaining and is governed by a panel of seven to ten teachers and administrators. The governing panel selects consulting teachers through a rigorous evaluation process that examines teaching skills and mentoring abilities. The panel also approves the assignment to intervention status (through self-referrals or referrals made by principals) of tenured teachers who are having difficulty, and it oversees appraisals of beginning and intervention teachers.

New teachers are designated *interns*, and they receive close mentoring from an expert consulting teacher who also evaluates them to determine if their employment contract will be renewed and if they will advance to the *residency* level. A less than satisfactory rating leads either to a second year of assistance or to termination. A satisfactory evaluation is needed to move up on the salary schedule. Consulting teachers are given release time so they can focus on this job. This ensures that they are able to provide extensive help and to document problems and progress over the course of a full academic year. They are selected for teaching excellence and generally matched by subject area and grade level with the teachers they are to help, which increases the value of the advice offered and the credibility of the judgment rendered.

Since the program began, overall attrition of beginning teachers has decreased and beginners become much more competent sooner. In

Rochester, for example, retention of interns is 90 percent, as compared with only 60 percent of beginners before the program was put in place. In Cincinnati, attrition of beginning teachers has been about 5 percent annually since the program was put into effect.[105]

Incentives for Expanding and Sharing Knowledge and Skills

In addition to mentoring supports, the Career-in-Teaching programs in Rochester, New York, and Cincinnati, Ohio, provide incentives to retain expert veteran teachers in the profession, to improve teachers' professional growth opportunities, and to give teachers broader roles and responsibilities that will improve student achievement and develop better schools. The program provides supports for learning, evaluation based on professional standards, and salary incentives. Teachers advance in their career in a series of steps—intern, resident, career teacher, and lead teacher—as they gain and demonstrate growing expertise.

After a new teacher graduates from intern status and is tenured, he or she becomes a resident teacher. Over the next three to four years, resident teachers develop their teaching skills and become active in professional decisionmaking. In Cincinnati, a formal evaluation by the principal is required at the third and fifth years, when the teacher applies for career status and tenure. Those who wish to can apply for lead teacher status after seven or more years. Lead teachers are not only excellent teachers, they also know how to mentor adults and facilitate school change. They serve as consulting teachers for beginners and veteran teachers who are having difficulty, as curriculum developers, as clinical faculty who work with student teachers in the districts' teacher education partnerships with local schools of education, and as leaders for school-based initiatives, all while continuing their own teaching.

To become a lead teacher in Rochester, candidates must provide confidential recommendations from five colleagues, including teachers and principals. Specific positions as mentors, curriculum designers, and project facilitators come with stipends ranging from 5 to 15 percent of total salaries—a range of about $3,000 to about $9,000. About thirty Rochester teachers are currently lead teachers. In Cincinnati, salary increments for lead teachers range from $4,500 to $5,000. About three hundred of Cincinnati's three thousand teachers have passed the rigorous evaluation process to attain lead teacher status—four to six classroom observations by expert teachers, interviews of colleagues about the applicant, and an extensive application that reveals the candidate's philosophy and experience.

The creation of these positions and processes also produces professional accountability for the overall quality of the teaching force. Although many claim it is impossible truly to evaluate teachers or get rid of those who are incompetent, these districts have transformed old, nonfunctional systems of teacher evaluation into peer review systems that improve teaching performance and counsel out those who should not be in the profession.

In each city, more teachers have been given help and have made major improvements in their teaching and more teachers have been dismissed than ever had occurred under the old systems of administrative review. In Cincinnati, roughly one-third of the teachers referred to intervention each year have left teaching by the end of the year through resignation, retirement, or dismissal. In Columbus, where a similar program was initiated, about 150 teachers (approximately 2 percent of the teaching force) were assigned to intervention over an eight-year period. Of those, about 20 percent retired or resigned; the other 80 percent have improved substantially. During the first five years of the program in Cincinnati, 61 percent of teacher dismissals for performance reasons resulted from peer review, as compared with 39 percent from evaluation by administrators. Five percent of beginning teachers under peer review were dismissed, as compared with 1.6 percent of those evaluated by principals. Of 60 Rochester teachers assigned to the Intervention Program since 1988, about 10 percent determined through their work with lead teacher mentors that they should leave the profession. (Rochester teachers may request the assistance of a lead teacher mentor voluntarily through the Professional Support Program, which has served about one hundred teachers each year since 1991.)

While some reformers have advocated the removal of teacher tenure as a means of getting rid of poor teachers, research suggests that these efforts to create a more accountable teaching force are more productive for retaining good teachers and weeding out poor ones than the removal of tenure would be.

Tenure provides not a guarantee of employment but protection against dismissal without cause. Statistics indicate that teacher dismissal rates are not correlated with the existence of tenure. The districts described above use focused evaluation to remove teachers who are not competent despite tenure. Meanwhile districts that have no collective bargaining or formal tenure generally do not evaluate many teachers out of the profession. The critical variable is the existence of a productive evaluation system that provides expertise and time for performance review and assistance while protecting due process.

Furthermore tenure provides an attraction to teaching that still operates: Tenure was introduced to provide protections for competent teachers against dismissal for political, patronage, and financial reasons—reasons that are still salient, especially in many highly politicized urban districts. Prior to tenure, it was not uncommon for administrators or school board members to dismiss a teacher in order to save money by hiring a less experienced one, to enforce a political ideology, or to place a friend or relative in the job instead. Whereas the removal of tenure could cost competent teachers their jobs, effective evaluation of the kind described above should push out incompetent teachers while maintaining protections for others who are doing an effective job.

When teachers take on the task of assuring professional accountability for themselves and their peers, it not only improves instruction but it profoundly changes the roles of teachers' unions. Rather than protecting incompetent teachers, unions take responsibility for assuring quality. "We can't legitimately protect teachers who are not performing," says Denise Hewitt, a Cincinnati Federation of Teachers member and director of Cincinnati's Peer Review Panel. At the same time, the improvements in teaching can sometimes be striking. According to Cincinnati consulting teacher Jim Byerly, "We had a teacher who was in intervention ten years ago, who . . . had considerable skills and experience but she had gotten lazy. . . . She needed to start planning the lessons and stick to them and do the hands-on stuff that was needed. . . . Her final appraisal was strong, better than average. I think she felt empowered by the outcome. She went on to be a lead teacher."[106] In addition, the chance to contribute to the profession in this way gives lead teachers a new lease on their own professional lives, while their work improves teaching quality throughout the district. The result is a career model that promotes the recruitment and retention of talented teachers while increasing professionwide knowledge and skill.

Redesigning Schools to Support Teaching and Learning

A final critical area for recruiting and retaining excellent teachers is the restructuring of school organizations and of teaching work, including a reallocation of personnel and resources so that teachers have time to work intensively with students and collaboratively with one another. Teaching in large, bureaucratic settings that do not enable teachers to come to know their students well or to work and plan with other teachers is exhausting work with few rewards. It is especially counterproductive in urban areas where students face many challenges and need a great deal of personal attention. Large, warehouse high schools in which teachers see 150 or more students daily, cycling anonymously through the classroom in fragmented forty-five-minute periods, create alienation and anomie because they support neither learning nor teaching well.

For more than thirty years, studies of school organization consistently have found that small schools (with enrollments of roughly three hundred to five hundred) promote higher student achievement, higher attendance, lower dropout rates, greater participation in school activities, more positive feelings toward self and school, more positive behavior, less violence and vandalism, and greater postschool success.[107] These outcomes also are found in settings where students have close sustained relationships with a smaller than average number of teachers throughout their school careers.[108] This can be achieved when teachers work for longer periods of time with smaller total numbers of students, either by teaching a core curriculum to one or two groups of students rather than a single subject to several groups or by teaching the same students for more than one year. Schools in which students remain with a cohort of their peers also foster a sense of community and a set of continuing relationships that are important to learning and to the affiliations needed to sustain trust and effort.

Evidence shows that better outcomes are achieved by "personal-communal" school models that foster common learning experiences, opportunities for cooperative work and continual relationships, and greater participation of parents, teachers, and students.[109] A recent study of 820 high schools in the National Education Longitudinal Study database found that schools that had restructured to personalize education and develop collaborative learning structures for adults and students produced significantly higher achievement gains that also were distributed much more equitably.[110] Their practices included keeping students in the same homeroom or advisory group throughout high school, establishing smaller school units through school-within-a-school structures, forming interdisciplinary teaching teams, giving teachers common planning time, involving staff in schoolwide problem solving, involving parents, and fostering cooperative learning. Not incidentally, schools with these features have lower teacher turnover and are easier to staff, regardless of the neighborhood or students they serve, since they provide teachers the opportunity to be successful.

Developing such schools requires rethinking organizational forms and norms that have developed over many decades. In contrast to European and Asian countries, which allocate 60 to 80 percent of their education personnel to classroom teaching, the extremely bureaucratic organization of U.S. schools means that only about 43 percent of education staff are regularly assigned as classroom teachers. This allocation of staff and resources to the periphery of the classroom maintains high class sizes and pupil loads for teachers and reduces their opportunity to plan and work together (see Figure 5.9). Successful urban schools not only have changed curriculum, assessments, and schedules to focus on providing longer periods of time for in-depth learning and teaching, they also have developed new patterns of staffing and resource use, including greater investments in teaching and technology rather

FIGURE 5.9. PROPORTIONS OF STAFF, BY FUNCTIONAL AREA

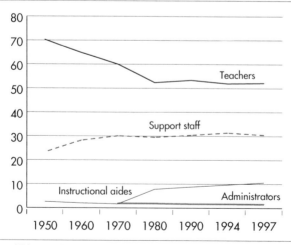

Source: *Digest of Education Statistics, 1996* (Washington, D.C.: National Center for Education Statistics, U.S. Department of Education, 1996), Table 81.

than in nonteaching functions.[111] In order to afford both smaller pupil loads for teachers and greater time for collegial work, these schools assign to the classroom more of the staff who in other schools work in pull-out programs and administrative and support roles.

All the strategies described above have been used in the more than one hundred new, small, restructured high schools in New York City that have been created since 1990 to replace failing comprehensive high schools. The new schools often create interdisciplinary teams of teachers who share students, and they establish block schedules that reduce teachers' pupil loads while creating more shared planning time. In one model, each teacher teaches two classes (either humanities or math/science) that meet for nearly two hours daily, four times per week. With class sizes of around 20 students, teachers have a total pupil load of 40 instead of the 160 to 170 students most New York City high school teachers face. Virtually everyone in the school works directly with students: about 75 percent of all staff are engaged full-time in classroom teaching, and 100 percent teach part-time or lead advisories—small groups of students who meet weekly with teacher advisers. This compares with the usual 55 percent of staff engaged in teaching in a large traditional high school. Teachers have about seven hours a week to plan together in addition to five hours of individual "prep" time. The codirectors (school leaders) teach some classes and counsel students in advisories. There are no guidance counselors, attendance officers, assistant principals, supervisors, or department heads, and few security guards are needed because students are so well known. Studies have found that attendance, grades, graduation rates, and the number of college-bound students are all higher in these restructured schools than in the traditional schools they are replacing.[112] In addition, teachers want to teach in these restructured schools. Whereas traditionally structured schools in these inner-city neighborhoods remain difficult to staff, these schools have a surplus of new and experienced teachers eager to teach in settings where they and their students are likely to succeed.

Recruiting School Leaders

Developing and leading the types of schools discussed here requires, in turn, efforts to recruit and train school principals who understand both the nature of good instruction and the strategies for developing collaborative organizations. Principals are gatekeepers of reform in schools. If schools are to become genuine learning organizations, school leaders must have a deep understanding of teaching and learning, for adults as well as children. In a learning organization, the primary job of management is professional development, which is concerned with the basic human resources of the enterprise and people's capacities to do the central job of the organization. For all members of the organization, that job is teaching and learning. To lead the schools of the future, principals will need to know how to nurture a collaborative environment that fosters continual self-assessment. Time and again, teachers confirm that the capacity of the school principal to lead in this way is critical to their desire to stay in a given school.

Successful efforts to recruit and train teachers and principals are embedded within the strategy of reform embraced by New York City's Community School District 2.[113] Far from seeing administrators as bureaucrats, the superintendent of District 2 expects all administrators to be instructional leaders in the schools. To develop this capacity, principals, like teachers, are engaged in mentoring and peer coaching, support and study groups, and opportunities for professional growth and learning.[114] With these supports, the principalship becomes an intellectual and personal challenge that can be satisfying and successful because it is supported, stemming the extraordinary attrition of urban principals. In addition, District 2 explicitly recruits excellent teachers with leadership abilities into principal training programs, paying for their credential programs and proactively grooming them for the job. This strategy both ensures that the people entering the principalships have the capacity to be credible and effective instructional leaders and that such individuals are given the supports and encouragement to make the transition into this challenging and critical job. With proactive policies for recruiting and supporting both high-quality teachers and principals, District 2 has become one of the most academically successful of New York's community school districts, even though most of its students are minority and come from low-income families, and a large share of them enter school without speaking English.

PUTTING IT ALL TOGETHER: HOW SUCCESSFUL URBAN SCHOOLS GET AND KEEP GREAT TEACHERS AND PRINCIPALS

The goal of offering caring, competent, and qualified teachers and administrators to all students in all communities is one that requires systemic strategies for improving the functioning of schools and school systems and the preparation of individuals for the real demands of the work. Quick fixes such as truncated training and combat pay have been tried for many decades without addressing the conditions that would prevent shortages in the first place: competitive salaries, proactive and streamlined recruiting that values teachers, preparation and professional development that enables success on the job, and supportive working conditions. With these parameters in place, districts that serve low-income and minority students have shown that they can provide excellent teaching and substantial success for all students.

6.

Charter Schools and Racial and Social Class Segregation: Yet Another Sorting Machine?

Amy Stuart Wells, Jennifer Jellison Holme,
Alejandra Lopez, and Camille Wilson Cooper

One of the most troubling contradictions of our time is that, as our society becomes more racially and ethnically diverse, our public schools are becoming more racially and ethnically homogeneous. Indeed, in the past twenty years, judges and policymakers have removed many of the formal mechanisms—such as court orders and student transfer policies—designed to create more desegregated public schools.

These developments are even more paradoxical in light of recent public opinion data that show more people in the United States than ever before say they believe that public schools should be racially diverse. For example, a 1994 Gallup poll found that the percentage of the

We would like to acknowledge the support of the Russell Sage Foundation. In particular, Elizabeth MacDaniel and Lisa Kahraman assisted with the analysis of the state-level data. In addition, Russell Sage provided the first author with the time to write this review.

American people who said "more should be done to integrate schools" had risen rapidly, from 37 percent in 1988 to 56 percent in 1994.[1] A 1998 survey found that 80 percent of African-American parents and 66 percent of white parents surveyed said that it was either "very important" or "somewhat important" that their children's schools be racially integrated. Only 8 percent of black parents and 17 percent of white parents said less should be done to achieve racial integration in schools.[2]

At the same time, there is a growing body of research demonstrating the positive impact of school desegregation on the social mobility and life chances of African Americans. For instance, a review of the literature on the long-term effects of school desegregation, found that African-American graduates of racially diverse schools had higher occupational aspirations and better understood the steps needed to obtain their goals than graduates of all-black schools. This review also noted that African-American graduates of desegregated high schools were more likely to attend predominantly white universities and earn higher degrees.[3] And finally, African Americans who had attended racially mixed schools were more likely to be working in white-collar and professional jobs in integrated corporations and institutions. They also had more integrated social and professional networks through which they learned about employment opportunities.[4]

Yet, despite opinion polls and research supporting integration, since 1988 public schools have become more racially and ethnically segregated as more districts are released from desegregation orders and urban schools become increasingly racially isolated. According to Gary Orfield and his colleagues, this shift has been most striking in the southern and border states and is most severe for Latino students—the fastest growing student population in the country.[5]

Thus, we are dismantling the mechanisms by which we desegregate public schools at the same time that the perceived need for more racially diverse schools is quite high and the positive, long-term impact of desegregation is better documented than ever before. Indeed, it seems as though this is an appropriate moment in the history of our country to question whether or not the goals of racial integration should be transferred to new educational policies. Yet to date, most policymakers remain resistant to crafting new policies, such as charter school laws, in ways that strongly support the goals of racial diversity in public schools. For instance, while virtually all thirty-six state charter school laws include anti-discrimination clauses and several give preference to schools that enroll "at-risk" students (often without defining what that means), very few laws specifically require racial or socioeconomic balance in charter schools. And even in states with laws requiring some racial balance for charter schools, there is little evidence that either state officials or local school districts are monitoring charter schools' compliance. In fact, in South Carolina—one of the states with the strictest racial balance guidelines for charter schools—a state judge recently declared these guidelines unconstitutional.[6] Furthermore, none of the laws provide meaningful incentives such as grants or other forms of support for people to create racially diverse schools.

But it is precisely this lack of regulation and requirement that is at the heart of charter school reform—a movement that allows schools to operate with public money but less government oversight. Given the laissez-faire nature of this very popular and rapidly expanding reform, skeptics fear that it will create greater racial/ethnic and socioeconomic segregation and stratification in the way that similar deregulated school choice policies in other countries have.[7]

Yet, charter school proponents claim that theirs is not an elitist movement that enables wealthy and white families to flee the regular public schools, thereby exacerbating racial and social class segregation.[8] Far from that, they say that charter schools are serving many disadvantaged students. Some even argue that a parent's right to choose a school, including a charter school, is the new civil rights issue of our time.[9]

Furthermore, several reports have shown that charter schools do indeed serve low-income students and students of color. In fact, in some states, comparisons of statewide averages demonstrate that charter schools serve these students at a higher rate than the public schools.[10] However, these data do not speak to the issue of racial/ethnic or socioeconomic isolation within and across charter schools. In fact, there is generally very little discussion of this isolation in most of these reports (many conducted by people and/or institutions that advocate charter school reform) or how its presence—or absence—relates to different students' opportunities to learn within these schools.

Thus, beyond the fears and proclamations of skeptics and proponents are a set of important questions about who is enrolled in charter schools in different states and local communities, how they got there, and why. In this chapter, we begin to answer some of these questions by reviewing more than twenty studies of charter schools—conducted by independent researchers—so that we can begin an informed dialogue about these important issues.[11] As far as we know, this is the most comprehensive review of the literature in this area to date.

After reviewing the literature and drawing from our own study of charter schools in ten California school districts, we argue that currently there is not sufficient evidence to support strongly either the assertion that charter schools will exacerbate segregation and inequality or that they will help to overcome them. Still, we note that there is enough evidence to suggest that charter schools are less racially and socioeconomically diverse than the already segregated public schools, albeit for different reasons in different states and communities. Thus, there is cause for concern that the current charter school legislation does not promote the creation of racially and socioeconomically diverse charter schools.

In the first section of this chapter, we examine the research on who is being served in charter schools. Here we report that despite the aggregated national data that show that low-income students and students of color are enrolled in charter schools, the context of the reform—where it is being implemented and why—matters a great deal in terms of who is served. It appears that in some states charter school reform is mostly an urban phenomenon, serving predominantly low-income students of color. In other states, it appeals to a much wider range of people and communities, including many that are disproportionately white and well-off.

In fact, our analysis suggests that, in many instances, states with more racially/ethnically and socioeconomically diverse K–12 student populations tend to have charter schools that enroll a disproportionate number of white and nonpoor students. Conversely, in many of the states with a general public school population that is predominantly white and less poor, charter schools are enrolling a disproportionate percentage of students of color and low-income students. These distinctions also relate to geography, with charter schools in northeastern states serving more poor students and students of color relative to their public schools than do the charter schools in the southwestern states. This may be due to differences in the size and diversity of the public school districts in these different regions. Also, across these different contexts, the more the data are broken down from national- to state- to district- and even neighborhood-level comparisons between charter schools and public schools, the more racially and socioeconomically segregated the charter schools appear to be. For instance, charter schools are often more racially and socioeconomically homogeneous than their local school districts as a whole. And a few studies suggest that charter schools tend to be less diverse than the closest public schools within their districts.

Furthermore, we explain in the section on access to charter schools, there is some evidence that even in poor communities, the relatively more advantaged of the disadvantaged students are enrolling in charter schools, and the percentage of the lowest-income students served in charter schools across the country is declining. Finally, there is some preliminary evidence to suggest that low-income students and students of color are frequently enrolled in some of the most impoverished charter schools or in those with the least challenging curriculum.

These findings do not necessarily imply that individual charter schools are intentionally segregating students by race and class. Rather, they suggest that the current charter school laws do not foster racial diversity. As we discuss in the section on charter school legislation and diversity, to the extent that the charter school laws vary across states, they almost all allow a great deal of leeway in terms of equity and student access to charter schools. Often the laws' language in these areas is vague and open to different interpretations, and, as we mentioned, rarely enforced. In other words, the laws leave room for many charter school founders and educators to do as they wish. Thus, we conclude this chapter with a discussion of implications for policy, noting that if policymakers were to pay attention to public opinion and research that favor less homogeneous schools, charter school laws would need to provide more support and incentives for founders who wanted to create racially/ethnically and socioeconomically diverse charter schools.

CHARTER SCHOOL REFORM AND DEMOGRAPHIC DIFFERENCES WITHIN AND ACROSS STATES

With charter school laws enacted in thirty-six states, the District of Columbia, and Puerto Rico, there is a wide range of demographic and political contexts into which this popular reform has been cast. Therefore, aggregated "national" data on who is served in the country's sixteen hundred charter schools is only partially helpful because hidden behind those average figures is a broad scope of charter school realities. Individual charter schools reside in very different parts of the country and different local communities, which means each has a unique interaction with its surrounding schools and community. To the extent that charter schools are exacerbating racial/ethnic and socioeconomic segregation, it is only visible within the state and local context of the school itself.

Thus, in this section, we examine available national-, state-, district-, and school-level data in order to demonstrate how one level of analysis can both inform and distort another.

National Data Show Racial and Socioeconomic Diversity

When data on charter school enrollment are aggregated to the national level they show that students of various races and ethnicities are enrolled in charter schools in similar proportions to their average enrollments in all the public schools in all the states studied. For instance, the U.S. Department of Education's Fourth-Year Report on charter schools nationwide in 1998–99 found that 48 percent of the students enrolled in 95 percent of the charter schools in twenty-seven states were white,[12] compared to about 59 percent of the students in the public schools in those same states.[13] The report also states that, on average, charter schools in these twenty-seven states were more likely to serve African-American, Latino, and American-Indian students than the public schools (see Table 6.1). For instance, while nearly 24 percent of all charter school students were African American, only 17 percent of all public school students in these states were African American. Similarly, 21 percent of the students in the charter schools were Latino, as opposed to 19 percent of students enrolled in the regular public schools. The difference for American-Indian students was about 3 percent. In fact, the only so-called minority racial/ethnic group that was not overrepresented in charter schools at the national level was Asian and Pacific Islanders.

In terms of the poverty rates of students in charter schools, the aggregated data on the twenty-seven states demonstrate that almost 39 percent of students in charter schools qualify for free or reduced-price lunch. This is about the same as the 37 percent of students who qualify in the regular public schools in these states.[14]

Thus, at the aggregated, national level, it appears as though charter schools look similar to regular public schools in terms of the students they enroll, with fewer white and more African-American students in charter schools. Yet, the more closely we break down this national information into state-, district-, and school-level data, the more complex the picture becomes. Because racial and socioeconomic demographics vary greatly across and within states, it is important to

TABLE 6.1. RACIAL/ETHNIC COMPOSITION OF CHARTER SCHOOL STUDENTS COMPARED TO ALL PUBLIC SCHOOL STUDENTS IN TWENTY-SEVEN STATES

RACIAL/ETHNIC CATEGORIES	# OF STUDENTS IN CATEGORY		% OF STUDENTS IN CATEGORY	
	CHARTER SCHOOLS	PUBLIC SCHOOLS	CHARTER SCHOOLS	PUBLIC SCHOOLS
Total number	230,299[a]	30,689,016	—	—
White, not of Hispanic origin	110,434	18,102,767	48.2	59.0
Black, not of Hispanic origin	53,926	5,289,814	23.5	17.2
Hispanic	48,352	5,657,976	21.1	18.4
Asian or Pacific Islander	7,687	1,354,509	3.4	4.4
American Indian or Alaska Native	5,976	283,930	2.6	1.0
Other	2,712	N/A	1.2	N/A

[a] This number is nearly 22,000 smaller than the total enrollment numbers for charter schools in these 27 states reported elsewhere in the DOE's Fourth-Year report. See page 18, for example, where the total enrollment number is 252,009.

Source: The State of Charter Schools 2000: Fourth-year Report, conducted by RPP International (Washington, D.C.: U.S. Department of Education, Office of Educational Research and Improvement, February 2000).

look at who is being served in which charter schools where. Also, because different states and different school districts contain vastly different numbers of charter schools and charter school students, it is critical to examine charter schools' racial, ethnic, and social class identifications within the states and communities with the most charter schools, versus those with very few charter schools.

State-Level Data and Important Cross-State Differences: Context Matters

When the national data are broken down state-by-state, some interesting findings emerge, namely huge variations in both the racial/ethnic and socioeconomic makeup of charter schools across the states analyzed in detail in the Department of Education's Fourth-Year report.[15] We found, for instance, in the twenty-one states enrolling more than one thousand students in charter schools, thirteen of these states housed charter schools that combined served a lower percentage of white students overall than the regular public schools in the same states. Conversely, in four states charter schools enrolled a disproportionately high percentage of white students. Furthermore, ten states were home to charter schools that serve a higher percentage of low-income students than their regular public schools. And in five of the twenty-one states charter schools enroll a disproportionately low percentage of poor students.

Obviously, across various state contexts charter schools are serving demographically distinct students. In this section, we explore these issues more fully to understand the demographic dimensions upon which charter schools differ, and the important trends and themes that emerge.

RACIAL/ETHNIC DIFFERENCES IN STATE-LEVEL DATA. Given the racial and ethnic diversity of statewide enrollments in charter schools, we have tried to tease out the distinctions and commonalities across states, especially as they relate to the public school enrollments in those states. Two major trends emerged. First, there were more students overall enrolled in charter schools in states in which charter schools serve the same or a higher percentage of white and nonpoor students. And second, in several, but not all, of the states there appears to be an inverse relationship between the percentage of white and nonpoor students in the public education system overall and the percentage of white and nonpoor students enrolled in charter schools.[16] This, we believe, says something about where the frustration with the regular public schools is lodged across these different state contexts and how that frustration relates to issues of race, class, and geography.

♦   THE CONCENTRATION OF CHARTER SCHOOLS AND STUDENTS. As we noted above, thirteen of the twenty-one states with more than one thousand charter school students enrolled a disproportionately high percentage of students of color, while another four states enrolled a disproportionately low percentage of these students. The remaining four states were within five percentage points of their state averages for white enrollment. While it is helpful to compare the number of states in which white students are over- or underrepresented in charter schools, the results are somewhat misleading in terms of how these schools impact the lives of children. Not all of the states have the same number of charter schools or, more importantly, the same number of students enrolled in charter schools.

Take, for instance, the thirteen states that have a higher percentage of students of color in their charter schools than in the public schools as a whole. Interestingly, while these states contain a little more than 50 percent of the charter schools in the twenty-one states included in our analysis, they enroll only 40 percent of the students attending charter schools in these states. The eight states/jurisdictions with either an overrepresentation of white students or a similar (within five percentage points) percentage of white students compared to the public schools enroll the majority of all charter school students in the twenty-one states (see Table 6.2, page 178).[17]

This analysis raises questions about the meaning of the aggregated data presented in the Department of Education's Fourth-Year report. As we mentioned above, those data show that overall, charter schools in twenty-seven states enroll a smaller percentage of white students and a larger percentage of African-American, Latino, and American-Indian students than do all the public schools in those states combined (see Table 6.1). But this report compares aggregated data from all charter schools to aggregated data from all the public schools in all twenty-seven states, whether those states had one hundred charter schools with more than twenty-five thousand students or twenty charter schools with fewer than two thousand students.

Thus, the overall racial/ethnic demographics of states such as Connecticut, Wisconsin, Ohio, and Kansas—each of which has a very high percentage of white students in their public schools—are averaged into the comparison even though they each enroll less than three thousand students in charter schools. In fact, many of the states that enroll the largest numbers of students in charter schools, including Arizona, California, Georgia, and Texas, have much lower percentages of white students in their regular public schools.

The aggregated enrollment numbers and percentages in the "All Public Schools" columns of Table 6.1, therefore, do not accurately reflect the racial/ethnic makeup of the public schools in the states in which the vast majority of the charter schools and charter

Charter Schools and Racial and Social Class Segregation

TABLE 6.2. CHARTER SCHOOL ENROLLMENTS BY STATES AND RELATIVE WHITE STUDENT ENROLLMENTS

STATES IN WHICH THE % WHITE ENROLLMENT IN CHARTER SCHOOLS IS HIGHER THAN OR THE SAME AS (BY 5 PERCENT OR MORE) THE REGULAR PUBLIC SCHOOLS OVERALL IN THAT STATE			STATES IN WHICH THE % WHITE ENROLLMENT IN CHARTER SCHOOLS IS LOWER THAN (BY 5 PERCENT OR MORE) THE REGULAR PUBLIC SCHOOLS OVERALL IN THAT STATE		
STATE	% DIFFERENCE	TOTAL ENROLLMENT	STATES	% DIFFERENCE	TOTAL ENROLLMENT
California	+10.5	73,905	Michigan	−31.3	25,294
Arizona	+1.1	32,209	Texas	−24.9	18,590
Georgia	+14.0	18,611	Florida	−7.2	10,561
Colorado	+4.2	13,911	Massachusetts	−20.4	9,673
New Mexico	−1.4	4,601	North Carolina	−14.0	9,513
Dist. of Col.	−3.9	3,364	Pennsylvania	−57.2	5,474
Alaska	+23.8	2,047	Minnesota	−30.3	4,670
Kansas	+5.1	1,545	New Jersey	−43.7	4,001
			Illinois	−60.8	3,333
			Ohio	−39.5	2,509
			Wisconsin	−10.7	2,060
			Connecticut	−38.9	1,613
			Louisiana	−24.4	1,589
Average difference = +6.6; combined enrollment = 150,193			Average difference = −31.0; combined enrollment = 98,880		
% of total enrollment/21 states = 60			% of total enrollment/21 states = 40		

Source: The State of Charter Schools 2000: Fourth-year Report, conducted by RPP International (Washington, D.C.: U.S. Department of Education, Office of Educational Research and Improvement, February 2000).

school students are located. As we noted above, this table reports that, on average, 59 percent of public school students in the twenty-seven states examined were white, while only 48 percent of charter school students were white. When we look more closely at the top two states in terms of student enrollment in charter schools—California (with 73,905 students) and Arizona (with 32,209 students)—we see that combined their total K–12 population in public schools is about 45 percent white. Yet the charter schools in these two states—educating about 46 percent of all charter school students across the country[18]—are 55 percent white. Furthermore, in both of these states, each with a large Latino population, Latino students are underrepresented in charter schools (see Table 6.3).

Clearly, further analysis must be conducted with more effort to separate out the data from states with large numbers of students—for example, more than ten thousand—enrolled in charter schools from those with far fewer students—say, fewer than fifteen hundred. It is a bit disingenuous to draw general conclusions about

TABLE 6.3. RACIAL/ETHNIC COMPOSITION OF CHARTER SCHOOL STUDENTS COMPARED TO ALL PUBLIC SCHOOL STUDENTS IN CALIFORNIA AND ARIZONA

RACIAL/ETHNIC CATEGORIES	# OF STUDENTS IN CATEGORY		% OF STUDENTS IN CATEGORY	
	CHARTER SCHOOLS	PUBLIC SCHOOLS	CHARTER SCHOOLS	PUBLIC SCHOOLS
Total Number	106,114[a]	6,543,729	—	—
White, not of Hispanic origin	58,025	2,960,779	54.7	45.2
Black, not of Hispanic origin	10,494	517,873	9.9	7.9
Hispanic	27,196	2,340,332	25.6	35.8
Asian or Pacific Islander	3,671	567,879	3.5	8.7
American Indian or Alaska Native	5,745	156,864	5.4	2.4
Other	942	N/A	0.8	—

[a] About 46 percent of the national total.

Source: *The State of Charter Schools 2000: Fourth-year Report*, conducted by RPP International (Washington, D.C.: U.S. Department of Education, Office of Educational Research and Improvement, February 2000).

who is and who is not being served by charter school reform when averaging data from twenty-seven states, as if these states were all equal in terms of charter school activities.

♦   THE RELATIONSHIP BETWEEN THE PERCENTAGES OF WHITES IN PUBLIC AND CHARTER SCHOOLS. Another issue that emerges from the 1998–99 state-level data is the tendency for charter schools in predominantly white states to serve a higher percentage of students of color. In other words, in looking at the thirteen states in which charter schools enroll a disproportionately high number of students of color, we see that ten of those states have a general public school population that is more than 60 percent white (see Table 6.4, pages 182–83).[19] In fact, half of these states have public school enrollments that are more than 80 percent white. Charter school enrollments in these ten states are, on average, about 35 percent less white than in the regular public schools overall.

In terms of their African-American student populations, the charter schools in these ten states enroll 31 percent more African-American students on average than do the public schools. In Illinois, for example, African-American enrollment in the eleven charter schools is, on average, 48 percent greater than in the regular public schools, while the white population is nearly 60 percent lower. The Latino student population in the charter schools in these ten states tends to be closer to the state averages, with a few states enrolling 9 percent or more greater Latino populations. Thus, in these ten predominantly white states, charter schools tend to enroll a disproportionate number of students of color.

Meanwhile, of the eight states/jurisdictions with charter school enrollments that are either higher or similar (within five percentage points) to the proportion of white students in the public schools,[20] six of them have general K–12 public school populations that are less than 60 percent white. For instance, California, which has a general public school population that is only 44 percent white, has a charter school population that is almost 55 percent white. While this percentage of white enrollment in charter schools is similar in terms of absolute percentage to the white enrollment in charter schools in states such as Massachusetts (58 percent), Michigan (50 percent), and Minnesota (52 percent), the latter three states have a much higher percentage of white students in their general public school population—78 percent, 81 percent, and 82 percent, respectively. Thus, the charter schools in these states serve a disproportionate number of African-American and/or Latino students, while the California charter schools serve a disproportionate number of white students (see Table 6.3). In other words, the larger context from which charter schools draw their enrollments give the racial/ethnic breakdown numbers their meaning. Therefore, it appears that there might be a relationship between a state context in which the public schools as a whole are predominantly white, such as Connecticut, Illinois, Michigan, Minnesota, and Pennsylvania, and a demand for charter schools that serve students of color.[21] On the other hand, there also appears to be a much weaker relationship between the demand for charter schools that serve white students and statewide public school demographics that are more diverse. Georgia provides a good case in point (see Table 6.3). There, according to Department of Education data, the K–12 public school population was about 56 percent white and 40 percent African American. Meanwhile, the aggregated data on Georgia charter schools show that almost 70 percent of the students were white and about 23 percent were African-American. In this state, therefore, white students were overrepresented in charter schools while African-American students were underrepresented. Thus, we see these interesting but uneven demographic relationships across states, with many of the racially diverse states enrolling relatively more white students in charter schools and most of the predominantly white states enrolling a higher percentage of students of color in charter schools than in the regular public schools.

Still, five of the twenty-one states—Texas, Colorado, Florida, Louisiana, and Kansas—do not fit this analysis. Colorado and Kansas have predominantly (greater than 60 percent) white public school populations in general and a very slight overrepresentation of white students in charter schools. Texas, Florida,[22] and Louisiana, on the other hand, have K–12 school-age populations that are less than 60 percent white and charter schools that enroll a disproportionately *high* percentage of students of color. But sixteen of the twenty-one states with the largest charter school enrollments fit the profile of either predominantly white states with

TABLE 6.4. COMPARISON OF ENROLLMENT IN CHARTER SCHOOLS AND ALL PUBLIC SCHOOLS IN THE TWENTY-ONE STATES WITH ONE THOUSAND OR MORE STUDENTS ENROLLED IN CHARTER SCHOOLS, 1998–99

States	# of students in charter schools^a / # of charter schools^b	% white enrollment in public schools/difference in % white enrollment in charter schools	% black enrollment in public schools/difference in % black enrollment in charter schools	% Hispanic enrollment in public schools/difference in % Hispanic enrollment in charter schools	% public school students who qualify for free and reduced-price lunch/difference in % of charter school students who qualify	% public school students who are LEP^c/difference in % of charter school students who are LEP^c	% public school students with disabilities/difference in % of charter school students with disabilities
California	73,905/143	44/+10.5	8.4/+2.4	36.4/−9.8	42.4/−11.3	24.6/−3.3	9.6/−3.2
Arizona	32,209/155	54/+1.1	4.5/+3.3	31.3/−7.9	40.1/+3.1	11.9/−4.1	9.2/−0.7
Michigan	25,294/121	81.3/−31.3	12.7/+28.7	3.3/+1.3	28.7/+10.6	1.6/+1.2	10.8/−5.3
Georgia	18,611/25	55.6/+14.0	39.5/−16.2	3.0/−0.4	40.6/−10.3	1.1/+0.8	9.7/−1.5
Texas	18,590/72	48/−24.9	13.9/+20	36.3/+3.2	46.1/+16.1	13.4/−3.8	11.4/−2.0
Colorado	13,911/57	72.4/+4.2	4.5/+1.5	19.8/−5.8	27.8/−9.6	7.4/−5.3	9.6/−1.6
Florida	10,561/60	56/−7.2	28.6/+11.7	13.8/−4.2	43.9/−1.5	12.2/−10.7	13.4/+4.3
Massachusetts	9,673/32	78.4/−20.4	8.7/+11.4	9.0/+4.8	25.6/+11.8	4.7/−1.1	15.6/−4.3
North Carolina	9,513/51	62.4/−14.0	31.8/+15.5	2.6/−1.0	36.5/−2.2	2.0/−0.6	11.5/+2.3
Pennsylvania	5,474/22	82.3/−57.2	12.9/+46.2	3.2/+10.6	31.1/+33	n.a./n.a.	11.2/+1.1

Minnesota	4,670/37	82.2/-30.3	7.2/+19.5	3.0/0.4	26.8/+33.3	3.4/+6.6	10.9/+2.7
New Mexico	4,601/5	36.7/-1.4	2.1/0	49.3/+7.5	49.6/-12.1	24.0/+1.6	13.7/+1.8
New Jersey	4,001/21	64.3/-43.7	17.7/+44.4	12.5/+1.0	28.3/+32.9	4.0/-3.4	15.1/-7.9
Dist. of Col.	3,364/14	4.9/-3.9	86.5/-12.2	7.1/+12.8	60.0/+2.3	6.2/+13.1	9.5/-3.8
Illinois	3,333/11	69.4/-60.8	19.0/+48	9.3/+13.9	30.8/+37.5	6.0/-4.5	12.5/-4.2
Ohio	2,509/7	83.6/-39.5	14.0/+35.8	1.4/-0.4	28.7/+39.9	0.7/-0.7	11.2/+5.7
Wisconsin	2,060/26	83.3/-10.7	8.8/+7.2	3.2/-0.5	24.9/+3.5	2.6/-1.7	11.3/-1.8
Alaska	2,047/13	46.9/+23.8	2.5/0.1	1.7/0.9	25.7/-21.4	27.7/-27.5	12.1/-6.5
Connecticut	1,613/16	71.4/-38.9	14.3/+30.7	11.8/+9.2	22.8/+24.6	3.8/-0.8	13.0/-6.2
Louisiana	1,589/10	49.4/-24.4	47.9/+24.5	1.1/-0.7	59.3/+16	0.9/-0.6	10.9/-5.6
Kansas	1,545/14	85.1/+5.1	6.5/-5.3	6.0/0.4	31.7/-0.9	2.8/-1.9	10.7/-0.6

[a] The enrollment numbers include "data for 1,010 charter schools and is based on responses from all 975 open charter schools that responded to the survey, supplemented with data from state departments of education" (see page 18 of the source).

[b] These numbers are based on responses from only 927 of the 975 open charter schools that responded to the survey (see p. 33 of the source). No explanation is given for why the other 48 schools are not included in the table.

[c] Limited English proficiency.

Note: The shaded rows mark those states in which the charter school enrollment is disproportionately less white (by 5 percent of more) than that of the statewide public school enrollment for that state.

Source: The State of Charter Schools 2000: Fourth-year Report, conducted by RPP International (Washington, D.C.: U.S. Department of Education, Office of Educational Research and Improvement, February 2000).

charter schools that enroll a disproportionate percentage of students of color or more racially diverse states that enroll a disproportionate percentage of white students in their charter schools.

It is also important to note, however, that in the eight states/jurisdictions where charter schools enroll the same or a higher percentage of white students than the public schools, their demographics, on average, tend to be less distinct from their statewide averages. In contrast, the racial/ethnic breakdowns of charter schools in the thirteen states where one or more "minority" groups were overrepresented were, in general, more distinct from the racial/ethnic breakdowns of the statewide public school enrollment (see states on the right side of Table 6.2). For instance, these states are more likely to have one or two racial/ethnic groups that are higher or lower than the state averages for those groups by more than 10 percent.

Furthermore, in terms of geographic distinctions, the eight states/jurisdictions with white charter school enrollments equal to or greater than the state population as a whole are all western, southern, and/or southwestern states/jurisdictions. Because the southern and western regions of the country tend to have geographically larger, countywide school districts, there could in fact be a relationship between the size *and* diversity of local school districts and the interest on the part of white parents and students in engaging in charter school reform. On the other hand, the majority of the thirteen states in which charter schools enroll a higher percentage of students of color are located in the north, east, and northeastern regions of the country. These states are more likely to have smaller and more racially homogeneous school districts.[23]

Thus, we can only speculate as to why the data look the way they do. For instance, one possibility is that in predominantly white and wealthy northeastern states such as Connecticut, where smaller city and suburban school districts have remained highly separate and unequal, the vast majority of frustration with public education is vested in the poor, urban school districts where most of the students of color reside. On the other hand, the more southern and western states, such as Arizona, have overall school-age populations that are more diverse—about 54 percent white and 31 percent Latino in Arizona—and less segregated across the larger, countywide school districts. Here, frustration with the public educational system could be less concentrated exclusively in poor, urban neighborhoods, as some white and more middle-class parents and students find themselves in school districts that are perceived to be not as good. In fact, in many places in these states it is more likely that white and wealthy parents and communities no longer see the public schools as places "for people like them."[24] And as we point out below, some of the strongest evidence in terms of intradistrict racial/ethnic segregation is emerging from research in California and Arizona.

Obviously, these issues need to be explored more carefully and in greater depth in future cross-state studies of charter schools.

POVERTY RATES IN STATE-LEVEL DATA. Compared to the data on the racial/ethnic make-up of charter schools, the socioeconomic data, as measured by eligibility for free and reduced-price lunch, are slightly more disparate. For instance, at the aggregated state level—only five of the twenty-one states with the largest charter school enrollments have smaller percentages (by 5 percent or more) of poor students in charter schools than in the regular public schools. In fact, all five of these states had a smaller percentage of poor students by *at least* 10 percent in charter schools.

While these are only five of the top twenty-one states with charter schools, they contained 45 percent of all students enrolled in charter schools nationally in 1998–99. Meanwhile, the six states that had equal (within five percentage points) low-income enrollments in charters and regular public schools were home to another 24 percent of the nation's charter school students. Thus, nearly 70 percent—more than two-thirds—of all charter school students were enrolled in the eleven states that had either fewer or an equal percentage of low-income students enrolled in charter schools than in the regular public schools. Once again, analyses of the aggregated national data can appear misleading upon closer examination of where the charter school students are located because these analyses include data on relatively nonpoor states that enroll very few charter school students.

◆   THE RELATIONSHIP BETWEEN THE PERCENTAGES OF POOR
STUDENTS IN PUBLIC AND CHARTER SCHOOLS. Similar to the findings on enrollments by race/ethnicity, charter schools are somewhat more likely to serve poor students in states with fewer poor

students in the public schools overall. In the eleven states in which charter schools serve a lower or equal percentage of poor students than the regular public schools, the overall percentage of students who qualify for free and reduced-price lunch is higher, on average, than in the other ten states. For instance, in seven of these states, 37 percent or more of students qualify for free or reduced-price lunch—thus at or above the average for all the states with charter schools studied by the Department of Education. Meanwhile only two of the ten states in which the percentage of poor students in charter schools is higher than the state average have more than 37 percent of their overall public school students eligible for free or reduced-price lunch (see Table 6.5).

What is perhaps most interesting, however, is the range of differences in poverty rates between the public schools and charter schools. For instance, as Table 6.5 illustrates, the difference between the percent of all public school students who qualify for free or reduced-price lunch and the percent of all charter school students who qualify is quite large in the less poor states. In fact, on average, the number of poor students enrolled in charter schools in these ten states is about 26 percent higher than in the public schools. Indeed, in five of these states, the difference is more than 30 percent.

In Ohio, for example, where almost 29 percent of all public school students are from low-income families, nearly 69 percent of charter school students are poor. And in Illinois, charter schools enroll on average about 37 percent more poor students than the regular public schools (68 percent poor students in charter schools almost 31 percent poor students in the regular public schools). As noted above, Illinois is a state with very low white enrollment in charter schools (9 percent of charter school students as opposed to 69 percent of all students in the public schools) and very high African-American enrollments (almost 67 percent of students in charter schools as opposed to only 19 percent in all public schools).

In comparison, in the five states in which charter schools enroll a smaller percentage of low-income students than do the public schools in the state, the average difference in the percentage of poor students between the charter schools and the statewide public school system is half that of the less poor states—about 13 percent (see Table 6.4). Therefore, as with the data on racial and

TABLE 6.5. CHARTER SCHOOL ENROLLMENTS BY STATES AND AND POVERTY RATES

States[a] in which the % of students who qualify for free or reduced-price lunch in charter schools is *LOWER THAN* the regular public schools overall in that state			States in which the % of students who qualify for free or reduced-price lunch in charter schools is *HIGHER THAN* (by 5 percent or more) the regular public schools overall in that state		
STATE	% DIFFERENCE	TOTAL ENROLLMENT	STATES	% DIFFERENCE	TOTAL ENROLLMENT
California	-11.3	73,905	Michigan	+10.6	25,294
Arizona	+3.1	32,209	Texas	+16.1	18,590
Georgia	-10.3	18,611	Massachusetts	+11.8	9,673
Colorado	-9.6	13,911	Pennsylvania	+33	5,474
Florida	-1.5	10,561	Minnesota	+33.3	4,670
North Carolina	-2.2	9,513	New Jersey	+32.9	4,001
New Mexico	-12.1	4,601	Illinois	+37.5	3,333
Dist. of Col.	+2.3	3,364	Ohio	+39.9	2,509
Wisconsin	+3.5	2,060	Connecticut	+24.6	1,613
Alaska	-21.4	2,047	Louisiana	+16	1,589
Kansas	-0.9	1,545			
Average difference = -5.5; combined enrollment = 172,327			Average difference = +25.6; combined enrollment = 76,746		
% of total enrollment/21 states = 69			% of total enrollment/21 states = 31		

[a] Of the 21 states with total enrollment in charter schools of more than 1,000.

Source: The *State of Charter Schools 2000: Fourth-year Report*, conducted by RPP International (Washington, D.C.: U.S. Department of Education, Office of Educational Research and Improvement, February 2000).

ethnic enrollment in charter schools, the data on poverty rates suggest that in the states with more poor students enrolled in charter schools, poverty rates of students in the charter schools differ more from the statewide public schools than in states with fewer poor students overall.

SUMMARY OF STATE-LEVEL DATA. The overarching finding here is that context matters. The tendency appears to be, with a few exceptions, that in states that are whiter and wealthier overall, charter schools are more likely to be serving a relatively high percentage of low-income students and students of color. In states that are more racially diverse overall and that have even a slightly higher percentage of low-income students enrolled in their public schools, charter schools are more likely to be drawing a relatively higher percentage of white and nonpoor students. This is not a perfect pattern; in fact, four of the twenty-one states—Texas, Colorado, Louisiana, and Kansas—do not fit *either* the race/ethnicity or the poverty trends. But in one way or another, the remaining seventeen states do.

As we noted above, we do not yet know what this means or why these phenomena are occurring. But we can begin to speculate from these data that in states where the public schools are organized into smaller school districts that are often more separate and unequal and the white and wealthy families are fairly content with their mostly segregated suburban schools, charter schools could be perceived mainly as a reform designed to help the most desperate students in poor, urban public schools. In more racially, ethnically, and socioeconomically diverse states where there are fewer white and wealthy public school district enclaves, charter school reform may represent more of a mixture of forces, including efforts by middle-class and white parents to create more quasi-private public schools, thereby pulling away from the larger public system. In doing so, these parents often create more racially/ethnically and socioeconomically homogeneous schools, whether they intend to or not.

These are possible explanations for a complicated pattern of charter school enrollments across states. Still, all of the data discussed thus far are aggregated at the national and state levels. Below we present data from several studies that look more closely at charter schools and their districts to suggest that even in states where charter school enrollment in the aggregate is more closely aligned to the statewide racial/ethnic averages in public schools, there is no evidence that white students and students of color or poor and nonpoor students are being served in the same charter schools.

District- and School-Level Data: Charter Schools within Their Local Contexts

The disparate state-level data point to the need to look more carefully at what is happening locally in school districts and in the charter schools within them. Thus it is clear that we need to know—despite the state averages—how many of the predominantly white charter schools are in school districts populated mostly by students of color. This is a very different picture than one in which the predominantly white charter schools are in predominantly white school districts.

In some states there are data that allow us to examine these issues—for example, reports that compare charter schools to their surrounding districts or, less frequently, nearby public schools within a local section of these districts. These reports tend to show a great deal of racial segregation across charter schools. Thus, even those states with relatively low percentages of white students enrolled in charter schools still often have some virtually all-white charter schools. They may also have many virtually all-African-American or all-Latino charter schools. Hence, it is extremely important to break down the state-level information when asking questions about racial/ethnic and social class segregation.

RACIAL DIVERSITY: COMPARING CHARTER SCHOOLS TO THEIR LOCAL DISTRICTS. The Department of Education's Fourth-Year report on charter schools states that 69 percent of all charter schools operating in twenty-seven states during the 1998–99 school year had white student populations that were within twenty percentage points (plus or minus) of their local school districts' average percentage of white students.[25] This was up from about 60 percent of all charter schools in the 1996–97 school year.[26] Meanwhile, another 17 percent of charter schools had a distinctly higher percentage of students of color and a lower percentage of white students than their surrounding districts. Thus, according to the report, only 14 percent of charter schools had a lower percentage of students of color and a higher percentage of white students than their districts.[27]

Unfortunately, the 20 percent range that the Department of Education report used to define charter school distinction along racial/ethnic enrollment lines seems quite broad compared to other reports that address these issues. Furthermore, the Department of Education's Fourth-Year Report fails to provide any further information on comparisons of charter schools to districts. For instance, there is no information on whether charter schools that are racially or ethnically distinct from their surrounding districts in one way or another are clustered in particular states or types of school districts—for example, urban or suburban. Nor is there any helpful school-level data to shed light on the racial makeup of individual charter schools as they compare to nearby public schools, and compared to districtwide averages.

In fact, the Department of Education's Second-Year Report included some of this information, comparing the proportion of white student enrollment in about 368 charter schools to white enrollment in all the public schools by ten percentage points—0 to 10 percent, 10 to 20 percent, 20 to 30 percent white, and so forth—in sixteen states.[28] This analysis showed that charter schools were much more likely to have 0 to 10 percent white enrollment than the regular public schools and somewhat more likely to have 90 to 100 percent white enrollments. Meanwhile, the public schools in these sixteen states were more likely to have 60 to 70, 50 to 60 or 20 to 30 percent white enrollment than were the charter schools, suggesting that the public schools were more racially diverse. Unfortunately, the Department of Education has not conducted this analysis in subsequent reports.

Still, these Second-Year Department of Education findings, which show that charter schools tend to be more racially isolated than the regular public schools, have been confirmed by subsequent studies conducted by other researchers. For instance, a study conducted by Carol Ascher, Robin Jacobowitz, and Yolanda McBride provides important cross-state information on charter school and district level enrollments.[29] They analyzed data from more than 550 charter schools in 317 school districts in twenty-six states. Like the Department of Education's Fourth-Year Report, they found that about 70 percent of all charter schools were not distinct (using plus or minus twenty percentage points) from their surrounding districts in the percentage of white students enrolled. Yet this report and others also reveal some interesting differences between the predominantly white and predominantly nonwhite charter schools, especially as they relate to their surrounding districts.

◆   CHARTER SCHOOLS ARE LESS RACIALLY/ETHNICALLY DIVERSE
THAN THEIR SURROUNDING DISTRICTS.[30] In breaking down the
data to examine charter schools in their local school district contexts, Ascher and her colleagues found that out of 552 charter
schools, 27 percent had a student population that was 0 to 20 percent white. Meanwhile, another 38 percent had an 81 to 100 percent white student population. Therefore, 64 percent, or almost
two-thirds, of all charter schools were either predominantly white
or predominantly students of color.[31]

In comparison, the racial makeup of the 317 school districts in
which these charter schools were located was more diverse. In fact,
only about 10 percent of these school districts were 0 to 20 percent
white, and another 37 percent were 81 to 100 percent white.
Therefore, only 47 percent of the school districts were either more
than 80 percent or less than 20 percent white, compared to 64
percent of the charter schools.

Thus, the percentage white is similar at one end of the spectrum, with about 38 percent of charter schools and 37 percent of
their host districts enrolling 80 to 100 percent white students.
Yet at the other end of the spectrum, charter schools and their districts are more disparate, with nearly three times as many charter
schools enrolling 0 to 20 percent white students as their home
districts.

Other reports examining charter school enrollment in different states also point to greater racial isolation in charter schools
than in their surrounding school districts, although the extent to
which this results in more predominantly white or more predominantly nonwhite charter schools differs across the states with
several state reports showing more predominantly white charter
schools.[32] For instance, in a comprehensive study of the enrollment of ninety-eight California charter schools from the 1996–97
school year,[33] SRI International found that while on the whole
charter schools served a population that was, demographically,
fairly similar to the student population statewide, intradistrict
comparisons showed greater discrepancies, especially in the predominantly white schools. More specifically, the report noted that
about 40 percent of the California charter schools enrolled a disproportionately high percentage of white students in comparison
to their surrounding school districts. In half of these cases, white

enrollment in charter schools exceed the district's by more than 25 percent. Meanwhile, the exact opposite was true for Latino students, who were underrepresented by at least 10 percent in almost 40 percent of all charter schools and by at least 25 percent in 18 percent of charter schools. These intradistrict discrepancies were far greater for white and Latino student populations than for African-American or Asian student populations.[34] This finding confirms an early finding in the Department of Education's First-Year Report on charter schools, which stated that 37 percent of the eighty-one charter schools in California during the 1995–96 school year, as opposed to 17 percent of all public schools in the state, had enrollments that were 80 to 100 percent white.[35]

Furthermore, these patterns of segregation in California charter schools do not appear to be changing. For instance, a study by Carol Muth Crockett examining data from the 123 California charter schools operating during the 1997–98 school year found only one charter school that reflected no difference at all in "whiteness" from its sponsoring district. "Of the remaining 122 charter schools, 78 (over 63 percent) were Whiter than their sponsoring districts." In fact, 22 of the charter schools (or 18 percent of the total studied) were at least 25 percent more white than the public schools in their districts.[36]

Meanwhile, paralleling the SRI findings, Crockett reported that while white students were often overrepresented in charter schools, in eighteen of the charter schools (15 percent), Latino students were underrepresented by at least 25 percent. And in about one-third of these schools, or 6 percent of the total, Latino students were underrepresented by 50 percent or more. Thus, once again, the state with by far the largest enrollment in charter schools is also the state with some of the most problematic demographic data.

In Colorado, where the aggregated charter school enrollment was about the same percentage white as the statewide K–12 public school enrollment, a 1998 evaluation of thirty-two charter schools showed that while differences between charter schools and regular school districts did not appear to be as great as they were in California, African-American and Latino students were underrepresented in charter schools.[37] For instance, twenty-six of the thirty-two charter schools studied—or 81 percent—served a lower percentage (by 5 percent or more) of students of color than their surrounding school districts.

On the other hand, Michigan is a predominantly white state (83 percent of the students in the public schools statewide are white; about 13 percent are African American), but white students were underrepresented in charter schools and African-American students were overrepresented. In all of the charter schools across the state combined, 50 percent of the students were white and 41 percent were African American.

A closer look at some of the preliminary data from two reports on Michigan charter schools suggests that, at least in some instances, African-American and white students were enrolling in separate charter schools.[38] These two studies of Michigan charter schools examined different areas of the state, and they come to different conclusions about how charter schools relate to their local districts in terms of racial/ethnic balance. Jerry Horn and Gary Miron, who studied sixty-two charter schools in all but the southeastern area of the state, showed that while there was a larger percentage of African-American students enrolled in these charter schools (39 percent) than in the state's public schools as a whole (17 percent), the percentage was lower than that of the districts surrounding the charter schools (51 percent). Meanwhile, the authors found the opposite was true in terms of white enrollment—that is, the percentage of white students enrolled in the charter schools was, on average, about 49 percent, compared to about 42 percent in the host districts.[39]

The second Michigan report examined the fifty-five charter schools in the Ann Arbor, Detroit, and Flint metropolitan areas.[40] Contrary to the Horn and Miron study, this study found that the percentage of students of color in the charter schools was higher than in the public schools in the surrounding districts. For instance, the report states that the charter schools in this southeastern section of Michigan enrolled a combined student population that was 68 percent students of color, while the surrounding school districts were only 54 percent students of color.[41] However, this analysis may have been confounded because data from one predominantly white school district that has only one charter school could have lowered this 54 percent average. Data are needed that break down these comparisons of charter schools and the surrounding districts to the district and community levels.

A study of Minnesota,[42] where the overall student population is predominantly white (86 percent) but the total charter school population is only about 52 percent white,[43] examined the range of racial diversity in charter schools and their surrounding school districts. This study found that the range of the percentage of white students enrolled was much wider in the charter schools—between 0 and 99 percent white—than it was in the host districts, where white enrollment ranged from 37 to 98 percent. This was also the case with African-American enrollment; while the surrounding or host school districts ranged from less than 1 to 40 percent African American, the charter schools ranged from 0 to 96 percent. Similarly, the range of Latino and Asian enrollments in charter schools was much wider in the host districts than in the public schools.

Following from the preliminary findings of several other reports, this study concludes that white students and students of color, for the most part, are enrolled in different charter schools. Thus, as of 1996 half of the sixteen charter schools operating in Minnesota were serving student populations that were less than 20 percent students of color, and the other half were serving more than 60 percent students of color. The authors write: "These data indicate that Minnesota charter schools, at this time, are not necessarily functioning as a desegregation tool."[44]

The third-year evaluation of charter schools in Texas conducted by a consortium of researchers, as well as the U.S. Department of Education, found that the eighty-nine charter schools operating in Texas during the 1998–99 school year enrolled a lower percentage of white students than the regular public schools overall.[45] But the report also makes clear that at the school level, the white students who were enrolled in Texas charter schools were rarely attending the same schools as African-American or Latino students. For instance, in 1998–99, the so-called at-risk charter schools had much higher concentrations of Latino and African-American students and a lower concentration of white or "Anglo" students. At the same time, the charter schools that were not targeted toward at-risk students enrolled a slightly lower percentage of Latino students and a higher percentage of

African-American students when compared to state averages. Although the percentage of white students in both types of charter schools—"at-risk" and "non-at-risk"—was lower than the statewide percentage of white students overall, they comprised 30 percent of the non-at-risk charter school population, as opposed to only 14 percent of the at-risk charter school population. In fact 84 percent of the at-risk charter schools had student populations that were less than 33 percent white. Meanwhile, 50 percent of the students enrolled in at-risk charter schools were Latino, even though Latinos comprise only 38 percent of the overall Texas public schools' student population.

Furthermore, the racial/ethnic breakdown of individual Texas charter schools shows that forty-four of them, one-half of the total, had enrollments that were more than 75 percent from only one racial/ethnic group. In fact, thirty of these schools had student bodies that were 90 percent or more from one racial/ethnic group, including four that were more than 90 percent white, twelve that were more than 90 percent African American, and fourteen that were 90 percent or more Latino.

Finally, the report examined the extent to which Texas charter school enrollments were within twenty percentage points of their local school districts' percentages for different racial/ethnic groups. The result was, once again, that Latino students are the most underrepresented group in the non-at-risk charter schools. Thus, while on average 85 percent of Texas public schools are within twenty percentage points of their district averages in terms of the percentage of Latino students, only 43 percent of the non-at-risk charter schools were within this limit. In fact, for every racial/ethnic group, enrollments in the regular public schools in Texas much more closely reflected the racial breakdowns of their local school districts than did the charter school enrollments.

In contrast, the Massachusetts data do not fully support the conclusion that charter schools are, for the most part, more racially segregated than their districts. In fact, many Massachusetts charter schools, particularly those that were predominantly white, closely reflected their school districts—that is, highly segregated by race and class. For instance, the data presented in the Massachusetts State Department of Education 1998 report show that eleven of the twenty-four operating charter schools had enrollments that were 88 percent or more white. While the statewide average white enrollment in the K–12 public school system was only 78 percent white, ten of these eleven schools were located in school districts that were at least 90 percent white. These ten charter schools, therefore, closely reflected the racial/ethnic makeup of their districts, even though they were disproportionately white compared to statewide averages in public schools. In fact, a recent study by the researchers at the Donahue Institute also found that Massachusetts's charter schools were not significantly different from their local school districts in terms of minority student enrollment.[46]

Still, even these Massachusetts data show that charter schools are segregated by race/ethnicity, even if, in this case, they are not more segregated than their surrounding school districts. Thus, the study by Ascher and her colleagues, combined with several of these state-by-state reports on charter schools, begin to show a trend of separate charter schools for white students versus students of color, even if they do not agree in terms of which types of charter schools—predominantly white or predominantly nonwhite—are more prevalent. Obviously, as with any aspect of charter school reform, more and better data are needed before firm conclusions can be drawn.

◆ PREDOMINANTLY WHITE CHARTER SCHOOLS ARE MORE SIMILAR TO THEIR SCHOOL DISTRICTS. Similar to the phenomenon discussed above regarding the state-level data, it appears that in at least some of the states examined the greatest racial/ethnic difference between the districts and the charter schools that operate within them occurred when charter schools served mostly students of color. According to the Ascher study, in terms of the racial makeup of the students, the predominantly white charter schools tend to be more similar to their districts.[47] In fact, the authors found that the makeup of 83 percent of the predominantly white charter schools nationwide was roughly equivalent to their districts' averages. And, as we noted earlier, while 37 percent of the districts had enrollments that were predominantly (81 to 100 percent) white, about the same percentage of charter schools—38 percent—were also predominantly white.[48] Meanwhile, the contrast between charter schools and school districts enrolling mostly students of color was much greater. For instance, while only 10 percent of all the school districts in the sample were 0 to 20 percent white, 27 percent of the charter schools were 0 to 20 percent white. The authors conclude:

> The higher the percentage of white students in the charter schools, the more likely charter schools are to be equivalent to their districts.... On the other hand, nearly half of all charter schools with more than two-thirds students of color are distinct from their districts. That is, charter schools may be offering students of color a more segregated environment than their districts as a whole.[49]

However, not all the research concurs on this point. For instance, in California Crockett found major differences between the predominantly white charter schools and their surrounding school districts; many of these charter schools were located in urban, predominantly nonwhite districts. She also found that 41 percent of all urban charter schools in California were more white by 20 percent or more as compared to their districts as a whole. Furthermore, she found that in urban districts, on average, the overrepresentation of white students in charter schools was two to three times greater than the overrepresentation of white students in suburban and rural charter schools.[50]

Still, despite some discrepancies, it appears as though some of the state reports concur with the two central findings of the Ascher national analysis of school- and district-level data. First, charter schools tend to be more racially segregated than their surrounding districts. Second, charter schools serving mostly students of color tend to enroll a higher percentage of these students than their surrounding school districts, whereas predominantly white charter schools tend to more closely match the demographic makeup of their surrounding school districts. Two very important exceptions are California and Texas.

◆ A SCHOOL-TO-SCHOOL LEVEL COMPARISON OF RACIAL COMPOSITION. Of course, the shortcoming of this analysis is that Ascher and her colleagues were comparing the demographics of individual charter schools to those of entire school districts. Obviously, within most school districts, individual public schools could be as racially/ethnically or socioeconomically segregated as any charter school. This issue is particularly problematic in large school districts where, despite districtwide racial diversity, individual schools are often quite racially homogeneous. Thus, a charter school enrolling mostly African-American students within a school district that is racially diverse could be located in a community in which the nearby public schools also enroll mostly African-American students.

One study by Casey Cobb and Gene Glass on Arizona's charter schools attempts to address this issue. This study employed a map analysis to compare the ethnic composition of every charter school in metropolitan Phoenix to that of "nearby" traditional public schools of comparable grade levels.[51] The analysis shows that time and time again charter schools enroll student populations that are a higher percentage white than their closest public schools. For instance, when the authors focused on Scottsdale, a predominantly white suburb of Phoenix, they found that in the southern section of the district, where the small population of ethnic minorities in that district reside, charter schools were enrolling a disproportionate percentage of white students. In fact, in the area surrounding two of the K–8 charter schools in Scottsdale, no public school enrolled as high a proportion of whites as these two schools. For instance, one Scottsdale charter school served 226 students in grades K–8, 87 percent of whom were white. Meanwhile the two closest public schools that spanned the same grades were only 62 percent white and 73 percent white.[52]

Similarly, in the suburb of Tempe, Cobb and Glass found that one elementary charter school had a higher percentage of white students enrolled than any of the nine other elementary schools in the area. A charter school serving middle-grade students in the same area was located less than a quarter of a mile from a public middle school that served nearly three times the proportion of ethnic minority students as the charter school.[53]

The authors also note that 75 percent of the students in the metropolitan Phoenix charter schools were in schools that were 70 percent white or more. In contrast, only 45 percent of the students in the public comparison group were in schools that were 70 percent white or more.[54] They conclude:

> The national and state evaluations which report that
> Arizona charter schools serve a proportion of ethnic

minority students at a level consistent with or greater than the traditional public schools are off the mark. Their methods produce numbers and percentages in the aggregate, techniques that conceal potential evidence of ethnic separation at the level at which it should be measured. The general picture of Arizona's charter schools is that they are significantly more segregated than the traditional public schools.[55]

The Cobb and Glass paper demonstrates why it is important to disaggregate the national-, state-, and even district-level data and to place charter schools within their local, community context to better understand issues of racial/ethnic segregation and isolation. Clearly, more research needs to be done in this area.

POVERTY RATES: A SCHOOL- AND DISTRICT-LEVEL COMPARISON. In terms of poverty rates at the school and district level, the Department of Education's Fourth-Year Report on charter schools is not helpful because the data are only broken down to the state level, not to the school or district level. The Department of Education's Second-Year Report is, however, much more helpful. These data, based on 1996–97 figures, showed that in about 52 percent of nearly four hundred charter schools, less than a third of students were eligible for free or reduced-price lunch, while in 29 percent of all charter schools more than two-thirds of the students were eligible. Thus, it looks as though charter school enrollments tend to cluster in both poor and less poor schools.

Yet the Ascher study, which used 1997–98 data, showed a decline in the percentage of charter schools—from 29 percent in 1996–97 to 19 percent in 1997–98—with more than two-thirds of their students eligible for free or reduced-price lunch.[56] At the other end of the spectrum, the percentage of charter schools with less than a third of students eligible had grown from 52 percent to 61 percent during that same year.

The Department of Education's Second-Year Report also compared the percentage of students in charter schools who qualified for free or reduced-price lunch to the average percentage of qualifying students in the surrounding school districts. The report states that 50 percent of the charter schools were not distinct from their districts in the percentage of qualified students, 23 percent had a higher percentage of students who were eligible, and 27 percent had a lower percentage of students who were eligible than their districts.

Likewise, in their more recent and broader based analysis, Ascher and her colleagues found that nearly half of all charter schools (48 percent) were equivalent to their districts in the percentage of poor students eligible for free or reduced-price lunch.[57] However, they also found that only 14 percent of charter schools had a higher percentage of students eligible, while the percentage of charter schools enrolling a smaller percentage of low-income students than their surrounding school districts had grown from 27 to 38 percent. Thus, the percentage of poor students enrolled in charter schools declined relative to the nearby public schools.

Below, we look at more specific findings related to comparisons of charter schools to their districts in terms of student poverty.

♦   CHARTER SCHOOLS TEND TO HAVE FEWER POOR STUDENTS THAN THEIR DISTRICTS. According to the Ascher report, 54 percent of the 483 charter schools for which they had data had 20 percent of students or less eligible for free or reduced-price lunch.[58] In fact, a third of all charter schools had no students eligible. (The authors note that this finding may be due, in part, to the bureaucratic obstacles to becoming part of the federal free and reduced-price lunch program.) Meanwhile, only 23 percent of the 314 school districts for which they had data had 20 percent of students or less eligible for free or reduced-price lunch.

This suggests that at one end of the continuum—low-poverty school districts—charter schools generally had even fewer poor students enrolled than their districts. Yet at the other end of the continuum—in high-poverty districts—there was a concentration of charter schools serving a disproportionately higher percentage of poor students than their surrounding school districts: while nearly 11 percent of charter schools had enrollments in which 80 percent of students or more were eligible for free or reduced-price lunch, only about 5 percent of the school districts that housed these charter schools served a student population that was 80 percent or more poor.[59]

Meanwhile, the percentage of charter schools in the Ascher study that were more socioeconomically diverse—with enrollments in which between 20 and 80 percent of the students qualified for free or reduced-price lunch—was relatively low, at about 35 percent. This compared to more than 72 percent of the school districts in which the charter schools resided.[60] Thus, like the data on the percentage of students of color, charter schools are more likely to be found on one end of the poverty continuum or the other, and the public school districts are more likely to be in the middle, with a greater mix of students.

Meanwhile, several of the individual state reports mentioned in the section above also provide information on charter schools and student poverty rates. Most show that charter schools tend to serve fewer poor students than their districts. For instance, the SRI report found that in about 60 percent of California charter schools, students were less likely to be from low-income families than other students in their sponsoring districts. In more than half of these instances—36 percent of all charter schools—the proportion of students eligible for the lunch program was more than twenty percentage points less than that in their districts' noncharter schools. Similar patterns hold in Colorado[61] and Massachusetts[62] and, to a lesser extent, in Michigan.[63]

The pattern of charter schools—regardless of their racial/ethnic makeup—serving smaller percentages of low-income students relative to their surrounding districts is strong. Some of this distinction between charter and noncharter public schools could be related to the subtle and often covert ways in which students and their families are recruited and admitted into charter schools. As we discuss in the following section, we learned a great deal about these practices in our in-depth study of ten school districts in California. Several other studies have raised these same issues.

SUMMARY OF SCHOOL- AND DISTRICT-LEVEL DATA. According to Ascher and her colleagues, while preliminary analyses of charter school enrollment data suggest that charter schools "mirror" their districts in the average percentage of students from different racial/ethnic or socioeconomic groups, a more careful analysis suggests that individual charter schools are serving more students at the extreme ends of the ethnicity and socioeconomic continuums. In particular, their data show that charter schools serving mostly students of color tend to be much less racially/ethnically diverse than their districts. Similarly, while a large number of charter schools do not serve very many students eligible for free or reduced-price lunch, in disadvantaged districts charter schools may serve even more eligible students than the district average. According to Ascher and colleagues, "[A] closer analysis suggests that charter schools may be proliferating at both the low and the high end of the race/ethnicity and affluent/poverty continuums."[64] The research from various states generally confirms these findings, although it shows some differences in terms of the specific distinctions between charter schools and their local school districts.

These findings offer an interesting twist to the story that emerged from the state-level data in the prior section. There it appeared that in states in which the overall public school enrollment was less white, charter schools were more likely to enroll an equal or disproportionately high percentage of white students. And in states where the overall public school enrollment was more white, the charter school enrollment was disproportionately students of color. The same inverse relationships between the charter schools and the statewide public schools existed, although not as strongly, for low-income students, suggesting that charter schools look different from the statewide public school system in terms of both the racial/ethnic and the socioeconomic makeup of the students who enroll.

The Ascher study as well as several of the state reports suggest that when you look at school- and district-level data, charter schools are more extreme in terms of racial and social class isolation and segregation than the districts in which they are located. Thus, in a predominantly white state such as Michigan, not only are charter schools more likely to enroll African-American students than white students, but they are also more likely to enroll a higher percentage of African-American students than their surrounding school districts—at least in the urban districts in the southeastern part of the state. Conversely, in a state such as California, in which the general K–12 public school population is very diverse, charter schools are more likely to enroll white students and more likely to have a higher percentage of white students then their surrounding school districts. The same would be true, on average, for poor and nonpoor students within their state and local context.

In this way, charter schools may well be exacerbating the racial/ethnic and socioeconomic segregation that is already quite pervasive in the public educational system. Of course, before such conclusions can be convincingly drawn, more data are needed comparing the racial/ethnic makeup of charter schools to that of nearby individual public schools. Indeed, for those charter schools located in large and diverse school districts, the charter school to school district comparisons are far less helpful.

ACCESS AND OPPORTUNITIES WITHIN CHARTER SCHOOL REFORM

Some of the most important findings from our study of charter schools[65] in California revealed that they can subtly garner increased control over who enrolls in them through their limited and targeted recruitment efforts and selective admissions policies. Other studies of charter schools across the country describe similar phenomena. These practices may be contributing to an increase in racial/ethnic isolation and segregation in charter schools.

Targeted and Word-of-Mouth Recruitment

A few of the charter schools we studied included information about their schools in districtwide school choice brochures that went to all parents. But more often the recruitment process was highly circumscribed. For instance, many more charter schools simply posted flyers in the local community or sent out mailers to families within their attendance boundaries. A few charter school directors took out ads in the local newspaper, and many gave tours of their schools to interested students and parents. Still other charter schools advertised by sending educators and/or students to attend various meetings or public forums to make presentations about the school. Finally, several charter schools in our study relied solely on word-of-mouth efforts to attract students and parents.

Though some of these recruitment tactics are utilized by other public schools, charter school founders and operators have much more flexibility to target these efforts in specific communities because of both the charter school legislation and the nature of this reform. Their methods can be especially effective when charter schools are new, start-up schools that are not serving an established attendance area. These start-up schools, which must recruit hundreds of students very quickly, are in a better position to market themselves strategically, and we found that many of them target specific communities, whether based on geographic location of residence, racial/ethnic composition, language proficiency, or "at-risk" characteristics.

In their discussion of such recruitment practices, David Arsen, David Plank, and Gary Sykes note that some Michigan charter schools have pursued locational, curricular, and marketing strategies that make them especially available or attractive to members of particular ethnic or racial groups. In some cases, the authors note, the "target market" is white students in districts where most of the students are members of minority groups.[66]

Furthermore, we learned in California that for schools that gain good reputations, the need for formal recruitment efforts often declines and more informal, word-of-mouth networks become the primary route through which people obtain information about the school. These word-of-mouth networks, often circumscribed by race, social class, and language, limit who finds out about these schools and their admissions policies.

Other studies point to the same phenomenon occurring outside of California. For instance, a study of Arizona charter schools reported that 53 percent of surveyed parents with children enrolled in charter schools said they found out about the school by word of mouth from a friend, relative, or neighbor. Another 22 percent said they had learned about the school because of its reputation in the community.[67] Similarly, the Texas study by Gregory Weiher and colleagues found that 97 percent of the students in the non-at-risk charter schools were recruited via word of mouth, as were nearly 80 percent of the at-risk charter school students.[68]

We posit that, in our segregated and stratified society, these targeted and word-of-mouth recruitment strategies, combined with the fairly selective admissions policies that charter schools employ, described below, work against racial/ethnic and socioeconomic diversity in many instances.

Selective Admissions Policies

Admissions requirements and processes exemplify another way in which charter schools have more control over their enrollments than most regular public schools. For instance, although many of the charter schools in our California study operated on a "first-come, first-served" basis, they still gave preferential treatment to certain students—that is, students who lived nearby, who had attended before the school went charter (in the case of a conversion school), who had siblings at the school, or whose parents worked there.

Furthermore, in most cases the degree of selection went beyond these "first-come" policies and preferences in part because almost every school we visited had a waiting list of students who wanted to enroll. Thus, most of the charter schools implemented some sort of admissions requirements to help them determine which of the "first come" students and parents best "fit" the philosophy and mission of the charter school. In fact, the SRI study found that 44 percent of the ninety-eight California charter schools surveyed cited student and/or parent lack of commitment to the school's philosophy as a factor for being denied admission.

In order to better assess the fit between the charter school and the families in terms of shared values and beliefs, several schools required some sort of pre-admissions meeting between school officials and parents and/or students. The meetings ranged, depending on the school, from informal discussions in which the school culture is described, to a more formal interview designed to assess students' abilities and interests as well as parents' level of commitment to education and school service. Charter school operators described to us how these meetings were often used as opportunities to assure that families would fit in at the schools.

Similarly, a report on charter school reform in New Jersey found that all seven charter schools studied required an interview of the applicants "to ensure that the goals and mission of the school are in concert with that of the parents and students."[69]

Another admissions requirement that gave the charter schools we studied more power to shape their educational communities were contracts compelling students and/or parents to abide by certain rules and expectations. These contracts are widespread in California charter schools. In fact, the SRI study found that 75 percent of California charter schools required a parent or adult to sign a contract with the school when enrolling a child.[70]

Seven of the seventeen charter schools we studied in depth required parents to sign contracts, which asked them to conduct a variety of tasks including reading to their children, going over homework, and encouraging "appropriate" student behavior in accordance with school behavior codes. However, the most common requirement in

these contracts was that parents volunteer at the school and participate in school activities a certain number either of hours or of events
per school year. Many of the schools reserved the right to ask families to
leave if parents did not meet the requirements specified in the contract. They could also deny families admission to the school if parents
did not agree ahead of time to fulfill the requirements of the charter.
According to the SRI report, 32 percent of California charter schools
had denied families admission to their schools because the parents were
not able to commit to the parental involvement requirement.[71]

Yet even more common than the parent contracts in our study
were the student contracts/requirements. All but four of the seventeen
charter schools we visited had such student contracts and/or requirements in place. Educators at these schools could ask students to leave if
they did not "live up to the charter" or the contract. In other words, students who were seen as not "trying hard enough," were frequently tardy
or absent, or misbehaved according to the school's conduct code could
be kicked out of their charter schools.

Again, this is not simply a California phenomenon. In fact, the
Arsen report noted that some Michigan charter schools appeared to
be developing increasingly aggressive strategies for selecting their students.[72] They cite mechanisms similar to those we documented in
California, including requiring parents to fill out elaborate application
forms and/or participate in an interview before enrolling their child.
The authors note that such practices make it possible for administrators
to discourage applications from students who might disrupt the school
community.[73]

Similarly, the New Jersey study found that although each of the
charter schools examined used a lottery system to ensure random selection
of its students, there were several components added to the application
process that undermined the intent of random selection, including parent
contracts and interviews.[74] In fact, one charter school in this study listed
"reasonable criteria" for admission which included "[i]nterview with parent (guardian) and child," "[a] review of past student school performance
to ascertain interest," and "[p]arent (guardian) agreement to, and signing
of, a contract regarding specific responsibilities."[75]

Setting admissions priorities for certain groups of students or
requiring that students and/or parents sign a contract and/or go through
an interview process illustrate some of the ways in which charter
schools, as schools of choice, can decide who attends them, more so

than other public schools. It is easy to see how these recruitment and admissions practices could lead to greater racial/ethnic and social class segregation and inequality at the school level, in part because of the way in which some charter school operators use them to create more homogeneous schools and in part because of the already existing segregation and inequality within local communities. And in fact, the majority of schools we studied were more racially/ethnically and socioeconomically isolated than the school districts in which they resided. In ten of the seventeen California charter schools we studied, at least one racial or ethnic group was over- or underrepresented by 15 percent or more in comparison to their districts' racial makeup. In eight of these schools, the percentages were off by more than 15 percent for two or more racial or ethnic groups.[76]

Still, we also suspect that the picture is more complicated than racial/ethnic demographic differences. We saw, for instance, how across various contexts these recruitment and admissions practices contributed to something we call "relative privilege": the way in which the ability of charter schools to control who comes to them more tightly assures that they enroll students who already have the resources, support, or best academic or behavioral records relative to other students in nearby public schools. In other words, even when charter schools look similar to regular public schools in terms of the racial/ethnic and even socioeconomic makeup of their students, they often may enroll the students from the local community with the most involved parents or the strongest support systems.

Thus, in addition to crude numbers on race/ethnicity and poverty rates, we also need to compare other characteristics of charter school and noncharter school students in the same community, especially parental support, prior achievement, and so forth. Similarly, as we discuss below, we also must compare the opportunities available to different children in different charter schools.

Opportunities to Learn across Charter Schools

Given the emerging evidence that poor students and students of color are often enrolled in separate charter schools from their more advantaged peers, a fundamental question that researchers should be pursuing is whether or not the opportunities to learn differ across charter schools, and, to the extent they do, which students have access to which opportunities. If indeed racial/ethnic and socioeconomic diversity within charter schools is not a high priority, then the issue of equality of opportunities to learn across racially and socioeconomically segregated charter schools is of utmost importance. Yet thus far, only a handful of researchers are trying to connect demographic information on charter school enrollments to an analysis of the educational opportunities available in different charter schools.

One of the best studies addressing this issue is the Cobb and Glass paper on Arizona charter schools, in which they examined the programmatic offerings, or "educational missions," of twenty-two charter high schools in the Phoenix metropolitan area.[77] They found that twelve of these schools offered a "college prep" curriculum, while the remaining ten offered a more vocational education program. Interestingly, the racial/ethnic breakdown of these two sets of schools is quite stark: 86 percent of the 1,865 students enrolled in the college-prep charter high schools were white, while less than 40 percent of the 1,635 students enrolled in the vocational high schools were white. The authors note that the proportion of white students in urban, college-bound charter high schools was well over two times the proportion of white students in urban, non-college-bound charter high schools.[78] Similar, although less dramatic, racial/ethnic distinctions between college-prep and vocational charter schools were found in the eleven rural charter high schools studied.

As we noted above, the Texas report by Weiher and his colleagues found that Latino students were overrepresented in the at-risk charter schools and somewhat underrepresented in the non-at-risk charter schools. Meanwhile, the student populations of the non-at-risk charter schools had two times as many white students as the at-risk charter schools—30 percent versus 14 percent. African-American students were about equally overrepresented in both the at-risk and the non-at-risk charter schools compared to their overall enrollment in the public schools statewide.[79]

These demographic differences for Latino and white students are more disturbing in light of another finding from the study, which showed that while 50 percent of the students in the non-at-risk charter schools intend to go on to a four-year college after graduation from high school, only 26 percent of the students in the at-risk charter schools have such plans.

Related to this issue of opportunity to learn, we found in our UCLA Charter Study of ten school districts in California that starting and operating a charter school required a substantial amount of resources of all kinds—material, in-kind, social, and political.[80] Access to these resources varied greatly depending on the location of the charter school in a given community and the school's relationship to various institutions, including the school districts, business community, policymakers, and so forth. While we saw charter school operators across the seventeen schools we studied engaged in one or more resource-generating strategies, we also witnessed substantial disparities in the resources they were able to attract with these strategies. For example, while a governance board member at a well-resourced charter school contemplated how to utilize the abundance of computers and a business manager at another wealthy charter school reflected on its $400,000 budget surplus, other charter schools were housed in barren facilities that sometimes had no running water, heat, or adequate classrooms for the students. In addition, usually there were very few, if any, computers or science equipment in the poor charter schools compared to the wealthier charter schools.

Generally speaking, schools located in predominantly middle- and upper-middle-class communities and serving a higher proportion of white students tended to have easier access to financial and in-kind resources due to their high-status connections. Meanwhile, educators in charter schools serving predominantly poor students and students of color were often overwhelmed by the day-to-day demands of running a school with limited resources and struggled to make similar connections. These findings raise important issues related to opportunities to learn that should be explored more fully in future research.[81]

Summary of Access and Opportunity Issues

It appears that many charter schools are able to engage in recruitment and admissions practices that in many cases may contribute to greater racial/ethnic and socioeconomic segregation across charter schools. These practices also seem to contribute to the self-selection of students into charter schools who are "relatively privileged" compared to students in the nearby public schools. Furthermore, there is some preliminary evidence that issues of opportunity to learn in charter schools are leading to a separate and unequal system in which poor students and students of color have less access to a challenging curriculum.

Lacking additional data and analysis, we argue that more attention needs to be paid to the mechanisms by which inequality is exacerbated by charter school reform. In the next section of this chapter we look more closely at the state charter school laws as they relate to this and other demographic information on charter schools in each state.

LEGISLATIVE LIMBO: CHARTER SCHOOLS AND DIVERSITY

Some charter school researchers have tried to relate their findings directly to the state laws governing charter school reform. They sometimes make a connection between the specifics of the legislation and the demographics of who enrolls in charter schools, arguing that the "rules matter" in terms of who is or is not served.[82] Given the diversity of charter school laws and charter school enrollments in different states, the search for a relationship between the two seems logical.

As part of our overall assessment of what is known thus far about racial/ethnic and socioeconomic diversity within charter schools, we also examined the charter school legislation of thirty-six states and the District of Columbia. We paid particular attention to provisions of these laws that would influence student access to charter schools, including who is eligible for charter schools, enrollment requirements and admissions criteria, selection criteria, racial balance guidelines, and desegregation compliance. We then compared what we learned about each state's law to what we knew from the above analysis of who is enrolling in charter schools and how those enrollments relate to the demographics of the regular public schools in the same states, districts, and communities.

We argue that at this stage in the process of researching and documenting charter school reform, it is very difficult to conclude that there is a direct, causal link between the specifics of a state charter school law and the reality of who founds and who enrolls in charter schools. This is because in most states, the laws leave room for equity and access issues to be dealt with—or not dealt with—at the local level. Also, we see little evidence that this highly deregulatory reform puts in place any mechanisms to monitor the equity or racial balance provisions in the laws.

Our hunch therefore, based on this analysis and our own research in California,[83] is that the specific context of different states and communities plays a larger role in shaping who engages in charter school reform than do rather subtle differences in the state laws. Given the generally weak nature of the equity and access provisions in most charter school laws, we see little evidence that they play a major role in shaping the race/ethnicity and socioeconomic demographics of most charter schools. This does not mean, however, that amended laws, with stronger diversity requirements and provisions, could not have a large impact.

In the following sections, we look more specifically at several domains of the legislation as they relate to the enrollment of charter schools in particular states.

Admissions Criteria and Enrollment Requirements

Theoretically, one of the most important ways state laws could shape the demographics of charter schools would be through the wording of admissions criteria. Thus, we examined the wording of the laws on admissions criteria in the thirty-six states we studied and related that to the data on charter school enrollments in the twenty-one states with the most students enrolled in charter schools. We tried to make connections between what we know about charter school legislation across the country and how these trends relate to who is enrolling in charter schools in the twenty-one states.

For the most part we saw no consistent pattern between the wording of a state's legislation on this issue and the race/ethnicity and poverty rates of students enrolled in charter schools in that state. Twenty-nine of the thirty-six state laws explicitly allow charter schools to have admissions criteria (although nine of these laws specify that these criteria cannot be based on intellectual ability, measures of achievement, or "aptitude"). Among these twenty-nine states several—for example, Alaska, California, Colorado, and Kansas—enroll either an equal or greater percentage of white students in charter schools compared to the regular public schools. These same states, as we noted above, also enroll equal or fewer poor students on average than the public schools in general. Meanwhile, many of the states that enroll a disproportionately high percentage of low-income students and students of color—for example, Connecticut, Pennsylvania, and Texas—also allow charter schools to apply admissions criteria. Therefore, whether or not charter schools can have admissions criteria does not appear to be the main variable in predicting the race/ethnicity and socioeconomic conditions of students who enroll.

It is interesting to note, however, that the majority of the nine states that allow charter schools to have admissions criteria that are not based on "intellectual ability" or "measures of achievement or aptitude" are all states in which charter schools enroll a disproportionately high percentage of low-income students and students of color. For instance, charter school laws in Massachusetts, Michigan, Minnesota, New Jersey, and Ohio all restrict the scope of charter school admissions criteria to nonacademic criteria. Thus, it may be that a more comprehensive "admissions criteria" policy that forces charter schools to select students based on nonacademic criteria impacts who enrolls in charter schools across the different contexts.

Another admissions and enrollment issue addressed in many of the laws is the selection method that charter schools can use if they are overenrolled. The vast majority of laws—twenty-five out of thirty-six—specify that students should be selected by random drawing if the school is overenrolled once the admissions criteria mentioned above have been applied. There is some variation across states, however, in terms of special preferences for various students in addition to the random selection. For instance, some laws specify that students will be selected randomly with preferences for siblings, for students living within the district boundary, or for students in particular grade levels.

But despite these particulars, once again no real pattern or relationship appears between the wording of the state laws in terms of enrollment and the demographics of the charter schools as compared to general K–12 public school enrollments. States that serve both disproportionately high *and* disproportionately low percentages of low-income students and students of color compared to the public schools in these states are among the twenty-five that call for random drawings.

Thus, there is little evidence that whether charter schools can have admissions criteria or whether they must select students randomly when they are overenrolled is a major mitigating factor in the broader demographic makeup of these schools. Additional research needs to be conducted in order to know whether a more restrictive law that forbids the use of "ability" or "prior achievement" as part of the criteria is more conducive to the development of charter schools that serve poor students and students of color. Another important part of that research agenda should be to examine "relative privilege" issues as they relate to charter schools in any states with admissions criteria. In other words, it is important to gather more information on how even the nonacademic criteria that charter schools use in admitting students can put some students at a disadvantage, regardless of race or poverty.

"At-Risk" Focus or Priority

A popular theme in charter school legislation is for charter schools to serve so-called at-risk students. Unfortunately, the legislation rarely defines what "at risk" means. Regardless of whether or not the laws specify that charter schools should serve these students does not appear to influence the proportion of low-income students or students of color served relative to the overall state enrollment.

For instance, among the nineteen states in which at-risk students are *not* mentioned or specified in the law are Arizona, California, Georgia, and Kansas—all of which enroll the same or a greater percentage of nonpoor and white students in their charter schools as in the regular public schools. On the other hand, also among these nineteen states are Michigan, Minnesota, New Jersey, and Pennsylvania —states that enroll a larger percentage of poor students and students of color in their charter schools. Conversely, states with laws that give priority to applications for charter schools designed to increase the educational opportunities of at-risk students include Colorado, where charter schools serve mostly white and nonpoor students. Similarly, the New Mexico law states that charter school applications "must" indicate how the charter schools will serve the needs of at-risk students, yet New Mexico's charter schools enroll students who are, on the average, significantly less poor than the students in the state's public schools.

One possible reason for an apparent lack of relationship between legislative provisions for serving at-risk students and the demographics of charter schools in various states is that the state laws tend to be rather vague. And, as with so many aspects of charter school legislation, it is not at all clear if or how such provisions are being monitored or enforced. In fact, it may be that only the laws with more specific criteria and requirements have any impact on charter school enrollments.

For instance, an argument could be made that a more specific requirement regarding at-risk students is one of the reasons why Texas does not fit the larger trend mentioned above of states with less white

and less wealthy overall public school populations housing more charter schools that serve white and more middle-class students. Unlike
legislation in other states, the Texas law specifies that the State Board
of Education may grant additional charters, above the 120-school cap,
if they go to schools that will serve at least 75 percent at-risk students.
Similarly, Connecticut, another state in which charter schools serve a
much higher percentage of low-income students and students of color
than the regular public schools, also has a law that is much more specific
about who will be served by this reform: the law states that preference
will be given to charter school applications for schools to be located in
school districts with concentrated child poverty or in which 75 percent or more of the students are "minorities."

Another state law that stands out is that of Rhode Island. This
law declares that the charter school population "must be reflective of
the student population of the district, including but not limited to special education children, children at risk, children eligible for free or
reduced cost lunch, and LEP [limited English proficiency] students."
More explicitly, the law states that "no charter shall be authorized" for
a school that does not include such students. Unfortunately, we do not
have demographic data on Rhode Island's two charter schools because
states with fewer than three schools were not included in the cross-
state analysis in the Department of Education's Fourth-Year report.
Thus, we argue that states such as Texas, Connecticut, and Rhode
Island should be monitored closely to assess the impact of these stronger
and more specific laws on charter school enrollments.

In closing, we do not see any evidence that charter school laws
that merely mention the education of at-risk students as a goal or a priority without any specific guidelines or requirements have much impact
on who enrolls in charter schools. We do, however, argue that more
attention should be paid to the relationship between the legislative
wording and at-risk student enrollment.

Racial Balance Requirements and Desegregation Policy Compliance

In looking at the racial balance and desegregation requirements of charter school laws, once again we see little evidence that the legislation has
much direct impact on who enrolls in charter schools in various states.

For instance, in terms of requiring charter schools to have any racial balance, twenty-six of the thirty-six states fall into two general categories: nineteen of the state laws say nothing about the racial balance of charter schools, and seven laws state that charter school applications should specify how the schools will achieve a racial and ethnic balance that is reflective of the population of the district in which it is located. Within each of these categories, states are mixed in terms of the students enrolled in their charter schools. For instance, under the category of states that require no racial balance are several states—including Alaska, Arizona, Colorado, Georgia, and New Mexico—in which the charter school population has an equal or higher percentage of white students and an equal or lower percentage of low-income students than the regular public schools. Yet there are also several states in this first category that have charter school populations with smaller percentages of white students and larger percentages of poor students, including Illinois, Louisiana, Michigan, and Texas. The same can be said of the second category of states, which includes California and Kansas as well as Florida, Ohio, and Wisconsin.

Of course, comparing state guidelines on the racial balance of individual schools to the aggregated data on statewide charter school enrollments is not entirely helpful because individual charter schools could be racially balanced in comparison to their local districts even if the state average for charter school enrollment is way off. But we do know from some of the state-by-state research that even in those states with laws that require charter school applications to specify how the schools will achieve a racial and ethnic balance reflective of their districts, there appears to be little compliance thus far. For instance, as we reported earlier, both our UCLA Charter School Study of seventeen charter schools in ten school districts in California[84] and the Crockett study of charter school segregation in California[85] show that in most cases, there is virtually no effort being made to assure that charter schools actually reflect the racial/ethnic makeup of their school districts.

Still, as with the at-risk requirements discussed above, some state legislation is more directive when it comes to racial balance requirements than others. And once again, the Connecticut legislation stands out as being more forceful on this issue than virtually any other state's legislation. The Connecticut law includes three provisions that should promote racial balance in charter schools: First, the law stipulates that once a charter has been approved at the local level (for district charters), the state review board must approve the charters as long as they do not have segregative effects on student assignments. Second, the law requires that charter proposals specify how the schools involved will promote a racially diverse student body. And third, the annual report that the state requires of each charter school must describe the schools' racial and ethnic composition and efforts taken to increase diversity. Thus, the Connecticut legislation stands out in terms of its stronger emphasis on creating more racial balance in charter schools. And as we have noted, large percentages of African-American and Latino as well as poor students are enrolled in charter schools in this state. Still, we currently do not have data to confirm whether or not these Connecticut charter schools are any more or less racially diverse than their local districts or nearby public schools.

In terms of the intersection between the relatively new charter school legislation and existing school desegregation policies, the charter school laws are particularly weak in the vast majority of states. A total of twenty-five state laws do not specify that charter schools must comply with school desegregation court orders or policies. And these twenty-five states are a mixture serving both more low-income students and students of color in the charter schools—for example, Connecticut, Massachusetts, Minnesota, and Texas—and those states with equal or more white students and/or fewer low-income students—for example, Alaska, California, Georgia, Kansas, and New Mexico.

The relatively small number of states with legislation that is more directive in this area are again a mixture of those states with charter school populations that are more and less reflective of the general public school populations, including Colorado, Louisiana, and Michigan. Yet once again, while no clear pattern emerges in terms of charter school racial balance and the specifics of the state legislation, it is also clear that we currently lack the more systematically collected data needed to examine these relationships.

Transportation

The final aspect of the legislation that potentially can have a strong impact on who is able to enroll in charter schools is whether or not transportation is provided for students. We found six states with legislation that guaranteed all students transportation to their charter schools. The laws in these states—Colorado, Illinois, New Mexico, New York, South Carolina, and Virginia—require charter schools to provide a plan for meeting the transportation needs of their students. Laws in another five states—Nevada, North Carolina, New Hampshire, New Jersey, and Pennsylvania—require charter schools to adhere to the same transportation policy as the district in which they are located but do not specify who pays for it. Only two states—Arizona and Minnesota—provide funds to help cover some of the cost of transportation for some students.

Another eight states have laws that require the charter schools or their local school districts to provide transportation to distinct groups of students—for example, those students residing in the district where the charter school is located or poor students who live a certain distance from the charter school. Again, these eight states represent a mixture of student enrollments, from Connecticut with its disproportionately high percentage of poor students and students of color in charter schools to Kansas with its disproportionately high percentage of white students and equal percentage of low-income students enrolled in charter schools as the regular public schools. Meanwhile, the laws in several states, which also have a mix of enrollments in their charter schools—including those of California, Georgia, and Michigan—require no transportation for charter schools.

Summary of Legislative Limbo

While we would never argue that the specifics of state legislation do not matter, when state charter school laws are so consistently weak in terms of student access, equity, and racial balance the relationship between the laws and students' experiences are more tangential. In other words, we see little correlation between the provisions of a charter school law with regard to admissions criteria, racial balance, at-risk focus, school desegregation compliance, or transportation provisions and the demographics of charter school enrollment.

Therefore, although Ascher and colleagues suggest that charter school enrollment in states such as Georgia and Minnesota may well be related to the weak equity provisions in the Georgia charter school law and the stronger provisions in the Minnesota law,[86] we see several examples that work in the other direction. For instance, the Colorado law is relatively strong in terms of an at-risk focus and required compliance with desegregation laws, but the charter schools underserve low-income students and (to a lesser extent) students of color. Meanwhile, Michigan is weak on the at-risk focus provisions but appears to enroll large percentages of poor students and students of color in its charter schools—students who, according to some definitions, are more likely to be at risk of failing in school.

It seems that the context of this reform as it interacts with the history and politics of each state and school district often has more to do with who is enrolled in charter schools and how the demographics of the schools relate to those of regular public schools than does the language in often vague and fairly deregulatory state legislation. At the same time, some of the particularly strong equity provisions in certain state laws— that is, the racial balance criteria in Connecticut and the at-risk focus criteria in Texas and Rhode Island—could very well have a direct impact on who enrolls and who is served by charter school reform.[87]

POLICY IMPLICATIONS AND CONCLUSIONS

The country is now at an important juncture, uncertain about what, if anything, will replace old race-specific policies, such as school desegregation, and address ongoing racial and social class inequality in our educational system and larger society. In part, charter school laws reflect this ambiguity. Charter schools could play an important role in setting an agenda around these issues, but only if policymakers and charter school movement leaders agree that such issues are worth addressing and amend charter school laws accordingly. If they do not, charter schools across the country will continue to reflect a wide range of local reactions to racial inequality and the national confusion about race and educational policy. Some, perhaps most, of these reactions will exacerbate existing problems.

This will occur because the state laws do not, for the most part, establish the support systems that many of the most disadvantaged students would need—for example, free and accessible transportation or a dissemination system to inform *all* parents about charter school options. Instead, most of the state laws allow charter schools to have some sort of admissions criteria, such as required parent involvement, which often are more difficult for the poorest and most disenfranchised parents to fulfill. And virtually all charter schools have a very limited and narrow method of recruitment that tends to tap into relatively better-off families, even in the low-income communities.

Meanwhile, the legislation generally does not encourage or provide support or incentives for charter school operators to serve a diverse group of students. Therefore, the vast majority of charter schools are created to serve students from a particular cultural or geographic community or those who share a similar educational philosophy or view of parental involvement. Thus, through various subtle recruitment and admissions mechanisms, charter schools are able to attract and admit more homogeneous—along several different dimensions—student bodies.

Layered on top of this are the state and local contexts that have shaped parents' and students' experiences in the regular public schools and their demand for alternatives. We argue that charter schools grow out of a strong sense of frustration with the regular public schools, wherever that frustration may be lodged. In predominantly white and wealthy states with smaller, more separate and unequal school districts—the profile of many of the northern and eastern states—we believe that frustration is housed primarily in the segregated and isolated urban school districts. Thus, we are likely to see charter schools serving poor students and students of color. In more racially and socioeconomically diverse southern and western states that generally contain larger and more diverse school districts, the frustration is likely to transcend a wider range of communities as whites in large urban school districts also want to participate in this reform. Obviously the racial/ethnic and social class inequality in the larger society has framed these frustrations, and if charter school legislation remains as laissez-faire as it has been, this will not be the reform to overcome such inequalities. In fact, it may well be the reform to exacerbate them.

For those charter school supporters who would like to see this reform movement achieve the more progressive goals of greater racial/ethnic and socioeconomic equality for all students, the first step is to reevaluate some of the popular rating systems that are currently applied to charter school laws. For instance, the conservative Center for Education Reform conducts a state ranking of charter school legislation in which the so-called strong laws are the more deregulatory laws that foster the "development of numerous genuinely independent charter schools."[88] The main criteria for these "strong" laws are that they place no (or a very high) limit on the number of charter schools that can open, provide for multiple charter granting agencies, allow students from all over the state to attend, and give schools a great deal of operational autonomy and whether laws allow for an "automatic" waiver from state and district laws and regulations. So-called weak laws, therefore, are those that are more regulatory in terms of all these criteria. The Center ranks all the state charter school laws according to these criteria, thereby designating the "strong" versus the "weak" laws.

Not mentioned in these rankings are any legislative provisions that advance equity or redistribute resources and opportunities to the students who have been the least well served by the public schools. Nor is there any value placed on provisions that would promote what the majority of parents say they want in their public schools—racial and ethnic diversity.

While the Center for Education Reform's ranking system appears to be popular with conservative backers of charter school reform, there are other more liberal and leftist charter school constituents who might be interested in supporting alternative ranking systems. One such system would give states more credit for legislation that requires a certain percentage of charter schools in a state to be racially/ethnically and socioeconomically diverse and then provides financial and resources incentives and supports to allow educators and parents to create such a school. A strong equity-focused law would provide money and resources to allow these diverse charter schools to have broader outreach and recruitment of students from different communities and to provide transportation for each student to and from school. It would restrict the use of parent contracts and disallow the use of admissions criteria, especially criteria based on perceived "ability" and prior achievement. It also would assure that white and wealthy families were not able to use charter school reform to escape racially and socioeconomically diverse public schools and school districts by creating predominantly white charter schools. Meanwhile, it would allow for the creation of some charter schools to enroll mostly African-American, Latino, American-Indian, or other students whose history and culture is often ignored in the regular public schools.

Extra resources and support services would be provided to such schools located in low-income communities to make up for the greater difficulty they face in raising the private resources available in wealthier communities. Still, these laws might want to restrict such extra resources to only those low-income charter schools that are run by community-based educators and parents as opposed to large for-profit educational management organizations (EMOs). Stronger and more specific legislative language giving preference to charter schools serving the most disadvantaged students is also needed.

While we believe that it is not fair to label charter school reform as an elitist movement, we are also aware that it is not realistic to declare charter schools, in their current manifestation, a viable solution to the inequitable educational opportunities available to poor students and students of color within the public schools. We fear that unless charter school laws change to promote more equity, access, and diversity within these more autonomous schools, this reform will become yet another sorting machine that exacerbates the existing system of segregation and isolation along racial/ethnic and social-class lines.

7.

UNEQUAL LEARNING ENVIRONMENTS: DISCIPLINE THAT WORKS

PAUL E. BARTON

Of all the commonly acknowledged reasons for inequality among American schools, policymakers often underemphasize the significance of student behavior. Schools in poor neighborhoods generally have higher levels of disorder, disruption, and fear, all of which impede the learning of low-income students. This chapter is about those behaviors: what they are, how they impact learning, what approaches are being tried to change them, and with what results.

EXTENT OF THE PROBLEM

Murder and Violence

Recently, the nation's attention has been riveted on media reports about serious injury and murder of students and teachers at school. In the combined school years of 1992–93 and 1993–94, the last time specific data on these events were collected, sixty-three students were murdered at school, an average of 31.5 per year. In addition, there were twenty-nine nonstudent personnel who met violent deaths, or 14.5 per year. Longer-term trend data are not available.[1]

During the 1996–97 school year, 12 percent of middle schools and 13 percent of high schools reported to police that a physical attack or fight with some type of weapon had taken place on school grounds. In 1993, 7.9 percent of twelfth-graders reported carrying some kind of weapon to school. This number declined to 5.7 percent in 1996. In 1994, just over 3 percent reported carrying a gun to school, about the same as in 1996.[2]

These incidents are horrifying and rightly warrant the attention of the education and policy communities. However, they are relatively infrequent for a country with some of the highest rates of violence in the developed world, one in which 99 percent of all child homicides occur off school grounds. The terrible acts of violence cited above certainly affect learning when they occur; in the case of the tragedy in Columbine, Colorado, the last two months of school were largely wiped out. But this chapter focuses on the problems that remain unseen and that affect the learning climate day-in and day-out. It is the less serious behaviors that are widespread—and growing—that have the largest adverse impact on students' learning.

Fear

The question beyond how much physical injury occurs is how much fear is engendered by the environment in schools. In 1996–97, about one in five middle and high schools—rising to over a third for city middle schools and almost half of city high schools—reported to police that "serious violent incidents" had occurred.[3] In 1996, 7 percent of male and 3 percent of female twelfth-graders reported that they had been injured with a weapon at school; 18 percent of males and 10 percent of females had been threatened with a weapon; another 13 percent of males and 11 percent of females had been injured without a weapon; and 27 percent of males and 17 percent of females had been threatened with injury. That adds up to two-thirds of males and two-fifths of females being threatened or injured. These figures have not changed much over the past twenty years. Such high levels of actual violence and weapons-carrying are bound to make students fearful for their safety. Street gangs also are a fact of life for a great many students. In 1989, 15 percent of twelve- to nineteen-year-old students reported that street gangs were present at their school, rising to 28 percent by 1995. For urban schools, the figure was 40 percent in 1995. While the number of students carrying weapons to school is down or stable, the presence of gangs has risen, and these are bound to contribute in some degree to the level of fear, tension, and distraction in schools.[4]

By all conventional measures, fear is rising in the nation's schools. In 1989, 6 percent of all twelve- to nineteen-year-old students reported fear of physical violence at school, and 4 percent feared going to and from school. These percentages had risen to 9 and 7 percent, respectively, by 1995. A similar percentage of students reported that they avoided one or more places in school out of fear. The percentages are considerably higher for minorities and students in urban schools. For black students in suburban schools, the figure is one in six who avoided places in school.[5]

Fear in urban schools parallels fear in the neighborhood. In a 1998 MetLife Survey, 44 percent of urban students said they were worried "about being physically attacked in or around" school, compared with 28 percent of suburban or rural students. Similarly, 45 percent of urban students were worried about the level of crime in their neighborhoods, while just 29 percent of suburban or rural students were.[6]

Disruption and Distraction

While murder, injury, and fear create disruption and distraction in schools and classrooms, many day-in and day-out student behaviors have an even greater impact on the teaching and learning processes. In Figure 7.1 (page 226), seventeen behaviors are arrayed by the degree to which public school principals believed the behaviors were serious problems in their schools. Student tardiness tops the list of disruptive behaviors, with half of the principals describing it as a serious or moderately serious problem in their schools in 1990–91. This figure rose to two in three in 1996–97. The more serious behaviors of absenteeism and cutting class were the second most frequently cited in 1996–97, identified by half the principals, and up from two in five from the previous period. Student use of tobacco, alcohol, and drugs

FIGURE 7.1. PERCENTAGE OF PUBLIC SCHOOL PRINCIPALS REPORTING THAT VARIOUS DISCIPLINE ISSUES WERE SERIOUS OR MODERATE PROBLEMS IN THEIR HIGH SCHOOLS, 1990–91 AND 1996–97

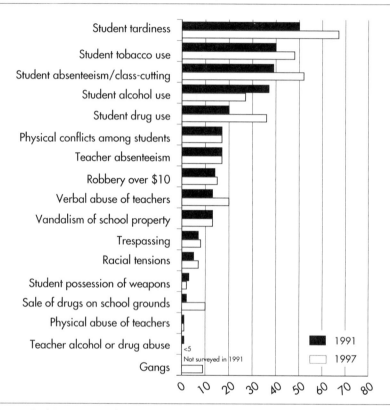

Source: Paul E. Barton, Richard J. Coley, and Harold Wenglinsky, "Order in the Classroom: Violence, Discipline, and Student Achievement," Educational Testing Service, Princeton, N.J., October 1998 [based on NCES, 1998].

are also high on the list, with a statistically significant increase in drug use from 1990–91 to 1996–97 (although alcohol use declined). There also was a significant increase in principals identifying drug sales on school grounds as a problem from 1990–91 to 1996–97. One in five principals identified verbal abuse of teachers as a problem in 1996–97, a significant increase from the prior period. The other ten behaviors showed no statistically significant differences between the two periods.

These national averages hide the considerable variation around the nation. To illustrate, Figure 7.2 shows the state-to-state variation in schools reporting that physical conflicts are a serious or moderate problem. Within the United States average of 14 percent, there was a low of 6 percent in North Dakota and a high of 44 percent in Hawaii. Of

FIGURE 7.2. PERCENTAGE OF EIGHTH-GRADERS WHOSE SCHOOLS REPORT THAT PHYSICAL CONFLICTS ARE A MODERATE OR SERIOUS PROBLEM IN THEIR SCHOOL, 1996

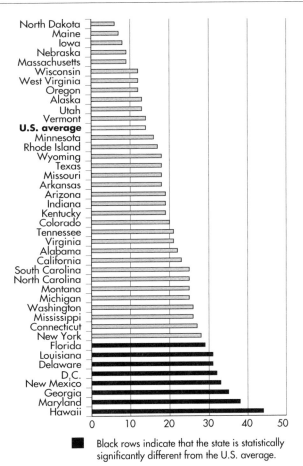

Black rows indicate that the state is statistically significantly different from the U.S. average.

Source: Paul E. Barton, Richard J. Coley, and Harold Wenglinsky, "Order in the Classroom: Violence, Discipline, and Student Achievement," Educational Testing Service, Princeton, N.J., October 1998 [based on *NAEP 1996 Mathematics Assessment*].

course, these are the schools' perceptions of the degree of the problem; there also may be variation in the degree to which principals view identical incidence of conflict as a problem.

It is not encouraging that in this decade of emphatic education reform, improvement was found only in the use of alcohol at school from 1990–91 to 1996–97. In terms of disruption in schools and classrooms, most negative behaviors are not trending in the right direction.

Concentration in Poorer Schools, Inner Cities, and Minority Populations

Most of the statistics provided above are averages for the United States or whole states. However, these disruptive behaviors are more severe in inner cities and in schools with high concentrations of minority students and students from low-income backgrounds.

There is great disparity between these less advantaged schools and their more advantaged counterparts in the most serious kind of violence. In the school years 1992–93 and 1993–94, the number of deaths by murder and suicide at school varied widely according to race. Of all murders and suicides, 50 percent were black and 25 percent were Hispanic. In inner-city public schools in 1993–94, 24 percent of teachers reported that they were either physically attacked or threatened with injury by a student, compared with only 13 percent for rural areas.[7]

In 1995, for ages twelve to nineteen, 16 percent of Hispanic students and 13 percent of black students feared being attacked or harmed at school. Only 6 percent of white students had the same fear. Fourteen percent of Hispanic, 13 percent of black, and 4 percent of white students reported such fear going to and from school.[8] And 13 percent of Hispanic, 12 percent of black, and 7 percent of white students avoided going to one or more places within their schools.

As noted before, street gangs became more prevalent from 1989 to 1995. While 23 percent of all twelve- to nineteen-year-old students reported street gangs in their school in 1995, 54 percent of urban Hispanics and 48 percent of suburban Hispanics reported their presence, as did 42 percent of urban blacks and 33 percent of suburban blacks. Older students were much more likely to report gang activity at school than younger students: 31 percent of nineteen-year-olds compared to 19 percent of twelve-year-olds. Among urban nineteen-year-olds, 54 percent reported street gangs.[9]

In reports from public schools of a composite of seventeen discipline issues in 1996–97, there was considerable disparity in incidence by school size, minority enrollment, and income of the surrounding areas. Of schools with fewer than three hundred students, 10 percent reported one or more discipline problems, compared to 38 percent of schools with one thousand or more students. This disparity existed irrespective of whether schools were in an urban, suburban, or rural area. Minority enrollment made a significant difference as well: schools that had minority levels at 50 percent or more were over twice as likely to report discipline problems as were schools that were less than 5 percent minority. Low income, defined by the percentage of students eligible for free or reduced-price lunches, affected discipline levels in rural areas and in the urban fringe.[10]

THE RELATIONSHIP BETWEEN DISCIPLINE AND ACHIEVEMENT

The late Albert Shanker used to say that if there is no discipline in the classroom there is no learning. Almost all teachers would likely agree. It is important, however, to examine the extent to which this is really true, as well as for what kind of behaviors it is true and how much changes in these behaviors improve or worsen student achievement. And, more specifically, how does disruptive behavior in schools and classrooms affect inner-city and minority youth, where the lags in achievement are the greatest?

Unfortunately, there have been no large-scale, national research studies specifically designed to answer these questions. One large study of school disorder was conducted in 1978 by the National Institute of Education, in response to a request by Congress. It found extensive problems of disorder in schools. There were, however, no corresponding measures of student achievement, so there is no way to explore the relationship between disorder and achievement through these data.

In 1998, Harold Wenglinsky of the ETS Policy Information Center specifically addressed disorder as it relates to achievement.[11] He analyzed the National Educational Longitudinal Survey,[12] which measured achievement and had extensive questionnaires about student behaviors and the policies that schools use to affect these behaviors. The survey was administered first in 1988, in the eighth grade, and then again in the tenth and twelfth grades. Wenglinsky ended up with usable information from 13,626 students. The frequency of both serious and non-serious offence was found to be negatively related to academic achievement in all four subject areas studied (mathematics, science, reading, and social science). The results from his analysis are summarized in Table 7.1.

Another critical issue is the role discipline and student behavior play in (1) whether people decide to go into teaching, (2) whether teachers move to other teaching locations, and (3) whether teachers leave the profession. While few data are available on the first two questions, a fair amount of information is available regarding teachers who leave the profession. Also, some data are available about the views of current teachers.

A first concern of teachers is the amount of disciplinary control they have over the classroom. In 1993–94, in the National Center for Education Statistics School and Staffing Survey,[13] teachers were asked specifically about areas over which they feel they have control. For the public school teachers surveyed, only 38 percent "thought that they had a great deal of influence on setting discipline policies." This is about the same degree of control they felt they had over the classroom curriculum. Meanwhile, more than 6 percent of teachers believed they had little or no influence. These statistics suggest that teachers have a considerable feeling of powerlessness in dealing with problems. But the public school data contrast sharply with that from private school teachers, of whom almost six in ten (the reverse) said they had a great deal of influence over discipline.

There is not a great deal of variation in the answers about discipline among teachers from central cities, urban fringes and large towns, and rural areas. However, school size does make an enormous difference, within each of these geographical categories. The percentage saying that they have influence over discipline in schools with fewer than 150 students is double the percentage who say this in schools of 750 or more (although much of this difference is due to the fact that many of the smaller schools are elementary schools, where teachers consistently say they have considerably more influence).

Given only one question asked in the survey about control, it is hard to interpret the results. Are teachers referring only to policies, such as the authority they have to deal with particular situations, or

TABLE 7.1. BETWEEN-SCHOOL COMPARISONS: THE NEGATIVE CORRELATION BETWEEN DELINQUENCY AND ACADEMIC ACHIEVEMENT

	SERIOUS	NONSERIOUS	DRUGS
MATH			
Urban		✓	✓
Nonurban	✓	✓	
Public	✓	✓	
Private			✓
READING			
Urban	✓		
Nonurban	✓	✓	
Public	✓	✓	
Private	✓		
SOCIAL SCIENCE			
Urban		✓	
Nonurban	✓	✓	
Public	✓	✓	
Private			
SCIENCE			
Urban		✓	✓
Nonurban	✓	✓	
Public	✓	✓	✓
Private			✓

Note: ✓ indicates a negative correlation.
Source: Paul E. Barton, Richard J. Coley, and Harold Wenglinsky, "Order in the Classroom: Violence, Discipline, and Student Achievement," Educational Testing Service, Princeton, N.J., October 1998 [based on Wenglinsky, unpublished tabulations derived from NELS:88].

are they speaking more broadly about the degree of control they are given? We need to know more about what they believe accounts for their lack of control.

Analysis of the School and Staffing Survey data leads to a firm conclusion that discipline does make a difference in whether teachers leave. Researchers at the American Institutes for Research and at the National Center for Education Statistics performed a statistical analysis with the data to identify factors associated with turnover (those factors were within the school, whether the exiting individual remained within the district, moved to another school elsewhere, or left education altogether). In each case, the turnover resulted in a decrease in teaching staff for the particular school.[14]

Differences in the rates of turnover were analyzed across different types of schools, including: "key characteristics of schools [such as size]; the level of poverty or affluence of the population served by the school (recipients of free lunch in public schools, tuition levels in private schools); some key demographic characteristics of the school faculty (levels of education, training, experience, and race); basic elements of faculty compensation packages; and important aspects of working conditions in schools." Two aspects of the working environment were found to be significant. Turnover rates in schools where teachers reported lower levels of control and influence were "distinctly" higher. Also, "higher levels in reported student discipline problems were associated with distinctly higher levels of turnover."

It is encouraging that the characteristics of being poor and urban themselves did not result in differences in turnover rates. Teacher control and student behavior contributed most. This suggests that we can keep more teachers if we can deal with the specific problems of student behavior, in inner cities as well as in suburbs.

When former teachers are asked why they left the profession, the four most common reasons are retirement, pregnancy/child rearing, pursuing another career, and a family or personal move. "Dissatisfied with teaching as a career" is the fifth most common reason, accounting for 9 percent of teachers leaving the profession in 1988–89 and 5 percent in 1994–95.[15] This figure is the same for teachers leaving both public and private schools. While many of the causes of turnover would be hard to alter, reviewing the causes of dissatisfaction could reveal avenues for reducing it.

Of those teachers who leave for reasons of dissatisfaction, how many are dissatisfied because of problems with student discipline and behaviors? In 1994–95, 18 percent of teachers leaving because of dissatisfaction attributed their departure to "student discipline problems," double the percentage in 1988–89. In addition, 18 percent cited "poor student motivation to learn," about the same as in 1988–89.[16] The relative importance of discipline problems also is revealed by teachers' responses to what steps they thought would be "most effective to encourage teachers to remain in teaching." Figure 7.3 shows that the

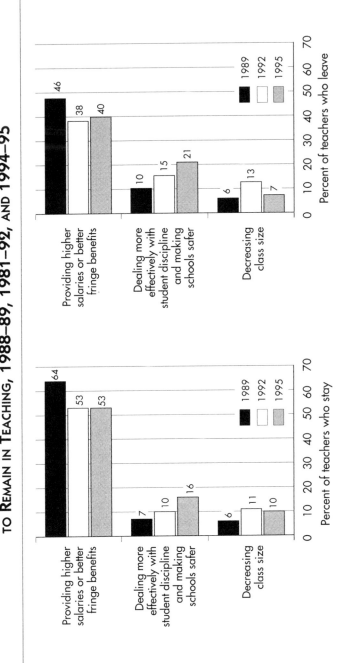

FIGURE 7.3. PUBLIC SCHOOL TEACHER OPINIONS ON EFFECTIVE STEPS TO ENCOURAGE TEACHERS TO REMAIN IN TEACHING, 1988–89, 1981–92, AND 1994–95

Source: Summer D. Whitener et al., *Characteristics of Stayers, Movers, and Leavers: Results from the Teacher Followup Survey: 1994–95,* NCES 97-450 (Washington, D.C.: U.S. Department of Education, National Center for Education Statistics, 1997), p. 17.

discipline problem falls between salaries/fringe benefits and decreasing class size in importance. Given the strong public interest in decreasing class size as a means to raise achievement, it is revealing that teachers think—at least from their own standpoint—that discipline is a more important matter. Moreover, the percentage citing discipline as important doubled from 1988–89 to 1994–95, both among teachers who stayed and among those who left.

The 1999 MetLife Survey sheds some light on where these concerns are most concentrated. The MetLife survey asked teachers, "How much of a factor would you say the problem of violence in your school is on teachers leaving your school—a major factor, a minor factor or not a factor?" Only 2 percent of teachers said it was a major factor, and 17 percent said a minor factor (81 percent said it was not a factor). But there was some variation. Most significantly, where the quality of education was judged only fair to poor, 18 percent called the problem of violence a major factor and 33 percent said it was a minor factor. Meanwhile, where many or all of the students were minority, 5 percent said violence was a major factor and 27 percent said it was a minor factor, roughly the same as when many or all of the students came from low-income families.[17]

APPROACHES TO DISCIPLINE

There is considerable variation in the methods used to improve discipline and reduce classroom disruption, ranging from statewide approaches to individual school district initiatives. Because many of these initiatives are new or not part of a research design, there is currently little scientific evaluation of them. However, some have been evaluated, and there is much anecdotal evidence about others.

New State Laws

Under the Constitution, the individual states are responsible for education. And in the last two decades, states have been very active in "education reform." In the 1980s, they required students to take more rigorous courses to graduate, and in the 1990s, they instituted "standards-based" reform, which spelled out what students should know and then subjected them to relentless standardized tests. But comprehensive approaches to school violence and discipline generally have not been part of the reform effort, and when there has been action taken, it is *safety* that has been the focus, not the day-in, day-out, disruptive behaviors that interfere with teaching and learning.

In the latter half of the 1990s, Texas and West Virginia enacted statewide laws that not only address safety but also give greater control to the classroom teacher. West Virginia passed the Productive and Safe Schools Act in 1995, specifying a wide range of disruptive behaviors and identifying who in the school system is responsible for correcting them. The law also included a zero tolerance policy for guns, violence, and drugs on school grounds and at school events. Students in violation of this policy could receive one-year mandatory suspension or expulsion.[18] Texas passed the Safe Schools Act, also in 1995. Under this law, school districts established codes of conduct that students could be removed from the classroom or the school for violating. These codes also specified the conditions for suspension or expulsion. The law gave legal authority to teachers to remove students from the classroom for unruly, disruptive behavior.

The American Federation of Teachers played a critical role in shaping these laws by polling and surveying teachers and by pressuring the state legislatures. The teacher surveys in particular disclosed strikingly high incidences of problem behaviors in classrooms and hallways before the laws were enacted. West Virginia teachers were surveyed in 1994, before the passage of the law, and then again after, in 1997. A major finding of the survey was that, in 1994, only 7 percent of teachers were satisfied with the discipline policies, and in 1997, 71 percent were satisfied. The proportion of teachers reporting that discipline policies had improved was 67 percent, weapons incidents were down 70 percent, assaults on teachers were down 50 percent, and threats of violence were down 41 percent.[19] Serious concerns among the teachers still existed, however. Seventy-five percent of teachers still said that they experienced some level of classroom disruption on a typical day, and 25 percent said that alternative education is not available in their county for students who must be removed from regular schools.

The Texas Federation of Teachers also surveyed teachers in 1993 and 1996. After the passage of the Safe Schools Act, there were reductions in threats of violence to students and teachers, in assaults on students and teachers, in abusive language directed to teachers, and in theft.[20] However, a troubling finding from the 1996 survey in Texas was that only 34 percent of teachers said that their school district had tried to enforce the Safe Schools Act, while 36 percent said it had not, and 30 percent were not sure. Still, it is impressive and encouraging to find that teachers in both states believe the situation is improving as a result of these laws.

Classroom Management

The media today talk a lot about the teaching skills of teachers: what their average SAT scores were when they applied to college compared to people going into other fields, how many are not certified, and how many are "teaching out of field." We hear little about the very difficult job they have of managing classroom behavior to ensure that students learn the subject matter being taught. In fact, almost all of standards-based reform is about subject matter content and standardized tests, but effective teaching and student learning involves a lot more.

Brenda Williams of the Broward Teachers Union of Broward County, Florida, summarizes the situation as follows:

> A teacher who has mastered these [classroom management] skills keeps students constructively engaged and learning from the moment they enter the room. Everything that occurs in the classroom is planned, from the seating arrangement to the instructions for students who finish their work early. To the untrained eye, a teacher's management skills may appear to be more art than science, leaving the impression that effective classroom management is instinctive rather than a learned craft. But let me assure you that effective classroom management can be taught and with time and effort, teachers can—and do—become more effective as managers.[21]

Williams describes the requirements for a complete classroom management approach, starting with districtwide codes covering discipline and containing "clear and precise language with specific examples of behaviors that will result in disciplinary action." The next steps, as outlined by the Alliance of Quality Schools (AQS) in Broward County, are consistent enforcement of the discipline code at the school level, ensuring that students learn how to correct their behaviors before they become ingrained, establishing alternative education sites for chronically disruptive and violent students, and wide-scale support for these policies in the broader community. The AQS is a comprehensive research-based model focusing on the interrelated areas of reading, writing, mathematics, parental involvement, and social behaviors. It has operated in Title I schools in Broward County, Seattle, and Cincinnati. To qualify for an AQS program, 80 percent of a school's teachers must vote for it to ensure that the effort has satisfactory support.

In 1994, twenty-five schools in the Ft. Lauderdale–area district were listed as "critically low performing." Now, "after intensive reform through the homegrown AQS program and an infusion of extra cash, all twenty-five low-performing schools are off the list."[22] This local effort was modeled after several nationally acclaimed programs, such as Success For All. Each school in the AQS is assigned a former teacher as a coach for half the week to help teachers develop the skills they need. This approach is viewed by the AQS as more effective than retreats or workshops.

Another program to deal with discipline and classroom behavior is Consistency Management and Cooperative Discipline (CMCD) in Houston, Texas.[23] CMCD is a classroom management program that incorporates a shared responsibility between teachers and students for learning and classroom organization. It is designed to "help students prepare for success, achieve self discipline, and develop responsibility . . . through an emphasis on prevention rather than intervention, shared responsibility, and cooperation between teacher and student, value based discipline, increased communication with parents, and effective instruction." Professor H. Jerome Freiberg has reported on the results of ten years of research and evaluation of CMCD, describing reductions in referrals to the principal's office, gains in student and teacher attendance, increases in student achievement, and improvements in classroom climate as reported by students, teachers, and principals.

Character Education and the Curriculum

The approaches described above are almost always in addition to the regular school curriculum designed to impart academic knowledge. But there is a substantial movement in the United States to include instruction within the curriculum that would build character and thereby change student behavior. American education took on the task of developing character when public schools began, and such directed effort reemerged in the 1980s under the terminology of moral development.

The idea of a curriculum approach to developing character gained momentum at the 1992 Aspen Conference on Character Education, which produced the Aspen Declaration. The declaration contained eight points and addressed society as a whole, not just the schools; one of its points states: "Character education is, first and foremost, an obligation of families; it is also an important obligation of faith communities, schools, youth, and other human service organizations." This declaration led to the Character Counts!™ approach and the Character Counts Coalition. This coalition is the product of the Josephson Institute of Ethics and combines national and regional education organizations, national youth development and service organizations, and community organizations. The goal of the coalition is to instill the right values in students, leading to the students becoming responsible citizens at school and in the community.

Another initiative is the Fund for the Improvement of Education, a division of the U.S. Department of Education, which since 1995 has administered the Character Education Partnership Grant in the amount of $10 million a year. These grants are made to partnerships of state education agencies and local schools, which together compete for the grants. So far, awards have been made in thirty-two states.

All programs must incorporate the following six elements of character: caring, civic virtue and citizenship, justice and fairness, respect, responsibility, and trustworthiness.[24] The state-school partnerships take many different approaches to advancing character education. Evaluation is emphasized in each program in order to help the states determine the most effective curricula.

The state of Maryland has completed a comprehensive evaluation covering the first year of its character education program, carried out with a Character Education Partnership Grant from the U.S. Department of Education. There was a dramatic improvement in school climate for all five districts participating. The large differences in perceptions between teachers and students narrowed during the year. Interestingly, school personnel saw the improvement in teacher-student relations as mainly coming from student improvement, the students saw it coming mainly from teacher treatment, and parents saw it in a safer school community.[25]

An important organization in the field of character education is the Character Education Partnership (CEP), a national nonprofit coalition of more than six hundred organizations and individuals. CEP is working to place character education at the top of the nation's agenda and to help create a new generation of "character educators" in schools throughout the country. CEP activities and projects include annual school and district awards for exemplary programs; a National Resource Center and website (www.character.org); a compilation of research studies, assessment surveys, and self-help materials; and advocacy for teacher preparation in character education.

Some Partners that Help

The programs described thus far are largely located in the school and run by the school administration, although outside organizations sometimes develop the approaches and assist the school in carrying them out and evaluating their effectiveness. But there are also programs that are run primarily by an outside organization.

COMMUNITY SERVICE LEARNING AND SCHOOL-TO-CAREER. Dr. Ann Southworth, the principal of Putnam Vocational Technical High School in Springfield, Massachusetts, was the driving force in reshaping her school. She describes her school before its improvement as "a school in danger of losing accreditation, wrought with violence and gang activity, with low attendance (70 percent) and high dropout rates." Now the school is described as safe and nonviolent; its students are in the National Honor Society and take advanced placement courses; the attendance rate is 93 percent; and students are "engaged, learning more, working in teams, respecting themselves and wanting to stay in school."[26]

Putnam combines community service projects (called Community Service Learning) with partnerships with employers in school-to-work programs (called School-to-Careers), utilizing the whole community for student learning and experience. The community projects include long-term activities, such as the rejuvenation of the Campanile, Springfield's bell tower, which was destroyed by fire ninety years ago.

This project was started by an honors English class that held a fund-raising drive, and students have been responsible for all phases of the project. Other projects include a comprehensive school-based health center and building a replica of a nineteenth-century trolley and trolley barn. In School-to-Careers, the teachers work with private and public employers to create integrated curriculum and internship opportunities.

A SCHOOL POLICE FORCE. The Los Angeles Unified School District (LAUSD) has its own, independent, school police force that cooperates with the regular police force. It costs $27 million per year to maintain its 312-member police department, which is paid out of the school budget. Los Angeles schools have had some form of security service for fifty years, but a school police department was not created until there was state authorizing legislation in 1984.[27]

The rate of violence in the LAUSD has fallen in recent years. Yet rather than focus on the incidence of violence, School Police Chief Wesley Mitchell says it is more prudent to focus "on the emotional security of students, staff, and the community. . . . It is the fear of violence that does the most harm to our educational system." In addition to normal policing duties and attendance at student functions, the school police do a variety of things, including speaking to classes, counseling teachers on working with students, and counseling students. They also provide counseling to parents. Officers rarely are hired from regular police departments in order to avoid hiring people with bad habits learned elsewhere; Los Angeles is looking for "individuals who want to make a difference in the lives of children rather than those who simply want to be police officers." So far there has been no specialized training available for the school policemen, but the National Organization of Black Executives has begun the development of a special curriculum.

BOYS AND GIRLS CLUBS WITH LOCAL SCHOOLS. Boys and girls clubs operate throughout the United States and have a positive track record in efforts to reduce crime and raise educational achievement. They also can partner with the schools. In Delaware, fifty young people who were about to be expelled or to quit school enrolled in the local club's educational program. Based on tests from before and after enrollment, 67 percent improved their grades and 68 percent showed improvements in their self-esteem.[28]

A Public Health Viewpoint

There are a number of lenses through which we can view student violence and classroom disruption. The media have highlighted the approach of building character through teacher initiatives, conflict resolution, school uniforms, and myriad other ways. But these problems also can be viewed as a public health issue: how to prevent injury due to violence.[29]

Four questions are commonly addressed in a public health approach: What is the problem? (called *surveillance*); What are the causes? (called *risk factor research*); What works to help prevent the problem? (called *intervention evaluation*); and, How do you do it? (called *program implementation*). However, while this is the desired sequence of action, it isn't always followed, according to Mark Rosenberg of the Centers for Disease Control and Prevention. "Violence among our youth is an urgent problem. Sometimes, the urgency of a problem forces us to take action before we have time to complete all the steps, and we must learn as we go how to refine our efforts and to provide the science base for our programs that others are implementing."

Based on the research that has been performed, Rosenberg identifies the following risk factors, or causes of violence among students:

◆ Individual factors: history of early aggression, beliefs supportive of violence, attributing hostility to others, and social cognitive deficits

◆ Family factors: problematic parental/caregiver behavior, low emotional attachment to parent/caregiver, poor monitoring and supervision of children, exposure to violence, and poor family functioning

◆ Peer/school factors: negative peer influences, low commitment to school, academic failure, and school environment problems such as undisciplined classrooms

◆ Environment/neighborhood factors: high concentrations of poor residents, high levels of transience, high levels of family disruption, low community involvement/participation, diminished economic opportunity, and access to firearms

This list illuminates the acute risk of school violence in central cities, where there are high rates of poverty and concentrations of minorities who have been deprived of supportive environments.

In 1993, Congress provided the Centers for Disease Control with $6.9 million to determine what interventions work to prevent violence among youth. Thirteen projects were carried out in thirteen cities and one county. Their primary targets were urban, high-risk youth. The principal findings of these projects were that (1) effective strategies emphasize the development of problem-solving skills, communication skills, and anger management; (2) in environments that are chaotic, where the administration does not support the efforts at intervention, and where communications are unclear, even otherwise sound approaches do not succeed; (3) outcomes vary across age groups, and it is important to match the intervention to the appropriate age and gender of the students; and (4) the interventions need to be intensive and have a long duration of student exposure. A few examples of current projects are provided below.

*   *Peace Builders in Tucson, Arizona,* works in elementary schools, using counselors and other specially trained instructors to teach students to interact socially in a positive way.

*   In *Chicago and Aurora, Illinois*, the University of Michigan is evaluating a three-tiered approach. The first level increases awareness and knowledge about factors that influence peer and other social relationships, the second tier adds training in small group environments, and the third tier adds family intervention. This approach has resulted in reduced aggressive behavior.

*   *The Youth Violence Prevention Program* in Richmond, Virginia, is a sixteen-session curriculum that teaches sixth-graders how to deal with violence and anger. The effort has resulted in substantial reductions in fights, weapons possession, suspensions, and threats to teachers, and in improvements in self-esteem.

*   *Self Enhancement, Inc.,* in Portland, Oregon, has provided adult mentors, as well as programs that have included approaches such as conflict resolution, social skills training, violence prevention skills, recreational opportunities, and academic tutoring. After two years

of the program there have been reductions in weapons possession and school fights, with no changes noted in the control group.

The Centers for Disease Control advocates a rigorous scientific approach. Del Elliott, author of *Violence in American Schools*, puts it this way: "When their costs are high or there are alternatives that are known to be effective, the absence of any evidence of effectiveness is a sufficient basis for challenging the use of these programs or policies. If there are no alternatives known to be effective and the costs are modest, a case can be made for using untested prevention programs for a time, pending careful evaluation."

Better Instruction, Better Behavior?

So far this chapter has looked at student behavior and achievement from the standpoint of how disruptive behaviors interfere with instruction and achievement. Another approach takes just the opposite view: that the way to improve student behavior is to engage students constructively through better methods of education. According to this theory, good instruction keeps students' attention, thus reducing disruptive behaviors, which are caused by boredom. Bad instruction produces bad behaviors, which undermine achievement. While there is some evidence to support this theory, not enough research has been done to provide conclusive results.

Several recent reports on major, national reform programs have demonstrated the potential behavioral effects of improving education. A study of the Accelerated Schools Project, which has about seven hundred participating schools, reported positive effects across the country. For example, suspensions dropped 50 percent in a participating Massachusetts middle school, and in one Missouri elementary school referrals to the principal's office dropped from ninety per year to just twenty-one.[30] There have been similar responses from school districts participating in the Coalition for Essential Schools, which report reductions in suspensions and discipline referrals and increases in attendance rates. After a long period of restructuring, Jefferson County, Kentucky, a participant in the coalition, reported improvements in attendance, parental and student satisfaction, and parental involvement.

The state of Kentucky has been undertaking a complete revamping of its education system since the early 1990s. While there has been no research directly examining the effects of this project, because it is the most serious, comprehensive, and sustained effort at education improvement in the country, it is useful to consider it in the context of this section.

Sample-based data available from the National Assessment of Educational Progress (NAEP) provide relevant statistics.[31] In 1992, 39 percent of Kentucky's schools reported that student absence was either a serious or a moderate problem. There was no improvement in 1998. This figure is higher than the 22 percent reported in 1998 for the nation as a whole, which also had little change over the same period. Meanwhile, from 1996 to 1998 the percentage of Kentucky schools reporting that 6 percent or more of their students were absent on an average day rose from 23 to 39 percent, while little changed in the nation's figures.

In 1992, 17 percent of Kentucky schools said that student tardiness was a serious or moderate problem, as did 13 percent in 1996, rising to 28 percent in 1998. Again, the figures in the same years in the nation as a whole were relatively stable. Reports in Kentucky of physical conflicts and negative attitudes toward academic achievement showed little change. In a new question for 1998, schools were asked about physical conflicts between students and teachers; 43 percent of Kentucky schools reported having such conflicts, compared with 19 percent of the nation's schools. Finally, 42 percent of Kentucky schools reported that student misbehavior was a serious or moderate problem in 1996, similar to the 47 percent that said so in 1998. On this count, the nation held steady at just over 30 percent.

In terms of student achievement, Kentucky has shown some improvement on NAEP math scores. While substantial improvement was initially reported in reading scores, analyses of students excluded from the test has raised questions about the validity of that report. Kentucky's own achievement tests would be a better measure for achievement, but they have changed over the decade, making it hard to measure trends in achievement.

In conclusion, the statistics show that on a statewide basis, we cannot assume that the reform approaches being carried out will be accompanied by improvements in the student behaviors that can retard achievement. Instead, more attention needs to be concentrated directly on disruptive behaviors.

School Codes of Behavior

Codes of behavior are common, although their application, adherence, and the extent to which they are actually applied nationally is unknown. Recently, the American Federation of Teachers (AFT) identified several school codes it thought were exemplary. One was in the Cincinnati school system. The entire code was reproduced in "Order in the Classroom: Violence, Discipline, and Student Achievement," published by the ETS Policy Information Center in 1998. The AFT also has singled out two schools in Toledo, Ohio, as well as the Oklahoma City Alternative Middle School.

The Cincinnati, Ohio, code of behavior covers matters such as time out of class, in-school suspension, supervision, expulsion, permanent exclusion, disorderly conduct, profanity, sexual harassment, smoking, and defacement of property, among others. It also spells out due process procedures to be followed and the rights of parents.

Alternative Schools

The state laws referred to earlier and the codes of behavior just described often state that disruptive students will be removed from the classroom and placed in "alternative schools," alternative classrooms, or special sections in regular schools. Descriptions of programs also suggest that the students are not always placed in adequate learning environments when they are removed from regular classrooms and schools. No statistics are available on how many alternative learning environments exist and how many students occupy them. If programs that depend on removing disruptive students are to work, there must be alternative arrangements that are conducive to learning for the students who are placed there.

The AFT supports alternative schools for students "who are violent and chronically disruptive." It believes that "both students who come to schools willing and ready to learn and those who are chronically disruptive benefit from such as arrangement."[32] It points out that costs per student are higher for students in alternative settings because smaller class sizes are required. The AFT estimates that the average cost per student in an alternative school is $7,000 per year, or 25 percent more than the national average. The cost varies considerably in different states and communities. It also has estimated that the benefits from increased time for learning that would otherwise have been lost and from reduced grade repetition would result in a total savings of over $20,000 per student.

One example of an alternative school is the Later Elementary Alternative Program (LEAP), created about fifteen years ago in Grand Rapids, Michigan. The LEAP school takes students with behavioral problems in grades four through six who have been recommended by their teachers. A group of ten students is assigned to one teacher and one full-time child care worker. LEAP attempts to return students to regular schools within three months. After studying the LEAP effort on behalf of the National Education Association, Elizabeth Metcalf urged Congress to support the creation of such alternative schools.[33]

Collective Bargaining

Another route to defining codes of behavior is collective bargaining contracts between teacher unions and school systems. These will, of course, vary from place to place. One example was reproduced in *Order in the Classroom*. It was the contract language of the Minneapolis Federation of Teachers #0059. The contract specifies authority to design a "Behavior Plan" to promote positive student behaviors, removing students from the classroom temporarily, expulsion for violent behavior, conferences with parents, and review panels to resolve questions about disciplinary actions.

Conflict Resolution

Since the early 1980s there have been programs to teach students how to deal with conflict. The state of Illinois now requires school districts to provide conflict resolution or violence prevention education to fourth-through twelfth-grade students. This service is provided through the Illinois Council for the Prevention of Violence.[34] Other efforts are under way in school districts in Minnesota, New York City, and Dayton, Ohio. These programs are described in "Youth Violence: A Policymakers Guide," published by the Education Commission of the States in 1996.

The Illinois law led to the creation of the Illinois Council for the Prevention of Violence to help the schools in the state teach the techniques of conflict resolution. In Minnesota, its Office of Community Collaboration issued a guide for the schools to follow. Dayton, Ohio, created the Positive Adolescents Training Program (PACT); a General Accounting Office study found less fighting and court referrals among PACT participants than in a control group. The New York City program is carried out in collaboration with Educators for Social Responsibility; the program has been in operation since 1985.

School Security Measures

There are a number of measures that schools have taken to control student movement and make schools safer. In 1996–97, based on a study of schools nationwide:

- almost all schools required visitors to sign in;

- four in five schools had a policy of not allowing students to leave the school grounds for lunch;

- over half of schools controlled access to the school building, and one-fourth to the school grounds;

- 1 percent of schools used metal detectors daily, and 4 percent used random metal detector checks; and

- 6 percent of schools had law-enforcement personnel in the schools thirty hours or more per week, and 4 percent had them for between one and twenty-nine hours.[35]

These ordinary measures can reduce problematic student behaviors, as was shown in the Wenglinsky study discussed earlier in this chapter.[36]

Limited, National-Level Analysis

The large-scale survey research approach is one way of elucidating both the prevalence of particular practices and their relative impact on behavior and achievement. The Wenglinsky study discussed above attempted to do this with data collected in 1990 and 1992 from the National Education Longitudinal Survey.[37] Based on the questions formulated at that time, Wenglinsky was able to draw conclusions about punishment. He found that the severity of the punishments used and preventative measures taken affected both serious and nonserious student offenses. For example, the more schools strictly monitor the movement of students during the school day, the less students are tardy or absent. Wenglinsky did not find any effect resulting from such policies as the use of uniforms or outlawing gangs. While the Wenglinsky analysis does not cover the breadth of approaches now in use, his research gives us good reason to believe that even fairly routine countermeasures can produce results.

Comparison of Different Approaches

With the incomplete information now available, it is not possible to say which approaches hold the most promise of being effective. Not only may some approaches produce more measurable gains than others, but some may work better with different student population groups, or in different school cultures. For example, the "conflict resolution" program may work better in inner-city schools than in rural areas. And aside from objective comparative effectiveness, localities likely will find differences in which approaches best fit their local culture and preferences. For example, a large police force may produce the most order but be judged unacceptable by the community. More research also is necessary to determine relative costs. A large-scale, national evaluation is recommended to address these issues.

CONCLUSIONS AND IMPLICATIONS

This chapter has highlighted an important problem in education that has not been given sufficient attention. Schools, districts, and statewide systems have instituted a variety of programs to help student achievement through improved student behavior, but more widespread action is still needed. The following steps are recommended:

*   The national preoccupation with the isolated school shootings that have occurred, as horrible as they are, needs to be balanced

with concern about the constant disorder and disruption that inter-feres with instruction in America's schools every day. Shootings and weapon possessions are becoming less prevalent in America, but disruption and disorder are increasing.

- The widespread standards-based education reform effort has focused on standards and standardized testing. It has virtually ignored student behaviors, which evidence has clearly shown to impede instruction and learning. In addition to subject matter content standards and large-scale testing, we need standards-based behavior goals to improve achievement.

- The situation is even more troubling and prevalent in inner-city schools, and the rate of problem behavior varies widely among the states. Changing student behaviors may be the principal opportu-nity to improve the learning environment in many locations. A change in student behavior may not be the single key to a large-scale turnaround, but it can lead to improvements, such as the willingness of capable people to enter and continue in the teach-ing profession or to teach in inner cities.

- There also is a need for more systematic knowledge of both student behaviors and their relationship to policy approaches and to stu-dent achievement. The last comprehensive survey on this topic was done in 1978 by the National Institute of Education. Not only is it now outdated, but that survey did not obtain information about student achievement. An updated survey should be done.

- There is, even without a new survey, more information that can be gathered about the effectiveness of some programs. All thirty-two grants made to states for character education have an evaluation component. While many of these grants are recent, some have been in place for several years. The evaluations should be collect-ed and synthesized.

- Beyond survey research, we also need more controlled experiments, similar to those run by the Manpower Demonstration Research Corporation (MDRC), which has, over the past couple of decades, run large-scale experiments with control groups based on random

assignment, in order to test program approaches in welfare, training, and youth employment.

While the recommendations and program approaches described
may not tell a school superintendent, school board, or governor the
best course of action to follow, they show the many options available.
After considering these options, discretionary judgment is needed, using
as much information as possible. School administrators and executives
need to investigate more fully what we know. Many people now have
experience with programs to improve discipline and behavior, and they
can make informed recommendations as to what will work best and
what would be acceptable. At the same time, those making the decisions are professionals with diverse training and substantial experience.
They need to come to conclusions of their own as to what will work
best in their communities, what their students most need, what their
communities will accept, and what they can afford.

While there remain many unanswered questions, we do know that
the problem of disruptive student behavior is greatest in school settings
with poor or inner-city children, and it is there that the achievement
gap is the largest and continues to grow. The need to act is urgent, and
the resource levels applied need to be substantial.

8.

CRITICAL SUPPORT:
THE PUBLIC VIEW OF PUBLIC EDUCATION

RUY TEIXEIRA

Public education is supposed to be the "great equalizer." While Americans oppose many redistributive social welfare efforts, they strongly believe in public education as a way of promoting social mobility. In recent years, a number of proposals have been floated to reform public education to address inequalities in educational opportunity stemming from unequal financial resources, unequal curriculum, unequal teacher quality, and the like. These reforms fall in seven broad areas of education policy, each of which will be discussed in this paper: standards, charter schools/public school choice and integration, teachers, discipline, social promotion/summer school, spending, and vouchers.

GENERAL VIEWS OF PUBLIC EDUCATION

Ratings of Public Schools

There is clearly significant current dissatisfaction with the public school system. As has been widely reported, public confidence in, and ratings of, the school system are now at a low level. For example, just

25 percent of Americans rate the nation's public schools as excellent or good, and 66 percent rate them only fair or poor.[1] Similarly, in a 1999 Gallup poll conducted for Phi Delta Kappa (PDK), just 24 percent of respondents gave the public school system a grade of A or B, and an astonishing 66 percent gave the system a grade of C, D, or fail (see Table 8.1).

Judging from Table 8.1, this dissatisfaction dates back at least to the early 1980s, abated somewhat in the mid-1980s, and dropped modestly in

TABLE 8.1. GRADING THE NATION'S PUBLIC SCHOOLS, 1981–99 (PERCENT)

How about the public schools in the nation as a whole? What grade would you give the public schools nationally—A, B, C, D, or Fail?

DATE	A	B	C	D	FAIL	DON'T KNOW
May 1981	2	18	43	15	6	16
May 1982	2	20	44	15	4	15
May 1983	1	17	38	16	6	21
May 1984	2	23	49	11	4	11
May 1985	3	24	43	12	3	15
April 1986	3	25	41	10	5	16
April 1987	4	22	44	11	2	17
April 1988	3	20	48	13	3	13
May 1989	2	20	47	15	4	12
April 1992	2	16	48	18	4	12
May 1993	2	17	48	17	4	12
May 1994	2	20	49	17	6	6
May 1995	2	18	50	17	4	9
May 1996	1	20	46	18	5	10
June 1997	2	20	48	15	6	9
June 1998	1	17	49	15	5	13
June 1999	2	22	46	16	4	10

Polls: All data from annual polls for Phi Delta Kappa conducted by Gallup.
Sources: Jennifer Hochschild and Bridget Scott, "The Polls—Trends: Governance and Reform of Public Education in the United States," *Public Opinion Quarterly* 62 (1998): 79–120; Phi Delta Kappa website: http://www.pdkintl.org.

the late 1980s and early 1990s to roughly its current level.[2] Note, however, that the total overall change from 1981 to 1999 is a matter of only a few percentage points, and it actually moves in a slightly optimistic direction. The public today is gloomy about the nation's schools, but not much more so than it has been for the past couple of decades.

One of the more intriguing findings of public opinion research on education is how optimistic the public tends to be about their own public schools. Indeed, the closer you get to the schools their children actually attend, the happier people say they are. For example, 49 percent give the schools in their local community an A or B, and a whopping 66 percent give the specific school their oldest child attends an A or B (see Table 8.2, page 254, and Table 8.3, page 255).[3]

As the tables show, this discrepancy is of long standing. As far back as we have data, respondents have been far more optimistic about their community's public schools than about the nation's, and downright sunny about the schools their own children attend.[4]

How can people rate the nation's public schools so poorly while rating their community's and especially their own children's schools so highly? Some analysts argue that the national ratings reflect people's true feelings and experiences, while people are reluctant to rate their own schools poorly because it makes them look bad for sending their children there. At the same time, others argue that the *local* ratings accurately reflect people's true experiences with the school system, while the national ratings are mostly a product of gloomy media coverage of problems in the schools. Academic analysts have reached no consensus on which, if either, of these hypotheses is correct. Therefore, until this issue is resolved, it would seem prudent for analysts to temper their alarm about low public esteem for the school system as a whole, with the knowledge that the public's views are considerably more positive about their own children's schools.

And there is another way to interpret these data: even allowing for considerable bias, people simply do not have the sense of crisis about their local public schools—reflecting fairly positive personal experiences with them—that they have about the national system. For example, they may have read about truly dysfunctional schools elsewhere (inner-city public schools would be the most common example) and consider this a very serious problem. So, when they rate the nation's public schools poorly, they may be expressing a sincere judgment about

TABLE 8.2. GRADING PUBLIC SCHOOLS IN LOCAL COMMUNITY, 1974–99 (PERCENT)

Students are often given the grades A, B, C, D, and Fail to denote the quality of their work. Suppose the public schools themselves, in this community, were graded in the same way. What grade would you give the public schools here—A, B, C, D, or Fail?

DATE	A	B	C	D	FAIL	DON'T KNOW/ NO ANSWER
May 1974	18	30	21	6	5	21
April 1976	13	29	28	10	6	4
April 1977	11	26	28	11	5	19
April 1978	9	27	30	11	8	15
May 1979	8	26	29	11	7	18
May 1980	10	25	29	12	6	18
May 1981	9	27	34	13	7	10
May 1982	8	29	33	14	5	11
May 1983	6	25	32	13	7	17
May 1984	10	32	35	11	4	8
May 1985	9	34	30	10	4	13
April 1986	11	30	28	11	5	15
April 1987	12	31	30	9	4	14
April 1988	9	31	34	10	4	12
May 1989	8	35	33	11	4	9
May 1991	10	32	33	10	5	10
April 1992	9	31	33	12	5	10
May 1993	10	37	31	11	4	7
May 1994	9	35	30	14	7	5
May 1995	8	33	37	12	5	5
May 1996	8	35	34	11	6	6
June 1997	10	36	32	11	6	5
June 1998	10	36	31	9	5	9
June 1999	11	38	31	9	5	6

Polls: Data from Kettering Foundation polls conducted by Gallup through 1980; thereafter from annual polls for Phi Delta Kappa conducted by Gallup.

Sources: Jennifer Hochschild and Bridget Scott, "The Polls—Trends: Governance and Reform of Public Education in the United States," *Public Opinion Quarterly* 62 (1998): 79–120; Phi Delta Kappa website: http://www.pdkintl.org.

TABLE 8.3. GRADING OWN CHILD'S
PUBLIC SCHOOL,[a] 1985–99 (PERCENT)

Using the A, B, C, D, and Fail scale again, what grade
would you give the school your oldest child attends?

DATE	A	B	C	D	FAIL	DON'T KNOW
May 1985	23	48	19	5	2	3
April 1986	29	37	24	4	2	4
April 1987	28	41	20	5	2	4
April 1988	22	48	22	3	2	3
May 1989	25	46	19	5	1	4
May 1991	29	44	21	2	4	—
April 1992	22	42	24	6	4	2
May 1993	27	45	18	5	2	3
May 1994	28	42	22	6	1	1
May 1995	27	38	23	8	3	1
May 1996	23	43	22	6	5	1
June 1997	26	38	23	7	4	2
June 1998	22	40	25	8	3	2
June 1999	24	42	21	7	5	1

[a] Public school parents only.

Polls: All data from annual polls for Phi Delta Kappa conducted by Gallup.
Sources: Jennifer Hochschild and Bridget Scott, "The Polls—Trends: Governance and Reform of Public Education in the United States," *Public Opinion Quarterly* 62 (1998): 79–120; Phi Delta Kappa website: http://www.pdkintl.org.

the failure of schools to lift up a substantial and disadvantaged proportion of society, rather than transferring their own personal dissatisfaction onto a national target. This contradicts a common picture of the
typical citizen as narrowly self-interested and unconcerned with the
collective welfare, but there is plenty of precedent for this view in the
academic literature.[5]

Of course, it is difficult to know where manipulation leaves off and
genuine concern begins. But, in a sense, it doesn't matter. The point is
that the public may see current educational problems, despite predominantly affecting others at present, as compromising the traditional role
of American education as a vehicle for economic opportunity and

upward mobility. And that disturbs them, particularly in an era when education is becoming more and more important to an individual's economic success. Not only do parents see that the system is failing for a substantial portion of American youth, thereby dooming them to be left behind economically, but how can these parents be sure their own children will not suffer the same fate later? After all, a system that fails for some may be on the verge of failing for others. Can they be sure that a school performing on a B level—the typical grade given by parents to their children's school—is truly adequate to the demands of the "new economy"? And can they really be sure current performance will not deteriorate, as the system is dragged down by its weakest links? In this way, concern for students currently being failed by the public schools merges into an enlightened self-interest for one's own children. As we shall see, this interpretation is consistent with other aspects of public opinion of public schools.

Support for Public Schools

Despite the public's negative feelings about the public school system as a whole—and consistent with relatively positive personal experiences—support for the institution of public schools remains strong. For example, in the 1999 Gallup/PDK poll, more than seven in ten respondents (71 percent) said that educational improvements should focus on reforming the existing public school system rather than finding an alternative to it.[6] Similarly, in a June 1999 Penn, Schoen, and Berland/Democratic Leadership Council (PSB/DLC) poll, 71 percent of the public endorsed using all available resources to improve public schools, compared to just 24 percent who preferred helping people go to private schools. Even more impressive, a staggering 98 percent say they favor continuing the guarantee of a free public education, and 96 percent say it is important that public schools be strengthened.[7] And the priority accorded improving the system has ranked at or near the top of the public's wish list for quite some time. Indeed, a June 1999 NBC/*Wall Street Journal* poll found that improving public education outranks such hardy perennials as guaranteeing the financial stability of Social Security, promoting strong moral values, and cutting taxes. Thus, general support for reforming and strengthening the public schools seems quite strong.

STANDARDS

One of the clearest public sentiments about school reform is the desire for higher standards, as well as the willingness to tolerate fairly strict guidelines and testing regimes to accomplish this goal. There is some evidence that support for standards today is substantially higher than it has been in the past. For example, a question dating back to the late 1950s (see Table 8.4) asks whether students should have to pass a standard, nationwide academic examination to graduate from high school. As the table shows, the public was split on the question through the mid-1960s, but by the mid-1970s (the next time the question was asked) a strong consensus had evolved: by more than two to one, people favored having such an examination. And closer to the present day, support is even more lopsided: 73 percent in favor

TABLE 8.4. SUPPORT FOR STANDARD ACADEMIC EXAMINATION TO GRADUATE FROM HIGH SCHOOL, 1958–96 (PERCENT)

Should all high school students in the United States be required to pass a standard nationwide examination in order to get a high school diploma?

DATE	YES/FAVOR	NO/OPPOSE	NO ANSWER
November 1958	50	40	11
March 1961	47	43	9
April 1965	48	43	8
September 1965	45	47	8
April 1976	65	31	4
June 1978	82	14	4
May 1984	65	29	6
April 1988	73	22	5
March 1996[a]	87	11	3

[a] 1996 question: Thinking about some different standards that some people have proposed— please listen as I read each one and tell me if you favor or oppose setting the standard. . . . Having students pass an academic examination in order to graduate from high school . . . [Prompt:] Do you favor or oppose this?

Polls: Gallup, 1958–65; Gallup for Kettering Foundation, 1976; CBS, 1978; Gallup for Phi Delta Kappa, 1984–88; Tarrance Group and Mellman/Lake/Lazarus for *U.S. News and World Report,* 1996.

Source: Jennifer Hochschild and Bridget Scott, "The Polls—Trends: Governance and Reform of Public Education in the United States," *Public Opinion Quarterly* 62 (1998): 79–120.

and 22 percent against in 1988, and an incredible 87 to 11 percent in 1996.[8]

While a nationwide examination for high school graduates is a specific and limited idea, other polling data show that the public has a broad and strong interest in the concept of national testing standards. For example, from 1970 to 1992 Gallup asked one form or another of a general question on using standardized national tests to measure and compare local student achievement, and support never dropped below 69 percent.[9] More recent polls tell the same story. A 1998 Gallup/PDK poll found that 71 percent of the public endorse a voluntary national program (as proposed by the Clinton administration) to measure the performance of public schools by testing fourth- and eighth-graders. The 1999 PSB/DLC poll found 69 percent supported a single, agreed-upon set of national standards, compared to just 27 percent who opposed it. Finally, a June 1999 National Public Radio/Kaiser Family Foundation (NPR/KFF) survey recorded 94 percent support for making students meet adequate academic standards to be promoted or graduated and 87 percent support for using standardized tests to ensure that students meet national academic standards. Note that these high levels of support for national standards occur in a public opinion environment where, to this day, there is strong public preference for local, rather than state or national, control of curricular content.

What leads people to override their basic preference for local control? Simply, they believe such standards will raise student achievement, something they apparently value more than the abstract principle of local control. For example, in a 1997 Gallup/PDK poll, 77 percent of the public said that national standards for the academic performance of public schools would help individual students either "a great deal" or "quite a lot." Similarly, 78 percent of respondents in a 1998 Zogby poll said that national testing standards would be very or somewhat effective in improving education.

So the public's preferences for higher standards are clear. But what about *flexibility* of standards: do they believe "one size fits all," or do they believe flexibility should be shown for students whose disadvantaged backgrounds provide barriers to achievement? The answer here is a clear no to the idea of flexibility in standards. By almost three to one (66 to 23 percent), parents believe inner-city students—the prototypical disadvantaged students—should be held to the same standards as kids from wealthier backgrounds.[10] Interestingly, support for this view is apparently stronger among blacks and Latinos than among whites: a 1998 Peter Harris/RNT poll found 79 percent of Latinos and 71 percent of blacks agreeing with the proposition that most children should be required to meet the same set of academic standards, compared to 68 percent of whites.

It is worth stressing that teachers overall share this view about the uniformity of standards (71 percent in favor and 27 percent opposed). However, data are not available on how teachers who actually teach these disadvantaged students—for example, in high-poverty neighborhoods—feel about this issue. It is possible that their views on standards are not as strict as teachers as a whole.

CHARTER SCHOOLS/PUBLIC SCHOOL CHOICE AND INTEGRATION

At this point, there are about 1,200 charter schools serving some 300,000 students. However, given that there are 88,000 schools and some 46 million students nationwide, it is perhaps not surprising that, until very recently, there has been very little polling data on public views about charter schools. One early exception was a question asked by Penn, Schoen, and Berland for the Democratic Leadership Council in July 1997 which suggested public support for an expansion of the charter school program (67 percent in favor to 26 percent opposed). Results from 1999 polls confirm this general picture, recording support levels of 68 percent (Public Agenda), 63 percent (PSB/DLC), and 62 percent (NPR/KFF) for the general concept of charter schools. Note, however, that each of these polls found that the majority of the public knows little to nothing about charter schools and is therefore expressing support for a concept, not a working reality. But as a concept it is appealing, and both the Public Agenda and PSB/DLC polls found that a majority of the public would at least consider sending their children to a charter school.

A more thoroughly tested proposition is public school choice. As shown in Table 8.5 (page 260), a variety of question wordings on this issue, reasonably neutral in all cases, have been used since 1987, and they all return strong evidence of public support—from a low of 60 percent (two to one) to a high of 82 percent (four to one) in favor of public school choice.[11] There is also some indication of increasing support from 1989 onwards. In terms of demographics, results from the 1997 survey indicate that support is stronger for this approach at lower education and income levels, which is not surprising given that the most affluent areas tend to have the best neighborhood schools. But even among the affluent, support is still strong—just not as strong as among the less privileged.

TABLE 8.5. SUPPORT FOR PUBLIC SCHOOL CHOICE, 1987–97 (PERCENT)

Do you favor or oppose allowing students and their parents to choose which public schools in this community the students attend, regardless of where they live?

DATE	FAVOR	OPPOSE	DON'T KNOW/ NO ANSWER
April 1987[a]	71	20	9
May 1989	60	31	9
1990	62	31	7
1991	62	33	5
August 1992[b]	69	29	2
1993	65	33	2
May 1995[c]	69	28	3
December 1996[d]	82	16	2
March 1997[e]	73	25	2

[a] 1987 question: Do you think that parents in this community should or should not have the right to choose which local schools their children attend?

[b] 1992 question: I'd like to read you a series of statements about public school education in this country (United States). Tell me whether you agree or disagree with each statement. . . . Children should be able to attend the public school of their choice including one outside of their district with government money going to the school they attend.

[c] 1995 question: Do you favor or oppose allowing students and their parents to choose which public schools in the community the students attend, regardless of where they live?

[d] 1996 question: I'm going to read you two education proposals, and for each one, please tell me whether you strongly favor, somewhat favor, somewhat oppose, or strongly oppose that proposal. . . . Giving parents choices in determining which public school their children will attend.

[e] 1997 question: I'm going to read you two education proposals, and for each one, please tell me whether you strongly favor, somewhat favor, somewhat oppose, or strongly oppose that proposal. . . . Allowing parents to send their children to any public school in their local school district.

Polls: Gallup for Phi Delta Kappa 1987–91, 1993–95; Harris/*Business Week*, 1992; NBC/*Wall Street Journal*, 1996–97.

Sources: Jennifer Hochschild and Bridget Scott, "The Polls—Trends: Governance and Reform of Public Education in the United States," *Public Opinion Quarterly* 62 (1998): 79–120; Stanley Elam, *How America Views Its Schools: The PDK/Gallup Polls, 1969–1994* (Bloomington, Ind.: Phi Delta Kappa Educational Foundation, 1995).

Can this apparently strong support for charter schools and, especially, public school choice be harnessed to further long-standing goals of integration, either by race, class, or both? Little beyond general public support or opposition to these proposals has been tested by pollsters, so we have no specific data on how people might react to linking either charter schools or public school choice to the goal of integration. We do know, however, that integration itself, as a general objective, is quite popular. Indeed, public support for the goal of integration by race has never been higher. On the most basic level, support is now consistently over 90 percent for the idea that whites and blacks should attend the same schools, which was certainly *not* true in the late 1960s and early 1970s. More significantly, the proportion of the public willing to send their children to a school where not just a few but half or even a majority of the students are of another race has continued to increase gradually over the past two decades (see Table 8.6, page 262).[12] As the most recent data in the table show, the public is almost unanimous in its lack of objection to sending its children to schools where a few students are of another race, and not far from that—an amazing 84 percent—in not objecting to sending its children to schools where half the student body is of another race. Finally, about two-thirds (65 percent) say they would not object to sending their children to a school where a majority of children were of another race.

These figures are largely traceable to the marked shift in American public opinion in the past several decades toward racial tolerance and respect for diversity. In most walks of life, including the public schools, Americans now tend to see diversity as a positive experience that, all else being equal, is a genuine benefit.

That said, the most widely used mechanism to enhance integration in the public schools is quite unpopular. Surveys in the 1990s have continued to show strong opposition to busing schoolchildren to achieve racial balance, chiefly among whites.[13] This is considerably less than the higher levels of opposition in the 1970s and 1980s, but it is clear that busing remains an unpopular policy mechanism, even though it is connected to the goal of integration that is, in and of itself, popular. Indeed, Public Agenda posed an explicitly integration-oriented question in April 1998: "Now I'm going to read you a way to achieve integrated schools and ask you if you favor or oppose it. How about busing children to achieve a better racial balance in the schools? Do you favor or oppose this?" The response was negative from three-quarters of whites.

TABLE 8.6. VIEWS ON LEVELS OF SCHOOL INTEGRATION, 1978–96 (PERCENT)

Would you have any objection to sending your children to a school where (a few/half/a majority) of the children are (black/white)?

DATE	FEW			HALF			MAJORITY		
	YES	NO	DON'T KNOW	YES	NO	DON'T KNOW	YES	NO	DON'T KNOW
April 1978	5	94	1	18	79	3	36	59	5
April 1982	6	93	1	17	80	3	37	57	6
April 1983	5	94	1	18	80	2	43	52	5
April 1985	4	95	1	16	82	2	40	56	5
April 1986	5	94	1	18	80	2	42	55	4
April 1988	4	95	1	16	82	2	37	58	6
April 1990	3	96	< 1	16	81	3	40	54	7
April 1991	3	96	1	15	83	2	34	60	6
April 1993	4	95	1	14	83	3	36	59	6
May 1994	4	96	1	12	86	2	35	60	5
May 1996	3	97	1	15	84	2	29	65	6

Note: Blacks were asked about whites; whites were asked about blacks.
Polls: All data from General Social Survey conducted by National Opinion Research Center.
Source: Jennifer Hochschild and Bridget Scott, "The Polls—Trends: Governance and Reform of Public Education in the United States," *Public Opinion Quarterly* 62 (1998): 79–120.

There is much debate on why this opposition exists. Some commentators tend to interpret it as evidence of covert racism; that is, whites say they like diversity, but in truth they still dislike blacks and try to avoid them wherever possible.[14] A simpler interpretation is that whites genuinely support integration but consider the costs associated with busing (sending their children to a different school with a typically more disadvantaged and lower-achieving student population, as well as longer commutes and fewer neighborhood friends) not worth the associated benefit.

Given the persistence of these not-irrational views, and given the demise of increasing numbers of desegregative busing plans in the 1990s, it seems fair to say that busing is on its way out as a method of promoting school integration. The broadly popular goal of integration therefore will have to be obtained in some other way, probably through linkage to some other broadly popular goal. Giving parents more choices within the public school system is a logical candidate.

Of course, providing choices requires that some restrictions be put on which choices parents can make so that the proper integrative effect can be obtained.[15] It may also be necessary, given the evolving legal climate, to base integration on class rather than racial criteria. And we simply do not know how these modifications of pure public school choice—particularly the idea of controlling choices—will play with parents. But since the public starts with general biases in favor of both integration and public school choice, there are some reasonable grounds for optimism. Consistent with this optimism, the 1998 Public Agenda poll found that 61 percent of white parents and 65 percent of black parents support the idea of "letting parents choose their top 3 schools, while the district makes the final choice, with an eye to racial balance." This contrasts with the current system for promoting integration, where there seems little possibility for the development of a solid popular support base (the same poll found that 76 percent of white parents oppose "busing children to achieve a better racial balance in the schools").

TEACHERS

Recent research suggests that teacher quality may be more important to student achievement than previously thought, particularly in terms of the relative achievement levels of black and white students. The public agrees that teacher quality is important and sees improving teacher quality as central to the project of improving the public schools.[16] Indeed, in a March 1997 NBC/*Wall Street Journal* poll, the proposal to "recruit and retain better teachers" easily topped a comprehensive list of school reforms presented to the public. More than four-fifths said that better teachers would produce a "big improvement" in public schools, eleven percentage points above the next most popular reform (improving computer equipment and training). Similarly, in the 1998 Peter Harris/RNT poll, 90 percent of the public said that "ensuring a well-qualified teacher in every classroom" was very important to lifting student achievement, higher than any other proposed measure in a long list except "keeping schools safe from violence."

But how can this goal of better teachers be accomplished? One approach the public favors is competency testing for teachers. In the 1998 Peter Harris/RNT poll, two-thirds of respondents said that requiring teachers to pass a competency test each year would be a big improvement. Consistent with this result, 72 percent of the respondents in a March 1998 Princeton Survey Research poll endorsed federally sponsored, national standardized tests to measure teacher competence. In addition, two 1999 polls showed very high support for some kind of teacher competency testing: 94 percent support in the PSB/DLC poll and 89 percent in the NPR/KFF poll. Related to this, there is support for some version of teacher accountability where, for example, teacher licensing standards are linked to student performance in classes they have taught (endorsed by 71 percent in the Peter Harris/RNT poll).[17] Finally, 97 percent of respondents in the 1999 Gallup/PDK poll said new teachers should be required to prove their knowledge in the subjects they will teach if they are hired.

Competency tests are one approach. Another, potentially complementary approach is to pay teachers more money, based on the market theory that if you are willing to pay a higher price, you will get a better "product." This is particularly apropos in an era where there is a serious teacher shortage, a shortage that can only be made worse by the push for smaller class size and the subsequent need for even more teachers. The public appears supportive of such an approach, reflecting their belief that teacher salaries are too low.[18] In the 1998 Peter Harris/RNT poll, for example, over three-quarters of respondents endorsed raising teacher salaries as a measure to deal with the teacher shortage. Similarly, 77 percent in the 1999 NPR/KFF survey favored paying teachers more as a way of improving public schools in their community. And, melding the accountability and higher pay approaches, 90 percent in the 1999 Gallup/PDK poll favored increased pay for teachers who demonstrate high performance as a method of attracting and retaining good public school teachers.

One of the key issues in teacher quality, of course, is its correlation with class and race; that is, the more disadvantaged the student body, the poorer the quality of teachers is likely to be. As mentioned above, this issue appears to loom large in the low achievement levels in high-poverty schools. The provision of higher salaries for teachers in these schools to attract higher-quality teachers might improve this situation. Does public support for improving teacher quality and increasing teacher salaries extend to a provision of such extra funds?

Apparently so. Consider the findings from the 1998 Gallup/PDK poll: 86 percent of respondents said it was "very important" to improve the nation's inner-city schools, and 66 percent said they would be willing to pay more in taxes to provide the requisite funds to improve these schools. (The latter finding reflects a long-standing public interest in spending more money on the public schools, even if that means higher taxes, providing the money is specifically targeted toward an educational goal they support.)[19]

Even more specifically, 68 percent of respondents in the 1998 Peter Harris/RNT poll said they favored providing tax credits for teachers who work in high-poverty areas as a measure to ease the teacher shortage. And an impressive 83 percent said they agreed *strongly* with the proposition that "we should ensure that all children, including those who are economically disadvantaged, have teachers who are fully qualified, even if that means spending more money to achieve that." Evidently, the public is quite willing to entertain the notion that teacher salaries should be raised more where such raises might be needed most: in failing inner-city public schools.

DISCIPLINE

Discipline and discipline-related issues in schools are very much in the front of the public mind—as they have generally been for the past three decades.[20] For example, in the 1999 Gallup/PDK poll, the most frequently mentioned problem afflicting schools in respondents' local communities was lack of discipline/more control (18 percent), followed by fighting/violence/gangs (11 percent). Similarly, 25 percent of respondents to a 1999 CBS poll put discipline/lack of discipline at the top of their list of biggest problems in schools today, followed by violence (14 percent) in second place.

Clearly, a safe, controlled learning environment in schools is a central educational priority for the public. Note, however, that when taken out of the realm of problems and put in the context of *solutions* for public schools, discipline does not necessarily top the list. For example, in a 1998 Peter Hart/Shell Oil poll, many more respondents selected "mak[ing] sure all elementary school students have mastered reading, writing and math" (55 percent) as an effective idea for educational improvement than selected "tak[ing] tough steps to improve discipline and safety in schools" (24 percent). This suggests that increased discipline is viewed as a means as much as an end—that is, lack of discipline hurts learning, so enhanced discipline is a necessary means to achieve high student achievement (rather than just being an end in and of itself.)[21]

Another striking feature of public opinion about discipline in the schools is the strong support for a hard-line approach toward disruptive students, up to and including a "zero tolerance" policy. In the April 1998 Public Agenda poll, parents overwhelmingly supported taking persistent troublemakers out of class and permanently removing youths caught with drugs or weapons from school grounds. Moreover, this support was almost equally strong among both white and black parents. For both removing troublemakers and suspending children caught with guns or weapons, 86 percent of white parents were in favor. And nearly as many black parents—81 and 78 percent, respectively—favored the same.

Nor is the public less supportive when an automatic suspension or "zero-tolerance" policy is described for drug, alcohol, or weapons violations in the schools. Indeed, it is more so. Support levels in recent Gallup/PDK polls were 90 percent for zero tolerance of drug/alcohol violations (1999) and 93 percent for zero tolerance of weapons violations (1997).

Linked to this strict position on removing discipline problems from the regular school system is support for alternative schools for such discipline problems. For example, in the 1997 Gallup/PDK poll, three-quarters of the public thought moving persistent troublemakers into alternative schools would help public school academic achievement "a great deal" or "quite a lot," just behind support levels for placing a computer in every classroom (81 percent) and establishing national standards for academic performance (77 percent). More recently, 64 percent of the public in the April 1999 CBS News poll expressed support for alternative schools for chronic behavioral problems.

Of course, these discipline problems tend to be worse in poorer schools and worst of all in high-poverty, inner-city schools. To what extent are Americans aware of this, and how does it influence their views toward poor and minority students?

A result from the 1997 Gallup/PDK poll indicates that the public acknowledges that discipline problems are found more often among poor and minority students. Participants were asked whether public schools in urban areas—where higher concentrations of poor and minority students are found—face more or less serious problems than nonurban schools; 69 percent said more serious, and 40 percent of those said much more serious. And this is among the same respondents whose views of school problems are dominated by discipline-related issues.

Might this perception be an influence on middle-class—particularly middle-class white—flight from schools that experience an influx of poor and minority students? Almost certainly. About half of white parents that venture an opinion explicitly say that the influx of a large number of black students into a white school will bring increased social problems in its wake. Conversely, more than four-fifths of white parents say they would not care about the race of students in their children's schools, provided they come from "good, hard-working families," a common euphemism for kids that do not pose discipline problems.[22] Finally, firm, well-maintained student discipline ranked second of twelve factors people would consider when choosing a school, if given free choice.[23] Clearly then, the perceived linkage between poor and minority students on the one hand, and discipline problems on the other, must reduce the desirability of schools with these students in the eyes of middle-class and white parents.

SOCIAL PROMOTION/SUMMER SCHOOL

To say Americans are merely supportive of ending social promotion is to understate the case considerably; they might fairly be characterized as adamant. For example, in a 1997 Wirthlin Worldwide poll, 93 percent of the public favored requiring students to meet basic standards before they can pass to the next grade, including 81 percent who strongly favored such a policy.[24] Consistent with this finding, in a November 1998 Public Agenda poll 81 percent of parents said it would be worse to pass a struggling student to the next grade and expect him or her to keep up than to have the student repeat a grade. Finally, 72 percent of respondents in the 1999 Gallup/PDK poll said they favored stricter standards for social promotion, even if significantly more students would be held back as a result.

Nor is there much difference between black and white parents on this issue. An August 1994 Public Agenda poll asked whether public schools should pass students to the next grade if they make an effort by attending classes regularly and working hard, or only pass them if they show they have gained the requisite knowledge and skills. Eighty percent of white parents and 77 percent of black parents rejected the social promotion option in favor of a results-based system of promotion.

So, the experts may not be clear on the merits of social promotion, but, for better or worse, the public is. As far as the public is concerned, student promotion should be merit based, period. But this view of the public runs headfirst into the considerable empirical evidence that holding back low-performing students by itself does little good academically, and may even do harm (by increasing dropout rates, and so on).

One way of satisfying the public's desire for ending social promotion, while at the same time avoiding the pitfalls of simply holding students back, is to make remedial summer school mandatory for these low-performing students. They can then acquire the skills needed to function at the next grade level without having to endure the social and other difficulties of being left behind their classmates (or at least so the theory goes).

At this point there is little polling data on the public opinion of the link between ending social promotion and mandatory summer school (that is, do people support the latter as a way of accomplishing the former?). Indeed, data are spotty, in general, on issues around school year extension. One of the only time series studies of summer school does show increasing support for a universal extended school year of 210 days over ten months, however. When the question was first asked by Gallup/PDK in 1982, the public opposed this proposition by a 53 to 37 percent margin. By the last time it was asked, in 1992, public opinion had almost exactly reversed; that is, it was favored by 55 to 35 percent.[25] Unfortunately, questions asked since then have typically conflated lengthening the school year and the school day and thus tell us little about how the specific idea of a 210-day school year may currently be faring in the court of public opinion.

And of course, such questions tell us nothing about the very specific idea of targeting summer school to low-performing students who otherwise could not or should not be promoted to the next grade. Since Americans are adamant about ending social promotion and apparently open to a general expansion of the school year into the summer, it would be unlikely that they would object to a specific extension of the school year designed to end social promotion. But we do not know for sure.

Likewise, we do not know whether the public would support "enrichment" summer school for disadvantaged children who are eligible for promotion without remedial work. It seems probable that such a measure would meet with public sympathy, but we have no specific measures with which to gauge these sympathies or to compare them with public support for mandatory summer school for low achievers. Here is an area where more public opinion research is genuinely needed.

SPENDING

One area where public opinion data are more available is in measuring support for spending on public education. And that support is overwhelming. As Table 8.7 (page 270) shows, Americans for the past quarter century have felt that too little rather than too much money is being spent on improving the nation's education system. Moreover, that sentiment has strengthened over time, so that support levels in the 1990s were generally higher than in the 1980s and much higher than in the 1970s.

The last survey in that series, conducted in 1998, well illustrates the current strength of support for education spending. Almost three-quarters of the public in that survey thought the government was spending too little on education, compared to a microscopic 7 percent who thought too much was being spent. This works out to a "net" spending figure (too little minus too much) of +66 percent—a very impressive support level indeed, and a full twenty-four percentage points higher than that recorded by the survey series in 1973.

So public support for increased education spending looks solid. But how solid is it really? Would Americans feel the same way about education spending if their taxes were to go up as a result?

They claim that they would. That is, when increased education spending has been linked specifically to higher taxes in survey questions, support for more spending has remained at a very high level.[26] In one test of this sentiment, respondents to the March 1997 NBC/*Wall Street Journal* poll were asked if they would be willing to pay more in taxes if the additional money was used specifically for education. The result: 70 percent said they would, compared to just 23 percent who would not. More recently, 84 percent of the public said they would be willing to pay from $100 to $500 more in taxes to support a package of reforms including increasing teacher salaries, placing more computers in classrooms, reducing class sizes, fixing run-down schools, and improving school security.[27]

TABLE 8.7. VIEWS ON GOVERNMENT SPENDING TO IMPROVE THE NATION'S EDUCATION SYSTEM, 1973–98

We are faced with many problems in this country, none of which can be solved easily or inexpensively. I'm going to name some of these problems, and for each one I'd like you to tell me whether you think we're spending too much money on it, too little money, or about the right amount. Are we spending too much, too little, or about the right amount on . . . improving the nation's education system?[a]

	TOO LITTLE (%)	ABOUT RIGHT (%)	TOO MUCH (%)	NET SCORE[b]
1973	51	39	9	+42
1974	54	38	8	+46
1975	52	37	12	+40
1976	53	38	9	+43
1977	50	40	10	+41
1978	53	35	12	+42
1980	56	34	10	+46
1982	57	34	9	+48
1983	62	32	6	+56
1984	64	31	5	+59
1985	65	29	6	+59
1986	65	30	5	+60
1987	65	29	6	+60
1988	69	28	4	+65
1989	71	26	3	+68
1990	75	23	3	+72
1991	71	25	5	+66
1993	71	23	6	+66
1994	73	22	6	+68
1996	73	22	6	+68
1998	73	21	7	+66

[a] From 1984–98, some respondents were asked an alternative wording of the question, in which the last phrase was changed to "on . . . education." Data for those years combine results from original wording and alternative wording.

[b] Net score is calculated by subtracting the percentage responding "too much" from the percentage responding "too little." Subtractions were made prior to rounding.

Polls: All data from National Opinion Research Center's General Social Survey, 1973–98.
Source: Tom W. Smith, "Trends in National Spending Priorities, 1973–1998," National Opinion Research Center, Chicago, 1999, p. 51.

The public's views also work the other way in the current budget surplus environment: Americans would rather see more money spent on the public schools than receive a tax cut. This has been shown by numerous national polls in 1998 and 1999 and extends to public views on the disposition of state surpluses. For example, in the 1998 Gallup/PDK poll, the public expressed a strong preference for spending state budget surpluses on public schools (50 percent), rather than tax cuts (31 percent) or saving the money in a "rainy day" fund (14 percent).

It is important to stress, however, that these positive views on education spending do not amount to a blank check from the public to the government. Far from it. The public has doubts about the efficacy of simply spending money to solve educational problems. This is shown by a series of polls over the years that show tepid faith in the effectiveness of a general increase in education funding, as compared to other education reform proposals. For example, in the 1997 NBC/*Wall Street Journal* poll, public support for a proposal to "spend more money on education" ranked only in the middle of the pack, behind nine other education reform items.

What these other proposals were sheds light on what the public means when it expresses support for increased education spending. The top three were recruiting and retaining better teachers, improvement of computer equipment and training, and reduction of class sizes. Of these three, the latter two unambiguously cost money, and the other would probably be hard to achieve without additional expenditures. So what the public really wants is not just increased education spending but increased spending on reforms it deems effective. This is confirmed by the 1999 PSB/DLC poll, which showed that "more funding *to reduce class size and raise teacher salaries*" (italics added) actually draws more support as a way of improving the public schools than hugely popular items like "more parental and community involvement" and "more emphasis on discipline."

Besides the three spending-related proposals just noted, the public is also heavily in favor of a program of school modernization and construction. In the 1998 Gallup/PDK poll, a proposal on "providing funds to help repair and replace older school buildings" received support from an overwhelming 86 percent of respondents, higher even than public support for the currently fashionable idea of class-size reduction in the early primary grades (80 percent). While the Gallup/PDK question did not mention a specific amount, other polling data show similar levels of support for proposals to spend $22 billion[28] (82 percent) or $30 billion[29] (74 percent) on modernization and construction efforts.

Besides supporting spending on the specific items mentioned here, would Americans support additional spending specifically designed to improve public schools for disadvantaged children? They say they would. Recall that two-thirds of respondents in the 1998 Gallup/PDK poll said they would pay higher taxes just to provide the revenues needed for such spending, and that 83 percent in the Peter Harris/RNT poll agreed strongly that, if necessary, more money should be spent to bring fully qualified teachers to the economically disadvantaged. And there is no reason to suppose that the public would not be similarly supportive of additional expenditures to bring other favored reforms (like small class size and modernized facilities) to poor children.

Indeed, the public is on record as strongly favoring equalization of funding across school districts, a measure that, in most areas, would result in significantly enhanced spending on poor children. This is even true when the survey question is framed in a zero-sum context, where equalizing spending means giving to students in poor districts by taking away from those in rich districts. For example, in the 1999 Gallup/PDK poll, 83 percent of the public said they favored equalizing the allocation of funds to students in their state, "even if it means taking funding away from some wealthy school districts and giving it to poor districts."

These data deserve some further discussion. Most obviously, how serious can the public be about its views on this subject when equalization of school funding has suffered such severe political difficulties in states like New Jersey and Texas? In New Jersey, although most districts and schools stood to gain funds under the equalization plan, it met stiff resistance and was quickly rescinded by the state legislature. In addition, then-governor Jim Florio lost his job in the next election, a defeat in which negative reaction to the school equalization plan was heavily implicated.

How can this disjuncture between public opinion and public reaction be explained? One factor was clearly public misapprehension about the plan. The New Jersey plan was complicated, involving not only redistribution of school funding but also property tax changes, pension shifts, and spending caps. This made it difficult for voters in many districts to discern their real gains from the plan, even those who probably *would* benefit overall from it. On the other hand, among those (wealthier) voters who did not stand to benefit from the plan, awareness of the plan's negative impact was probably extremely high.[30] This imbalance in perceptions seriously undermined support for the plan.

The other important factor, as mentioned earlier, is that voters want more spending on education, but they do not want to give government a blank check. There was therefore considerable suspicion of what the simple provision of more money would really do for schools in poor and minority areas. And lacking adequate assurance that the additional funds would be wisely spent, many voters, predominantly whites of moderate income, turned against the plan.

This suggests several lessons about attempts to equalize school funding. One is that the plan should not be zero sum, but rather should harmonize upward. That is, it should be clear to the public that equalization will take place primarily by giving new money to poorer districts to make them equal to rich districts, not by taking away money from rich districts and giving it to nonrich districts. It is probable that few survey respondents who said they supported the latter approach really saw themselves as being in the kind of rich districts that would lose funding. Even the possibility of this was enough to make New Jersey voters angry when such zero-sum equalization schemes were put into effect.

Second, equalization should be linked to popular spending items like small class size, better teachers, and school modernization, rather than simply providing more money to schools in poor and minority districts. In addition, the extra funding should be linked to educational reform and accountability measures in areas like standards and discipline, where the public tends to believe schools in poorer districts are falling woefully short. In this way, citizens can be assured that funding equalization is not harming them as individuals, and that the additional monies for poorer districts will be spent effectively instead of wasted.

VOUCHERS

Here we come to perhaps the most contentious proposal for reforming public schools: allowing parents simply to opt out of the public school system with taxpayer support in the form of vouchers. The vouchers can then be used to attend whatever nonpublic schools parents prefer (and can successfully enroll their children in). While the monetary magnitude is ill-defined and some legal controversy persists about the constitutionality of using vouchers to attend church-related schools, the basic concept of providing taxpayer support to parents wishing to send their children outside of the public school system is clear enough— and, by now, a familiar part of the national education debate.

The theory supporting the voucher approach is also clear enough: parents who are stuck with a poorly functioning public school will benefit by allowing their children to escape to a superior alternative, while the general ability of students to exit the public schools will provide a bracing tonic of discipline to the system and force it to improve to meet parents' expectations and the needs of their children. Opponents vigorously argue that the only certain result of this process will be to drain public schools of financial and political support, leaving them with the most difficult students to educate, while not markedly improving the educational outcomes for those students who leave the system.

The public, at this point, does not clearly endorse either side of this dispute. For example, the June 1999 NBC/*Wall Street Journal* poll asked respondents to choose between two positions: government should give parents more educational choices by providing taxpayer-funded vouchers to help pay for private or religious schools, or government funding should be limited to children who attend public schools. The result was a dead-even 47 percent–47 percent split. Similarly, an August 1998 *Washington Post*/Kaiser Family Foundation/Harvard University survey asked, "do you favor or oppose providing parents with tax money in the form of school vouchers to help pay for their children to attend private or religious schools?" The poll found 49 percent in favor and an identical 49 percent opposed.

Of course, not all voucher questions produce a dead-even split. But those that are reasonably fair do tend to show the public evenly divided about vouchers, with only very slight majorities for or against. More specifically, questions that emphasize taxpayer or public expense and full funding of private school tuition tend to elicit slightly negative responses, while those that deemphasize the taxpayer/public source of voucher money and allude to partial rather than full coverage of tuition tend to generate slightly positive responses. But the very weak majorities in either case indicate a public that has not made up its mind.[31]

Would the weight of public opinion be more decisively in one camp or the other if vouchers were means tested; that is, tilted toward low-income families who are presumably most in need of escaping bad public schools? Available data do not allow us to consider this possibility, despite the fact that most current voucher programs are, in fact, means tested. The best we can say is that, given the existence of a voucher program, the public is opposed to having that program available only to low-income families (72 to 22 percent in the 1999 Public Agenda poll),[32] but mildly in favor of having the program give poor children more money than wealthier children (47 to 37 percent in a 1998 Joint Center poll). But there is no basis for concluding that making vouchers means tested would move the public away from its current ambivalence.

However, while the public may now be split about vouchers, the trend over time appears to be favorable to the voucher cause. Consider the data in Table 8.8. In 1993, when the Gallup/PDK survey first asked, "Do you favor or oppose allowing students and parents to choose a private school to attend at public expense?" the public was overwhelmingly opposed, by a 74 to 24 percent margin. But opposition to the proposal dropped between 1993 and 1999: in the latter year, opposition to the proposal was only 55 percent, compared to 41 percent actually favoring the proposal. This is quite a significant shift in a short period of time.

Not all voucher questions with consistent wording show a shift of this magnitude. But they do tend to show a shift in the same direction. For example, Table 8.9 (page 276) shows responses to a voucher question regarding allowing parents to send children to any "public, private or church-related school," with the government picking up all or part of the tuition for nonpublic school choices. As the table shows,

TABLE 8.8. CHOOSING A PRIVATE SCHOOL TO ATTEND AT PUBLIC EXPENSE, 1993–99 (PERCENT)

Do you favor or oppose allowing students and parents to choose a private school to attend at public expense?

	FAVOR	OPPOSE	DON'T KNOW
May 1993	24	74	2
June 1995	33	65	2
May 1996	36	61	3
June 1997	44	52	4
June 1998	44	50	6
June 1999	41	55	4

Polls: All data from Gallup polls conducted for Phi Delta Kappa.
Source: Phi Delta Kappa website: http:://www.pdkintl.org.

TABLE 8.9. VIEWS ON GOVERNMENT PAYING ALL OR PART OF NONPUBLIC SCHOOL TUITION, 1994–99 (PERCENT)

A proposal has been made that would allow parents to send their school-age children to any public, private, or church-related school they choose. For those parents choosing nonpublic schools, the government would pay all or part of the tuition. Would you favor or oppose this proposal in your state?

	FAVOR	OPPOSE	DON'T KNOW
May 1994	45	54	1
May 1996	43	54	3
June 1997	49	48	3
June 1998	51	45	4
June 1999	51	47	2

Polls: All data from Gallup polls conducted for Phi Delta Kappa.
Source: Phi Delta Kappa website: http:://www.pdkintl.org.

opposition dropped by seven points in the 1994–99 period, to the point where a slight majority (51 to 47 percent) now favors the proposal.

Similarly, a series of questions (with only minor wording variations) asked by NBC/*Wall Street Journal* on providing vouchers for sending children to private schools shows opposition dropping from 61 percent in 1994 to 52 percent in 1998. Finally, a March 1999 CNN/*Time* poll found 54 percent saying the government should only spend money on children attending public schools (as opposed to the government spending money to assist those families who want to send their children to private or religious schools), down from 64 percent in favor of such a restriction in 1992.

So the trend clearly favors the provoucher side of this debate,[33] even if the current balance of public opinion does not. And, of course, if the trend of the last six or seven years continues, that balance will shift and we *will* see a public opinion climate that is basically provoucher.

How can we explain this trend? What is making vouchers more attractive over time to an initially skeptical public? One reason is the perceived superiority of private over public schools in key areas like standards and discipline, areas that, as established earlier in this paper, are of critical importance to the public. For example, in a May 1995 Public Agenda poll, 53 percent of respondents said private schools in their area were likely to have higher academic standards, compared to just 24 percent who selected public schools as having higher academic standards. Similarly, the public preferred local private schools over public schools in terms of discipline and order in the classroom 61 to 18 percent, in terms of smaller class size 67 to 13 percent, and in terms of promoting good values 54 to 17 percent.

Thus, the public not only believes that public schools have failed in certain areas outside their communities (inner cities), they also believe that, within their communities, local public schools come up short in key respects when compared to local private schools. This makes it easier to understand why the public is increasingly willing to entertain the notion of vouchers for private schools. In the public's view, private schools provide a very credible alternative, as public schools appear to be making little progress addressing their chronic problems. Indeed, so credible are private schools as an alternative that the public strongly believes public school students choosing to switch to private schools will gain academically (65 percent), rather than remain the same (28 percent) or get worse (only 4 percent).[34] Almost against their will, this forces the public to scrutinize the voucher alternative closely.

And it really is almost against their will. Consider this result from the 1999 Gallup/PDK poll: when asked to evaluate two different plans, improving and strengthening the existing public schools or providing vouchers for parents to use to send their children to private or church-related schools, the public overwhelmingly selected reforming the public schools over vouchers, 70 to 28 percent. Similarly, in the 1998 Peter Harris/RNT poll, 84 percent of the public chose "doing what it takes to get a fully-qualified teacher in every classroom" over "allowing parents to use money spent on their child's education in public schools for a private education" (only 14 percent). Finally, even when asked to think specifically of parents with children in low-performing schools, respondents preferred allowing these parents to send their children to the public school they think best, rather than allowing them to send their children to alternative schools, including private schools (58 to 33 percent in the 1999 PSB/DLC poll).

Clearly, the public must be dissatisfied with the pace of reform for the voucher option to be gaining strength in the face of such pro–public school sentiment. And, to underscore the seriousness of this situation, support for vouchers is strongest among those most directly served by the public schools (public school parents), those whose schools are generally viewed as having the most problems (blacks), and those whose views will shape the future political environment (youths).[35] Without serious—and widely perceived—change, therefore, the public schools seem likely to face the unpredictable consequences of large-scale voucher use in the near future.

CONCLUSION: THE PUBLIC VISION FOR PUBLIC SCHOOLS

Americans remain supportive of the public school system, despite being very critical of the current performance of the system. They want that performance improved in a number of ways, reflecting their vision of what a good public school system should be. To begin, they want higher standards and are willing to tolerate fairly strict guidelines and testing regimes to accomplish this goal. This ranges from support for requiring students to pass a standard nationwide exam to graduate from high school, to support for current proposals to set national standards for academic achievement as a measure for public school performance.

The public also wants to see the quality of public school teachers substantially improved and believes this is central to the goal of reforming public schools. It endorses competency testing for teachers and is willing to see teacher salaries raised to counter the teacher shortage and attract better applicants.

The public is adamant about the importance of discipline in the public schools and wants to see this problem vigorously addressed. This includes overwhelming support for a zero-tolerance policy toward drug, alcohol, or weapons violations in the schools, and for putting persistent troublemakers into alternative schools.

The public also believes that the practice of promoting students from grade to grade whether or not they have learned the appropriate material must be stopped. Social promotion, in the public view, is a far worse evil than holding students back until they meet standards.

Americans also would like to see more money spent on the public schools, with the proviso that it go to reforms and programs they deem important. Topping the list of such spending priorities are smaller class size, technological infrastructure, school modernization and construction, and attracting better teachers.

In addition to these general improvements in the nation's schools, the public's vision of change includes doing something about failing schools, particularly in troubled areas like the nation's inner cities. Americans are willing to see extra resources allocated to such schools, provided such resources are used for critically needed improvements like better teachers. They are even willing to see poor districts' funding equalized with that of rich districts—though again the public needs assurance that poor districts' additional funding will be used for reform, rather than to support the status quo and that their own school districts will not lose funding as a result.

Finally, the public wants to see more choice in the system. Given the problems that do exist in the current system, as well as the broad challenges of today's economy, the public wants the option of rejecting their traditional neighborhood school in favor of a school where the curriculum and practices suit their children's needs.

All these changes together constitute the public's vision of a reformed public school system. Implementing that vision would go far toward reestablishing the public school system as the general engine of upward mobility, a role that has been called into question by the system's widely publicized shortcomings.

Conversely, failure to implement that vision risks a crisis of confidence in the public schools. Given recent public opinion trends, that can only result in the implementation of a voucher system in place of the vision just articulated. And the result of *that* could be the end of public schools' historic role as the chief engine of upward mobility in American society. The time for change, therefore, is now. The risks of delay—especially for those who champion the cause of greater equality in American society—are simply unacceptable.

NOTES

Chapter 1

1. Peter Schrag, "Education and the Election," *The Nation*, March 6, 2000.

2. U.S. Department of Education, *NAEP 1998 Reading Report Card for the Nation*, March 1999, p. 59.

3. For further discussion of this idea, see Richard D. Kahlenberg, "Economic School Desegregation," *Education Week*, March 31, 1999, p. 52; and Kahlenberg, *All Together Now: Creating Middle-Class Schools through Public School Choice*, a Century Foundation Book (Washington, D.C.: Brookings Institution Press, 2000).

Chapter 2

1. See Doris R. Entwisle, Karl L. Alexander, and Linda Steffel Olson, *Children, Schools, and Inequality* (Boulder, Colo.: Westview Press, 1997); Doris R. Entwisle and Karl L. Alexander, "Summer Setback: Race, Poverty, School Composition, and Mathematics Achievement in the First Two Years of School," *American Sociological Review* 57 (February 1992): 72–84; Doris R. Entwisle and Karl L. Alexander, "Winter Setback: School Racial Composition and Learning to Read," *American Sociological Review* 59 (June 1994): 446–60.

2. See Jeanne Brooks-Gunn, Greg J. Duncan, and Nancy Maritato, "Poor Families, Poor Outcomes: The Well-Being of Children and Youth," in Greg J.

Duncan and Jeanne Brooks-Gunn, eds., *The Consequences of Growing Up Poor* (New York: The Russell Sage Foundation, 1997).

3. For example, see Irwin Garfinkel and Sara S. McLanahan, *Single Mothers and Their Children: A New American Dilemma* (Washington, D.C.: Urban Institute Press, 1986); Robert H. Haveman and Barbara L. Wolfe, *Succeeding Generations: On the Effects of Investments in Children* (New York: Russell Sage Foundation, 1994); Glen H. Elder, Jr., *Children of the Great Depression: Social Change in Life Experience* (Chicago: University of Chicago Press, 1974); Vonnie McLoyd, "Socialization and Development in a Changing Economy: The Effects of Paternal Income and Job Loss on Children," *American Psychologist* 44 (February 1989): 293–302; Vonnie C. McLoyd, "The Impact of Economic Hardship on Black Families and Children: Psychological Distress, Parenting, and Socioemotional Development," *Child Development* 62 (April 1990): 311–46.

4. Haveman and Wolfe, *Succeeding Generations*.

5. U.S. Bureau of the Census, *Statistical Abstract of the United States: 1998* (Washington, D.C.: Government Printing Office, 1998), Tables 296, 297.

6. National Center for Education Statistics, *The Condition of Education 1994*, NCES 94-149 (Washington, D.C.: U.S. Department of Education, 1994).

7. Susan E. Mayer, *What Money Can't Buy: Family Income and Children's Life Chances* (Cambridge, Mass.: Harvard University Press, 1997), Table 3.1.

8. *National Urban Education Goals: 1992–93 Indicators Report* (Washington, D.C.: Council of Great City Schools, 1994).

9. U.S. Bureau of the Census, *Statistical Abstract: 1998*, Table 299.

10. Duane F. Alwin and Arland Thornton, "Family Origins and the Schooling Process: Early versus Late Influence of Parental Characteristics," *American Sociological Review* 49 (December 1984): 784–802; Kevin Marjoribanks, *Families and Their Learning Environments* (London: Routledge, 1979).

11. For example, see Richard J. Murnane, *The Impact of School Resources on the Learning of Inner City Children* (Cambridge, Mass.: Ballinger, 1975); Marjoribanks, *Families and Their Learning Environments*; Karl L. Alexander and Doris R. Entwisle, "Educational Tracking in the Early Years: First Grade Placements and Middle School Constraints," in Alan C. Kerckhoff, ed., *Generating Social Stratification: Toward a New Research Agenda* (New York: Westview Press, 1996); Greg J. Duncan et al., "How Much Does Childhood Poverty Affect the Life Chances of Children?" *American Sociological Review* 63 (June 1998): 406–23.

12. Marshall S. Smith, "Equality of Educational Opportunity: The Basic Findings Reconsidered," in Frederick Mosteller and Daniel P. Moynihan, eds., *On Equality of Educational Opportunity* (New York: Vantage Books, 1972), pp. 230–342; Aletha C. Huston, *Children in Poverty: Designing Research to Affect Policy*, Social Policy Report, Society for Research in Child Development (Ann Arbor: University of Michigan, 1994).

13. Mayer, *What Money Can't Buy.*

14. This research is a prospective longitudinal study of children's academic and social development beginning in first grade and continuing through high school graduation and beyond. Data collection began in 1982 and is ongoing. In 1982 a two-stage random sample of youngsters beginning first grade in the Baltimore City Public Schools was selected for study. First, a sample of twenty schools, stratified by racial mix (six predominantly African American, six white, eight integrated) and by socioeconomic status (fourteen inner city or working class and six middle class) was selected. Second, within each school students were randomly sampled from every first-grade classroom by using kindergarten lists from the previous spring supplemented by class rosters after school began in the fall. Parents' permission was obtained for 97 percent of the children so chosen, resulting in a final sample of 790 youngsters beginning first grade for the first time in 1982. See Entwisle, Alexander, and Olson, *Children, Schools, and Inequality,* for an overall presentation of the Beginning School Study (BSS) and for more information on the study design and procedures.

15. California Achievement Test (CAT) Form C, Reading Comprehension and Mathematics Concepts and Applications subtests. For documentation on test see California Achievement Test, *Technical Bulletin 1, Forms C and D, Levels 10–19* (Monterey, Calif.: McGraw-Hill, 1979).

16. Students qualified for the federal meal subsidy program based on income and family size guidelines developed by the Department of Agriculture. The guidelines are obtained each year by multiplying the federal income poverty level by 1.85 for reduced-price meals and by 1.30 for free meals. Sixty-seven percent of the sample qualified for either reduced-price meals or a full subsidy.

17. In BSS data, reading scores at the beginning of first grade for meal subsidy students were lower by about three months in terms of annual growth than those for non–meal subsidy students. Likewise, for math, meal subsidy students were about five months below more affluent students.

18. Karl L. Alexander, Doris R. Entwisle, and Susan L. Dauber, *On the Success of Failure: A Reassessment of the Effects of Retention in the Primary Grades* (Cambridge: Cambridge University Press, 1994).

19. Susan M. Bianchi, "Children's Progress through School: A Research Note," *Sociology of Education* 57 (July 1984): 184–92.

20. National Center for Education Statistics, *A Profile of the American Eighth Grader: NELS 88 Student Descriptive Summary,* U.S. Department of Education, Office of Educational Research and Improvement (Washington, D.C.: U.S. Government Printing Office, 1990).

21. The Beginning School Study often is referred to as the "Baltimore Study."

22. Alexander, Entwisle, and Dauber, *On the Success of Failure.*

23. Consortium of Longitudinal Studies, *As the Twig Is Bent: Lasting Effect of Preschool Programs* (Hillsdale, N.J.: Erlbaum, 1983); Aaron M. Pallas, *School*

Dropouts in the United States, issue paper CS87-426, Center for Education Statistics, Office of Educational Research and Improvement (Washington, D.C.: U.S. Government Printing Office, 1987); R. W. Rumberger, "High School Dropouts: A Review of Issues and Evidence," *Review of Educational Research* 57, no. 2 (1987): 101–21; T. C. Wagenaar, "What Do We Know about Dropping Out of High School?" in A. C. Kerckhoff, ed., *Research in Sociology of Education and Socialization* (Greenwich, Conn.: JAI, 1987), pp 161–90.

24. J. B. Grissom and L. A. Shepard, "Repeating and Dropping Out of School," in L. A. Shepard and M. L. Smith, eds., *Flunking Grades: Research and Policies on Retention* (London: Falmer, 1989), pp. 34–63; Aaron M. Pallas, "The Determinants of High School Dropouts," Ph.D. diss., Johns Hopkins University, Baltimore, Md., 1984.

25. See Table 25 in National Center for Education Statistics, NCES 97-473, *Dropout Rates in the United States: 1995* (Washington, D.C.: U.S. Government Printing Office, 1995).

26. Robert B. Cairns, Beverley D. Cairns, and Holly J. Neckerman, "Early School Dropout: Configurations and Determinants," *Child Development* 60 (December 1989): 1437–52; D. N. Lloyd, "Prediction of School Failure from Third-Grade Data," *Educational and Psychological Measurement* 38, no. 4 (Winter 1978): 1193–1200; Atlee L. Stroup and Lee N. Robins, "Elementary School Predictors of High School Dropout among Black Males," *Sociology of Education* 45 (Spring 1972): 212–22; Karl L. Alexander, Doris R. Entwisle, and Carrie S. Horsey, "From First Grade Forward: Early Foundations of High School Dropout," *Sociology of Education* 70 (April 1997): 87–107.

27. Barbara Heyns, *Summer Learning and the Effects of Schooling* (New York: Academic, 1978); Geoffrey B. Saxe, Steven R. Guberman, and Maryl Gearheart, "Social Processes in Early Number Development," *Monographs of the Society for Research in Child Development* 52, no. 2, serial No. 216 (1987); Barbara L. Schneider and James S. Coleman, *Parents, Their Children, and Schools* (Boulder, Colo.: Westview, 1993); Doris R. Entwisle and Karl L. Alexander, "A Parent's Economic Shadow: Family Structure versus Family Resources as Influences on Early School Achievement," *Journal of Marriage and the Family* 57 (May 1995): 399–409.

28. Entwisle, Alexander, and Olson, *Children, Schools, and Inequality*, p. 40.

29. For Beginning School Study children, borrowing books from the library in the summer and children's socioeconomic status correlate 0.37. See also Heyns, *Summer Learning*, p. 119.

30. Mayer, *What Money Can't Buy*, p. 2.

31. Elizabeth G. Menaghan and Toby L. Parcel, "Stability and Change in Children's Home Environments: The Effects of Parental Occupational Experiences and Family Conditions," paper presented at the meeting of the Society for Research on Child Development, Seattle, Wash., April 1991.

32. Robert D. Hess and Virginia C. Shipman, "Early Experience and the Socialization of Cognitive Modes in Children," *Child Development* 36, no. 4 (1965): 869–88.

33. Entwisle, Alexander, and Olson, *Children, Schools, and Inequality*, Table 3.4, p. 41.

34. Ibid., Table 3.5, p. 43.

35. See Karl L. Alexander and Doris R. Entwisle, "Achievement in the First Two Years of School: Patterns and Processes," *Monographs of the Society for Research in Child Development* 53, no. 2, serial No. 218 (1988); Doris R. Entwisle and Karl L. Alexander, "Beginning School Math Competence," *Child Development* 61 (April 1990): 454–71; Karl L. Alexander, Doris R. Entwisle, M. Jane Sundius, and Susan L. Dauber, "Developmental Trends in Academic Self-Image and Marks: Lessons from the Experience of Repeaters," Johns Hopkins University, Baltimore, Md., 1994; Aaron M. Pallas et al., "Ability-Group Effects: Instructional, Social or Institutional?" *Sociology of Education* 67 (January 1994): 27–46; Doris R. Entwisle and Karl L. Alexander, "Family Type and Children's Growth in Reading and Math over the Primary Grades," *Journal of Marriage and the Family* 58 (May 1996): 341–55.

36. Entwisle and Alexander, "Family Type and Children's Growth."

37. Heyns, *Summer Learning*.

38. Valerie Lee, Anthony S. Bryk, and Julia B. Smith, "The Organization of Effective Secondary Schools," in Linda Darling-Hammond, ed., *Review of Research in Education* (Washington D.C.: American Educational Research Association, 1993), pp. 171–67; Entwisle and Alexander, "Family Type and Children's Growth."

39. Heyns, *Summer Learning*; Murnane, *Impact of School Resources*; Harris Cooper et al., "The Effects of Summer Vacation on Achievement Test Scores: A Narrative and Meta-Analytic Review," *Review of Educational Research* 66 (Fall 1996): 227–69.

40. Family socioeconomic status is measured as a composite, using information on student participation in the school meal subsidy program and mother's and father's educational levels and occupational status. A three-category version of this measure was derived, with the low-status group averaging 10.0 years of education for mothers and a 95 percent rate of participation in the school meal subsidy program. For the high-status group, mothers averaged 14.6 years of education and 13 percent of students received a meal subsidy.

41. See top half of Table 3.1 in Entwisle, Alexander, and Olson, *Children, Schools, and Inequality*, p. 34.

42. See ibid., lower panel of Table 3.1.

43. Multivariate analyses of variance show that these seasonal differences vary significantly with family socioeconomic status over the first two years of school. See Entwisle and Alexander, "Summer Setback"; Entwisle and

Alexander, "Winter Setback"; Entwisle, Alexander, and Olson, *Children, Schools, and Inequality.*

44. Heyns, *Summer Learning.*

45. Murnane, *Impact of School Resources.*

46. See Donald P. Hayes and Judith Grether, "The School Year and Vacations: When Do Students Learn?" paper presented at the annual meeting of the Eastern Sociological Association, New York, April 1969; Jane L. David, "Follow-Through Summer Study: A Two-Part Investigation of the Impact of Exposure to Schooling on Achievement Growth," Ed.D. diss., Harvard Graduate School of Education, Cambridge, Mass., 1974; Donald P. Hayes and J. P. King, *The Development of Reading Achievement Differentials During the School Year and Vacations,* Cornell University, Ithaca, N.Y., 1974; Sol H. Pelavin and Jane L. David, *Evaluating Long-Term Achievement: An Analysis of Longitudinal Data from Compensatory Educational Programs,* EPRC 4537-15, prepared for the Office of the Assistant Secretary for Education, Department of Health, Education and Welfare (Washington, D.C.: SRI International Educational Policy Research Center, 1977); Jane L. David and Sol H. Pelavin, "Secondary Analysis: In Compensatory Education Programs," *New Directions for Program Evaluation* 4 (1978): 31–44; Pierce A. Hammond and Joy A. Frechtling, "Twelve, Nine and Three Month Achievement Gains of Low and Average Achieving Elementary School Students," paper presented at annual meeting of the American Educational Research Association, San Francisco, April 8, 1979.

47. Beginning School Study schools were located in neighborhoods which ranged from very low socioeconomic status (close to 40 percent of families in poverty, the average parent a drop-out, and only 5 percent of workers in professional/managerial jobs) to relatively high socioeconomic status (2 percent of families in poverty, the average parent close to a college graduate, and 64 percent of workers in professional/managerial jobs).

48. The gains also corresponded to the average number of children *not* on meal subsidy in the (neighborhood) school the child attended. See Table 3.8 in Entwisle, Alexander, and Olson, *Children, Schools, and Inequality,* p. 50.

49. See ibid., left side, Table 3.8.

50. Paul A. Jargowsky and Mary Jo Bane, "Ghetto Poverty: Basic Questions," in Laurence E. Lynn and Michael G. H. McGeary, eds., *Inner-City Poverty in the United States* (Washington, D.C.: National Academy Press, 1990); Entwisle, Alexander, and Olson, *Children, Schools, and Inequality.*

51. Annette Lareau, "Social Class Differences in Family-School Relationships: The Importance of Cultural Capital," *Sociology of Education* 60 (April 1987): 73–85.

52. Joyce L. Epstein, "Effects on Student Achievement of Teachers' Practices of Parent Involvement," in S. Silvern, ed., *Literacy Through Family, Community,*

and School Interaction, vol. 6 (Greenwich, Conn.: JAI Press, 1991), pp. 261–76; Joyce L. Epstein, "School and Family Partnerships," in Marvin Alkin, ed., *Encyclopedia of Educational Research*, 6th ed. (New York: Macmillan, 1992), pp. 1139–51.

53. Hess and Shipman, "Early Experience and the Socialization of Cognitive Modes in Children."

54. Lareau, "Social Class Differences in Family-School Relationships." Also see Entwisle, Alexander, and Olson, *Children, Schools, and Inequality*, p. 52; Karl L. Alexander, Doris R. Entwisle, and Samuel D. Bedinger, "When Expectations Work: Race and Socioeconomic Differences in School Performance," *Social Psychology Quarterly* 57, no. 4 (1994): 283–99.

55. Doris R. Entwisle and Leslie A. Hayduk, *Too Great Expectations: The Academic Outlook of Young Children* (Baltimore: Johns Hopkins University Press, 1978); Doris R. Entwisle and Leslie A. Hayduk, *Early Schooling: Cognitive and Affective Outcomes* (Baltimore: Johns Hopkins University Press, 1982); Doris R. Entwisle and Leslie A. Hayduk, "Lasting Effects of Elementary School," *Sociology of Education* 61 (July 1988): 147–59.

56. See Alexander, Entwisle, and Bedinger, "When Expectations Work."

57. See Doris R. Entwisle and Leslie A. Hayduk, "Academic Expectations and the School Attainment of Young Children," *Sociology of Education* 54 (January 1981): 34–50; Entwisle and Hayduk, *Too Great Expectations*.

58. DuBois and his colleagues, for instance, found that school-based supports buffered or compensated for hazards in the home and other places outside school, and that disadvantaged youths had a greater potential than their better-off classmates to benefit from adults' social support in school achievement. See David L. DuBois et al., "A Prospective Study of Life Stress, Social Support, and Adaptation in Early Adolescence," *Child Development* 63 (June 1992): 542–57; David L. DuBois et al., "Prospective Investigation of the Effects of Socioeconomic Disadvantage, Life Stress, and Social Support on Early Adolescent Adjustment," *Journal of Abnormal Psychology* 103, no. 3 (1994): 511–22.

59. Robert C. Pianta, L. Alan Sroufe, and Byron Egeland, "Continuity and Discontinuity in Maternal Sensitivity at 6, 24 and 42 Months of Age in a High-Risk Sample," *Child Development* 60 (April 1989): 481–87;

60. Steven Parker, Steven Greer, and Barry Zuckerman, "Double Jeopardy: The Impact of Poverty on Early Child Development," *Pediatric Clinics of North America* 35 (December 1988): 1227–40.

61. Entwisle and Alexander, "Family Type and Children's Growth."

62. See Entwisle, Alexander, and Olson, *Children, Schools, and Inequality*, Table 3.7, p. 47.

63. The rank-order correlation is 0.71.

64. That is, three standard deviations below the average interest and participation rating of students in the same school.

65. For early studies see Hayes and Grether, "School Year and Vacations"; Hayes and King, *Development of Reading Achievement Differentials*; M. M. Shapiro, J. L. Bresnahar, and I. J. Knopf, cited by Heyns, *Summer Learning*; Murnane, *The Impact of School Resources*; David, "Follow-Through Summer Study."

66. For an overview of this research see, for example, Charles Ballinger, "Prisoners No More," *Educational Leadership* 53 (November 1995): 28–31; Harris Cooper et al., "Making the Most of Summer School: A Meta-Analytic and Narrative Review," *Monographs of the Society for Research in Child Development* 65, pt. 1 (2000). Importantly, the Cooper et al. review tallies only studies sponsored by schools, school districts, or colleges and universities. Other studies, also cited in this chapter, address more clearly the picture for social class differences in summer school effects.

67. See Cooper et al., "Making the Most of Summer School"; and earlier research by G. R. Austin, B. G. Rogers, and H. H. Walbesser, "The Effectiveness of Summer Compensatory Education: A Review of the Research," *Review of Educational Research* 42 (1972): 171–81; Barbara Heyns, *Summer Programs and Compensatory Education: The Future of an Idea*, Working paper, National Institute of Education, Chapter One Study Team, Conference on the Effects of Alternative Designs in Compensatory Education, Washington, D.C., 1986, ERIC Document Reproduction Service No. ED 293906; C. Ascher, "Summer School, Extended School Year, and Year-Round Schooling for Disadvantaged Students," *ERIC Clearinghouse on Urban Education Digest* 42 (1988): 1–2. Cooper and his colleagues (p. 46) conclude that students from middle-class homes gained more from summer school than students from disadvantaged homes when student socioeconomic status (SES) is defined as a "moderator variable" affecting summer school outcomes. This approach signifies finding a difference between summer school gains of "middle SES and low SES" students. The conclusion is based on three samples limited to middle-class students, that is, no comparison of middle with low SES. M. Welch and J.B. Jensen, "Write P.L.E.A.S.E.: A Video-Assisted Strategic Intervention to Improve Written Expression of Inefficient Learners," *Remedial and Special Education* 12 (January/February 1991): 37–47; R. Geis, *A Preventive Summer Program for Kindergarten Children Likely to Fail First Grade Reading* (La Canada, Calif.: La Canada Unified School District, 1968), ERIC Document Reproduction Service No. ED 1029427; H. S. Leviton, "The Effect of a Summer Compensatory Education Program on Academic Achievement and Self-Concept of Primary Grade Learning Disabled Children with Follow-up Study," Ph.D. diss., University of Iowa, Iowa City, 1973; plus a fourth study (D. Doss et al., *Interim Evaluation Report: The 1979 Summer School Program* [Washington, D.C.: Department of Health, Education, and Welfare, 1979], ERIC Document Reproduction Service No. ED 188823) showing *no*

effects for either middle-class or migrant/Title I students who took part in a randomized experiment. Two other studies are based on children of migrant workers: V. J. Garafolo, *Evaluation of Migrant Summer School Programs Supported by the New York Department of Education During 1968*, Final Report (Albany: New York State Education Department, 1968), ERIC Document Reproduction Service No. ED 026162; D. M. Baxley and M. Hinton, *The Eloy Story. A Report from the Eloy Elementary School Summer Migrant Program for Kindergarten through Second Grade Level Children* (Phoenix: Arizona State Department of Education, 1971), ERIC Document Reproduction Services No. ED 067217. The 1971 report is based on eight students.

68. See Cooper et al., "Making the Most of Summer School."

69. Ibid.

70. See Launor F. Carter, "The Sustaining Effects Study of Compensatory and Elementary Education," *Educational Researcher* 13 (August/September 1984): 4–13; Leonard S. Klibanoff and Sue A. Haggart, *Report # 8: Summer Growth and the Effectiveness of Summer School*, technical report to the Office of Program Evaluation, U.S. Department of Education (Mountain View, Calif.: RMC Research Corporation, 1981), which is entirely devoted to summer growth.

71. Barbara Heyns, "Schooling and Cognitive Development: Is There a Season for Learning?" *Child Development* 58 (October 1987): 1151–60. See especially pp. 1153, 1158.

72. Heyns, *Summer Learning*.

73. See Thomas D. Cook et al., *"Sesame Street" Revisited* (New York: Russell Sage, 1975), especially Chapter 1, which points out how difficult evaluations are to conduct and the kinds of stumbling blocks that researchers encounter. It also lists Matthew effects, such as that more viewing of *Sesame Street* by disadvantaged children was associated with less parental reading to children, and viewing itself was positively correlated with parents' income and education. For another example, see Carter, "Sustaining Effects Study." Students who entered Title I programs at near-average achievement levels profited most, whereas those entering at a low level profited only little or not at all. More recently, in 1997 the New York State Legislature enacted a universal kindergarten for four-year-olds, but there has been *underenrollment* in the communities with limited access to quality preschools. See Foundation for Child Development, *March 1999 Update* (New York: Foundation for Child Development, 1999).

74. See Heyns, *Summer Learning*, p. 128.

75. National Center for Education Statistics, *The Condition of Education 1998*, NCES 98-013 (Washington, D.C.: U.S. Government Printing Office, 1998), Indicator 1: Preprimary Education Enrollment.

76. Achievement test data for Beginning School Study children and for national samples as well show that their scores increase most in first grade, next most in second grade, and continue to decelerate each year thereafter.

These decreasing rates are visible in the upper (winter) portions of Table 3.1 (Entwisle, Alexander, and Olson, *Children, Schools, and Inequality*, p. 34), but are visible as well in standardized test data more generally. While psychometric issues of how these tests are scaled are complex and worrisome, the general observation that there is a spurt in children's cognitive growth at the time formal schooling begins is not in doubt. See also Doris R. Entwisle and Karl L. Alexander, "Further Comments on Seasonal Learning," in Alan Booth and Judith F. Dunn, eds., *Family-School Links: How Do They Affect Educational Outcomes?* (Mahwah, N.J.: Lawrence Erlbaum Associates, 1996), pp. 125–36; Barbara L. Schneider, "Production Analysis of Gains in Achievement," paper presented at the annual meeting of the American Educational Research Association, Boston, 1980.

77. See Irving Lazar and Richard Darlington, "Lasting Effects of Early Education: A Report from the Consortium for Longitudinal Studies," *Monographs of the Society for Research in Child Development* 47, nos. 2–3 (1982): ix–139; Consortium for Longitudinal Studies, *As the Twig Is Bent*.

78. Alexander, Entwisle, and Dauber, *On the Success of Failure*.

79. This analysis of the effects of first-grade retention on later high school dropout included controls on race, gender, family socioeconomic status, and reading and math CAT scores at the beginning of first grade.

80. See Doris R. Entwisle, "The Role of Schools in Sustaining Benefits of Early Childhood Programs," *The Future of Children* 5, no. 3 (Winter 1995): 133–44.

81. See W. Steven Barnett, "Long-Term Effects of Early Childhood Care and Education on Disadvantaged Children's Cognitive Development and School Success," *The Future of Children* 5, no. 3 (1995): 36–39, Table 2.

82. This will not be easy because in 1996 roughly twice as many three- and four-year-old children in families with incomes above $50,000 were enrolled in center-based programs as in families with incomes of $10,000 or less. National Center for Education Statistics, *The Condition of Education 1998*, Indicator 1.

83. Maryland State Department of Education, *Maryland School Performance Report, 1994: State and School Systems* (Baltimore: Maryland State Department of Education, 1994).

84. National Center for Education Statistics, *The Condition of Education 1995*, NCES 95-273 (Washington, D.C.: U.S. Department of Education, 1995), pp. 24, 30.

85. Doris R. Entwisle et al., "Kindergarten Experience: Cognitive Effects or Socialization?," *American Educational Research Journal* 24 (Fall 1987): 337–64.

86. See Arthur J. Reynolds, "Effects of a Preschool Plus Follow-On Intervention for Children at Risk," *Developmental Psychology* 30 (December 1994): 787–804; Arthur J. Reynolds and Judy A. Temple, "Extended Early Childhood Intervention and School Achievement: Age Thirteen Findings from the Chicago Longitudinal Study," *Child Development* 69 (1998): 231–46;

Judy A. Temple, Arthur J. Reynolds, and Wendy T. Miedel, "Can Early Intervention Prevent High School Dropout? Evidence from the Chicago Child-Parent Centers," Institute for Research on Poverty, discussion paper no. 1180-98 (Madison: University of Wisconsin, 1998). Primary-grade (follow-on) programs that are school-based operate five days a week during the school year and are tailored to increase children's learning opportunities through reduced class size, parental involvement activities, and instructional coordination. A major focus is child-centered attention to develop reading comprehension and writing skills.

87. Heyns, *Summer Learning*, p. 191.

88. Regression analyses predicting summer test score gains controlled on race, sex, and family socioeconomic status.

89. For a discussion of the link between organized sports and academic progress, see Doris R. Entwisle, Karl L. Alexander, and Linda Steffel Olson, "The Gender Gap in Math: Its Possible Origins in Neighborhood Effects," *American Sociological Review* 59 (December 1994): 822–38.

90. James S. Coleman, *The Adolescent Society: The Social Life of the Teenager and Its Impact on Education* (New York: Free Press, 1961).

91. In fact, the pooled psychological capital of adults in better-off neighborhoods probably explains some of the summer growth of children in those neighborhoods. Entwisle, Alexander, and Olson, *Children, Schools, and Inequality*, p. 51.

92. See Ballinger, "Prisoners No More."

93. See Reynolds and Temple, "Extended Early Childhood Intervention."

94. Lazar and Darlington, "Lasting Effects of Early Education."

95. Entwisle, Alexander, and Olson, *Children, Schools, and Inequality*.

96. Barnett, "Long-Term Effects."

97. Christopher Jencks estimates that children's cognitive growth rate in first grade may be ten times as great as the rate in high school. See Christopher Jencks, "How Much Do High School Students Learn?" *Sociology of Education* 58 (April 1985): 128–35.

98. Alan C. Kerckhoff, *Diverging Pathways: Social Structure and Career Deflections* (New York: Cambridge University Press, 1993).

Chapter 3

1. Paul Minorini and Stephen D. Sugarman, "School Finance Litigation in the Name of Educational Equity: Its Evolution, Impact and Future," in Helen Ladd, Rosemary Chalk, and Janet S. Hansen, eds., *Equity and Adequacy in Education Finance: Issues and Perspectives* (Washington, D.C.: National Academy Press, 1999), pp. 34–71.

2. U.S. Department of Education, Office of Educational Research and Improvement, *NAEP 1998 Reading Report Card for the Nation and the States*, NCES 1999-500, National Center for Education Statistics, 1999, Table 3.6. Scores on the National Assessment of Educational Progress (NAEP) are disaggregated by children's eligibility for the free and reduced-price lunch program. Children are eligible for the free lunch program if their families have income equal to or less than 130 percent of the federal poverty line. Children are eligible for the subsidized ("reduced-price") lunch program if their families have income equal to or less than 185 percent of the federal poverty line. While NAEP is administered to fourth-, eighth-, and twelfth-grade students, schools apparently enroll fewer eligible children at higher grade levels, partly because children themselves are less willing to sign up for the program and identify themselves as poor or near-poor. Therefore, only fourth-grade scores can provide reasonably valid indications of the relative performance of poor and near-poor children. There is no expert consensus regarding the validity of the National Assessment Governing Board's cut-off points for "basic" or "proficient" scores. See Richard Rothstein, *The Way We Were? The Myths and Realities of America's Student Achievement* (New York: The Century Foundation Press, 1998), pp. 70–74. But even if the cut-off points are invalid, the relative, properly measured proficiency of poor and near-poor children on the one hand and nonpoor children on the other would probably be similar to that reported.

3. Estimated from data reported in Christopher Jencks and Meredith Phillips, eds., *The Black-White Test Score Gap* (Washington, D.C.: Brookings Institution Press, 1998), p. 3. In 1971, the black-white seventeen-year-old reading score gap was 1.25 standard deviations. In 1996 it was 0.69 standard deviations.

4. David W. Grissmer et al., *Student Achievement and the Changing American Family* (Santa Monica, Calif.: RAND, 1994). It also possible that better-specified background characteristics could explain some additional portion of the gains.

5. U.S. Department of Education, Office of Educational Research and Improvement, *NAEP Trends in Academic Progress*, NCES 97-985, National Center for Education Statistics, 1997, Figures 3.6, 3.8, 5.6, 5.8.

6. Thomas B. Parrish, Christine S. Matsumoto, and William J. Fowler, Jr., *Disparities in Public School Spending, 1989-90*, NCES 95-300, National Center for Education Statistics, 1995.

7. Parrish, Matsumoto, and Fowler do not use the terms "affluent," "moderately affluent," "moderate poverty," and "high poverty." These terms are utilized here for ease of reference. The cut-off points used to categorize them are defined as follows: Affluent districts are those where less than 5 percent of children are poor—such districts enroll 11 percent of the nation's students. Moderately affluent districts are those where from 5 to 15 percent of children are poor—such districts enroll 36 percent of the nation's students. Moderate-poverty districts are

those where from 15 to 25 percent of children are poor—such districts enroll 26 percent of the nation's students. High-poverty districts are those where 25 percent or more of children are poor—such districts enroll 26 percent of the nation's students.

8. Districts with a "large" percentage of students at risk are those where more than 5 percent of students are classified so, constituting 39 percent of the nation's students; districts with a "moderate" share are those where from 3 percent to 5 percent of students are at risk, making up 15 percent of the nation's students; districts with "few" students in this category are those where less than 3 percent of students are at risk, representing 45 percent of the nation's students.

9. Henry M. Levin, "Financing the Education of At-Risk Students," *Education Evaluation and Policy Analysis* 11, no. 1 (Spring 1989): 47–60.

10. Penny L. Howell and Barbara B. Miller, "Sources of Funding for Schools," *The Future of Children* 7, no. 3 (Winter 1997): 39–51.

11. Allan Odden, "School Finance Reform in Kentucky, New Jersey and Texas," *Journal of Education Finance* 18, no. 4 (Spring 1993): 293–317; Allan R. Odden and Lawrence O. Picus, *School Finance: A Policy Perspective* (New York: McGraw-Hill, 1992), Figure 8.1.

12. William H. Clune, "The Shift from Equity to Adequacy in School Finance," *Educational Policy* 8, no. 4 (December 1994): 376–94; Andrew Reschovsky and Jennifer Imazeki, "The Development of School Finance Formulas to Guarantee the Provision of Adequate Education to Low Income Students," in William J. Fowler, Jr., ed., *Developments in School Finance, 1997* (Washington, D.C.: National Center for Education Statistics, 1998).

13. See, for example, Thomas A. Downes and Thomas F. Pogue, "Adjusting School Aid Formulas for the Higher Cost of Educating Disadvantaged Students," *National Tax Journal* 47, no. 1 (March 1994): 89–110.

14. See, for example, John Augenblick, John Myers, and Amy Anderson, "Equity and Adequacy in School Funding," *The Future of Children* 7, no. 3 (Winter 1997): 63–78.

15. While districts with high poverty concentrations spend 93 percent as much as affluent districts after figures are cost- and need-adjusted, it was noted above that they spend 79 percent as much without such adjustment. These figures relate to district spending comparisons not within states but when all states are lumped together in a single national pool. The cost- and need-adjusted disparity is probably less than the unadjusted disparity because states probably spend their compensatory funds (both federal and state generated) disproportionately in districts, or in schools within districts, with high concentrations of poverty. Thus, even if compensatory funds do not reduce interstate inequality, they could reduce inequality in spending among districts on a national basis.

16. See, for example, Jay Mathews, *Class Struggle: What's Wrong (and Right) with America's Best Public High Schools* (New York: Times Books, 1998); Jeannie

Oakes, *Keeping Track: How Schools Structure Inequality* (New Haven: Yale University Press, 1985); Nicola Alexander, "Race, Poverty, and the Student Curriculum, 1975–1995: Implications for Public Policy," in William J. Fowler, Jr., ed., *Developments in School Finance, 1996* (Washington, D.C.: National Center for Education Statistics, 1997); among others, for discussion of resource differences in tracked schools. Because there is not a true market for teachers, school districts with a uniform salary schedule pay the same price for teachers of varying quality. However, despite the equality in teacher salaries for teachers with similar education and experience, assignment of teachers of greater quality to some students can represent greater real resources applied to the education of those students. This differential application of teacher resources can contribute to Type IV inequalities. It also contributes to Type III inequalities, something that is discussed below.

17. These data are for public elementary and secondary school revenues, not expenditures, because it is not possible to distinguish school expenditures by the source of funds. Even categorical programs mix funds from federal, state, and local sources. However, if school district budgetary carryovers remain fairly constant from year to year, total revenues and total expenditures will be roughly equivalent, and so state and local "revenues" can be deemed equivalent to state and local "expenditures." In the discussion that follows, the words "school spending" should be understood to refer precisely to revenues, not expenditures.

18. How to adjust for regional differences in the cost of education is a matter of great theoretical complexity. Lawrence Mishel and Richard Rothstein, "Measurement Issues in Adjusting School Spending across Time and Place," paper presented at the annual Data Conference of the National Center for Education Statistics, Washington, D.C., July 1997. A common approach is to adjust for differences in teacher salaries, with additional adjustments for differences in consumer prices (see, for example, "Quality Counts: A Report Card on the Condition of Public Education in the 50 States," *Education Week*, January 22, 1997). This method, however, involves problems of endogeneity—salaries for teachers with comparable experience could differ because of regional differences in cost but also because states choose to hire teachers of different quality. In Table 3.1 of this chapter, adjustments for state cost of education differences in column 3 were calculated by adjusting first for differences in "cost of living" between states in 1990, as estimated in Walter W. McMahon, "Intrastate Cost Adjustments," in William J. Fowler, Jr., ed., *Selected Papers in School Finance, 1994* (Washington, D.C: National Center for Education Statistics, 1995) utilizing census data on population growth, the price of housing, and per capita personal income. (McMahon does not, however, make an adjustment for "amenities of location," leaving open the possibility that the prices of housing in high-price states reflect a higher unmeasured value of

housing location.) Column 3 then inflates McMahon's index numbers for 1990 by changes from 1990 to 1996–97 in the "all services" component of the consumer price index for the census region in which each state was located. U.S. Department of Labor, Bureau of Labor Statistics, "BLS Homepage," Series ID: CUUS0100SAS; CUUS0200SAS; CUUS0300SAS; CUUS0400SAS, 1999; http://146.142.4.24/cgi-bin/dsrv. For a discussion of using a services index for this purpose rather than the full consumer price index, see Richard Rothstein with Karen Hawley Miles, *Where's the Money Gone? Changes in the Level and Composition of Education Spending* (Washington, D.C.: Economic Policy Institute, 1995).

19. Because taxation of a state's residents is the primary source of support for public education, this chapter uses a state's total personal income per pupil, rather than a state's gross product per pupil, as a measure of fiscal capacity. However, this measure is not equally valid for all states. Some states (Alaska and Wyoming, for example) raise revenues primarily from mineral severance taxes, not taxes on individuals. The General Accounting Office estimates a state's fiscal capacity to pay for education by taking into account both personal income and gross state product per enrolled student (see note 22, below). While there is merit to this approach, it also entails some double-counting. The value of oil extracted in Alaska, for example, contributes both to Alaska's gross state product and to the personal income of Alaska oil workers and New York oil executives.

20. The methodology for column 8 is the same as for column 3, except that McMahon's 1990 estimates were inflated for 1996–97 using regional consumer price indices for all goods and services, not for services alone, U.S. Department of Labor, Bureau of Labor Statistics, "BLS Homepage," Series ID: CUUS0100SA0; CUUS0200SA0; CUUS0300SA0; CUUS0400SA0, 1999; http://146.142.4.24/cgi-bin/dsrv.

21. Here and subsequently, "PIPS" refers to cost-adjusted personal income per student, not to nominal personal income per student.

22. There is no single appropriate method for making these calculations and adjustments. In an analysis of 1992 data, the General Accounting Office calculated an "ability to raise revenue for schools," utilizing a measurement of taxable resources that included both personal income and gross state product per child. U.S. General Accounting Office, *School Finance: Trends in Education Spending*, GAO/HEHS 95-235, September 1995. Unlike the analysis in this chapter, which applies a cost-of-living adjustment to personal income per capita, the GAO analysis accounted for regional differences in the value of the dollar by application of an adjustment to 75.5 percent of its taxable resources measure, utilizing an index derived from relative differences in teacher salaries, adjusted for differences in teacher experience (75.5 percent was the GAO's estimate of the share of school expenditures consumed by personnel resources).

Of course, relative fiscal capacity could have changed substantially from 1989, for which year the GAO report used data, and 1996, the year for data used in this chapter; nonetheless, the GAO's identification of states with low fiscal capacity was similar but not identical to that in Table 3.1, column 9. For example, probably because PIPS does not account for revenue from mineral severance taxes, Table 3.1 shows Alaska has low capacity, while the GAO report does not. GAO's identification of states with high fiscal capacity is also similar to that in Table 3.1, with some exceptions; for example, the GAO included Hawaii in this group, whereas Table 3.1 shows Hawaii to have relatively low fiscal capacity.

23. In a linear regression, the standard error is $5.

24. In a linear regression, the standard error is $17.

25. Throughout this chapter, the District of Columbia is referred to as a state. The rankings of "states," therefore, include fifty-one jurisdictions.

26. Having relatively less need for spending does not mean that the state spends "too much." Without a determination about how much spending is the right amount, we cannot make such a judgment. It is possible that all states should spend the amounts spent by states with relatively high spending and relatively little need. However, while many advocates of school spending make this assumption, there is little research evidence to support or refute it.

27. U.S. Department of Education, Office of Educational Research and Improvement, *Statistics in Brief: Revenues and Expenditures for Public Elementary and Secondary Education, School Year 1996-97*, NCES 1999-301, National Center for Education Statistics, 1999; Howell and Miller, "Sources of Funding for Schools," Table 1.

28. Adjustments are limited to between 80 percent and 120 percent of the national average.

29. As noted above, however, great significance should not be attributed to small change or lack of change in rank because each step in rank does not necessarily represent an equal interval. These statistics are only suggestive.

30. Costs were adjusted for regional differences in the cost of living, using the same methodology as that described above for Table 3.1, column 8 (but for 1998, not 1996–97).

31. The adjustment is accomplished by calculating per pupil spending taking an enrollment figure that has been increased above actual enrollment by 50 percent of the total number of children in poverty. This does not imply that 1.5 is the appropriate weight for disadvantaged students. It is used here for illustrative purposes only.

School finance analysts typically use the coefficient of variation to measure spending inequality between jurisdictions. The coefficient of variation of district spending within a state is calculated by taking the standard deviation of spending as a percentage of the mean spending level. The standard deviation of spending is a measure of how "spread out" the spending levels are; specifically, it is the absolute value of the average variation from the mean (with positive and negative variations treated equally). To calculate the standard deviation, first square the difference of each unit's spending (in this case, each state's average per pupil spending) from the mean, and add these differences together. This is the total variance. Then, divide this total variance by the number of observations (states) and take the square root of this result.

A coefficient of variation is conventionally expressed as an absolute value, not as a percent. However, for purposes of clarity, because conceptually the coefficient of variation can be thought of as the average "spread from the mean" as a percent of the mean, this chapter expresses these as percents.

32. Their multivariate analysis reveals similar differences in federal aid received by high-poverty, affluent, moderately affluent, and moderate-poverty districts.

33. In 1989–90, districts at the ninety-fifth percentile of spending distribution in Kentucky spent $3,520, while districts at the fifth percentile of the spending distribution in Wisconsin spent $4,289. U.S. General Accounting Office, *School Finance*, Table III-4. (On a cost-adjusted basis, employing the methodology of this chapter, the amounts were $3,825 and $4,517.) This analysis includes all spending, from federal as well as state and local funds.

34. These calculations of potential subsidy are not adjusted for geographical cost differences nor for variation in student need (disadvantage) by state.

35. In 1969–70, the state at the twenty-fifth percentile was Texas, and the state at the seventy-fifth percentile was Iowa. These data were adjusted for interstate cost differences using the methodology described in note 18, based on a McMahon index for 1981, except that, because the Bureau of Labor Statistics does not publish regional services indexes for 1970, these indexes were estimated utilizing national services index numbers, adjusted by regional CPI (all items) numbers for the period from 1970 to 1978. Walter W. McMahon and Shao-Chung Chang, "Geographical Cost of Living Differences: Interstate and Intrastate, Update, 1991," Center for the Study of Educational Finance, Illinois State University, 1991.

36. Sheila Murray, William N. Evans, and Robert Schwab, "Education Finance Reform and the Distribution of Education Resources," *American Economic Review* 88, no. 4 (September 1998): 789–812, Table 2.

37. U.S. Department of Education, Office of Educational Research and Improvement, *120 Years of American Education: A Statistical Portrait*, NCES 93-442, National Center for Education Statistics, 1993, Table 21.

38. U.S. Department of Education, Office of Educational Research and Improvement, *Statistics in Brief*, Figure 1, http://nces.ed.gov/pubs99/1999301.pdf.

39. Michael Heise, "State Constitutions, School Finance Litigation, and the 'Third Wave': From Equity to Adequacy," 68 *Temple Law Review* 1151–76, 1995.

40. Discussions of school finance conventionally refer to this U.S. Supreme Court decision as the "Rodriguez" case. However, because another important school finance case, discussed extensively below, is also conventionally referred to as the "Rodriguez" case, in this chapter the 1973 Supreme Court ruling will be referred to as the *San Antonio* decision. The second case, *Rodriguez* v. *LAUSD*, settled in Los Angeles County Superior Court in 1992, will be referred to as the "LAUSD" case or the "LAUSD consent decree."

41. The Supreme Court in the *San Antonio* decision described the "rights of speech" and "full participation in the political process" as fundamental rights. Therefore, a school system that failed to provide each child with the skills necessary to exercise these rights might be constitutionally inadequate. But unequal outcomes above this minimum would not be consitutionally suspect, and there have been no subsequent successful challenges to school finance systems under this theory. Another possible constitutional lever to improve resources for disadvantaged students was suggested by a 1984 Federal Eleventh Circuit decision, *Debra P.* v. *Turlington* (730 F. 2d 1405). Here, the court concurred that if a state requires passage of a minimum competency test to receive a high school diploma, it must show that it "actually taught" minority students the skills necessary to pass this test. However, the court found that the state of Florida had complied with this standard, and no remedy was required. The substantial resource inequalities within Florida did not alter the court's reasoning—indeed, they were not considered. Because a minimum competency test is a fairly low standard, and because "actually teaching" skills is a much lower standard than effectively teaching them, the *Debra P.* decision has led to no further federal cases to equalize school resources. However, if the current trend continues of states raising standards for awarding of high school diplomas, it is conceivable that the federal constitutional right implicit in *Debra P.* could become a more powerful lever.

42. Robert Berne, "Equity Issues in School Finance," *Journal of Education Finance* 14 (Fall 1988): 159–80.

43. In two of these, Hawaii and the District of Columbia, intrastate considerations do not apply, as they are unitary systems.

44. Heise, "State Constitutions, School Finance Litigation, and the 'Third Wave.'"

45. Deborah A. Verstegen and Terry Whitney, "From Courthouses to Schoolhouses: Emerging Judicial Theories of Adequacy and Equity," *Educational Policy* 11, no. 3 (September 1997): 330–52.

46. Personal communication with Greg Scieszka, superintendent, Bennington-Rutland Supervisory District, Bennington, Vt., 1999.

47. It is not entirely clear that *Serrano* was responsible, or partly responsible, for the taxpayers' revolt or if the revolt developed independently. See Peter Schrag, *Paradise Lost: California's Experience, America's Future* (New York: New

Press, 1998); William A. Fischel, "How *Serrano* Caused Proposition 13," *Journal of Law and Politics* 12 (Fall 1996): 607–36.

48. Lonnie Harp, "Broad Coalition in Michigan Backing Tax Reform and Finance Amendment," *Education Week*, May 26, 1993.

49. Steve Stecklow and Krystal Miller, "Michigan's Plan for Financing Schools May Spread, but Not to Certain States," *Wall Street Journal*, March 18, 1994; "Rich Are Wary of Michigan's Revolt," *New York Times*, March 23, 1994.

50. Harp, "Broad Coalition in Michigan Backing Tax Reform."

51. With food and heating fuel exempt, the sales tax was not fully regressive, but liberal groups like the teachers' union, allied with the tobacco industry, opposed the sales tax hike in favor of the income tax proposal. William Celis 3d, "Michigan Debates What Tax Is Best to Pay for Education," *New York Times*, March 14, 1994; William Celis 3d, "Michigan Votes for Revolution in Financing Its Public Schools," *New York Times*, March 17, 1994. The field coordinator for the referendum campaign, however, was a teachers' union lobbyist on loan. See Harp, "Broad Coalition in Michigan Backing Tax Reform."

52. "Rich Are Wary of Michigan's Revolt"; "In Michigan, Uncertainty and Unhappiness over New Method to Finance the Schools," *New York Times*, January 18, 1995.

53. "Rich Are Wary of Michigan's Revolt."

54. Calculations include state and local funds only, and state spending was adjusted for estimated regional cost differences in 1969–70 and 1996–97. Inflation was estimated utilizing regional services indices from 1978 to 1996 and the CPI-U from 1970 to 1978.

55. Murray, Evans, and Schwab, "Education Finance Reform." This is an estimate of per capita education spending increase, not per pupil spending increase. Per capita spending increases would differ from per pupil spending increases to the extent that the ratio of children to the general population differed from state to state.

56. G. Alan Hickrod, "The Effect of Constitutional Litigation on Educational Finance: A Further Analysis," in National Center for Education Statistics, *Selected Papers in School Finance, 1995* (Washington, D.C.: Government Printing Office, 1997). Hickrod's analysis not only reflects his judgment about whether a mixed judicial decision is a "victory" or a "loss" for equalization but also is insensitive to the timing of a decision. Thus, a "victory" won in 1989 is presumed to affect 1980–90 spending trends in the group of "victorious" states. This is the same problem as that which limits the significance of Table 3.5.

57. Specifically, they found an increase of 11 percent in districts spending at the fifth percentile of districts in their states and an increase of 8 percent in districts at the fiftieth percentile after court-ordered reform.

58. Jonathan Kozol's *Savage Inequalities: Children in America's Schools* (New York: Crown Books, 1991) highlighted resource inequalities and has given new

impetus to Type II finance litigation. However, the inequalities he described may not reflect a consistent relationship between student and community poverty. The relationship may exist in East St. Louis but not in the South Bronx.

59. For a more extensive discussion of alternative ways of calculating "adequacy," see James W. Guthrie and Richard Rothstein, "Enabling 'Adequacy' to Achieve Reality: Translating Adequacy into State School Finance Distribution Arrangements," in Ladd, Chalk, and Hansen, *Equity and Adequacy in Education Finance*.

60. Chris Pipho, "Finance Potpourri," *Phi Delta Kappan*, June 1997, pp. 737–38.

61. John Augenblick, Kern Alexander, and James W. Guthrie, "Report of the Panel of Experts: Proposals for the Elimination of Wealth Based Disparities in Education," submitted by Ohio chief state school officer Theodore Sanders to the Ohio Legislature, June 1995; John Augenblick, "Recommendations for a Base Figure and Pupil-Weighted Adjustments to the Base Figure for Use in a New School Finance System in Ohio," School Funding Task Force, Ohio Department of Education, July 17, 1997.

62. Personal communication with Robert Greenwald, Searle Fellow, Department of Education, University of Chicago, March 19–20, 1998.

63. Augenblick, Myers, and Anderson, "Equity and Adequacy in School Funding."

64. James W. Guthrie et al., *A Proposed Cost-Based Block Grant Model for Wyoming School Finance* (Sacramento: Management Analyst & Planning Associates, L.L.C., May 1997). The author of this paper was a member of Guthrie's team.

65. *Essential Programs and Services: Equity and Adequacy in Funding to Improve Learning for All Children*, Maine Department of Education, January, 1999.

66. Odden, "School Finance Reform in Kentucky." Considering these 30 special needs districts and 110 wealthy suburban districts in New Jersey as a group, the coefficient of variation declined by one-third (from 18 percent to 12 percent) from 1991 to 1993. Douglas S. Reed, "Court-ordered School Finance Equalization: Judicial Activism and Democratic Opposition," in William J. Fowler, Jr., ed., *Developments in School Finance, 1996* (Washington, D.C.: National Center for Education Statistics, 1997), Figure 3.

67. Jennifer Preston, "Ending 28-Year Battle, Court Backs Whitman's Plan to Improve Urban Schools," *New York Times*, May 22, 1998; Maria Newman, "Full-Day Preschool for Poor in New Jersey," *New York Times*, January 9, 1999.

68. This (seven to ten years) seems to be the consensus estimate of education research professionals. There is little solid evidence to confirm this, primarily because research on the relationship between teacher experience and student achievement generally compares a cross section of teachers with different amounts of experience at the same point in time. Such cross-sectional analyses do not generally control for the fact that different cohorts of teachers may

have different levels of initial ability, in part because of differences in the supply and demand for teachers in different years (teacher "vintage effects"). Cross-sectional analyses also do not generally account for the fact that higher-quality teachers may be more likely to leave the cohort to become administrators. One analysis that attempted to control for vintage effects found an increase in teacher effectiveness with experience: "the size of the estimated coefficient, when translated into grade equivalents, implies that children taught by a teacher with five years of experience make three to four months more of progress in acquiring reading skills during a school year than do children taught by a first year teacher." Richard J. Murnane and Barbara R. Phillips, "Learning by Doing, Vintage, and Selection: Three Pieces of the Puzzle Relating Teaching Experience and Teaching Performance," *Economics of Education Review* 1, no. 4 (Fall 1981): 453–65.

69. Anemona Hartocollis, "Crew to Close 13 Poorly Performing Schools and Take Control of 43 Others," *New York Times*, June 24, 1999.

70. Donald L. Horowitz, *The Courts and Social Policy* (Washington, D.C.: Brookings Institution, 1977).

71. For example, the Washington, D.C., schools still had a policy in the mid-1960s of permitting white students to transfer to predominantly white schools if those students claimed that attending school in an integrated setting would cause them "psychological upset."

72. Peter Schmidt, "L.A. Decree Would Equalize Resources among All Schools," *Education Week*, December 11, 1991; "News Update," *Education Week*, March 25, 1992; Ann Bradley, "Equation for Equality," *Education Week*, September 14, 1994; Amy Pyle, "L.A. Schools Wrestle with Realities of '92 Money Pact," *Los Angeles Times*, February 14, 1995; Amy Pyle, "More Schools Meeting Spending Decree Goals," *Los Angeles Times*, March 3, 1998.

73. Richard Rothstein, "Blaming Teachers," *American Prospect*, December 6, 1999, pp. 40–45.

74. Research evidence here is sparse, however. The "Student-Teacher Achievement Ratio" (STAR) experiment in Tennessee seems to show that reducing class sizes from about twenty-four to about fifteen in the primary grades has a bigger positive impact on disadvantaged than on other children. Alan Krueger found that smaller class sizes from kindergarten to third grade increased third-grade test scores by 0.24 standard deviations for whites and by 0.33 standard deviations for blacks. Alan B. Krueger, "Experimental Estimates of Education Production Functions," Working Paper no. 379, Industrial Relations Section, Princeton University, May 1997. Nationwide, average elementary class sizes declined from twenty-eight in 1966 to twenty-four in 1996. U.S. Department of Education, Office of Educational Research and Improvement, *Digest of Education Statistics 1998*, NCES 1999-036, National Center for Education Statistics, 1999, Table 70. The increase in

instructional and professional staff has been even greater. Pupils per teacher went from 22.6 in 1970 to 17.1 in 1997, and the use of instructional aides increased by a like percentage. The number of pupils per guidance counselor went from 934 in 1970 to 513 in 1997 (*Digest of Education Statistics*, Table 83). While much of the increase in teachers and instructional staff was devoted to special education, some of the increase, at least in certain school districts, went to specialist teachers, and this may have benefited disproportionately the education of disadvantaged children. See Rothstein and Miles, *Where's the Money Gone?*

75. Barbara Heyns, "Schooling and Cognitive Development: Is There a Season for Learning?" *Child Development* 58, no. 5 (October 1987): 1151–60; Doris Entwisle and Karl L. Alexander, "Summer Setback: Race, Poverty, School Composition, and Mathematics Achievement in the First Two Years of School," *American Sociological Review* 57 (February 1992): 72–84.

76. Rothstein, "Blaming Teachers."

77. Leanna Stiefel et al., *The Effects of Size of Student Body on School Costs and Performance in New York City High Schools* (New York: Institute for Education and Social Policy, New York University, April, 1998).

78. James S. Coleman et al., *Equality of Educational Opportunity* (Washington, D.C.: U.S. Government Printing Office, 1966).

79. Nick Anderson, "With a Gift for Dialogue, Education Chief Gets Congress Talking," *Los Angeles Times*, July 6, 1999.

80. Ulric Neisser et al., "Intelligence: Knowns and Unknowns," *American Psychologist* 51, no. 2 (February 1996): 77–101.

81. In the "Section 8" program, families can receive subsidies equal to the difference between 30 percent of their income and "fair market value" of their rental unit. Participating landlords must charge only the "fair market value."

82. Alan Meyers et al., "Housing Subsidies and Pediatric Undernutrition," *Archives of Pediatrics and Adolescent Medicine* 149 (October 1995): 1079–84.

83. M. C. Wang, G. D. Haertel, and H. J. Walberg, "Educational Resilience in Inner Cities," in Margaret C. Wang and Edmund W. Gordon, eds., *Educational Resilience in Inner-City America: Challenges and Prospects* (Hillsdale, N.J.: Lawrence Erlbaum Associates, 1994).

84. U.S. General Accounting Office, *Elementary School Children: Many Change Schools Frequently, Harming Their Education*, GAO/HEHS 94-45, February 1994, p. 5.

85. David Kerbow, "Patterns of Urban Student Mobility and Local School Reform," *Journal of Education for Students Placed at Risk* 1, no. 2 (1996): 147–69.

86. James Bruno and Jo Ann Isken, "Inter and Intraschool Site Student Transiency: Practical and Theoretical Implications for Instructional Continuity at Inner-City Schools," *Journal of Research and Development in Education* 29, no. 4 (Summer 1996): 239–52.

87. U.S. General Accounting Office, *Elementary School Children*, p. 12.

88. Bruno and Isken, "Inter and Intraschool Site Student Transiency," p. 243.

89. Kerbow, "Patterns of Urban Student Mobility."

90. Jennifer Daskal, "In Search of Shelter. The Growing Shortage of Affordable Rental Housing," Center for Budget and Policy Priorities, Washington, D.C., June 15, 1998, p. 28.

91. U.S. General Accounting Office, *Elementary School Children*; Kerbow, "Patterns of Urban Student Mobility."

92. David B. Schuler, "Effects of Family Mobility on Student Achievement," *ERS Spectrum* (Educational Research Service) 8, no. 4 (Fall 1990): 17–24.

93. Marybeth Shinn et al., "Predictors of Homelessness among Families in New York City: From Shelter Request to Housing Stability," *American Journal of Public Health* 88, no. 11 (November 1998): 1651–57.

94. Daskal, "In Search of Shelter," Table 1.

95. U.S. General Accounting Office, *Section 8 Tenant-Based Housing Assistance: Opportunities to Improve HUD's Financial Management*, GAO/RCED 98-47, February 1998, Table 3.1.

Chapter 4

1. Mary H. Metz, "How Social Class Differences Shape Teachers' Work," in Milbrey W. McLaughlin, Joan E. Talbert, and Nina Bascia, eds., *The Contexts of Teaching in Secondary Schools* (New York: Teachers College Press, 1990), pp. 40–107; Michael S. Knapp and associates, *Teaching for Meaning in High-Poverty Classrooms* (New York: Teachers College Press, 1995); Michael J. Puma et al., *Prospects: Final Report on Student Outcomes* (Cambridge, Mass.: Abt Associates, 1997).

2. Barbara Heyns, *Summer Learning* (New York: Academic Press, 1978), found that 71 percent of the black-white achievement gaps occurs during summer; Doris Entwistle, Karl L. Alexander, and Linda Steffel Olson, *Children, Schools, and Inequality* (Boulder, Colo.: Westview Press, 1997), found that virtually all of the black-white achievement gap occurs during the summer.

3. Michael S. Knapp, "The Teaching Challenge in High-Poverty Classrooms," in Michael S. Knapp and associates, *Teaching for Meaning in High-Poverty Classrooms*, pp. 5–6.

4. Puma et al., *Prospects*.

5. Entwistle, Alexander, and Olson, *Children, Schools, and Inequality*.

6. Ibid., pp. 69–70.

7. Robert Dreeben and Adam Gamoran, "Race, Instruction, and Learning," *American Sociological Review* 51, no. 5 (1986): 660–69.

8. Entwistle, Alexander, and Olson, *Children, Schools, and Inequality*; J. S. Coleman et al., *Equality of Educational Opportunity* (Washington, D.C.: U.S. Government Printing Office, 1966); C. L. Jencks et al., *Inequality: A Reassessment of the Effects of Family and Schooling in America* (New York: Basic Books, 1972).

9. Tom Loveless, *The Tracking and Ability Grouping Debate* (Washington, D.C.: Fordham Foundation, 1998).

10. Jeannie Oakes, Adam Gamoran, and Reba N. Page, "Curriculum Differentiation: Opportunities, Outcomes, and Meanings," in P. W. Jackson, ed., *Handbook of Research on Curriculum* (New York: Macmillan, 1992), pp. 570–608.

11. Brian Rowan and Andrew J. Miracle, Jr., "Systems of Ability Grouping and the Stratification of Achievement in Elementary Schools," *Sociology of Education* 56, no. 3 (1983): 133–44.

12. Rebecca Barr and Robert Dreeben, *How Schools Work* (Chicago: University of Chicago Press, 1983).

13. Adam Gamoran, "Instructional and Institutional Effects of Ability Grouping," *Sociology of Education* 59, no. 4 (1986): 185–98.

14. Emile J. Haller and Sharon Davis, "Does Socioeconomic Status Bias the Assignment of Elementary School Students to Reading Groups?" *American Educational Research Journal* 17, no. 4 (1980): 409–18; Emile J. Haller, "Pupil Race and Elementary School Ability Grouping: Are Teachers Biased Against Black Children?" *American Educational Research Journal* 22, no. 4 (1985): 456–83; Dreeben and Gamoran, "Race, Instruction, and Learning"; Adam Gamoran, "Rank, Performance, and Mobility in Elementary School Grouping," *Sociological Quarterly* 30, no. 1 (1989): 109–23; for a contrary view see Ray Rist, "Student Social Class and Teacher Expectations: The Self-Fulfilling Prophecy in Ghetto Education," *Harvard Educational Review* 40, no. 3 (1970): 411–51.

15. Robert E. Slavin, "Ability Grouping and Student Achievement in Elementary Schools: A Best-Evidence Synthesis," *Review of Educational Research* 57, no. 3 (1987): 293–336.

16. Oakes, Gamoran, and Page, "Curriculum Differentiation."

17. Coleman et al., *Equality of Educational Opportunity*; Jencks et al., *Inequality*; Entwistle, Alexander, and Olson, *Children, Schools, and Inequality*.

18. Philip Kaufman and Denise Bradby, *Characteristics of At-Risk Students in NELS:88*, NCES 92-042 (Washington, D.C.: U.S. Department of Education, 1992).

19. Kaufman and Bradby, *Characteristics of At-Risk Students in NELS:88*, author's computations based on Table 2.3, p. 8.

20. David H. Monk and Emile J. Haller, "Predictors of High School Academic Course Offerings: The Role of School Size," *American Educational Research Journal* 30, no. 1 (1993): 3–21.

21. Jeannie Oakes, *Multiplying Inequalities* (Santa Monica, Calif.: RAND, 1990), p. 32, emphasis in the original.

22. Julie Smith, "Does an Extra Year Make a Difference? The Impact of Early Access to Algebra on Long-Term Gains in Mathematics Attainment," *Educational Evaluation and Policy Analysis* 18, no. 2 (1996), 141–53; Richard Riley, "Mathematics Equals Opportunity" (Washington, D.C.: U.S. Department of Education, 1997).

23. Oakes, *Multiplying Inequalities*, p. 49.

24. Ibid.

25. Mary Metz, "Real School: A Universal Drama amid Disparate Experience," *Politics of Education Association Yearbook* (1989): 75–91.

26. Ibid., p. 78.

27. Adam Gamoran, "The Stratification of High School Learning Opportunities," *Sociology of Education* 60, no. 3 (1987): 135–55.

28. Oakes, Gamoran, and Page, "Curriculum Differentiation."

29. Alan C. Kerckhoff, "Effects of Ability Grouping in British Secondary Schools," *American Sociological Review* 51, no. 6 (1986): 842–58; Adam Gamoran and Martin Nystrand, "Tracking, Instruction, and Achievement," *International Journal of Educational Research* 21, no. 2 (1994): 217–31; Thomas Hoffer, "Middle School Ability Grouping and Student Achievement in Science and Mathematics," *Educational Evaluation and Policy Analysis* 14, no. 3 (1992): 205–28.

30. National Center for Education Statistics, *Curricular Differentiation in Public High Schools*, NCES 95-360 (Washington, D.C.: U.S. Department of Education, 1994).

31. Adam Gamoran, "The Stratification of High School Learning Opportunities," *Sociology of Education* 60, no. 3 (1987): 135–55.

32. Robert E. Slavin, "Achievement Effects of Ability Grouping in Secondary Schools: A Best-Evidence Synthesis," *Review of Research in Education* 60, no. 3 (1990): 471–99.

33. Adam Gamoran, "Organization, Instruction, and the Effects of Ability Grouping: Comment on Slavin's 'Best-Evidence Synthesis,'" *Review of Educational Research* 57, no. 3 (1987): 341–45.

34. Adam Gamoran, "The Variable Effects of High School Tracking," *American Sociological Review* 57, no. 6 (1992): 812–28.

35. Adam Gamoran, "The Stratification of High School Learning Opportunities."

36. Ibid.

37. Jeannie Oakes, *Keeping Track* (New Haven: Yale University Press, 1985); Adam Gamoran, "Alternative Uses of Ability Grouping in Secondary Schools: Can We Bring High-Quality Instruction to Low-Ability Classes?" *American Journal of Education* 101, no. 1 (1993): 1–22.

38. Adam Gamoran and William J. Carbonaro, "High School English: A National Portrait" (paper presented at the annual meeting of the American Educational Research Association, San Diego, April 1998).

39. Jeannie Oakes, *Keeping Track*; Adam Gamoran et al., "An Organizational Analysis of the Effects of Ability Grouping," *American Educational Research Journal* 32, no. 4 (1995): 687–715.

40. Adam Gamoran and Mark Berends, "The Effects of Stratification in Secondary Schools: Synthesis of Survey and Ethnographic Research," *Review of Educational Research* 57, no. 4 (1987): 415–435; Oakes, Gamoran, and Page, "Curriculum Differentiation," pp. 570–608.

41. Gamoran et al., "An Organizational Analysis of the Effects of Ability Grouping."

42. James Rosenbaum, *Making Inequality* (New York: John Wiley and Sons, 1976).

43. Reba N. Page, *Lower-Track Classrooms* (New York: Teachers College Press, 1991).

44. Ibid., p. 91.

45. Merrilee K. Finley, "Teachers and Tracking in a Comprehensive High School," *Sociology of Education* 57, no. 4 (1984): 233–43.

46. Thomas Hoffer and Adam Gamoran, *Effects of Instructional Differences among Ability Groups on Student Achievement in Middle-School Science and Mathematics* (Madison, Wis.: Center on Organization and Restructuring of Schools, 1993); Oakes, *Multiplying Inequalities*.

47. Oakes, *Multiplying Inequalities*, p. 66.

48. Adam Gamoran and Robert D. Mare, "Secondary School Tracking and Educational Inequality: Compensation, Reinforcement, or Neutrality?" *American Journal of Sociology* 94, no. 5 (1989): 1146–83.

49. Maureen T. Hallinan, "Tracking: From Theory to Practice," *Sociology of Education* 67, no. 2 (1994): 79–84.

50. Gamoran, "The Variable Effects of High School Tracking"; Anthony S. Bryk, Valerie E. Lee, and Peter B. Holland, *Catholic Schools and the Common Good* (Cambridge, Mass.: Harvard University Press, 1993).

51. Bryk, Lee, and Holland, *Catholic Schools and the Common Good*.

52. Adam Gamoran and Matthew Weinstein, "Differentiation and Opportunity in Restructured Schools," *American Journal of Education* 106, no. 3 (1998): 385–415.

53. Paula A. White et al., "Upgrading the High School Math Curriculum: Math Course-Taking Patterns in Seven High Schools in California and New York," *Educational Evaluation and Policy Analysis* 18, no. 4 (1996): 285–307; Adam Gamoran et al., "Upgrading High School Mathematics Instruction: Improving Learning Opportunities for Low-Income, Low-Achieving Youth," *Educational Evaluation and Policy Analysis* 19, no. 4 (1997): 325–38; Paula A. White et al., "Upgrading High School Math: A Look at Three Transition Courses," *NASSP Bulletin* 81 (Fall 1997): 72–83.

54. Hanna Ayalon and Adam Gamoran, "Stratification in Academic Secondary Programs and Educational Inequality: Comparison of Israel and the

United States," *Comparative Education Review* 44, no. 1 (2000): 54–80. Note that Israeli high schools are also divided into academic and vocational programs, which have the same stratifying effects as American tracking. It is the divisions into levels *within* the academic, examination-oriented program that has beneficial effects.

55. Oakes, Gamoran, and Page, "Curriculum Differentiation."

56. Ibid.

57. Jeannie Oakes, "Can Tracking Research Inform Practice? Technical, Normative, and Political Considerations," *Educational Researcher* 21, no. 4 (1992): 12–22.

58. Jeannie Oakes and Amy Stuart Wells, "Detracking for High Student Achievement," *Educational Leadership* 55 (March 1998): 38–41; Jeannie Oakes et al., "Equity Lessons from Detracking Schools," *ASCD Yearbook 1997* (1997): 43–72; Amy Stuart Wells and Irene Serna, "The Politics of Culture: Understanding Local Political Resistance to Detracking in Racially Mixed Schools," *Harvard Educational Review* 66, no. 1 (1996): 93–118.

59. Oakes and Wells, "Detracking for High Student Achievement," p. 41.

60. Tom Loveless, "The Influence of Subject Areas on Middle School Tracking Policies," *Research in Sociology of Education and Socialization* 10 (1994): 147–75; Gamoran and Weinstein, "Differentiation and Opportunity in Restructured Schools."

61. Tom Loveless, *The Tracking Wars* (Washington, D.C.: Brookings Institution Press), p. 143.

62. Gamoran and Weinstein, "Differentiation and Opportunity in Restructured Schools."

63. Ibid., p. 393.

64. Ibid., p. 402.

65. L. Alper et al., "Designing a High School Mathematics Curriculum for All Students," *American Journal of Education* 106, no. 1 (1997): 148–79; Norman L. Webb, "The Impact of the Interactive Mathematics Program on Student Learning," in S. L. Senk and D. R. Thompson, eds., *Standards-Oriented School Mathematics Curricula: What Does the Research Say about Student Outcomes?* (Mahwah, N.J.: Lawrence Erlbaum Associates, forthcoming).

66. Norman L. Webb, "The Impact of the Interactive Mathematics Program on Student Learning."

67. *Equity 2000—Impact* (New York: The College Board, 1999). Available at: http://cbweb1.collegeboard.org/index_this/equity/html/impact html.

68. Adam Gamoran and Eileen C. Hannigan, "Algebra for Everyone? Benefits of College-Preparatory Mathematics for Students of Diverse Abilities in Early Secondary School," *Educational Evaluation and Policy Analysis*, forthcoming.

69. Rebecca Herman et al., *An Educators' Guide to Schoolwide Reform* (Arlington, Va.: Educational Research Service, 1999).

70. Slavin, "Ability Grouping and Achievement in Elementary Schools."

71. Susan J. Bodilly and Mark Berends, "Necessary District Support for Comprehensive School Reform," in Gary Orfield and Elizabeth H. DeBray, eds., *Hard Work for Good Schools* (Boston: The Civil Rights Project, Harvard University, 1999), pp. 111–19; Mark Berends, "Teacher-Reported Effects of New American Schools' Designs: Exploring Relationships to Teacher Background and School Context," RAND, Washington, D.C., 1999.

72. Herman et al., *An Educators' Guide to Schoolwide Reform.*

73. Bodilly and Berends, "Necessary District Support for Comprehensive School Reform."

74. Elliot W. Eisner, "Standards for American Schools: Help or Hindrance?" *Phi Delta Kappan* 76, no. 10 (1995): 758–60, 762–64.

75. Gary Natriello, "National Standards for Assessments and Performance: Reactions, Knowledge Base, and Recommendations for Research, " in K. M. Borman et al., eds., *Implementing Educational Reform: Sociological Perspectives on Educational Policy* (Norwood, N.J.: Ablex, 1996), pp. 65–79.

76. Adam Gamoran, Andrew C. Porter, and Tae-joong Gahng, "Teacher Empowerment: A Policy in Search of Theory and Evidence," in W. J. Fowler, B. Levin, and H. J. Walberg, eds., *Organizational Influences on Educational Productivity*, vol. 5 (Greenwich, Conn.: JAI Press, 1995), pp. 175–93.

77. Kenneth R. Howe, "Standards, Assessment, and Equality of Educational Opportunity," *Educational Researcher* 23, no. 8 (1994): 27–33; Kevin J. Dougherty, "Opportunity to Learn Standards: A Sociological Critique," *Sociology of Education* Special Issue (1996): 40–65.

78. Jomills H. Braddock II and Mary M. Williams, "Equality of Educational Opportunity and the Goals 2000, Educate America Act," in K. M. Borman et al., eds., *Implementing Educational Reform: Sociological Perspectives on Educational Policy* (Norwood, N.J.: Ablex, 1996), pp. 89–109; Dougherty, "Opportunity to Learn Standards."

79. Tom Loveless, "The Politics of National Standards," *Education Week*, October 6, 1993, pp. 40, 31.

80. Andrew C. Porter, "The Uses and Misuses of Opportunity-to-Learn Standards," *Educational Researcher* 24, no. 1 (1995): 21–27.

81. Diane Massell, Michael Kirst, and Margaret Hoppe, *Persistence and Change: Standards-Based Reform in Nine States* (Philadelphia: Consortium for Policy Research in Education, 1997); Diane Massell, *State Strategies for Building Capacity in Education: Progress and Continuing Challenges* (Philadelphia: Consortium for Policy Research in Education, 1998).

82. Andrew C. Porter and associates, *Reform of High School Mathematics and Science and Opportunity to Learn*, document no. RB-13-9/94 (New Brunswick, N.J.: Consortium for Policy Research in Education, 1994); Bruce Wilson and Gretchen Rossman, *Mandating Academic Excellence* (New York: Teachers College Press, 1993).

83. Thomas Hoffer, "High School Graduation Requirements: Effects on Dropping Out and Student Achievement," *Teachers College Record* 98, no. 4 (1997): 584–628.

84. Diane Massell and Susan Fuhrman, *Ten Years of State Education Reform, 1983–1993: Overview with Four Case Studies* (New Brunswick, N.J.: Consortium for Policy Research in Education, 1994); Massell, Kirst, and Hoppe, *Persistence and Change*; Massell, *State Strategies for Building Capacity in Education*.

85. David Grissmer and Ann Flanagan, *Exploring Rapid Achievement Gains in North Carolina and Texas* (Washington, D.C.: National Educational Goals Panel, 1998).

86. John Bishop, "The Power of External Standards," *American Educator* 19, no. 3 (1995): 10–18, 42–43; John Bishop, *Do Curriculum-Based External Exit Exam Systems Enhance Student Achievement?* (Philadelphia: Consortium for Policy Research in Education, 1998).

87. Adam Gamoran, "Curriculum Standardization and Equality of Opportunity in Scottish Secondary Education, 1984–1990," *Sociology of Education* 29, no. 1 (1996): 1–21; Adam Gamoran, "Curriculum Change as a Reform Strategy: Lessons from the United States and Scotland," *Teachers College Record* 98, no. 4 (1997): 608–28.

88. Grissmer and Flanagan, *Exploring Rapid Achievement Gains in North Carolina and Texas*.

89. Ibid., pp. 33–34.

90. Recent criticisms of the validity of rising scores on Kentucky's statewide examinations have raised questions about whether the gains are meaningful; see Dan Koretz and Sheila Barron, *The Validity of Gains in Scores on Kentucky Instructional Results Information System (KIRIS)* (Washington, D.C.: RAND, 1999). However, NAEP scores for Kentucky have also risen (see Table 4.1), and these gains are not subject to the same criticism.

91. Massell, Kirst, and Hoppe, *Persistence and Change: Standards-Based Reform in Nine States*; Jason Shepard, "Only a Test," *Isthmus* (Madison, Wisconsin), May 7, 1999, pp. 9–10.

92. Jane L. David and Patrick M. Shields, "Standards are Not Magic," *Education Week*, April 14, 1999, pp. 40–42.

93. Appalachian Educational Laboratory, "Evolution of the Primary Program in Six Kentucky Schools," *Notes from the Field: Education Reform in Kentucky* 6, no. 1 (1998): 1–11.

94. June Kronholz, "If You Have Brains, You Might Decide to Skip This Test," *Wall Street Journal*, March 28, 1997, p. A1.

95. Massell, Kirst, and Hoppe, *Persistence and Change*.

96. Lake et al., *Making Standards Work*, pp. 11–12.

97. David and Shields, "Standards Are Not Magic."

98. Lake et al., *Making Standards Work*; Kenneth K. Wong et al., "Implementation of an Educational Accountability Agenda: Integrated Governance in the Chicago Public Schools Enters Its Fourth Year" (Chicago: Department of Education, University of Chicago, 1999).

99. David and Shields, "Standards Are Not Magic," 42.

100. Wong et al., "Implementation of an Educational Accountability Agenda"; Kerry A. White, "Chicago Centers Target 8th Graders in Transition," *Education Week,* April 21, 1999, pp.1, 16; Randall C. Archibold, "Without Much Data on Success, Mandatory Summer School Grows," *New York Times,* June 17, 1999, pp. A1, A29.

101. Jay P. Heubert and Robert M. Hauser, *High Stakes: Testing for Tracking, Promotion, and Graduation* (Washington, D.C.: National Research Council, 1999), p. 286.

Chapter 5

1. Recent analyses of data prepared for school finance cases in Alabama, New Jersey, New York, Louisiana, and Texas have found that on every tangible measure—from qualified teachers to curriculum offerings—schools serving greater numbers of students of color have significantly fewer resources than schools serving mostly white students. Not only do funding systems allocate fewer resources to poor urban districts than to their suburban neighbors, but studies consistently show that within these districts schools with high concentrations of low-income and minority students receive fewer instructional resources than others in the same district. In addition, tracking systems exacerbate these inequalities by segregating many low-income and minority students within schools. See Jonathan Kozol, *Savage Inequalities* (New York: Crown, 1991); William L. Taylor and Diane Piche, *A Report on Shortchanging Children: The Impact of Fiscal Inequity on the Education of Students at Risk,* prepared for the Committee on Education and Labor, U.S. House of Representatives (Washington, D.C.: U.S. Government Printing Office, 1991).

2. William L. Sanders and June C. Rivers, "Cumulative and Residual Effects of Teachers on Future Student Academic Achievement" (Knoxville: University of Tennessee Value-Added Research and Assessment Center, November 1996). See also S. Paul Wright, Sandra P. Horn, and William L. Sanders, "Teacher and Classroom Context Effects on Student Achievement: Implications for Teacher Evaluation," *Journal of Personnel Evaluation in Education* 1, no. 11 (1997): 57–67; Heather R. Jordan, Robert L. Mendro, and Dash Weerashinghe, *Teacher Effects on Longitudinal Student Achievement* (Dallas: Dallas Public Schools, July 1997).

3. Sanders and Rivers, "Cumulative and Residual Effects of Teachers on Future Student Academic Achievement."

4. Ronald F. Ferguson, "Paying for Public Education: New Evidence on How and Why Money Matters," *Harvard Journal of Legislation* 28 (Summer 1991): 495–98.

5. Ronald F. Ferguson and Helen F. Ladd, "How and Why Money Matters: An Analysis of Alabama Schools," in Helen Ladd, ed., *Holding Schools Accountable* (Washington, D.C.: Brookings Institution Press, 1996), pp. 265–98.

6. Robert P. Strauss and Elizabeth A. Sawyer, "Some New Evidence on Teacher and Student Competencies," *Economics of Education Review* 5, no. 1 (1986): 41–48.

7. Ibid., p. 47.

8. Rob Greenwald, Larry V. Hedges, and Richard D. Laine, "The Effect of School Resources on Student Achievement," *Review of Educational Research* 66 (Fall 1996): 361–96.

9. Eleanor Armour-Thomas et al., *An Outlier Study of Elementary and Middle Schools in New York City: Final Report* (New York: New York City Board of Education, 1989).

10. National Assessment of Educational Progress, *1992 NAEP Trial State Assessment* (Washington, D.C.: U.S. Department of Education, 1994); *Teachers with Advanced Degrees Advance Student Learning* (Atlanta: Council for School Performance, Georgia State University, 1997); G. A. Knoblock, "Continuing Professional Education for Teachers and Its Relationship to Teacher Effectiveness," Ph.D. diss., Western Michigan University, Dissertation Abstracts International 46(02), 3325A (University Microfilms No. AAC 8529729), 1986; S. L. Sanders, S. D. Skonie-Hardin, and W. H. Phelps, "The Effects of Teacher Educational Attainment on Student Educational Attainment in Four Regions of Virginia: Implications for Administrators," paper presented at the Annual Meeting of the Mid-South Educational Research Association, November 1994.

11. National Assessment of Educational Progress, *1992 NAEP Trial State Assessment.*

12. Patricia Ashton and Linda Crocker, "Does Teacher Certification Make a Difference?" *Florida Journal of Teacher Education* 3 (1986) 73–83; Patricia Ashton and Linda Crocker, "Systematic Study of Planned Variations: The Essential Focus of Teacher Education Reform," *Journal of Teacher Education* 38, no. 3 (1987): 2–8; Linda Darling-Hammond, "Teaching and Knowledge: Policy Issues Posed by Alternate Certification for Teachers," *Peabody Journal of Education* 67, no. 3 (1992): 123–54; Cynthia A. Druva and Ronald D. Anderson, "Science Teacher Characteristics by Teacher Behavior and by Student Outcome: A Meta-Analysis of Research," *Journal of Research in Science Teaching* 20, no. 5 (1983): 467–79; Carolyn Evertson, Willis Hawley, and Marilyn Zlotnick, "Making a Difference in Educational Quality through

Teacher Education," *Journal of Teacher Education* 36, no. 3 (1985): 2–12; James D. Greenberg, "The Case for Teacher Education: Open and Shut," *Journal of Teacher Education* 34, no. 4 (1983): 2–5.

13. Evertson, Hawley, and Zlotnick, "Making a Difference in Educational Quality through Teacher Education," p. 8.

14. For a review, see Linda Darling-Hammond, "Teaching and Knowledge: Policy Issues Posed by Alternate Certification for Teachers," *Peabody Journal of Education* 67, no. 3 (1992): 123–54.

15. Victor A. Perkes, "Junior High School Science Teacher Preparation, Teaching Behavior, and Student Achievement," *Journal of Research in Science Teaching* 6 (1968): 121–26; J. B. Hansen, "The Relationship of Skills and Classroom Climate of Trained and Untrained Teachers of Gifted Students," Ph.D. diss., Purdue University, West Lafayette, Ind., 1988; Parmalee Hawk, Charles R. Coble, and Melvin Swanson, "Certification: It Does Matter," *Journal of Teacher Education* 36, no. 3 (1985): 13–15.

16. Kathy Cater and Walter Doyle, "Teachers' Knowledge Structures and Comprehension Processes," in J. Calderhead, ed., *Exploring Teacher Thinking* (London: Cassell, 1987), pp. 147–60; Walter Doyle, "Content Representation in Teachers' Definitions of Academic Work," *Journal of Curriculum Studies* 18 (1986): 365–79; Eric Cooper and John Sherk, "Addressing Urban School Reform: Issues and Alliances," *Journal of Negro Education* 58, no. 3 (1989): 315–31.

17. Ronald Edmonds, "Effective Schools for the Urban Poor," *Educational Leadership* (October 1979).

18. Ronald Edmonds, cited in G. Weber, *Inner-City Children Can Be Taught to Read: Four Successful Schools* (Washington, D.C.: Council for Basic Education, 1971).

19. Edmonds, "Effective Schools for the Urban Poor," 22.

20. K. D. Peterson and J. L. Martin, "Developing Teacher Commitment: The Role of the Administrator," in P. Reyes, ed., *Teachers and Their Workplace: Commitment, Performance, and Productivity* (Newbury Park, Calif.: Sage Publications, 1990), pp. 225–40.

21. Mark A. Smylie, "Teacher Participation in School Decision Making: Assessing Willingness to Participate," *Educational Evaluation and Policy Analysis* 14, no. 1 (1992): 53–67.

22. Michael Fullan, "Visions that Blind," *Educational Leadership* 49, no. 5 (1992): 19–20; Thomas J. Sergiovanni, *The Principalship* (Boston: Allyn & Bacon, 1987); Thomas J. Sergiovanni, "Why We Should Seek Substitutes for Leadership," *Educational Leadership* 49, no. 5 (1992): 41–45.

23. Elizabeth Ashburn, "The Nature of Teachers' Commitment and Its Relationship to School Workplace Conditions," paper presented at the annual meeting of the American Educational Research Association, San Francisco, 1989.

24. E. Anderman, S. Belzer, and J. Smith, "Teacher Commitment and Job Satisfaction: The Role of School Culture and Principal Leadership," paper presented at the annual meeting of the American Educational Research Association, Chicago, 1991.

25. Eileen M. Sclan, "The Effect of Perceived Workplace Conditions on Beginning Teachers' Work Commitment, Career Choice Commitment, and Planned Retention," Ph.D. diss., Teachers College, Columbia University, New York (University Microfilms No. 9400594).

26. Edmonds, "Effective Schools for the Urban Poor"; Sclan, "The Effect of Perceived Workplace Conditions on Beginning Teachers' Work Commitment, Career Choice Commitment, and Planned Retention"; Anderman, Belser, and Smith, "Teacher Commitment and Job Satisfaction"; Peterson and Martin, "Developing Teacher Commitment."

27. Linda Darling-Hammond and Eileen M. Sclan, "Who Teaches and Why: The Dilemmas of Building a Profession for 21st Century Schools," in John Sikula, ed., Handbook of Research on Teacher Education (New York: Macmillan, 1996), pp. 67–101.

28. "America's Teachers: Profile of a Profession, 1993–94," National Center for Education Statistics, U.S. Department of Education, Washington, D.C., 1993, pp. 97–98. About 75 percent of graduates who applied for teaching positions received offers and 90 percent of those who received offers accepted them (about 67 percent of all applicants). Interestingly, a number of recent bachelor's degree recipients who had prepared to teach reported they had not completed all requirements for entering teaching, probably reflecting the fact that many states now require tests and some graduate study before licensure. Of those who prepared to teach in undergraduate school but did not do so in the year after graduation, 33 percent said they had not taken or passed the necessary tests, 24 percent said they needed to obtain more education, and 2 percent felt they were not yet ready.

29. Ibid., Table A8.11.

30. Susan P. Choy et al., Schools and Staffing in the United States: A Statistical Profile, 1990–91 (Washington, D.C.: National Center for Education Statistics, U.S. Department of Education, 1993) [hereafter Schools and Staffing Survey, 1990–91].

31. Ibid.

32. In 1994, these statistics included 10.7 percent of newly hired, nontransferring public school teachers (new hires who had not been teaching the year before) who had no license in their main field, plus 16.3 percent who were hired on substandard licenses (emergency, temporary, provisional, or alternative licenses). Tabulations conducted by the National Commission on Teaching and America's Future using data from the Schools and Staffing Surveys, 1990–91 and Robin R. Henke et al., Schools and Staffing in the United States: A

Statistical Profile, 1993–94 (Washington, D.C.: National Center for Educational Statistics, U.S. Department of Education, 1996), "Public School Teacher Questionnaires."

33. Jeannie Oakes, "Multiplying Inequalities: The Effects of Race, Social Class, and Tracking on Opportunities to Learn Mathematics and Science" (Santa Monica, Calif.: RAND Corporation, 1990).

34. "America's Teachers," p. 30.

35. Ibid., Tables 3.5 and A3.

36. Ibid., p. 29.

37. Michael Andrew, "The Differences between Graduates of Four-Year and Five-Year Teacher Preparation Programs," *Journal of Teacher Education* 41, no. 2 (1990): 45–51; Thomas Baker, "A Survey of Four-Year and Five-Year Program Graduates and their Principals," *Southeastern Regional Association of Teacher Educators (SRATE) Journal* 2, no. 2 (Summer 1993): 28–33; Michael Andrew and Richard L. Schwab, "Has Reform in Teacher Education Influenced Teacher Performance? An Outcome Assessment of Graduates of Eleven Teacher Education Programs," *Action in Teacher Education* 17 (Fall 1995): 43–53; Jon J. Denton and William H. Peters, "Program Assessment Report: Curriculum Evaluation of a Non-Traditional Program for Certifying Teachers," Texas A&M University, College Station, 1988; Hyun-Seok Shin, "Estimating Future Teacher Supply: An Application of Survival Analysis," paper presented at the annual meeting of the American Educational Research Association, New Orleans, April 1994.

38. Linda Darling-Hammond, "Inequality in Access to Knowledge," in James Banks and Cherry A. McGee Banks, eds., *Handbook of Research on Multicultural Education* (New York: Macmillan, 1995).

39. *Doing What Matters Most: Investing in Quality Teaching* (New York: National Commission on Teaching and America's Future, November 1997), Appendix B.

40. Linda Darling-Hammond, "Teacher Quality and Student Achievement: A Review of State Policy Evidence," *Education Policy Analysis Archives* 8, no. 1 (January 2000).

41. *Doing What Matters Most*, Appendix B.

42. *Schools and Staffing Surveys, 1993–94*, "Public School District Survey," tabulations conducted by the National Commission on Teaching for America's Future.

43. F. Howard Nelson and Krista Schneider, *Survey and Analysis of Teacher Salary Trends, 1998* (Washington, D.C.: American Federation of Teachers, 1998).

44. "America's Teachers."

45. *What Matters Most: Teaching for America's Future* (New York: National Commission on Teaching and America's Future, 1996); Nelson and Schneider, *Survey and Analysis of Teacher Salary Trends*.

46. Adam Gamaron and Richard Mare, "Secondary School Tracking and Educational Inequality: Compensation, Reinforcement or Neutrality?" *American Journal of Sociology* 94 (1989): 1146–83; Jeannie Oakes, *Keeping Track: How Schools Structure Inequality* (New Haven: Yale University Press, 1985); Jeannie Oakes, "Tracking in Secondary Schools: A Contextual Perspective," *Educational Psychologist* 22 (June 1986): 129–54; Adam Gamoran, "The Consequences of Track-Related Instructional Differences for Student Achievement," paper presented at the meeting of the American Educational Research Association, Boston, April 1990.

47. Oakes, *Keeping Track*; Oakes, "Tracking in Secondary Schools"; Thomas B. Hoffer, "Middle School Ability Grouping and Student Achievement in Science and Mathematics," *Educational Evaluation and Policy Analysis* 14, no. 3 (1992): 205–27; C. C. Kulik and J. A. Kulik, "Effects of Ability Grouping on Secondary School Students: A Meta-Analysis of Evaluation Findings," *American Education Research Journal* 19 (1982): 415–28; Robert. E. Slavin, "Achievement Effects of Ability Grouping in Secondary Schools: A Best Evidence Synthesis," *Review of Educational Research* 60, no. 3 (1990): 471–500.

48. Oakes, "Tracking in Secondary Schools"; D. G. Davis, "A Pilot Study to Assess Equity in Selected Curricular Offerings across Three Diverse Schools in a Large Urban School District: A Search for Methodology," paper presented at the meeting of the American Educational Research Association, San Francisco, Calif., 1986; M. K. Finley, "Teachers and Tracking in a Comprehensive High School," *Sociology of Education* 57 (1984): 233–43; J. E. Rosenbaum, *Making Inequality: The Hidden Curriculum of High School Tracking* (New York: John Wiley & Sons, 1976); Joan E. Talbert, "Teacher Tracking: Exacerbating Inequalities in the High School," Center for Research on the Context of Secondary Teaching, Stanford University, Stanford, Calif., 1990; Lorraine M. McDonnell et al., "Discovering What Schools Really Teach: Designing Improved Coursework Indicators," U.S. Department of Education, Washington, D.C., 1990; J. E. Kaufman and J. E. Rosenbaum, "Education and Employment of Low-Income Black Youth in White Suburbs," *Educational Evaluation and Policy Analysis* 14, no. 3 (1992): 229–40; Anne Wheelock, *Crossing the Tracks* (New York: New Press, 1992).

49. Linda Darling-Hammond, *The Right to Learn* (San Francisco: Jossey-Bass, 1997), p. 268.

50. Oakes, *Keeping Track*; Davis, "A Pilot Study to Assess Equity in Selected Curricular Offerings across Three Diverse Schools in a Large Urban School District"; Mary H. Metz, *Classrooms and Corridors: The Crisis of Authority in Desegregated Secondary Schools* (Berkeley: University of California Press, 1978); K. Trimble and R. L. Sinclair, "Ability Grouping and Differing Conditions for Learning: An Analysis of Content and Instruction in Ability-Grouped Classes,"

paper presented at the meeting of the American Educational Research Association, San Francisco, 1986; Cooper and Sherk, "Addressing Urban School Reform."

51. "America's Teachers," Tables A4.15–A4.16.

52. *Characteristics of Stayers, Movers, and Leavers: Results from the Teacher Followup Survey, 1994–95* (Washington, D.C.: National Center for Educational Statistics, U.S. Department of Education, 1997).

53. Ibid., pp. 6–7.

54. "America's Teachers," p. 109.

55. Low-poverty schools are those with less than 5 percent of their students receiving free or reduced-price lunch. High-poverty schools are those with more than 50 percent of their students receiving free or reduced-price lunch. *Schools and Staffing Surveys*, "Teacher Followup Survey 1994–95," National Center for Education Statistics, tabulations conducted by the National Commission on Teaching and America's Future.

56. "America's Teachers," p. 93.

57. Ibid., p. 90.

58. Susan M. Johnson, *Teachers at Work: Achieving Success in Our Schools* (New York: Basic Books, 1990).

59. Sharon Conley, "Review of Research on Teacher Participation in School Decisionmaking," in Gerald Grant, ed., *Review of Research in Education* (Washington, D.C.: American Educational Research Association, 1991), pp. 225–66.

60. "America's Teachers," p. 53.

61. *The Condition of Teaching, A State-by-State Analysis* (New York: Carnegie Foundation, 1990).

62. Sclan, "The Effect of Perceived Workplace Conditions on Beginning Teachers' Work Commitment, Career Choice Commitment, and Planned Retention."

63. "The American Teacher 1993," Metropolitan Life, New York, 1993.

64. *Schools and Staffing Surveys, 1993–94*, "Public School Teacher Questionnaires," tabulations conducted by the National Commission on Teaching and America's Future.

65. "America's Teachers," Table A4.15.

66. For a review, see Darling-Hammond, *The Right to Learn.*

67. Linda Darling-Hammond, Arthur E. Wise, and Tamar Gendler, "The Teaching Internship: Practical Preparation for a Licensed Profession" (Santa Monica, Calif.: RAND Corporation, 1990).

68. *Schools and Staffing Surveys, 1993–94*, "Public School Teacher Questionnaires," tabulations conducted by the National Commission on Teaching and America's Future.

69. *Schools and Staffing Survey, 1990–91*, p. 8.

70. Linda Darling-Hammond, "Teacher Professionalism: Why and How," in Ann Lieberman, ed., *Schools as Collaborative Cultures: Creating the Future Now* (Philadelphia: Falmer Press, 1990); Linda Darling-Hammond, "Teachers and Teaching: Signs of a Changing Profession," in Robert Houston, Martin Haberman, and John Sikula, eds., *Handbook of Research on Teacher Education* (New York: Macmillan, 1990); A. M. Huberman and Matthew Miles, "Rethinking the Quest for School Improvement: Some Findings from the DESSI Study," *Teachers College Record* 86, no. 1 (1984): 34–54; Ann Lieberman, "Expanding the Leadership Team," *Educational Leadership* 45, no. 5 (1988): 4–8; Lieberman, *Schools as Collaborative Cultures*; Karen S. Louis and Matthew B. Miles, *Improving the Urban High School: What Works and Why* (New York: Teachers College Press, 1990); Milbrey W. McLaughlin et al., "Why Teachers Won't Teach," *Phi Delta Kappan* 67, no. 6 (1986): 420–26.

71. George A. Johanson and Crystal J. Gips, "The Hiring Preferences of Secondary School Principals," *High School Journal* 76 (October/November 1992): 1–16; Susanna W. Pflaum and Theodore Abramson, "Teacher Assignment, Hiring, and Preparation: Minority Teachers in New York City," *Urban Review* 22 (March 1990): 17–31; Martin Haberman, "Selecting 'Star' Teachers for Children," *Phi Delta Kappan* 76 (June 1995): 777–81; Janice Poda, "1994–95 Annual Report for the South Carolina Center for Teacher Recruitment" (Rock Hill: South Carolina Center for Teacher Recruitment, 1995); Beverly A. Browne and Richard J. Rankin, "Predicting Employment in Education: The Relative Efficiency of National Teacher Examinations Scores and Student Teacher Ratings," *Educational and Psychological Measurement* 46 (Spring 1986): 191–97; Arthur E. Wise, Linda Darling-Hammond, and Barnett Berry, *Effective Teacher Selection, from Recruitment to Retention* (Santa Monica, Calif.: RAND Corporation, 1987); P. C. Schlechty, "Reform in Teacher Education: A Sociological View," American Association of Colleges for Teacher Education, Washington, D.C., 1990.

72. Wise, Darling-Hammond, and Berry, *Effective Teacher Selection.*

73. Ibid.

74. Ibid.

75. Jon Snyder, *New Haven Unified School District: A Teaching Quality System for Excellence and Equity* (New York: National Commission on Teaching and America's Future, 1999); Wise, Darling-Hammond, and Berry, *Effective Teacher Selection*, 1987.

76. J. Norris, personal communication with Barnett Berry, May 22, 1998.

77. Barnett Berry, *Keeping Talented Teachers: Lessons Learned from the North Carolina Teaching Fellows*, commissioned by the North Carolina Teaching Fellows Commission (Raleigh, N.C.: Public School Forum, 1995).

78. Ferguson, "Paying for Public Education."

79. James E. Bruno, "Teacher Compensation and Incentive Programs for Large Urban School Districts," *The Elementary School Journal* 86, no. 4 (March 1986): 441.

80. *Doing What Matters Most.*

81. Ibid.

82. Snyder, *New Haven Unified School District.*

83. For a vivid illustration of the problem, see the John Merrow report featuring Oakland and nearby New Haven, California, *Teacher Shortages: False Alarm?* videocassette, Minow Reports, New York, 1999.

84. *Schools and Staffing Survey, 1990–91.*

85. For citations see Leslie Huling-Austin, "Research on Learning to Teach: Implications for Teacher Induction and Mentoring Programs," *Journal of Teacher Education* 43, no. 3 (May–June 1992): 174.

86. Thomas J. Buttery, Martin Haberman, and W. Robert Houston, "First Annual ATE Survey of Critical Issues in Teacher Education," *Action in Teacher Education* 12, no. 2 (Summer 1990): 1–7.

87. Metropolitan Life Survey of Teachers, 1991.

88. Sandra J. Odell and Douglas P. Ferraro, "Teacher Mentoring and Teacher Retention," *Journal of Teacher Education* 43, no. 3 (May–June 1992): 203. See also Joel A. Colbert and Diana E. Wolff, "Surviving in Urban Schools: A Collaborative Model for a Beginning Teacher Support System," *Journal of Teacher Education* 43, no. 3 (May–June 1992): 193–99; Leslie Huling-Austin and S. C. Murphy, "Assessing the Impact of Teacher Induction Programs: Implications for Program Development," paper presented at the meeting of the American Educational Research Association, Washington, D.C., 1987; S. Odell, "Induction Support of New Teachers: A Functional Approach," *Journal of Teacher Education* 37, 26–30; David P. Wright, Mark McKibbon, and Priscilla Walton, *The Effectiveness of the Teacher Trainee Program: An Alternate Route into Teaching in California* (Sacramento, California: Commission on Teacher Credentialing, 1987).

89. See for example, Linda Darling-Hammond with Eileen Sclan, "Policy and Supervision," in Carl Glickman, ed., *Supervision and Transition* (Alexandria, Va.: Association for Supervision and Curriculum Development, 1992); Judith Warren Little, "Teachers as Colleagues," in Virginia Richardson-Koehler, ed., *Educator's Handbook: A Research Perspective* (New York: Longman, 1987), pp. 491–518; Susan J. Rosenholtz, "Effective Schools: Interpreting the Evidence," *American Journal of Education* 93, no. 3 (1985): 352–88.

90. Gayle A. Wilkinson, "Support for Individualizing Teacher Induction," *Action in Teacher Education* 16, no. 2 (Summer 1994): 52–61.

91. Ibid., p. 59.

92. Terry M. Wildman et al., "Teacher Mentoring: An Analysis of Roles, Activities, and Conditions," *Journal of Teacher Education* 43, no. 3 (May–June 1992): 212.

93. Joan M. Hofmann and Harriet Feldlaufer, "Involving Veteran Teachers in a State Induction Program," *The Clearing House* 66, no. 2 (November/December 1992): 101–3.

94. Ibid., p. 102.

95. Ibid.

96. Huling-Austin, "Research on Learning to Teach," 175.

97. Ibid.

98. Ibid.

99. Ibid., p. 177; Wildman et al., "Teacher Mentoring," 210.

100. Colbert and Wolff, "Surviving in Urban Schools," 193–99.

101. Ibid., p. 194.

102. Ibid., p. 197.

103. Ibid., pp. 193–99.

104. Ibid., p. 197.

105. *What Matters Most*, p. 97.

106. Ibid.

107. Emil J. Haller, "High School Size and Student Discipline: Another Aspect of the School Consolidation Issue," *Educational Evaluation and Policy Analysis* 14, no. 2 (1992): 145–56; Emil J. Haller, "Small Schools and Higher-Order Thinking Skills," *Journal of Research in Rural Education* 9, no. 2 (1993): 66–73; William J. Fowler, "What Do We Know about School Size? What Should We Know?" paper presented at the meeting of the American Educational Research Association, San Francisco, Calif., April 1992; Craig B. Howley and Gary Huang, "Extracurricular Participation and Achievement: School Size as Possible Mediator of SES Influence among Individual Students," *Resources in Education* (July 1991); Craig B. Howley, "Synthesis of the Effects of School and District Size: What Research Says about Achievement in Small Schools and School Districts," *Journal of Rural and Small Schools* 4, no. 1 (1989): 2–12; G. Green and W. Stevens, "What Research Says about Small Schools," *Rural Educators* 10, no. 1 (1988): 9–14; P. Lindsay, "The Effect of High School Size on Student Participation, Satisfaction, and Attendance," *Educational Evaluation and Policy Analysis* 4 (1982): 57–65; P. Lindsay, "High School Size, Participation in Activities, and Young Adult Social Participation: Some Enduring Effects of Schooling," *Educational Evaluation and Policy Analysis* 6, no. 1 (1984): 73–83; D. Oxley, "Smaller Is Better," *American Educator* (Spring 1989): 28–31, 51–52; R. Pittman and P. Haughwout, "Influence of High School Size on Dropout Rate," *Educational Evaluation and Policy Analysis* 9 (1987): 337–43; J. Garbarino, "The Human Ecology of School Crime: A Case for Small Schools," in E. Wenk, ed., *School Crime* (Davis, Calif.: National Council on Crime and Delinquency, 1978), pp. 122–33.

108. National Institute of Education, *Violent Schools—Safe Schools: The Safe School Study Report to Congress* (Washington, D.C.: National Academy Press, 1977); Gary D. Gottfredson and D. C. Daiger, "Disruption in 600 Schools,"

Center for Social Organization of Schools, Johns Hopkins University, Baltimore, 1979.

109. For a review see Valerie E. Lee, Anthony Bryk, and Julia B. Smith, "The Organization of Effective Secondary Schools," in Linda Darling-Hammond, ed., *Review of Research in Education* 19 (Washington, D.C.: American Educational Research Association, 1993), pp. 171–267.

110. Valerie E. Lee and Julia B. Smith, "Effects of High School Restructuring and Size on Gains in Achievement and Engagement for Early Secondary School Students" (Madison: Wisconsin Center for Education Research, University of Wisconsin, 1995).

111. Darling-Hammond, *The Right to Learn*.

112. Ibid.

113. Richard F. Elmore with Deanna Burney, *Investing in Teacher Learning: Staff Development and Instructional Improvement in Community School District #2* (New York: National Commission on Teaching and America's Future and the Consortium for Policy Research in Education, 1997).

114. Elmore, *Investigating Teacher Learning*, p. 6.

Chapter 6

1. Gary Orfield, "Public Opinion and School Desegregation," *Teachers College Record* 96, no. 4 (1995): 654–70.

2. *Time to Move On* (Washington, D.C.: Public Agenda, 1998).

3. Amy Stuart Wells and Robert L. Crain, "Perpetuation Theory and the Long-term Effects of School Desegregation" *Review of Educational Research* 64, no. 4 (1994): 531–55.

4. Ibid.

5. Gary Orfield et al., "Deepening Segregation in American Public Schools," Harvard Project on School Desegregation Report, Harvard University, 1997.

6. Darcia Harris Bauman, "South Carolina Charter School Law Still in Limbo," *Education Week*, July 12, 2000, p. 28.

7. Geoff Whitty, "Creating Quasi-Markets in Education: A Review of Recent Research on Parental Choice and School Autonomy in Three Countries," *Review of Research in Education*, vol. 22 (1997): 3–47.

8. See, for example, Bruno V. Manno et al., "How Charter Schools Are Different: Lessons and Implications from a National Study," *Phi Delta Kappan* 79, no. 7 (March 1998): 488–98; Louann Bierlein, "Charter Schools: A New Approach to Public Education," *NASSP Bulletin* 79, no. 572 (September 1995): 12–20.

9. See Roselyn Tantraphol, "Debater Says School Choice Is a Question of Civil Rights," *The Union-News*, March 2, 2000, http://www.massline.com;

Nina Shokraii, "Free at Last: Black American Signs up for School Choice," *Policy Review* 80 (November–December 1996): 20–26; Lynn Schnaiberg, "Justice Department Accused of Obstructing Charter Schools" *Education Week*, October 20, 1999.

10. See, for example, Gregg Vanourek et al., *Charter Schools in Action: Charter Schools as Seen by Those Who Know Them Best: Students, Teachers, and Parents* (Washington, D.C.: The Hudson Institute, June 1997), http://www.edexcellence.net/chart/chart2html; *The State of Charter Schools: Third-year Report 1999*, conducted by RPP International (Washington, D.C.: U.S. Department of Education, Office of Educational Research and Improvement, May 1999), http://www.ed.gov/pubs/charter3rdyear/title.html.

11. We draw from a number of independently conducted studies of charter schools in various states. Thus, we have excluded reports by partisan think tanks that simultaneously support charter school reform. The problem with this analysis is that each of these studies was designed to answer a different set of research questions, each draws from a different body of data, and employs different definitions and measures. For instance, in some reports the researchers did not consider a charter school's enrollment to be racially or ethnically distinct from that of the state or district enrollment unless they differed by 20 percent or more. Other researchers considered charter school to be distinct if their enrollments in one or more racial/ethnic category differed by only 10 percent. Also, depending on the way in which the data are presented in the reports, it was often impossible to reanalyze them to make the findings more uniform. Still, we have made the effort to contrast and compare the information in each report as best we can.

12. A total of 927 of the 975 open charter schools during the 1998–99 school year responded to the survey.

13. *The State of Charter Schools 2000: Fourth-year Report*, conducted by RPP International (Washington, D.C.: U.S. Department of Education, Office of Educational Research and Improvement, February 2000), p. 33.

14. *The State of Charter Schools 2000.*

15. Ibid. According to the report, only the twenty-three states that had three or more charter schools during the 1998–98 school year were included in this part of the analysis. It is not always clear why the authors sometimes chose to focus on these twenty-three states and sometimes on all twenty-seven states in this report. We chose, therefore, to examine the data from the twenty-one states with charter school enrollments of more than one thousand. It seemed more appropriate to focus on enrollments than on the number of schools given that we believe what matters most is how this reform impacts the lives of students. Also, the average enrollments per school vary widely across states; thus, some states with more than three charter schools had smaller overall charter school enrollments than did states with less than three charter schools.

16. A scatter plot of all twenty-one states examined in this chapter shows a weak relationship between the percentage of white students in the public schools and the percentage of white students in the charter schools (the correlation coefficient is 0.43). Thus, the regression analysis indicates that only 18.5 percent of the variance in the percentage of white students in charter schools in any given state is explained by the percentage of white students in the public schools in general. Still, a close look at the demographics in each state reveals evidence of a trend toward states with more white students in general enrolling more students of color in charter schools, particularly in many of the states with the highest charter school enrollments.

17. California, Arizona, Georgia, Colorado, District of Columbia, New Mexico, Alaska, and Kansas.

18. This depends on which total charter school enrollment numbers you use. When using the Department of Education's Fourth-Year Report numbers cited in Table 1 of this chapter, the percentage of charter school students in California and Arizona is about 46 percent.

19. The thirteen states, in order of the number of students they enroll in charter schools, are: Michigan, Texas, Florida, Massachusetts, North Carolina, Pennsylvania, Minnesota, New Jersey, Illinois, Ohio, Wisconsin, Connecticut, and Louisiana. The only three states that have a higher percentage of students of color in charter schools and a less than 60 percent white general public school population are Texas, Florida, and Louisiana. We used 60 percent as our cut-off for "predominantly" white because, according to the Department of Education's Fourth-Year Report, 59 percent was the average for white enrollment in the twenty-seven states with charter schools during the 1998–99 school year. It is also close to the national average of the percent of all students enrolled in public schools who are "white," which is 66 percent.

20. These eight include the District of Columbia, which is an anomaly due to its extremely small white population. About 5 percent of the students in the District of Columbia public schools were white, and only 1 percent of the students enrolled in charter schools there were white. Still, it fits this larger category of jurisdictions in which the white population in charter schools is either equal to (within five percentage points) or greater than the white population in the public schools in general.

The seven states, in order of their charter school enrollment size, are: California, Arizona, Georgia, Colorado, New Mexico, Alaska, and Kansas.

21. For instance, in New Jersey, the overall public school population is about 63 percent white, 19 percent African American, and 14 percent Latino. But the charter schools in New Jersey are only 29 percent white, 30 percent African American, and about 36 percent Latino. In fact, of the ten states in which white students are underrepresented in charter schools, seven contain charter schools in which both African-American and Latino students are

overrepresented. In the other three states, African-American students only are overrepresented and the Latino charter school enrollments are either equal to or slightly lower than the general public school population.

22. The picture from Florida is a little less clear-cut because white students are only slightly underrepresented—by about 7 percent—in charter schools, while Latino students are also slightly underrepresented.

23. See Gary Orfield and Susan Eaton, *Dismantling Desegregation*, the Harvard Project on School Desegregation (New York: New Press, 1996), pp. 15, 60.

24. Obviously, the District of Columbia does not fit this theme, given its very small white enrollment in charter or regular public schools. Still, the hypothesis is worth exploring in the seven states that fit this profile.

25. *The State of Charter Schools 2000*. Although the report does not provide any specific information about how many charter schools were considered in this particular analysis or what year the data are from, it appears as though this analysis is based on data from 920 out of the 975 charter schools open during the 1998–99 school year.

26. *A National Study of Charter Schools: Second-year Report*, conducted by RPP International (Washington, D.C.: U.S. Department of Education, Office of Educational Research and Improvement, 1998).

27. *The State of Charter Schools 2000*.

28. *A National Study of Charter Schools*.

29. Carol Ascher, Robin Jacobowitz, and Yolanda McBride, *Charter School Access: A Preliminary Analysis of Charter School Legislation and Charter School Students* (New York: Institute for Education and Social Policy, New York University, 1999).

30. We acknowledge the shortcomings in comparing the racial balance of individual charter schools to those of an entire school district. We realize that many school districts may be racially, ethnically, and socioeconomically diverse but that there is a great deal of segregation within these districts and that individual public schools are generally less diverse than the districts as a whole. Still, we think that these analyses of charter school and district-level data provide us with yet another layer of information and that the findings here are as valuable as those related to aggregated state and national data.

31. Ascher, Jacobowitz, and McBride, *Charter School Access*.

32. While the separate state-level reports are extremely important, as we mentioned above they oftentimes present very different data, making cross-state comparisons difficult.

33. *Evaluation of Charter School Effectiveness*, prepared for the State of California Office of Legislative Analyst (Menlo Park, Calif.: SRI International, 1997).

34. Ibid.

35. *A Study of Charter Schools: First-year Report,* conducted by RPP International (Washington, D.C.: U.S. Department of Education, Office of Educational Research and Improvement, 1997).

36. Carol Muth Crockett, "California Charter Schools: The Issue of Racial/Ethnic Segregation," PhD. diss., Arizona State University, 1999, p. 37.

37. Clayton Foundation, *1998 Colorado Charter Schools Evaluation Study* (Denver, Colo.: Colorado Department of Education, January 1999).

38. It is too early to draw conclusions about the racial/ethnic makeup of charter school enrollments as compared to those of other public schools in Michigan because the data have not yet been analyzed fully in that way. In fact, each of the three reports relies on slightly different data and each research team analyzed the available data differently.

39. Jerry Horn and Gary Miron, "Evaluation of the Michigan Public School Academy Initiative" (Kalamazoo, Mich.: The Evaluation Center, Western Michigan University, 1999).

40. Public Sector Consultants, Inc., and Maximus, Inc., *Michigan's Charter School Initiative: From Theory to Practice* (Lansing, Mich.: Department of Education, 1999).

41. The authors note that the charter school data are from the 1997–98 school year, while the district data are from the 1995–96 school year.

42. *Minnesota Charter Schools Evaluation,* final report (Minneapolis: Center for Applied Research and Educational Improvement, College of Education and Human Development, University of Minnesota, 1998).

43. The Department of Education *Third-year Report* and the University of Minnesota report differ somewhat in their reporting of the percentage of white students in the public schools in general and in charter schools total for Minnesota. The Department of Education report lists the overall statewide white enrollment as 86 percent and the charter school white enrollment as 53 percent. The University of Minnesota report lists the statewide white enrollment as 84 percent and the charter school white enrollment as 55 percent. Such small discrepancies between the U.S. Department of Education report and the various state reports are common.

44. *Minnesota Charter Schools Evaluation,* p. 4, Section Five.

45. Gregory Weiher et al., *Texas Open-Enrollment Charter Schools: Third Year Evaluation* (Arlington, Tex.: School of Urban and Public Affairs, University of Texas at Arlington, 2000).

46. *The Massachusetts Charter School Initiative 1998 Statistical Portrait,* (Boston: Massachusetts State Department of Education, 1998), http://www.doe.mass.edu/cs.www/report98/stats.html; Jennifer Wood, *An Early Examination of the Massachusetts Charter School Initiative* (Amherst, Mass.: Donahue Institute, University of Massachusetts, 1999). This finding could also be related to the smaller, more homogeneous make-up of Massachusetts school districts.

47. Ascher, Jacobowitz, and McBride, *Charter School Access*.

48. Ibid.

49. Ibid., p. 9.

50. Crockett, "California Charter Schools."

51. Casey D. Cobb and Gene V. Glass, "Ethnic Segregation in Arizona Charter Schools," *Educational Policy Analysis Archives* 7, no. 1 (1999).

52. Ibid., p. 16.

53. Ibid., p. 17.

54. Ibid., pp. 22–23.

55. Ibid., p. 29.

56. Ascher, Jacobowitz, and McBride, *Charter School Access*, p. 10.

57. This section of the Ascher report is based on data from 483 charter schools and 314 school districts. The second-year Department of Education report is based on data from 225 charter schools and their surrounding districts, the number of which is not revealed.

58. Ascher, Jacobowitz, and McBride, *Charter School Access*.

59. Ibid., p. 11.

60. Ibid., p. 12.

61. Clayton Foundation, *1998 Colorado Charter Schools Evaluation Study*, p. 27.

62. *The Massachusetts Charter School Initiative 1998 Statistical Portrait*; Wood, *An Early Examination of the Massachusetts Charter School Initiative*.

63. Horn and Miron, *Evaluation of the Michigan Public School Academy Initiative*; Public Sector Consultants, Inc., and Maximus, Inc., *Michigan's Charter School Initiative*.

64. Ascher, Jacobowitz, and McBride, *Charter School Access*, p. 13.

65. *Beyond the Rhetoric of Charter School Reform: A Study of Ten California School Districts* (Los Angeles: UCLA Graduate School of Education and Information Studies, 1998). This was a two-and-a-half-year study of ten California school districts engaged in charter school reform.

66. David Arsen, David N. Plank, and Gary Sykes, *School Choice Politics in Michigan: The Rules Matter* (East Lansing: Michigan State University, 1999).

67. Lori A. Mulholland, "Arizona Charter School Progress Evaluation," Morrison Institute for Public Policy, Tucson, Ariz., March 1999.

68. Weiher et al., *Texas Open-Enrollment Charter Schools*.

69. Monique Campbell et al., *NJ Charter School Law in Implementation: 1st Year Case Study* (New York: Robert F. Wagner Graduate School of Public Service and the Institute for Education and Social Policy, New York University, 1998).

70. Powell, *Evaluation of Charter School Effectiveness*.

71. Ibid.

72. Arsen, Plank, and Sykes, *School Choice Politics in Michigan*.

73. Ibid.

74. Campbell et al., *NJ Charter School Law in Implementation*, p. 16.

75. Ibid., p. 8.

76. *Beyond the Rhetoric of Charter School Reform.*

77. Cobb and Glass, "Ethnic Segregation in Arizona Charter Schools."

78. Ibid., p. 23.

79. Weiher et al., *Texas Open-Enrollment Charter Schools.*

80. *Beyond the Rhetoric of Charter School Reform.* Also see Janelle Scott and Jennifer Jellison Holme, "Private Resources, Public Schools: The Role of Social Networks in California Charter School Reform," AERA Conference Paper, San Diego, Calif., 1998. Also Amy Stuart Wells and Janelle Scott, "Privatization and Charter School Reform: The Rich Get Richer," in Henry M. Levin, ed., *Setting the Agenda for the National Center for the Study of Privatization in Education* (San Francisco: Westview Press, forthcoming).

81. Ibid.

82. See, for example, Arsen, Plank, and Sykes, *School Choice Politics in Michigan*; also Ascher, Jacobowitz, and McBride, *Charter School Access.*

83. *Beyond the Rhetoric of Charter School Reform.*

84. Ibid.

85. Crockett, "California Charter Schools."

86. Ascher, Jacobowitz, and McBride, *Charter School Access.*

87. This is not to say that the legislation does not matter, particularly in areas of funding and governance. Rather, we are suggesting that there is less of a direct link between the legislation as it is currently written and who has access to charter schools.

88. See the Center for Education Reform's website for information on their state ranking system: http://edreform.com/charter_schools/laws/ranking.htm.

Chapter 7

1. Phillip Kaufman et al., *Indicators of School Crime and Safety, 1998,* NCES 98-251/NCJ-172215, U.S. Departments of Education and Justice, Washington, D.C., 1998.

2. Ibid.

3. Ibid.

4. Ibid.

5. Ibid.

6. *The Metropolitan Life Survey of the American Teacher, 1999: Violence in America's Public Schools: Five Years Later* (New York: MetLife, 1999), p. 51.

7. Ibid.

8. Ibid.

9. Ibid.

10. Ibid.

11. Paul E. Barton, Richard J. Coley, and Harold Wenglinsky, "Order in the Classroom: Violence, Discipline, and Student Achievement," Educational Testing Service, Princeton, N.J., October 1998.

12. National Education Longitudinal Survey, National Center for Education Statistics (conducted in 1988, with subsequent follow-up surveys) [hereafter NELS:88].

13. Robin R. Henke et al., *Schools and Staffing in the United States: A Statistical Profile, 1993–94* (Washington, D.C.: National Center for Educational Statistics, U.S. Department of Education, 1996), pp. 120–21.

14. Richard M. Ingersoll, Mei Han, and Sharon Bobbitt, *Teacher Supply, Teacher Qualifications, and Teacher Turnover: Aspects of Teacher Supply and Demand in the U.S., 1990–91* (Washington, D.C.: U.S. Department of Education, National Center for Education Statistics, 1995).

15. Summer D. Whitener et al., *Characteristics of Stayers, Movers, and Leavers: Results from the Teacher Followup Survey: 1994–95*, NCES 97-450 (Washington, D.C.: U.S. Department of Education, National Center for Education Statistics, 1997), p. 13.

16. Ibid., p. 15.

17. *The Metropolitan Life Survey of the American Teacher*, p. 51.

18. American Federation of Teachers, *AFT School Discipline Resource Manual* (Washington, D.C., 1997).

19. Letter from Judy Hale and Bob Brown to the West Virginia Federation of Teachers, January 16, 1998.

20. Remarks of Texas Federation of Teachers president John Cole, Safe Schools Press Conference, November 19, 1996.

21. Testimony of Brenda Williams, Broward, Florida, Teachers Union/American Federation of Teachers, before the House Subcommittee on Early Childhood, Youth and Families Committee on Education and the Workforce, March 9, 1999.

22. In *What Works in Teaching and Learning* 30, no. 15, July 29, 1998 (newsletter).

23. This description is drawn from a presentation made by H. Jerome Freiberg, Professor of Education at the University of Houston, at the National Education Association Conference, March 1999.

24. Information taken from the fiscal year 1999 budget request of the United States Department of Education to the Congress of the United States.

25. "Evaluation of the Maryland Partnership in Character Education," One Year Report, West Mesa Associates, Inc., Hardy, Va., January 19, 1999.

26. This description is taken from a "Forum Brief" provided by the American Youth Policy Forum, Washington, D.C., January 15, 1999.

27. The description provided here is drawn from the testimony of Wesley C. Mitchell, Chief of Police, Los Angeles School Police Department, before the House Committee on Education and the Workforce, May 1999.

28. Materials supplied by George Krupanski, Executive Director, Boys and Girls Clubs of America.

29. This discussion draws from a presentation by Mark L. Rosenberg of the National Center for Injury Prevention and Control, Centers for Disease Control and Prevention, Department of Health and Human Services, before the House Subcommittee on Early Childhood, Youth and Families, March 11, 1999. Unless otherwise noted, all information used in this section comes from Rosenberg's presentation.

30. Education Commission of the States, *Youth Violence: A Policymaker's Guide*, Denver, Colo., March 1996.

31. The data used here is derived from the assessments of the National Assessment of Educational Progress for the years 1992, 1996, and 1998. NAEP is a project of the National Center for Education Statistics of the U.S. Department of Education. The data used here can be found on the Center's website at http://nces.ed.gov/.

32. Statement provided by the American Federation of Teachers, April 22, 1999.

33. Statement of Elizabeth Metcalf before the House Committee on Education and the Workforce, Subcommittee on Early Childhood, Youth and Families, March 9, 1999.

34. *Youth Violence.*

35. Sheila Heaviside et al., "Violence and Discipline Problems in U.S. Public Schools, 1996–97," NCES 98-030, U.S. Department of Education, National Center for Education Statistics, Washington, D.C., 1998.

36. Barton, Coley, and Wenglinsky, "Order in the Classroom," pp. 11–19.

37. NELS:88.

Chapter 8

1. July 1998 Peter Hart/Shell Oil poll.

2. Judging from a related data series about confidence in the public schools, the real decline in the public's ratings of the nation's public schools occurred in the 1970s and early 1980s; since then there has been relatively little overall change. Tom Loveless, "The Structure of Public Confidence in Education," *American Journal of Education* 105 (February 1997): 127–59.

3. This too appears to be a sentiment of long standing. For example, a question in the 1998 Shell poll asked how people rated public schools in the area or neighborhood where they lived; the response was 12 percent excellent, 40 percent good, 26 percent only fair, and 15 percent poor. This is virtually identical to responses to the same question asked by Gallup in 1972 (13 percent excellent, 40 percent good, 26 percent only fair, and 13 percent poor).

4. It is also worth noting that this long-standing gap between ratings of the nation's and local community schools has widened since 1988. See the detailed discussion in Loveless, "Structure of Public Confidence in Education."

5. Lawrence R. Jacobs and Robert Y. Shapiro, "Public Opinion and Health Care: Individualism, Government and the Market," paper presented at the annual meeting of the American Political Science Association, September 2–5, 1993.

6. This essentially duplicates the result of the 1997 Gallup/PDK poll, where the same question was asked.

7. Peter Harris/Recruiting New Teachers (RNT) poll, 1998, cited in David Haselkorn and Louis Harris, *The Essential Profession: A National Survey of Public Attitudes toward Teaching, Educational Opportunity and School Reform* (Belmont, Mass.: Recruiting New Teachers, Inc., 1998).

8. However, note that the question was worded differently in the 1996 reading, possibly accounting for the unusually lopsided result in that year.

9. Note, however, that public endorsement of a national test to set standards does not imply a high comfort level with the federal government as the creator and administrator of the test. For example, a March 1997 NBC/*Wall Street Journal* poll found the public split on a question that explicitly mentions the federal government as creator of a national reading/math test and poses the arguments both for and against such a proposition. And a 1999 National Public Radio/Kaiser Family Foundation poll found little support, in general, for the federal government having primary responsibility for developing standardized tests. This suggests that a national standardized test may need to be, in one way or another, somewhat disassociated from the federal government, perhaps through a quasi-independent agency or commission.

10. Public Agenda poll, October 1997.

11. Two 1999 polls also asked about public school choice, though they used radically different question wording and are not included in the table. The Penn, Schoen, Berland/Democratic Leadership Council poll framed public school choice as a method of forcing competition among schools, while the Public Agenda poll counterposed free choice by parents to retention of some control by the school district. In each case, however, the polls still recorded majority (54 percent) support for public school choice.

12. Note that the choice is framed exclusively in terms of blacks and whites; but since the most incendiary controversies are precisely about blacks and whites this should, if anything, bias the question conservatively (that is, toward the display of racial bias).

13. See cross-tabular data cited in Jennifer Hochschild and Bridget Scott, "The Polls—Trends: Governance and Reform of Public Education in the United States," *Public Opinion Quarterly* 62 (1998): 79–120.

14. For example, Donald Kinder and Lynn Sanders, *Divided by Color: Racial Politics and Democratic Ideals* (Chicago: University of Chicago Press, 1996).

15. Michael J. Alves and Charles V. Willie, "Controlled Choice Assignments: A New and More Effective Approach to School Desegregation," *The Urban Review* 19, no. 2 (1987): 67–88.

16. However, oddly enough, poor teacher quality does not typically rank very high in the public's rankings of problems that currently bedevil the public schools.

17. Note, however, that a stronger version of teacher accountability, where teacher pay is tied directly to student performance, received only weak support (33 percent) in the same poll.

18. According to data cited in Hochschild and Scott, "Polls—Trends," pp. 110–11. Note, however, that their most recent data on this issue comes from 1992. More recently a 1998 Peter Harris/RNT poll found 70 percent of the public characterizing teachers as "just adequately paid" or "inadequately paid." Unfortunately, the survey report provides no breakdown between these two responses.

19. See the section on spending later in this chapter for more detail.

20. See Stanley Elam, *How America Views Its Schools: The PDK/Gallup Polls, 1969–1994* (Bloomington, Ind.: Phi Delta Kappa Educational Foundation, 1995), p. 41, and Hochschild and Scott, "Polls—Trends," Table A7.

21. Of course, the closer the issue gets to the specific question of safety within schools, the more it is, in fact, an end in itself. In the 1998 Gallup/PDK poll, about one-third of respondents reported fearing for the safety of their oldest child at school (though note that 31 percent also feared for the safety of that child when just playing in their local neighborhood). In the wake of the Littleton, Colorado, school massacre, parents' fears about school safety have gone up substantially from the level just cited, but, as these events recede, it is probable that fears will recede to something like their 1998 levels.

22. Public Agenda poll, April 1998.

23. 1991 poll cited in Elam, *How America Views Its Schools*, p. 47.

24. February 1997 poll cited on Public Agenda website, http://publicagenda.org.

25. A much broader question in the 1999 PSB/DLC poll finds 54 percent opposition to and 45 percent support for "lengthening the school year to year-round schooling."

26. See data in Hochschild and Scott, "Polls—Trends," Tables D6 and D7.

27. Respondents were asked this question only in reference to the components of this package, which they had previously said they supported.

28. Luntz Research poll, January 1999.

29. Greenberg Research/Tarrance Group/American Federation of Teachers/National Education Association poll, January 1998.

30. Jennifer Hochschild and Deidre Kolarick, "Public Involvement in Decisions about Public Education," unpublished manuscript prepared for the National Academy of Sciences, 1997, provides data along these lines for the somewhat similar Texas case.

31. It also is worth noting that the 1999 Public Agenda poll establishes, fairly definitively, that most Americans still know relatively little about vouchers and how they work in the real world.

32. Reported in *On Thin Ice: How Advocates and Opponents Could Misread the Public's Views on Vouchers and Charter Schools* (New York: Public Agenda, 1999).

33. However, note that in the very short term (1998 to 1999) the Gallup/PDK data do show a slight increase in opposition to vouchers (see Tables 8 and 9 and the report on the 1999 Gallup/PDK survey on the PDK website, http://www.pdkintl.org). On the other hand, the 1999 Joint Center for Political and Economic Studies poll shows an increase in support for vouchers over the same time period.

34. 1997 Gallup/PDK poll.

35. Based on the 1999 Gallup/PDK poll and the 1999 Joint Center for Political and Economic Studies poll.

INDEX

Ability grouping: and achievement gap, 97–98, 102–103; arguments for and against, 105; in elementary schools, 97–98; with modifications, in whole-school reform, 112; most rigid forms of, 106–107; reform to eliminate, 107–111; in secondary schools, 102–103; successful use of, 105–106; and teacher inequalities, 103–104, 141, 142

Absenteeism, 225

Accelerated Schools Project, 243

Access: to advanced courses, 99–100, 142; to books, socioeconomic status and, 13; to charter schools, 203–207, 209–210

Accountability: professional, 161, 162; standards and, 114, 122; teacher, public support for, 264

Achievement, student: advanced courses and, 101; of black students, 33; discipline and, 229–230; factors determining, 129–130, 131; first-grade similarities in, 20–21, 22; as performance standard, 116; vs. starting level, 21; summer school and, 23; teacher quality and, 129–133, 263

Achievement gap, 32–33; blame for, sources of, 31–32; curriculum inequality and, 106–107; between elementary schools, 95–96; within elementary schools, 97–98; further enhancements needed for narrowing, 33–34; growth over time, 98; home environment and, 9; ineffective attempts at reducing, 10; litigation strategy for reducing, 31, 65–67, 73, 74–79, 81–84; narrowing of, since 1960s, 31, 33; persistence of, 86, 90; preschool programs for reducing, 25–26; resource weighting system for reducing, 34–35; between secondary schools, 99–101; within secondary schools, 101–107; social capital improvements and reduction of, 86–89;

ABOUT THE CONTRIBUTORS

KARL L. ALEXANDER is the John Dewey Professor of Sociology, The Johns Hopkins University. For more than fifteen years he has conducted the Beginning School Study with Doris Entwisle, keeping track of children at twenty public schools in Baltimore in an effort to examine the effects of early schooling on the later performance and welfare of children. With Doris Entwisle and Susan Dauber, he is working on an update of their 1994 volume, *On the Success of Failure: A Reassessment of the Effects of Retention in the Primary Grades* (to be reissued by Cambridge University Press in 2000).

PAUL E. BARTON is senior associate in the research division at Educational Testing Service (ETS), where he was formerly director of the Policy Information Center and associate director of the National Assessment of Educational Progress. He has been a president of the National Institute for Work and Learning, a member of the U.S. secretary of labor's policy planning staff, and was a member of the staff of the Office of Management and Budget.

CAMILLE WILSON COOPER is a doctoral candidate in educational policy studies at the Graduate School of Education and Information Studies at the University of California, Los Angeles (UCLA). She studies issues related to school choice, race, equity, and the politics of educational change.

DORIS R. ENTWISLE is professor emerita of sociology, The Johns Hopkins University. Her main area of interest is the sociology of human development over the life course, with an emphasis on issues of inequality. With Karl Alexander and Linda Olson, her most recent book is *Children, Schools, and Inequality* (Westview Press, 1997). A former Guggenheim Fellow, in 1997 she received the Society of Research in Child Development Award for Distinguished Scientific Contributions to Child Development.

LINDA DARLING-HAMMOND is Charles E. Ducommun Professor of Education at Stanford University. She is also executive director of the National Commission on Teaching and America's Future, which produced the 1996 report *What Matters Most: Teaching for America's Future* outlining a blueprint for policies that have been adopted by many states and districts working to assure well-qualified teachers for all children. Her research, teaching, and policy work focus on teaching quality, school restructuring, and educational equity.

ADAM GAMORAN is professor of sociology and educational policy studies at the University of Wisconsin-Madison. His research focuses on inequality in education, effects of curriculum differentiation on student outcomes, and school organization as a context for reform.

JENNIFER JELLISON HOLME received her doctorate in educational policy studies at UCLA. She has worked as a researcher on the UCLA Charter School Study and she is currently working as a research associate on the UCLA Understanding Race and Education Study, a study of graduates of racially mixed high schools. Her research focuses on school desegregation, school choice, and the relationship between housing and educational access.

RICHARD D. KAHLENBERG is a senior fellow at The Century Foundation, where he writes about education and civil rights. He is the author of *All Together Now: Creating Middle Class Schools through Public School Choice* (Brookings Press, 2000); *The Remedy: Class, Race, and Affirmative Action* (Basic Books, 1996); and *Broken Contract: A Memoir of Harvard Law School* (Hill and Wang, 1992). He has been a fellow at the Center for National Policy, a visiting associate professor of constitutional law at George Washington University, and a legislative assistant to Senator Charles S. Robb (D-Va.).

ALEJANDRA LOPEZ is a doctoral candidate at the UCLA Graduate School of Education and Information Studies. Her current research focuses on mixed-race and multiethnic adolescents' experiences with racial and ethnic identification, particularly in the schooling context, and issues around "measuring" or collecting data about race and ethnicity.

LINDA STEFFEL OLSON is a senior research assistant in the Department of Sociology at The Johns Hopkins University. She has been associated with the Beginning School Study for the past thirteen years. Her interests center on the effects of social structure on schooling outcomes.

LAURA POST is a doctoral student in the School of Education at Stanford University. She received her M.A. from Stanford in 1998 and her B.A. from the University of Wisconsin-Madison in 1991. Prior to coming to graduate school, she taught elementary school for five years in Pasadena, California. Her research interests include teacher education and professional development, teacher professional communities, and issues of equity in schooling.

RICHARD ROTHSTEIN is a research associate of the Economic Policy Institute and the national education columnist of the *New York Times*. He is the author of *The Way We Were? The Myths and Realities of America's Student Achievement* (The Century Foundation Press, 1998).

RUY TEIXEIRA is a senior fellow at The Century Foundation and formerly director of the Politics and Public Opinion Program at the Economic Policy Institute. He is the coauthor (with Joel Rogers) of *America's Forgotten Majority: Why the White Working Class Still Matters* (Basic Books, 2000) and the author of *The Disappearing American Voter* (Brookings Institution Press, 1992).

AMY STUART WELLS is a professor of educational policy at UCLA's Graduate School of Education and Information Studies. She was the principal investigator of a two-and-a-half-year study of charter school reform in ten school districts in California and currently is directing a study of adults who attended racially mixed high schools. She is the author and editor of numerous books and articles, including editor of *Multiple Meanings of Charter School Reform: Lessons from Ten California School Districts* (forthcoming, Teachers College Press); coauthor with Robert L. Crain of *Stepping Over the Color Line: African-American Students in White Suburban Schools* (Yale University Press, 1997); and author of *Time to Choose: America at the Crossroads of School Choice Policy* (Hill and Wang, 1993).